Walking in Truth™

A Biblical Worldview and Bible Survey Curriculum for Grades 6–8

Competing Worldviews

Student Textbook
Grade 7

Summit Ministries

Acknowledgements

Vice President of Publishing: Jason Graham

Managing Curriculum Editor: Macki Jones

Authors
John Hay, Jr.
Kim Pettit
Lorraine Wadman
Macki Jones

Editorial Team
John Conaway
Kim Pettit
Lorraine Wadman
Macki Jones
Nancy Sutton

Design Team
Claire Coleman
Mike Riester

Illustrator
Aline Heiser

Worldview Model Design
Randy Bounds
Steven Myasoto

Published by Summit Press, P.O. Box 207, Manitou Springs, CO 80829
Printed in USA

ISBN: 978-1-7330256-4-5

Walking in Truth Table of Contents—Student Textbook

Christianity

Lesson 1   The House of Truth

Getting Started—What Is the House of Truth?

Have you ever built a model—perhaps a model airplane, car, boat, or something for a science fair? Even if you haven't, you know that a model is made to represent something real. An architect, for example, may draw plans for a new home. Then, to help people envision what it might look like if it were built, he or she may build a

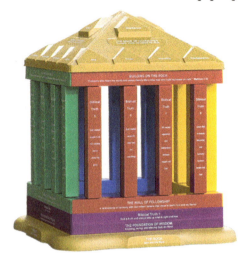

three-dimensional model of the house. Although the model is not the real building, it helps people visualize what the finished structure will look like. It may also help them consider changes that need to be made in the design or help them estimate the cost of the structure.

The Bible is a guide to living a life that pleases God. It contains principles, or truths, that we can use to build a strong life. In order to represent these truths in a way that is easy to see and understand, we will use a model called *the House of Truth*. This model functions much like an architect's model—it will help us see what we need to include in our lives, and the character traits we need to develop. The House of Truth is a representation of biblical Christianity—a theistic worldview that affirms God's Word as the ultimate source of truth.

> **Biblical Christianity**
> A theistic worldview centered in Jesus Christ,
> deriving its understanding of the world
> through the teachings of the Holy Bible

Topic 1—The Foundation of Wisdom

It's important to remember that a model can never tell God's great story completely or perfectly. Only the Bible can do that. Still, pictures and models can help us see and understand important truths from the Bible that we need to know as we live our lives. As we review each part of the House of Truth model, we'll always confirm it with God's Word. We'll start with the most important part of the structure—the foundation. God's Word tells us that he is the Rock and the Truth on which we are to build our life. We make God the foundation of our lives by knowing, loving, and obeying him. On the model, we call this foundation *The Foundation of Wisdom* because wise builders know that the fear of the LORD is the foundation of wisdom. Knowledge of the Holy One results in good judgment (Proverbs 9:10). God's Word is true, instructive, and eternal.

Every word of God proves true. He is a shield to all who come to him for protection.   Proverbs 30:5

Jesus replied, "But even more blessed are all who hear the word of God and put it into practice."   Luke 11:28

The grass withers and the flowers fade, but the word of our God stands forever.   Isaiah 40:8

There are four Biblical Truths that make up the Foundation of Wisdom, the base of the model.

Biblical Truth 1: God is Truth and always tells us what is right and true. God's great story begins, of course, with God. The very first words of the story, In the beginning God . . . (Genesis 1:1), tell us that the story is God's story and that it has a definite beginning. This doesn't mean God had a beginning. God is eternal. But it does mean that God's creation

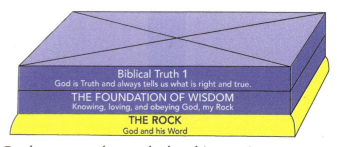

had a beginning that was possible only because of him. But how can we know whether this story is true or not? We know it's true because God tells us, "I, the LORD, speak only what is true and declare only what is right" (Isaiah 45:19).

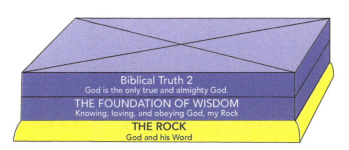

Biblical Truth 2: God is the only true and almighty God. People have many different beliefs about God. Some people believe in many gods. But the God who speaks the truth of his great story to us says, "Remember the things I have done in the past. For I alone am God! I am God, and there is none like me" (Isaiah 46:9).

For you are great and perform wonderful deeds. You alone are God.   Psalm 86:10

Biblical Truth 3: God is God the Father, God the Son, and God the Holy Spirit. God assures us that he is only one God. In a way that we cannot fully understand as human beings, God tells us that he is one God in three Persons—the Father, the Son, and the Holy Spirit. All three Persons are equally God, and they work in harmony in all that God does. All three Persons created the

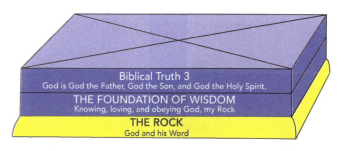

heavens and the earth. Christians use the word *Trinity* to refer to this Biblical Truth. The word *trinity* is a combination of a prefix and a smaller word: *tri* meaning *three* and *unity* meaning *united as one*. The following Scriptures show us the three Persons of the Trinity:

May the grace of the Lord Jesus Christ, the love of God [the Father], and the fellowship of the Holy Spirit be with you all.   2 Corinthians 13:14

Therefore, go and make disciples of all the nations, baptizing them in the name of the Father and the Son and the Holy Spirit.   Matthew 28:19

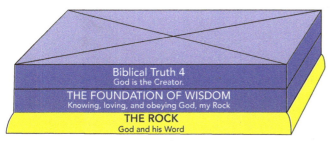

Biblical Truth 4: God is the Creator. The only true and almighty God created everything in heaven and on Earth. He created the visible, material things. And he created the invisible, immaterial things. Because he is almighty, he created all that exists simply by speaking. He did not need any special materials to create. In fact, he created out of nothing. Just by the command of his all-powerful voice, everything came into existence. And because God the Father, Son, and Holy Spirit have lived eternally in a relationship of harmony, the world they created was a world of harmonious relationships. God created people to live in harmonious relationships with God, themselves, others, and the earth.

For in six days the LORD made the heavens, the earth, the sea, and everything in them.

Exodus 20:11

I was chosen to explain to everyone this mysterious plan that God, the Creator of all things, had kept secret from the beginning.

Ephesians 3:9

For through him God created everything in the heavenly realms and on earth. He made the things we can see and the things we can't see—such as thrones, kingdoms, rulers, and authorities in the unseen world. Everything was created through him and for him.

Colossians 1:16

Not only do Christians build truth into their lives through knowing, loving, and obeying God, they also grow in character. Four character traits related to the first four Biblical Truths are obedience, reverence, loyalty, and gratitude, which are defined below.

Obedience	Reverence	Loyalty	Gratitude
The act of doing what I am told with a willing and loving heart	An attitude of respect and honor for God	Continuing faithfulness in loving and serving God and others	Thankfulness in my heart that I express to God and others for the blessings that I receive from them

Topic 2—The Wall of Fellowship

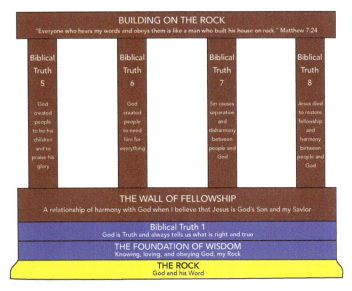

Now that our model for living has a foundation, it's time to add walls. Each wall of the worldview model represents a human relationship. The first wall is *The Wall of Fellowship*. It represents our relationship with God. There are four Biblical Truths and four character traits that are related to the Wall of Fellowship.

Biblical Truth 5: God created people to be his children and to praise his glory. Have you ever wondered why God created you? Do you think God needed you? Was there something he wouldn't have been able to do without you? Was he lonely? As you know, God has never been alone. God the Father, Son, and Holy Spirit have been in a relationship of unity for all eternity. And God certainly doesn't need you to do things for him. He's all-powerful, and he can do anything. So why did he create you? He created you as a person on whom he can lavish his love. Loving you brings God great joy and pleasure. And God is blessed when you love him, honor him, and praise him for his glory. In other words, he created you for the joy of fellowship, and as you know, that fellowship was absolutely perfect in the beginning.

God's purpose was that we Jews who were the first to trust in Christ would bring praise and glory to God.

Ephesians 1:12

Biblical Truth 6: God created people to need him for everything.
God's plan in the beginning was for us to enjoy fellowship with him forever. He created us as his image-bearers so that we could not only receive his love, but we could also love him. Even though God created us to bear his image, he did not create us to live independently of him. He did not create us as all-powerful, all-knowing, and all-present beings. Rather, God created us to depend completely on him for everything we need. This doesn't mean that we can't do things for ourselves, but it does mean that our very lives and every breath we take depend on God, our Creator.

He himself gives life and breath to everything, and he satisfies every need.   Acts 17:25

If God were to take back his spirit
and withdraw his breath, all life would cease,
and humanity would turn again to dust.   Job 34:14–15

Biblical Truth 7: Sin causes separation and disharmony between people and God. When God created Adam and Eve in his image, they were perfectly holy, just like God. Because they were holy, they enjoyed perfect fellowship with God in a garden that he had made specifically for them. Sadly, Adam and Eve chose to disobey God's command to not eat from the Tree of the Knowledge of Good and Evil. Once they chose to eat the fruit from the one tree God forbade, they were no longer the holy image-bearers God had created them to be. As sinful people, they lost the ability to have fellowship with God because a holy God cannot have fellowship with unholy people. We call this event in human history *the fall*.

It's your sins that have cut you off from God.
Because of your sins, he has turned away
and will not listen anymore.   Isaiah 59:2

Biblical Truth 8: Jesus died to restore fellowship and harmony between people and God. If Biblical Truth 7 were the end of God's great story, we would have no hope. We would be eternally separated from God. Every relationship of creation would have remained forever in disharmony. But the fall is not the end of the story. After Adam and Eve sinned, God promised them that one day a child would be born who would defeat or crush Satan and his evil works. We know that Jesus Christ is that Child.

Christ suffered for our sins once for all time. He never sinned, but he died for sinners to bring you safely home to God. He suffered physical death, but he was raised to life in the Spirit.   1 Peter 3:18

The Wall of Fellowship also has four character traits related to the Biblical Truths. They are joy, trust, humility, and compassion.

Joy	Trust	Humility	Compassion
A delight in my life that comes not from my circumstances, but from being in fellowship with God as his child	A complete confidence in God that he will always do everything he promises	An attitude in my heart that I am not better than any other of God's image-bearers	Acts of tenderness and love I give to those who are hurting

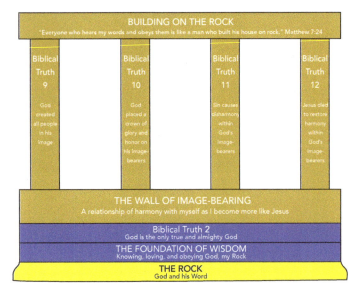

The second relationship is the relationship God created us to have within our own hearts. In the House of Truth model, this relationship is represented by a yellow wall with four pillars, *The Wall of Image-Bearing*. As with the other walls, each pillar represents a different Biblical Truth.

When people ask the question "Who am I?" they generally look for the answer within themselves. They may imagine the kind of person they think they should be or would like to be. Then they try to make themselves into that kind of person, or they may try to become like someone they idolize. Most people don't succeed at either of these attempts, or if they do, they're never happy with the person they become. They may think their looks or their clothes or their possessions or their actions will make them happy and define who they are, but they discover that they still don't know their identity. This discovery often leads them to try new ways to find out who they are, and these ways fail too. Of course, with each failure, people continue to experience increasing disharmony within themselves.

The only way people can end the disappointments that come from trying to find their identity by looking inside themselves is to discover that God created them as his image-bearers. This is who they truly are. Only as they become more and more like Jesus and bear his image, as they were created to do, will they find peace and joy within.

Biblical Truth 9: God created people in his image. To bear someone's image means to carry that person's likeness. We say that children bear or carry the image of their parents, meaning that children often resemble their parents' appearance. Children also often act and speak like their parents. In a similar sense, God is our heavenly Father, and he created us in his image.

When God created human beings, he made them to be like himself.   Genesis 5:1b

Biblical Truth 10: God placed a crown of glory and honor on each of his image-bearers. God created us in his image, and he also crowned us with glory and honor. This crown is not a physical crown that we can see and touch. Instead, God uses this metaphor of a crown of glory and honor to help us understand that he created us as the crown of all his creation. God gives us, his image-bearers, a position of honor higher than any other earthly creature.

5 Yet you made them only a little lower than God
    and crowned them with glory and honor.
6 You gave them charge of everything you made,
    putting all things under their authority—
7 the flocks and the herds
    and all the wild animals,
8 the birds in the sky, the fish in the sea,
    and everything that swims the ocean currents.   Psalm 8:5–8

Biblical Truth 11: Sin causes disharmony within each of God's image-bearers. God created all of his image-bearers as holy people. He also created them with the freedom to make their own choices. Adam and

Eve were holy because they were created by a holy God. At first, their thoughts were pure, their emotions pleasant, and their choices were in line with God's will. Their hearts had harmony within—until they made the choice to sin by disobeying God.

Sadly, since the fall of Adam and Eve, all people on Earth are born with sinful hearts. And because all people have sinful hearts, all people are guilty of sinning. Our guilt is the responsibility we bear for intentionally or unintentionally disobeying God's laws or commands. Most of the time, we're aware of our guilt. This is because guilt causes several kinds of guilty feelings, including shame, worry, and fear.

"There is no peace for the wicked," says my God.   Isaiah 57:21

My guilt overwhelms me—it is a burden too heavy to bear.   Psalm 38:4

Biblical Truth 12: Jesus died to restore harmony within each of God's image-bearers. If Biblical Truth 11 were the end of God's great story, we'd have no hope of ever finding personal harmony. As much as we might try, we would not be able to make the emotional disharmony caused by guilt to go away. Only God can remove our guilt, and only God can make us into new people and fill our hearts with harmony. And just as Jesus died and was raised from death to redeem and restore our relationship with God, he also died to redeem and restore the relationship of harmony God created us to have with ourselves.

When you receive Jesus as God's Son and your Savior, God replaces your guilt with innocence. He does not hold you guilty for the sins you have committed. And if you are no longer guilty, then you are no longer subject to eternal punishment and separation from God.

So now there is no condemnation for those who belong to Christ Jesus.   Romans 8:1

The Bible tells us that God not only removes our guilt, he also makes us a "new person."

This means that anyone who belongs to Christ has become a new person. The old life is gone; a new life has begun!   2 Corinthians 5:17

There are four character traits related to *The Wall of Image-Bearing*. They are holiness, confidence, self-control, and peace.

Holiness	Confidence	Self-Control	Peace
Purity in my heart in everything I think, say, and do	A strong belief that God will help me do all the things I need to do	An ability to do the right thing even when I don't feel like it	A quietness in my heart because Jesus is with me and has forgiven my sins

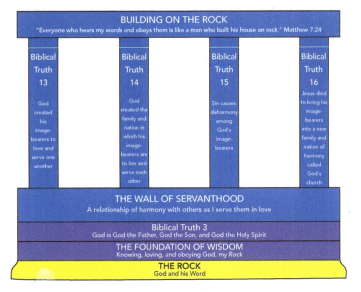

The third relationship described in God's great story is the relationship God created us to have with others. On the House of Truth model, this relationship is represented by the blue wall, *The Wall of Servanthood*. We were not created to live alone. We cannot live alone. Only as we live and work in loving relationships of service to and with others can we fulfill God's plan for our lives and for his creation.

In order to serve, we must be willing to be more concerned about others than we are about ourselves. This is not always easy because most people like being served instead of serving. But God himself showed us how to serve each other. He did this by sending Jesus to humbly serve us. His Son was the perfect obedient Servant, who cared more about us than even his own life. If you understand and imitate Jesus' example of serving others, you can become the servant that God created you to be. Jesus said, [43] "But among you it will be different. Whoever wants to be a leader among you must be your servant, [44] and whoever wants to be first among you must be the slave of everyone else" (Mark 10:43–44).

Biblical Truth 13: God created his image-bearers to love and serve one another. God said that everything he created was good. But after he created Adam, he said something was not good. It wasn't Adam; it was the fact that Adam was alone. By himself, Adam was incomplete. One person could not fulfill the plans God intended for his creation. So, God created Eve, Adam's wife. Together, Adam and Eve would begin to fill the earth with people and care for it, serving not only God, but also each other. It's true today; no individual can fulfill God's plan for creation. We were created to need others and to meet each other's needs as servants.

[6] But 'God made them male and female' from the beginning of creation. [7] 'This explains why a man leaves his father and mother and is joined to his wife.'
Mark 10:6–7

Biblical Truth 14: God made the family and nation in which his image-bearers are to live and serve each other. When God created Adam and Eve, he created the first family and gave the family the responsibility of filling the earth. One family eventually became many families.

From one man he created all the nations throughout the whole earth. He decided beforehand when they should rise and fall, and he determined their boundaries.
Acts 17:26

The families of the earth multiplied, and they moved to new places, forming extended families, such as tribes or clans. As these small, societal communities grew, they spread out and became states and nations. Nations were part of God's plan. From the very beginning, he designed the nation to consist of a large group of people, living together in their own land with their own laws and their own government. His purpose for the nations, especially his chosen nation of Israel, was that they serve each other in love.

Biblical Truth 15: Sin causes disharmony among God's image-bearers. The fall caused disharmony in Adam and Eve's relationships with God and themselves. It also brought disharmony into their relationship with each other. When God asked Adam if he had eaten the fruit, he admitted that he had. But what did he do next? He blamed Eve for giving it to him. This act of blaming Eve for his own sin shows us that their sin caused disharmony between them.

Since all people have a sinful nature, families and nations are also filled with disharmony. In our nation, we see many of God's blessings and many good citizens who do what is just and right. But we also see many problems that cause disharmony. People commit crimes against other people. Government leaders often argue with each other. Sometimes they make unjust laws. Nations have disagreements with other nations, and these disagreements always lead to unfriendly relationships and sometimes even to war.

Godliness makes a nation great,
  but sin is a disgrace to any people.

Proverbs 14:34

Biblical Truth 16: Jesus died to bring his image-bearers into a new family and nation of harmony called God's church. When Adam and Eve gave in to Satan's temptation in the garden of Eden and disobeyed God, they immediately experienced disharmony with God, themselves, each other, and the earth. Because Satan is not omniscient and omnipotent like God, he must have thought he had destroyed God's plan for families and nations. But the Bible tells us that even before God created the world, he had an eternal plan to destroy all Satan's works and restore harmony in every relationship of creation. This included the plan to restore harmony among people living in families and nations. God's plan was accomplished through the death and resurrection of Jesus.

So now you Gentiles are no longer strangers and foreigners. You are citizens along with all of God's holy people. You are members of God's family.

Ephesians 2:19

But you are not like that, for you are a chosen people. You are royal priests, a holy nation, God's very own possession. As a result, you can show others the goodness of God, for he called you out of the darkness into his wonderful light.

1 Peter 2:9

Like *The Wall of Fellowship* and *The Wall of Image-Bearing*, *The Wall of Servanthood* has four character traits related to its Biblical Truths. They are friendliness, honesty, kindness, and forgiveness.

Friendliness	Honesty	Kindness	Forgiveness
Kind actions, words, and smiles that show others how special they are	Truthfulness in everything I think, say, and do	Loving acts of service and courtesy I give to others	A choice to love those who have been unkind to me

Topic 5—The Wall of Stewardship

The Wall of Stewardship, the green wall, is the last wall on the House of Truth model. All stewardship begins with a steward, someone who is called to take care of property belonging to someone else. God created us to be stewards of his property, the earth.

The earth is the LORD's, and everything in it. The world and all its people belong to him.   Psalm 24:1

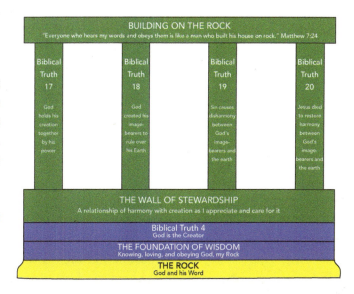

BUILDING ON THE ROCK
"Everyone who hears my words and obeys them is like a man who built his house on rock." Matthew 7:24

Biblical Truth 17
God holds his creation together by his power

Biblical Truth 18
God created his image-bearers to rule over his Earth

Biblical Truth 19
Sin causes disharmony between God's image-bearers and the earth

Biblical Truth 20
Jesus died to restore harmony between God's image-bearers and the earth

THE WALL OF STEWARDSHIP
A relationship of harmony with creation as I appreciate and care for it

Biblical Truth 4
God is the Creator

THE FOUNDATION OF WISDOM
Knowing, loving, and obeying God, my Rock

THE ROCK
God and his Word

You gave them [human beings] charge of everything you made, putting all things under their authority.

Psalm 8:6

There are four Biblical Truths that relate to our relationship of stewardship of the earth.

Biblical Truth 17: God holds his creation together by his power. Only God could have created the universe and the earth where we live. And only God can make the earth and everything he created continue. The Bible tells us that God holds everything together through his Son, Jesus.

The Son radiates God's own glory and expresses the very character of God, and he sustains everything by the mighty power of his command. When he had cleansed us from our sins, he sat down in the place of honor at the right hand of the majestic God in heaven.

Hebrews 1:3

Biblical Truth 18: God created his image-bearers to rule over his Earth. God created the heavens and the earth and everything in them, and he owns everything he created. There is nothing that God did not create, and there is nothing he does not own, including you. But just because God owns everything doesn't mean he's selfish. In fact, he created the things of the earth for his image-bearers to use and enjoy. The Bible tells us that God gave the earth to human beings—not to own, but to enjoy and care for as his stewards.

The heavens belong to the LORD, but he has given the earth to all humanity.

Psalm 115:16

Then God blessed them [Adam and Eve] and said, "Be fruitful and multiply. Fill the earth and govern it. Reign over the fish in the sea, the birds in the sky, and all the animals that scurry along the ground.

Genesis 1:28

Biblical Truth 19: Sin causes disharmony between God's image-bearers and the earth. When Adam and Eve disobeyed God, the harmony in all their relationships was broken—even their harmony with the earth. Adam and Eve began to grow old, and they slowly began to die as God had told them they would.

[16] But the LORD God warned him, "You may freely eat the fruit of every tree in the garden— [17] except the tree of the knowledge of good and evil. If you eat its fruit, you are sure to die."

Genesis 2:16–17

Not only did God punish Adam and Eve with death, he also cursed the ground. This means that God took away his full blessing from the earth itself. Instead of easily producing the food Adam and Eve needed, the earth began to grow weeds and plants with thorns. When Adam and Eve planted and harvested a crop, they had to work hard.

[17] And to the man [Adam] he [God] said, "Since you listened to your wife and ate from the tree whose fruit I commanded you not to eat, the ground is cursed because of you. All your life you will struggle to scratch a living from it. [18] It will grow thorns and thistles for you, though you will eat of its grains. [19] By the sweat of your brow will you have food to eat until you return to the ground from which you were made. For you were made from dust, and to dust you will return."

Genesis 3:17–19

Biblical Truth 20: Jesus died to restore harmony between God's image-bearers and the earth. The fall did not bring an end to God's plan for his image-bearers to live forever in harmony with the earth. Though God cursed the earth, he promised Adam and Eve that one day Jesus would crush Satan's head and defeat his evil works. God kept this promise and sent Jesus to die on the cross to redeem and restore our harmony with God, ourselves, and others. Jesus also died to restore harmony with the earth. God promises a new earth, one without the decay that we see now.

And the one sitting on the throne said, "Look, I am making everything new!" And then he said to me, "Write this down, for what I tell you is trustworthy and true."

Revelation 21:5

In this verse, "everything" includes the earth as well as our physical bodies. Not only will God create a new heaven and earth, he will also create new bodies for us. In our new bodies, we'll live eternally on the new earth where we'll serve God and reign with him over it.

But we are looking forward to the new heavens and new earth he has promised, a world filled with God's righteousness.

2 Peter 3:13

There are four character traits that relate to *The Wall of Stewardship*. They are orderliness, dependability, perseverance, and initiative.

Orderliness	Dependability	Perseverance	Initiative
The ability to conduct the activities of my life in an orderly and harmonious way	An ability to complete everything I am responsible for with a willing attitude	An ability to continue fulfilling my responsibilities even when it is hard to do so	An ability to see what needs to be done and do it without being told

The Biblical Christian Worldview

Getting Started—What Christians Believe

In the previous lesson, we examined the biblical Christian worldview by using a model called *the House of Truth*. Although all models have limitations, the House of Truth gives us a sense of what we, as Christians, believe about our relationship with God, ourselves, others, and with the earth. The foundation and each wall contain truth statements about human relationships. The model presents a general picture of how each relationship intersects with the others. When we learn the truths from the Bible about our relationships—including who God is and who we are as his image-bearers—we begin to see how they apply to our personal life story.

While the worldview model presents general biblical truths, it does not provide all the answers to questions asked about the world and God. People often ask, What is truth? How do we know what is true and what is not? How does God reveal truth to us? How can we be sure the Bible is true? Who is God? What is he like? Is there really one God? Who am I? Why am I here? Where did the universe come from? How can I know what is right and what is wrong? These and other questions will be answered in this lesson.

Topic 1—The Biblical Christian View of Truth

What Is Truth? Truth may be defined as *that which agrees with and accurately describes what is real*. A belief that is true conforms to reality rather than fantasy.

There are several ways we can know if something is true. One way is through our senses. If someone were to tell you that it is freezing outside, you could easily determine the truth of the statement by going outside to feel the air for yourself, or you might consult an outdoor thermometer. If someone suggests that unicorns are real, you could ask to see or touch one. Yet our senses may not always be reliable. If we hear a shout in the mountains, the sound will echo, and we may not realize its source. Our sense of smell is easily confused when a stronger scent overpowers a weaker one. Optical illusions can trick our eyes.

Which way is the target facing?

We can also know certain truths through reason. For example, if today is Monday and a friend says that tomorrow is Thursday, could the statement be true? Of course not! Logic and reason will lead us to many true or accurate conclusions, but sometimes we don't have all the facts, or we jump to conclusions that are simply not true. Ultimately, the combination of what we can sense and what we can understand logically helps us to know truth. Our experiences can also help us know what is true. And we, as Christians, believe that God reveals truth to us. We know what is true is through our senses, reason, experiences, and revelation.

God Reveals Truth through His Creation: Most of us have observed the stars on a clear night and wondered how they got there. Were they placed in the sky by an all-powerful Creator, or are they the result of a cosmic accident? Ancient people observed the moon and realized that its phases followed a logical, predictable pattern. Could this be an accident? Or was the pattern evidence of a Designer? Thousands of years ago, a psalmist thought about the moon and stars and concluded that they must have had a Creator.

¹ The heavens proclaim the glory of God.
   The skies display his craftsmanship.
² Day after day they continue to speak;
   night after night they make him known.
³ They speak without a sound or word;
   their voice is never heard.
⁴ Yet their message has gone throughout the earth,
   and their words to all the world.   Psalm 19:1–4

The creation is a powerful testimony to God's existence. It is difficult to deny that. Anyone who has seen God's work has also seen his greatness and power. In the book of Romans, the apostle Paul also tells us how creation speaks truth about God.

¹⁹ [People] know the truth about God because he has made it obvious to them. ²⁰ For ever since the world was created, people have seen the earth and sky. Through everything God made, they can clearly see his invisible qualities—his eternal power and divine nature. So they have no excuse for not knowing God. Romans 1:19–20

STATUE OF ISAIAH BY
SALVATORE REVELLI

God Reveals Truth through the Bible and the Holy Spirit: Christians believe the Bible is God's Word. The Bible's veracity has been proven time and time again. Prophecies about the coming Messiah were fulfilled in Jesus. Bible scholars say that there are 61 specific Old Testament prophecies about the Messiah that were fulfilled in the New Testament by Jesus. God revealed himself to the writers of the Bible through the inspiration of the Holy Spirit, assuring us that the Bible is both his Word and completely true. Isaiah 45:19 says, "I, the LORD, speak only what is true and declare only what is right."

Paul, inspired by the Holy Spirit, wrote, all Scripture is inspired by God and is useful to teach us what is true and to make us realize what is wrong in our lives. It corrects us when we are wrong and teaches us to do what is right (2 Timothy 3:16).

We also know from Paul that God revealed these things by his Spirit. For his Spirit searches out everything and shows us God's deep secrets (1 Corinthians 2:10).

God Reveals Truth through His Son: Everything that creation, the Holy Spirit, and Scripture reveal to us about God was shown to be true through the life and words of Jesus. The writer of Hebrews affirms that God spoke, and continues to speak, through his Son, Jesus.

[1] Long ago God spoke many times and in many ways to our ancestors through the prophets. [2] And now in these final days, he has spoken to us through his Son. God promised everything to the Son as an inheritance, and through the Son he created the universe.

Hebrews 1:1–2

Jesus said of himself, "I am the way, the truth, and the life" (John 14:6). In Revelation, the last book of the Bible, Jesus is called *the Word of God* (Revelation 19:13). It is this Jesus—the Word of God and the Way, the Truth, and the Life—who came to Earth that we might know God himself personally, in the flesh, as John wrote:

[1] In the beginning the Word already existed.
   The Word was with God,
      and the Word was God.
[2] He existed in the beginning with God.
[3] God created everything through him,
      and nothing was created except through him.
[4] The Word gave life to everything that was created,
      and his life brought light to everyone.

John 1:1–4

Topic 2—The Biblical Christian View of God

Truth describes what is real, and we know it through our senses, reason, experiences, and revelation. God reveals himself to us through creation, the Bible, Jesus, and the Holy Spirit. Who is God? What is he like? The study of God is called theology. People also use the word *theology* more broadly to talk about topics related to God, such as belief, faith, and religion. The term *theology* is based on *theos*, the Greek word for God.

> **Theology**
> The study of God

Part 1—Who Is God?

Christians base their faith on the truths that God has revealed about himself through his creation, his Word, his Holy Spirit, and his Son. What do these sources of revelation tell us about God? First, they tell us that he is a personal Being who is both like and unlike us. Like us, God communicates. He has thoughts and feelings and he can make choices. Unlike us, God is perfectly holy. He always acts in accordance with his nature. We, in contrast, do not always do what is right because of our sinful nature.

God Is a Personal Being: We know God is a Person rather than an impersonal force. A force cannot communicate, but God speaks to his image-bearers. Because all human beings bear God's image, they can therefore understand and reply to God. One famous example of God's communication is found in Exodus 3. In that passage, God spoke to Moses through a burning bush and told him, [14] ". . . I AM WHO I AM. Say this to the people of Israel: I AM has sent me to you." [15] God also said to Moses, "Say this to the people of Israel: Yahweh, the God of your ancestors—the God of Abraham, the God of Isaac, and the God of Jacob—has sent me to you. This is my eternal name, my name to remember for all generations" (Exodus 3:14–15).

God Has Thoughts: God communicates his ideas and plans to us, yet we cannot understand all of God's thoughts because they are very different from ours.

8 "My thoughts are nothing like your thoughts," says the LORD. "And my ways are far beyond anything you could imagine. 9 For just as the heavens are higher than the earth, so my ways are higher than your ways and my thoughts higher than your thoughts."

Isaiah 55:8–9

God Has Emotions: As a personal Being, God expresses emotions. He always does this in a pure and holy way. He expresses love, joy, sorrow, and even anger. God reveals his emotions to us throughout the Bible, perhaps most clearly in the accounts of his relationship with the Israelites. God gave them laws to follow as his chosen nation. Sadly, they rebelled against God and refused to follow his laws. The prophets Hosea and Isaiah wrote about God's love and sorrow for his chosen people. God is speaking in the following verse:

1 "When Israel was a child, I loved him,
  and I called my son out of Egypt.
2 But the more I called to him,
  the farther he moved from me,
offering sacrifices to the images of Baal
  and burning incense to idols."

Hosea 11:1–2

Isaiah tells of God's righteous anger against sin in the following verses:

24 [The Israelites] have rejected the law of the LORD of Heaven's Armies; they have despised the word of the Holy One of Israel. 25 That is why the LORD's anger burns against his people, and why he has raised his fist to crush them.

Isaiah 5:24–25

God also feels sadness and happiness.

Oh, how often they . . . grieved his heart in that dry wasteland.

Psalm 78:40

"The joy of the LORD is your strength!"

Nehemiah 8:10

God Makes Choices: In Genesis 1–2, we see that God made a choice to create the universe. But even before he created the heavens and the earth, God had already decided to choose us as his children.

4 Even before he made the world, God loved us and chose us in Christ to be holy and without fault in his eyes. 5 God decided in advance to adopt us into his own family by bringing us to himself through Jesus Christ. This is what he wanted to do, and it gave him great pleasure.

Ephesians 1:4–5

God chose Jesus to be our Savior. God chose to create a special nation through which Jesus would be born. God's choices are carefully and thoughtfully related to his great plan for creation. His choices are perfect and always lead to the praise of his glory.

God Is Spirit and Invisible: Although God is a personal Being, he is not a physical one. The Bible tells us that God is Spirit (John 4:24). The Bible also tells us that God has no form of any kind (Deuteronomy 4:15). God is invisible, and this is why no one has ever seen God face to face, nor can they ever see him (1 Timothy 6:16). Even so, he has revealed his presence to us on several occasions and in several ways. One of those ways was through Jesus Christ.

[10] "Don't you believe that I am in the Father and the Father is in me? The words I speak are not my own, but my Father who lives in me does his work through me. [11] Just believe that I am in the Father and the Father is in me. Or at least believe because of the work you have seen me do."

John 14:10–11

No one has seen God the Father, but people have seen God the Son, Jesus. Just before Jesus was crucified, he met with his disciples for the Passover meal. That night, he explained that anyone who had seen him physically had seen the Father. Jesus was not denying that he and the Father were two distinct Persons within the one true God. Rather, he was saying that he himself is the fullest revelation of the Father that the world has ever seen.

Part 2—What Is God Like?

God Is Triune: One of the things that we as human beings find the most difficult to understand about God is his triune existence. God is one God in three Persons—God the Father, God the Son, and God the Holy Spirit. Together, we refer to one God in three Persons as *the Trinity*. It is one of the great mysteries of God that Christians accept by faith through a careful study of Scripture. As we study the Bible, we come to understand that God is, indeed, one God existing in three Persons—not three gods nor one god with three personalities. The three Persons exist in perfect unity—unchanging, coeternal, and coequal.

The apostle Peter described their work together in the following verse:

God the Father knew you and chose you long ago, and his Spirit has made you holy. As a result, you have obeyed him and have been cleansed by the blood of Jesus Christ.

1 Peter 1:2

Jesus commanded the disciples to make disciples and baptize them in the name of the Father and the Son and the Holy Spirit (Matthew 28:19). The Trinity is also present in Paul's prayer for the church in Corinth:

May the grace of the Lord Jesus Christ, the love of God, and the fellowship of the Holy Spirit be with you all.

2 Corinthians 13:14

In 1826, Reginald Heber wrote the words to a Christian hymn that is still sung in many churches today. In 1861, John Dykes wrote the music. The name of the hymn is "Holy, Holy, Holy."

Holy, Holy, Holy! Lord God Almighty!
Early in the morning our song shall rise to Thee.
Holy, Holy, Holy! Merciful and mighty!
God in three Persons, blessed Trinity!

God the Son, Jesus, took on flesh and was born as a human being. He is completely God and completely human. John emphasized both the deity and the humanity of Jesus in his gospel:

THE HOLY TRINITY, WOODCUT, 1881

[Jesus] became human and made his home among us. He was full of unfailing love and faithfulness. And we have seen his glory, the glory of the Father's one and only Son.   John 1:14

After Jesus ascended into heaven, he and the Father sent the Holy Spirit to God's people. The prophet Joel wrote about this event. The day it took place was Pentecost—the birthday of the church.

In those days I will pour out my Spirit
  even on servants—men and women alike.   Joel 2:29

God is always for our good. The three Persons of the Trinity work together to help, teach, and, ultimately, establish an everlasting relationship with us.

God Has Unique Attributes: The Bible reveals that God is eternal, immutable, omnipotent, omniscient, and omnipresent. This means that God has no beginning or end, does not change, is all-powerful, all-knowing, and in all places at all times.

The Psalms speak to the eternal nature of God:

Before the mountains were born,
  before you gave birth to the earth and the world,
  from beginning to end, you are God. Psalm 90:2

The prophet Isaiah affirms God is eternal:

Trust in the LORD always, for the LORD GOD is the eternal Rock.   Isaiah 26:4

Through the prophet Malachi, God declares he is immutable:

"I am the LORD, and I do not change."   Malachi 3:6

The prophet Jeremiah attested to God's omnipotence saying, "O Sovereign LORD! You made the heavens and earth by your strong hand and powerful arm. Nothing is too hard for you!" (Jeremiah 32:17). Jeremiah also wrote about God's omnipresence. "Am I not everywhere in all the heavens and the earth?" says the LORD (Jeremiah 23:24).

The apostle John revealed God's omniscience when he wrote that God knows everything (1 John 3:20).

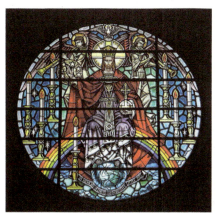

God is also transcendent, meaning that although God is deeply interested in his creation, he is not a part of it. He is above all he created, as Isaiah says:

God sits above the circle of the earth.
  The people below seem like grasshoppers to him!
He spreads out the heavens like a curtain
  and makes his tent from them.   Isaiah 40:22

God is greater than we can imagine (Isaiah 55:8), and he is worthy of our worship.

Yours, O LORD, is the greatness, the power, the glory, the victory, and the majesty. Everything in the heavens and on earth is yours, O LORD, and this is your kingdom. We adore you as the one who is over all things.

1 Chronicles 29:11

Topic 3—The Biblical Christian View of People

People from every race and culture, at some time in their lives, ask at least four personal questions: *Where did I come from? Who am I? Why am I here?* and *Where am I going?* The biblical Christian worldview holds specific beliefs about these questions.

Part 1—Where Did I Come From?

The Origin of Humankind: The mystery of the beginning of the human race is solved in Genesis. The Bible reveals that on the sixth day of creation, God himself created a man and a woman.

[18] Then the LORD GOD said, "It is not good for the man to be alone. I will make a helper who is just right for him." [19] So the LORD GOD formed from the ground all the wild animals and all the birds of the sky. He brought them to the man to see what he would call them, and the man chose a name for each one. [20] He gave names to all the livestock, all the birds of the sky, and all the wild animals. But still there was no helper just right for him.

[21] So the LORD GOD caused the man to fall into a deep sleep. While the man slept, the LORD GOD took out one of the man's ribs and closed up the opening. [22] Then the LORD GOD made a woman from the rib, and he brought her to the man.

Genesis 2:18–22

When Does Human Life Start? Biblical Christianity asserts that human life begins at conception. All life is precious, from the womb until natural death.

[8] "'You formed me with your hands; you made me,
   yet now you completely destroy me.
[9] Remember that you made me from dust—
   will you turn me back to dust so soon?
[10] You guided my conception
   and formed me in the womb.
[11] You clothed me with skin and flesh,
   and you knit my bones and sinews together.
[12] You gave me life and showed me your unfailing love.
   My life was preserved by your care.'"   Job 10:8–12

Part 2—Who Am I?

The biblical Christian worldview sees all people as immensely valuable. Their value is not based on whether they are male or female, black or white, talented or untalented, attractive or unattractive. Everyone's value is based on one thing and one thing only. All people are equally valuable because God created all people as his image-bearers. We read this truth in Genesis: So God created human beings in his own image. In the image of God he created them (Genesis 1:27). People of all races, all ages, all shapes and sizes, and even all worldviews are God's image-bearers. This truth alone gives all people equal worth and value! Jesus said, [6] "What is the price of five sparrows—two copper coins? Yet God does not forget a single one of them. [7] And the very hairs on your head are all numbered. So don't be afraid; you are more valuable to God than a whole flock of sparrows" (Luke 12:6–7).

I Am God's Image-Bearer. People bear God's image in several ways. Of course, we do not have his divine attributes of omniscience, omnipotence, omnipresence, or transcendence, but we do share some qualities with God. For example, people have and express emotions (Ephesians 4:26), and have the ability to make choices (Psalm 39:1) and think rationally (Romans 8:6).

Another attribute we share with God is the ability to know right from wrong. The Bible tells us that as God's image-bearers, we are endowed with a conscience. God revealed this truth about the conscience to Paul, who wrote about it in a letter to the Christians in Rome.

[People] demonstrate that God's law is written in their hearts, for their own conscience and thoughts either accuse them or tell them they are doing right.   Romans 2:15

Sadly, people don't always act according to their conscience. They get angry and lash out at others and neglect God's command to be holy. Peter wrote you must be holy in everything you do, just as God who chose you is holy (1 Peter 1:15). That is why we are dependent upon God for his grace and forgiveness. In fact, we are dependent upon God for everything.

As God's image-bearers, we also have an eternal soul, or spirit that will continue to live after our physical death. The Holy Spirit communicates with our spirits.

[10] Create in me a clean heart, O God.
    Renew a loyal spirit within me.
[11] Do not banish me from your presence,
    and don't take your Holy Spirit from me.   Psalm 51:10–11

I Am Dependent on God. Since God created us—giving us life and breath—we are truly dependent on him for everything. Our bodies belong to him.

[19] Don't you realize that your body is the temple of the Holy Spirit, who lives in you and was given to you by God? You do not belong to yourself, [20] for God bought you with a high price. So you must honor God with your body.   1 Corinthians 6:19–20

Sometimes people think they are in control of their own lives, but it is actually God who is in control. It is he who supplies all of our needs (Philippians 4:19) and sustains the universe (Hebrews 1:3).

I Am Relational. God created people to be in a relationship with him; he also made people to have relationships with others. The first social unit that God created was the relationship between husband and wife. Adam and Eve formed the first family. Later, they followed God's command to be fruitful and multiply. They had children and those children had children. Families became tribes, and tribes became cities, states, and eventually, nations. All of this was part of God's plan for humankind to rule over the earth.

All the nations of the earth descended from these clans [the families of Noah] after the flood.
Genesis 10:32

I Am a Sinful Image-Bearer. Although God created Adam and Eve as perfect image-bearers, since the fall all image-bearers are imperfect or marred. We now carry God's image imperfectly because we have inherited the sinful nature of Adam, our first father.

UNITED NATIONS BUILDING
MANHATTAN, NEW YORK

All of us, like sheep, have strayed away.
We have left God's paths to follow our own.
Isaiah 53:6

Part 3—Why Am I Here?

God created people for a reason. No one is here by accident. God specifically designed each person to be a part of his eternal plan for life on earth now and, later, in heaven.

At some point in their lives, most people wonder why they are here on Earth. They may ask if their life has a purpose. If so, what is that purpose?

God Created Me Because It Gave Him Pleasure. Some people say that God created people because he was lonely. This is not true! He created you to be his child because it pleased him to do so.

⁴ Even before he made the world, God loved us and chose us in Christ to be holy and without fault in his eyes. ⁵ God decided in advance to adopt us into his own family by bringing us to himself through Jesus Christ. This is what he wanted to do, and it gave him great pleasure.
Ephesians 1:4–5

God Created Me to Praise His Glory. Because God is so amazing, he not only created us because it gave him great pleasure to do so, but he created us to praise his glory.

¹¹ We were also chosen . . . ¹² in order that we, who were the first to put our hope in Christ, might be for the praise of his glory.
Ephesians 1:11–12, NIV

To praise God's glory means to worship, adore, and honor his perfect excellence, splendor, majesty, and greatness. What a wonderful privilege and responsibility God gives his image-bearers!

God Created Me to Glorify Him. Not only did God create us to praise him, he also created us to glorify him. When God commands us to give him glory, he means we are to acknowledge the glory he already has. How do we do this? We glorify God when we praise him, worship him, thank him, and tell others about him. We also glorify God when we take care of ourselves and others, when we live according to his Word, and when we do good works.

So whether you eat or drink, or whatever you do, do all for the glory of God. 1 Corinthians 10:31

I Am Here to Serve Others. The biblical Christian worldview teaches that God created people to live in relationships with others. One aspect of those relationships is loving our fellow image-bearers and serving them as Jesus served us. In Paul's letter to the Galatians, God commanded us to serve one another. And we are to serve others for God's glory, not ours. Since the fall, our sinful nature makes us focus more on ourselves than

on others. But in order to follow Jesus' example, we need to put selfishness aside. Jesus taught us this truth in his Sermon on the Mount when he said, "Let your good deeds shine out for all to see, so that everyone will praise your heavenly Father" (Matthew 5:16).

Service requires patience, love, time, and often sacrifice. Jesus, of course, is our perfect Example of a loving, selfless Servant. While eating the Passover meal with his disciples on the night before he was crucified, Jesus demonstrated what it means to be a servant when he washed his disciples' feet.

Part 4—Where Am I Going?

For people who hold the biblical Christian worldview, death is not the end of life. Life continues beyond the grave—either in the presence of God or in the absence of his presence. How can we be sure we will be in God's presence when we die? God made the answer to this question very clear because of his great love and mercy to us.

²⁵ Jesus told her [Martha], "I am the resurrection and the life. Anyone who believes in me will live, even after dying. ²⁶ Everyone who lives in me and believes in me will never ever die." John 11:25–26

Where I Go Is My Choice. Since people were created in the image of God with an eternal spirit, everyone has life after death. Are all people going to live with God in the new heavens and earth after they die a physical death? Jesus answered this question. John wrote the answer in his gospel.

²⁴ "I tell you the truth, those who listen to my message and believe in God who sent me have eternal life. They will never be condemned for their sins, but they have already passed from death into life. . . .

²⁸ Don't be so surprised! Indeed, the time is coming when all the dead in their graves will hear the voice of God's Son, ²⁹ and they will rise again. Those who have done good will rise to experience eternal life, and those who have continued in evil will rise to experience judgment. John 5:24, 28–29

What did Jesus mean when he said that those who have continued in evil will experience judgment? He meant that people who have not accepted him as their Savior will be condemned. Condemnation is eternal separation from God. Being separated from God will be sad and painful forever.

Topic 4—The Biblical Christian View of the Universe

People often ask questions about the universe—the heavens and the earth. Let's explore the biblical Christian answers to some of these questions.

Where Did the Universe Come From? The biblical Christian view of the universe is based on God's revelation that the universe is not eternal. Before it came into existence, there was no eternal matter waiting to suddenly come together and accidentally make a universe. The materials that God used to make the universe were themselves created by him, and he then shaped them into the heavens and the earth.

The Trinity—Father, Son, and Holy Spirit—created everything that exists. Absolutely nothing exists that was not made through Jesus, the Word. God revealed this truth in John's gospel.

[1] In the beginning the Word already existed. The Word was with God, and the Word was God. [2] He existed in the beginning with God. [3] God created everything through him, and nothing was created except through him.

John 1:1–3

Why Did God Create the Universe? In Genesis 1, we read the words "Then God said" before every one of God's creative acts. At his command, things came into existence from nothing—the earth, light, sky, sun, moon, and stars. The land produced plants and living creatures, the waters filled with creatures of the deep, and the air filled with birds. But why did God create all these amazing things?

1. God Created the Universe Because It Pleased Him. God created the universe because he wanted to; it pleased him to do so. He revealed this to John through a vision of heaven, in which John saw God's servants praising God for what he had done.

You are worthy, O Lord our God,
    to receive glory and honor and power.
For you created all things,
    and they exist because you created what you pleased.

Revelation 4:11

2. God Created the Universe for Himself. When God created the universe, he made it to be his own possession.

The earth is the LORD's, and everything in it.
The world and all its people belong to him.   Psalm 24:1

The heavens are yours, and the earth is yours;
everything in the world is yours—you created it all.
                                                    Psalm 89:11

3. God Created the Universe to Reveal His Existence and to Show Us What He Is Like. Just as every video game, airplane, and delicious ice cream sundae could not exist without someone to design and make it, neither could the universe exist without a Maker. Creation not only reveals that God exists; it also shows his divine nature.

King David understood that the creation reveals God's existence and nature. He understood that without saying one word, the universe shows us God's glory—his perfect excellence, majesty, honor, and greatness that cannot be compared to anything else. Let's look at how David explained this truth in one of his psalms.

[1] The heavens proclaim the glory of God.
The skies display his craftsmanship.
[2] Day after day they continue to speak;
night after night they make him known.
[3] They speak without a sound or word;
their voice is never heard.
[4] Yet their message has gone throughout the earth,
and their words to all the world.   Psalm 19:1–4

4. God Created the Earth to Be the Home for His Image-Bearers. Although God created the universe as his own possession, he created it for his image-bearers. God created the earth to be our home.

The heavens belong to the LORD,
but he has given the earth to all humanity.   Psalm 115:16

Even though this present Earth was cursed by God because of the fall, a day is coming when he will make new heavens and a new earth. That new earth will also be our home. God will create it for all people who repent of their sins and believe in Jesus as God's Son and their Savior. The new earth and the people who live on it will never grow old, wear out, or die. And best of all, God himself will live there with us.

[2] And I saw the holy city, the new Jerusalem, coming down from God out of heaven like a bride beautifully dressed for her husband. [3] I heard a loud shout from the throne, saying, "Look, God's home is now among his people! He will live with them, and they will be his people. God himself will be with them." Revelation 21:2–3

What Is God's Relationship to the Universe? Since God created the universe, he has never abandoned it. He didn't create it with a battery to keep it going until it runs down. No, God created the universe by the power of his word, and he sustains it by his word. He created the laws that govern our existence on Earth—including gravity, water and rock cycles, the tides, the seasons, planetary movement, and many other natural laws. God sustains the entire universe.

[Jesus] existed before anything else, and he holds all creation together. Colossians 1:17

God also revealed this truth to the writer of Hebrews.

The Son radiates God's own glory and expresses the very character of God, and he sustains everything by the mighty power of his command. Hebrews 1:3

What Is My Relationship with the Universe? God created us to have a relationship with the universe. He designed our relationship to be with a small part of the universe—the earth. God created Earth to be our home and for us to be its stewards. To rule over, or steward, the works of God on the earth is a huge responsibility—one that no animal could possibly fulfill. Only people, God's image-bearers, have this ability. God crowned us with glory and honor, giving us the ability to rule. We can think and reason, make choices, and act on God's behalf to manage and care for everything he made. King David understood this when he wrote this psalm:

⁵Yet you made them [people] only a little lower than God
  and crowned them with glory and honor.
⁶You gave them charge of everything you made,
  putting all things under their authority—
⁷the flocks and the herds
  and all the wild animals,
⁸the birds in the sky, the fish in the sea,
  and everything that swims the ocean currents.
⁹O LORD, our Lord, your majestic name fills the earth! Psalm 8:5–9

Topic 5—The Biblical Christian View of Moral Laws and Values

We began our study of the biblical Christian worldview by examining questions that people have about truth, the existence of God, the purpose and nature of people, and our relationship to the universe. Now it is time to look at one more category of beliefs that make up a worldview—beliefs about what is right and what is wrong.

Moral Awareness: Moral awareness is a God-given inner knowledge that all people possess of behaviors and attitudes that are right and good. We have moral awareness through our conscience. Our conscience is an inner voice that either accuses us when we do wrong or tells us when our actions are right. This is how Paul explained this truth in the book of Romans.

⁹There will be trouble and calamity for everyone who keeps on doing what is evil—for the Jew first and also for the Gentile. ¹⁰But there will be glory and honor and peace from God for all who do good—for the Jew first and also for the Gentile. ¹¹For God does not show favoritism. Romans 2:9–11

Although we have a "sense" of what is right or wrong, our consciences are not always perfect moral indicators. People who constantly go against their consciences can actually shut off their internal alarm system so that it no longer warns them of sin. Paul wrote about the danger of ignoring one's conscience in a letter to Timothy.

¹ Now the Holy Spirit tells us clearly that in the last times some will turn away from the true faith; they will follow deceptive spirits and teachings that come from demons. ² These people are hypocrites and liars, and their consciences are dead.

1 Timothy 4:1–2

Because of our sinful nature and our imperfect conscience, God lovingly reveals his moral nature and truth about right and wrong to us through Scripture. He does not leave us alone to figure it out. King David knew and loved the Scriptures and the laws of God they contained. He knew how morally perfect they were, and he knew that God gave them to help people do what is right. Like a compass, God's laws in Scripture help everyone find the right way to live.

⁷ The instructions of the LORD are perfect,
  reviving the soul.
The decrees of the LORD are trustworthy,
  making wise the simple.
⁸ The commandments of the LORD are right,
  bringing joy to the heart.
The commands of the LORD are clear,
  giving insight for living.
⁹ Reverence for the LORD is pure,
  lasting forever.
The laws of the LORD are true;
  each one is fair.   Psalm 19:7–9

God's Moral Laws: What are God's moral laws like? How do we know they are right? Well, as a perfect moral Being, God is absolutely holy and sinless. Therefore, God's moral laws are based on the perfect moral nature of God himself. If God is holy, then his laws must be holy. God is also righteous and just.

He is the Rock; his deeds are perfect.
  Everything he does is just and fair.
He is a faithful God who does no wrong;
  how just and upright he is!

Deuteronomy 32:4

God's moral laws are also objective and absolute. When we say that God's moral laws are objective, we mean that they are real and that they exist apart from or independently of us. Regardless of whether we think they exist or not, they still exist. In contrast to human laws that are often imperfect and changeable, God's moral laws are absolute. This means they are absolutely perfect in every way, and they never change. They are not true one day and untrue the next. Many people believe that whether something is right or wrong depends on individual opinions or situations. They may hold this view in order to justify sinful actions, claiming that decisions are a personal matter. Yet, God's laws are for all people at all times. They are universal—they apply to everyone, wherever and whenever they live on earth.

The Ten Commandments (Exodus 20:1–21, also in Deuteronomy 5:6–21) in the Old Testament are some of God's moral laws. It is important to know that Jesus did not come to remove or replace any of God's laws. In his gospel, Matthew wrote about Jesus' teaching on morality.

^{37} Jesus replied, "'You must love the LORD your God with all your heart, all your soul, and all your mind.' ^{38} This is the first and greatest commandment. ^{39} A second is equally important: 'Love your neighbor as yourself.' ^{40} The entire law and all the demands of the prophets are based on these two commandments."

Matthew 22:37–40

So, morality demands that we love God with all our heart, soul, and mind and that we love others as we love ourselves. If we consider our thoughts, words, and actions in light of what Jesus said, then we will avoid wrong behaviors and do what is right.

Our Responsibility to God's Moral Laws: We know that we are imperfect people with sinful natures, yet God holds us accountable for knowing and following his laws. But the wonderful message of the Christian faith is that our holiness before God does not depend on our ability to become perfectly holy by ourselves. This is impossible. Jesus' selfless sacrifice on our behalf makes us holy in God's eyes. Jesus was perfectly holy, and by his mercy and love, he places his holiness on us. God revealed this wonderful truth to the writer of the book of Hebrews.

For God's will was for us to be made holy by the sacrifice of the body of Jesus Christ.

Hebrews 10:10

If God sees us as holy through Jesus, can't we just do whatever we want? The answer is no! We are still responsible to grow in holiness. We are to perfect our holiness. God commands us to purify our hearts and to work toward perfect or complete holiness.

Let us cleanse ourselves from everything that can defile our body or spirit. And let us work toward complete holiness because we fear God.

2 Corinthians 7:1

Paul gave commands against immoral behavior; he also commanded moral behavior. As Paul made clear, such commands are intended to help God's children conform to Jesus' holiness. Notice that Paul emphasizes that all of God's moral laws are held together by love. Why? Because God's laws are based on his perfect character, and God's character is perfect love.

^{5} Put to death the sinful, earthly things lurking within you. Have nothing to do with sexual immorality, impurity, lust, and evil desires. Don't be greedy, for a greedy person is an idolater, worshiping the things of this world. ^{6} Because of these sins, the anger of God is coming. . . .

^{9} Don't lie to each other, for you have stripped off your old sinful nature and all its wicked deeds. ^{10} Put on your new nature, and be renewed as you learn to know your Creator and become like him. . . .

^{12} Since God chose you to be the holy people he loves, you must clothe yourselves with tenderhearted mercy, kindness, humility, gentleness, and patience. ^{13} Make allowance for each other's faults, and forgive anyone who offends you. Remember, the Lord forgave you, so you must forgive others. ^{14} Above all, clothe yourselves with love, which binds us all together in perfect harmony.   Colossians 3:5–6, 9–10, 12–14

© Walking in Truth Grade 7

Unit 2

Islam
An Unbiblical View of
God and the World

Getting Started—What Is Islam?

Over 1,400 years ago—600 years after Christianity was born—one of the world's largest monotheistic religions came into existence. This religion is called Islam. In the year 610 in the desert of present-day Saudi Arabia, a man named *Muhammad* reported that he received a special revelation of truth from God through the angel Gabriel. Other revelations followed, continuing for 23 years. After each revelation, Muhammad recited the words he heard to friends who wrote them down. Many who heard the revelations believed that Muhammad's words were truths from God, and they submissively obeyed them. *Islam* is the Arabic word for *submission*, and people who submit to the revelations Muhammad claimed to have received from God are known as *Muslims*. The word Muslim is derived or taken from the word *Islam*, and it means *one who submits*.

Eventually all of Muhammad's revelations were combined in one book, and this book is called the Quran (Koran). Today, approximately 1.6 billion people, about 23 percent of the world's population in 2009, believe that the Quran is a holy book, a truthful revelation from God. They believe that the Quran contains truth about truth, God, people, the universe, and right and wrong. These beliefs, of course, are the "glasses" through which Muslims look at and interpret the world around them. These beliefs form their worldview, and their worldview determines how they think, dress, eat, raise their families, build their communities, and worship the God they believe is the only true God.

The Islamic worldview is a monotheistic worldview because it holds that only one all-powerful creator God exists, but it is not a biblical worldview. Islam's views about God the Father and his Son, Jesus, are very different from biblical Christianity's views. Islam's views about the nature of people are also unlike biblical Christianity's which says people are God's image-bearers These and other differences between Christianity and Islam are important to understand as we study how Islam has spread throughout the world, sometimes peacefully and sometimes by force.

In the lessons of Unit 2, we'll explore the Islamic views in each category of beliefs common to all worldviews. Then we will compare the beliefs of the Islamic worldview with the beliefs of the Christian worldview.

Before we begin our comparative study, it's important to understand a little of Islam's history. This lesson presents facts about Muhammad: Who was he? How did he become the founder of Islam? What basic message did he preach? And the lesson presents some basic facts about Islam: How quickly did it grow? How did it spread around the world? How far did it spread? What does Islam look like in the world today?

Islam
A monotheistic worldview religion founded by Muhammad

Muslim
One who submits

Quran
The holy book of Islam said to contain Allah's revelations to Muhammad

Topic 1—Who Was Muhammad?

Muhammad's Childhood: Muhammad was born in about 570. His name means *praised*. At the time of his birth, Christianity was over 500 years old and had spread to many parts of the world, including Europe, Africa, parts of Asia, and throughout the Middle East, including the Arabian Peninsula.

Muhammad was born in the city of Mecca on the western side of the Arabian Peninsula. His early life was one of tragedy and struggle. His father died before he was born, and his mother died when he was only six years old. He was placed in the care of his grandfather, who also soon died. Then he was taken in by his uncle, Abu Talib, who raised him until he was a young adult.

Muhammad's First Marriage and Business: Although Muhammad belonged to a very powerful Arabic tribe called *the Quraysh*, he lived a simple life until he was 25 years old. Then, in 595, he married a wealthy 40-year-old businesswoman named *Khadijah*. She owned many large trade caravans whose camels and riders traveled hundreds of miles through the Arabian desert to buy, sell, and trade with merchants. Her caravans traveled as far north as the modern-day country of Syria and as far south as the modern-day country of Yemen (see maps on page 30).

A MEDAL OF KHADIJAH, ALSO KNOWN AS MOTHER OF THE BELIEVERS

Muhammad worked with his wife in this very profitable trading business and served as her representative or agent on many of the trading journeys. Through Khadijah, Muhammad was introduced to some of the most important people of Mecca. As he traveled throughout Arabia, he became acquainted with the religions and politics of his country. Although most Arabs he encountered along the trade routes were polytheistic idol worshippers, he also encountered small communities of Jews and Christians. What Muhammad saw and learned about Arabia's religions affected him deeply and led him on the spiritual journey that eventually gave birth to Islam.

Muhammad's Spiritual Journey: The city of Mecca was an important trade center. It was the resting place for trade caravans traveling both north and south through Arabia. Mecca was also the center of Arabia's polytheistic religion. Inside the city was a cube-shaped shrine or building called the Ka'aba, meaning *cube*. It was 45 feet high, 33 feet wide, and 50 feet long. Inside was a statue of the moon god, Hubal, the main god of the Arab people. Inside, or possibly around, the Ka'aba stood 360 other idols that the Arabs also worshipped.

CARAVAN TRADE ROUTE
OF ANCIENT ARABIA

SAUDI ARABIA AND SURROUNDING
NATIONS TODAY

THE KA'ABA AND PILGRIMS AT THE
MECCA GRAND MOSQUE

Each year, the polytheistic Arabs from different tribes made a *hajj—a religious journey or pilgrimage—*to Mecca to honor their gods. The pilgrims entered the large arena that surrounded the Ka'aba and walked around it in circles seven times. On the eastern corner of the Ka'aba was a black stone that they believed fell from heaven, possibly as a gift or sign from a god. As the pilgrims passed the stone, they gave it special honor by kissing it. Next, the pilgrims traveled about one mile from the Ka'aba to a pillar that represented the devil. There they threw rocks at the pillar.

For some people, including Muhammad, the annual pilgrimage to Mecca revealed just how divided the Arab tribes were. Each tribe not only worshipped its own special god, but each also had its own customs and laws. These religious and political differences caused major strife among the tribes and resulted in tribal arguments and wars.

When Muhammad was 40 years old, he began retreating to a cave in a mountain near Mecca. Here he spent time meditating and praying about the problems he saw within and among the polytheistic Arab tribes. During one of his retreats for meditation, he is said to have been visited by the angel Gabriel, who commanded him to recite a few sentences. This was the first of many revelations Muhammad claimed to have received over the next 23 years. These recitations were eventually written down by friends of Muhammad and compiled in a book called *the Quran* or *Koran.* The word *Quran* means *recitation.* The Quran contains 114 chapters, or *surahs,* but no individual books as the Bible does. Each surah is divided into several verses. The reference Quran 33:9, for example, simply refers to the 33rd chapter (surah) and 9th verse. We will explore the Quran in more detail in Lesson 4.

At first, Muhammad was not sure about the source of the revelations he received in the cave. He told his wife, Khadijah, that perhaps he had been possessed by a demon. He was not sure that the messages he was hearing were really from the supreme or one high God, whom the Arabs called Allah. Muhammad's wife, however, assured him that the messages were from Allah, and she encouraged him to teach others the things he was hearing and reciting. Soon other close family members, including his adopted son Zaid and a young cousin, accepted Muhammad's recitations as truth from Allah. Within a short time, about 100 people from Mecca had accepted Muhammad's teachings and submitted to them.

MUHAMMAD PREACHING ISLAM
TO HIS FOLLOWERS

Ka'aba
The cube-shaped shrine in Mecca
designated as the house of Allah

Allah
The Islamic name for God

MUSLIM CHILDREN STUDYING THE QURAN

MUHAMMAD RECEIVES
REVELATION FROM GABRIEL

The Main Message: Muhammad is said to have received many messages from God over many years. But the main message he heard and recited was this: There is no God but Allah, and Muhammad is the prophet of God. In fact, Muhammad believed that Allah had revealed that he, Muhammad, was the seal, or last, of all the prophets to whom Allah would speak. There would be no prophets after Muhammad, and the messages he received would be the very last messages God would ever reveal.

The People's Response: Now think for a minute about how most people in Mecca would have responded to Muhammad's message. Remember that the Arabs were polytheists. They worshipped not only Hubal, the moon god, but they also worshipped 360 other gods. They believed these gods helped and protected them. And when thousands of pilgrims from all over the country made the annual hajj to worship at the Ka'aba, they bought food and other supplies from the shop owners in Mecca. Perhaps they paid innkeepers, and no doubt some bought idols from the silversmiths and goldsmiths who crafted them. For Mecca, polytheism was good for business and the economy.

Now imagine that they suddenly hear this contradictory message from Muhammad: "There is no God but Allah! You must repent and turn from worshipping your idols and turn to Allah. Oh, and by the way, the Ka'aba belongs only to Allah and to none of the other gods."

Consider how the people of Mecca would have responded to such a message. Except for Muhammad's immediate family and a few friends, everyone in Mecca rejected it. In fact, leaders of his own tribe warned him not to preach it. Muhammad's message was a great threat to the Arabs' polytheistic way of life. His message threatened not only their lifestyle, but also their income. The people of Mecca began to accuse the new prophet of witchcraft and lying. They even accused him of copying his ideas from the Jews and Christians who were scattered throughout Arabia.

During these difficult years of opposition to his message, many changes were occurring in Muhammad's family. In 620 when Muhammad was 50 years old, his wife, Khadijah, died. A few weeks later Abu Talib, the uncle who had raised him, also died. Two months after that, Muhammad married his second wife, a widow of one of his followers. He also married a six-year-old girl, who stayed with her parents until she moved in with Muhammad when she was just nine. She was the daughter of one of his close friends. Later in his life, Muhammad married many more women because he believed that Allah had given him special permission to do so (Quran 33:50). However, he told other men that Allah had given them permission to marry only four wives (Quran 4:3).

The Flight from Mecca: The opposition in Mecca to Muhammad's message became so violent that he and about 100 new Muslim families fled the city for their safety. In the year 622, two years after Khadijah's death, Muhammad and his followers traveled north to the city of Yathrib. Yathrib is called *Medina* today. Muslims call this flight from Mecca to Medina the *hijrah*. In Arabic, *hijrah* means *flight* or *migration*.

For all Muslims, 622 is an important date. Not only is it the date of the hijrah, it is also considered the date for the true beginning of Islam. This date is so important that Muslims created their own calendar. Whereas most western nations use calendars that begin with the time Jesus was born about 2,000 years ago, Muslim calendars begin with the year 622, the year of the hijrah. In the Christian calendar, the year 2000 refers to the approximate number of years since the birth of Christ. For Muslims, the year 2000 is 1420, the approximate number of years since the hijrah.

MUHAMMAD'S FLIGHT TO MEDINA

The Return to and Conquest of Mecca: Muhammad and his followers lived in Medina for eight years after they fled from Mecca. During these years, more and more people submitted to Allah and the teachings of Islam. However, there was still great resistance in Mecca and throughout Arabia to the new religion. One day, however, Muhammad reportedly received another revelation from Allah. The new message was that Allah was giving Muslims permission to fight for the cause of Islam (Quran 9:5). With this new teaching, Muhammad began building a powerful army. In January 630, Muhammad led an army of over 10,000 men south toward Mecca. He took control of the city by force. He destroyed all the images and idols at the Ka'aba and executed many of the people who resisted him.

MUHAMMAD CONQUERS MECCA

Muhammad became the undisputed political and religious leader of Mecca. He made Mecca the center of Islam—the world's newest monotheistic religion.

Muhammad's conquest of Mecca was only the beginning of Islam's growth. Within one year, the prophet had forcefully united most of the tribes of Arabia under his control and the religion of Islam. For the polytheistic tribes, there was only one choice when confronted with Islam—convert or be killed by the sword.

Christian and Jewish communities that did not completely resist Muhammad's armies were allowed some freedom of worship. Yet in order to have this freedom, they had to pay high taxes and be in subjection to the new Islamic laws and powers (Quran 9:29).

Muhammad's conquest of Arabia was the first step toward Islam's goal of bringing the entire world under its control. Within two or three generations, Islam became a global power spreading across three continents. It absorbed Christian and other cultures under its power and become a threat to European nations as far west as France. We'll explore more about the spread and growth of Islam in Topic 4.

Topic 3—The Death of Muhammad and Division within Islam

The Death of Muhammad: Muhammad conquered Mecca in 630. He died two years later at the age of 62. Muhammad had no living son to become his heir and the next leader of Islam. Although Muhammad could have appointed someone to succeed him as leader before he died, he failed to do so. The question of who would become the next leader of Islam became a divisive problem.

ABU BAKR—ISLAM'S FIRST CALIPH

Some Muslims believed Muhammad's successor should be a blood relative such as his cousin Ali. Some even believed that Muhammad had appointed Ali to succeed him. Others disagreed. As the Muslim community debated who should become their next leader, the majority chose Muhammad's father-in-law and good friend, Abu Bakr. The new leader was called *a caliph*. His responsibility was to carry out the leadership and rule of Islam throughout Arabia and other parts of the world.

The choice of Abu Bakr and later two more caliphs who were not Muhammad's blood relatives angered many Muslims. A great division occurred within Islam that remains to this day. Those who believe Muhammad's successor should have been a blood relative are known as *Shiite Muslims*. Those who believe that his successor should be elected are known as *Sunni Muslims*.

MUSLIM MAN IN PRAYER

Today, about 80 percent of the world's Muslims are Sunni, and only about 12 percent are Shiite. The remaining 8 percent include smaller groups of Muslims, each with unique beliefs that set them apart from the others. Although worldwide the Shiite Muslims are in the minority compared to the Sunni Muslims, in some nations like Iran and Iraq, the Shiites are in the majority. Over 90 percent of Iranians and 65 percent of Iraqis are Shiite. In nations where one branch is in the majority, there is often persecution of the minority group(s). Not only do Shiite and Sunni Muslims disagree over Muhammad's successor, they also disagree over other things. Shiites believe that their leaders should have both political and religious power. Sunnis believe that the authority over religious and political affairs should be separate.

Topic 4—The Growth and Spread of Islam

The First One Hundred Years: After Muhammad's death, the first caliph, Abu Bakr, continued his work. He brought all the tribes of Arabia into one community of believers. They became essentially one religious, cultural, and political group with a unified army. All of this occurred within one year of Muhammad's death. Abu Bakr ruled for only two years before he died. In 634, a second caliph was chosen. His name was *Umar*, or *Omar*. During Umar's reign, amazing things began to happen. The Islamic empire grew rapidly. In just 10 years, the Muslim armies led by Umar conquered Mesopotamia (Iraq today) and parts of Persia (Iran today). They marched west, conquering Egypt, and north, conquering Syria and Palestine, including the city of Jerusalem. They swept across North Africa and moved as far north as Armenia, just south of modern-day Russia. In 644, Umar was murdered by a man from Persia (Iran). His successor was Uthman, who continued to lead Islam's march across the world.

UMAR THE GREAT: ISLAM'S
SECOND CALIPH

By the year 732, just 100 years after Muhammad's death, Muslim armies had conquered lands from as far east as India to as far west as modern-day Morocco in northwest Africa. They had also moved into Europe, ruling most of Spain. But in 732, their move into Europe was stopped as they tried to conquer France. At the famous Battle of Tours, the Muslim conquest of Europe was halted. Nevertheless, Islam was well established in Africa, the Middle East, and Asia.

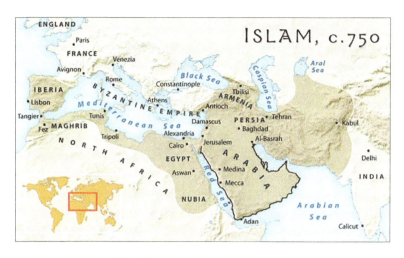

ISLAM, c. 750

THE SPREAD OF ISLAM FOLLOWING
MUHAMMAD'S DEATH 632–750

The Later Years: Although Islam's westward march was stopped in France, Muslims established powerful empires in later centuries. The most powerful was the Ottoman Empire, which ruled from Anatolia or modern-day Turkey. Once again, the Muslim armies marched against Europe. This time they conquered Hungary and moved all the way into Austria. However, their armies were again stopped, this time at the gates to the city of Vienna, Austria, in 1529. Had the Muslim armies not been defeated, most historians believe that Europe would be a completely Muslim continent today.

Islam Around the World Today: Today over 1.6 billion people or 23 percent of the world's population practice the Islamic religion, hold an Islamic worldview, and identify as Muslims. (Approximately 2 billion people or about 32 percent of the world's population today identify as Christian.) Although Islam began in Arabia, most Muslims today are not Arabs. In fact, the countries with the largest Muslim populations today are found outside the Middle East. These include Indonesia, Pakistan, Bangladesh, and India. Muslims are in the majority in Northern Africa as well as in all the countries of the Middle East except Israel. (Lebanon is also a Muslim-majority nation, but it is more tolerant of other faiths than other Muslim countries.)

Beyond these countries, Islam is growing rapidly, so rapidly that some believe the Muslim population of the world will equal or even outnumber the Christian population by the year 2025. For example, in England in 1945 there was only one mosque. A *mosque* is *a special building where Muslims worship.* Today there are thousands of mosques in the United Kingdom and many thousands more are being built around the world from the Americas to Africa.

THE JAMA MASJID MOSQUE IN DELHI, INDIA

Most of the Islamic growth today is peaceful. As Muslim families move or emigrate to traditionally non-Muslim parts of the world such as Europe or North America, they raise their children, who in turn grow up, marry, and have their own children, thus increasing the Muslim population.

But some of the growth of Islam is not peaceful. Some Muslims are called *militants*. They work to spread their religion and worldview by force through terrorism and war with non-Islamic groups and countries. Militant Islam causes much tension in today's world. Efforts to coexist peacefully with Islam's militant groups often fail. While most Muslims want to live in peace with their Christian and non-Christian neighbors, the clash between militant Islam and other cultures and worldviews is a difficult reality that affects many nations of the world today.

Comparing Islam to Biblical Christianity: In the lessons of Unit 2, we'll continue to explore Islam as a worldview shaped by its beliefs about truth, God, people, the universe, and values. As we explore each category of beliefs, we will always compare them with what God's revelation in the Bible says. Some people say that Muslims and Christians believe exactly the same things. While Christians and Muslims do share some common beliefs, their differences are so great that Islam cannot be called a biblical Christian view of God and the world. For this reason, we must evaluate Islam and all other worldviews in light of the truths God revealed to us in Scripture.

It is important to remember that Muslims are God's image-bearers. They may be your neighbors, or they may be people you know about only through newspapers or television. But either way, you must study their worldview with respect and with prayer. Guard against basing your personal opinions on what you read or hear others say. Always search for the truth within God's Word. And if you have an opportunity to share your faith and biblical Christianity with a Muslim, remember to do so with love and respect.

The apostles Paul and Peter instructed the Christians of the early church to speak to non-Christians with the love of Christ—never belligerently or defensively.

⁵ Live wisely among those who are not believers, and make the most of every opportunity. ⁶ Let your conversation be gracious and attractive so that you will have the right response for everyone.
Colossians 4:5–6

¹⁵ If someone asks about your Christian hope, always be ready to explain it. ¹⁶ But do this in a gentle and respectful way.
1 Peter 3:15–16

THE MOSQUE AND KA'ABA IN MECCA, SAUDI
ARABIA—ISLAM'S MOST HOLY SITE

THE PROPHET'S MOSQUE IN MEDINA, SAUDI
ARABIA—ISLAM'S SECOND MOST HOLY SITE
BUILT ON THE SITE OF MUHAMMAD'S ORIGINAL
MOSQUE AND HOME

DOME OF THE ROCK SHRINE IN JERUSALEM—ISLAM'S
THIRD MOST HOLY SITE BUILT ON THE SITE OF
KING SOLOMON'S TEMPLE IN 690 AFTER THE ISLAMIC
CONQUEST OF JERUSALEM IN 637

Getting Started—The Quran

Worldviews are formed by people's beliefs about God, people, the universe, and values. Worldviews are also influenced by what people believe about truth itself. Most people, for example, believe that truth is that which agrees with, accurately describes, and accurately explains what is real. You learned that you can know much truth through your senses even though they don't always tell you the truth. And you learned that you can come to know truth through reasoning. But again, reasoning doesn't always lead to a perfect knowledge of truth. You also learned that monotheists—people who believe in only one personal, living, creator God—believe that there is some truth that can be known only as this one God reveals it.

Christians believe God reveals truth through creation, through his written Word, the Bible, through the Holy Spirit, and through the living Word, Jesus, his Son. When you studied the biblical Christian worldview, you learned that what one believes about God, people, the universe, values, and truth itself must always agree with God's revealed Word in Scripture. Without this perfect guide to truth from a God who speaks only truth, we would very likely believe many things are true when actually they are not. In other words, God's written Word is the foundation for evaluating everything we believe about God and our world. This is why we call our worldview *a biblical Christian worldview.*

As we study Islam, it is important for us to understand that Muslims, like Christians, base their worldview on what they believe is true about God, people, the universe, and values. Ultimately, like Christians, they believe that their worldview must be in harmony with God's revealed truth. A major difference between Muslims and Christians, however, is that Muslims believe God revealed his final truth to Muhammad. And they believe that this truth has been recorded in their holy book, the Quran. This, of course, raises an important question: Is the Quran a true holy book? Is it God's final revelation to the world? Are the Quran and the Bible the revealed Word of God?

In this lesson, we will explore further what Muslims believe about the Quran. We will investigate where and when Muhammad is said to have received his revelations from God. We will explore how Muhammad received his revelations and how the Quran became the book Muslims believe is the final truth from God, whom they call *Allah.* As we explore the Quranic foundation of the Islamic worldview, we will investigate how this foundation compares with the biblical foundation of the Christian worldview. Unless the Quran agrees with God's revealed truth in the Bible, we cannot accept it as God's final revelation of truth to his creation.

The Quran—Islam's Most Important Source of Truth: The Quran is the foundation of Islam and stands at the heart of Muslims' worldview and practices. For Muslims, no other book on Earth is equal to it. Although Muslims believe that God revealed truth to Jews and Christians in the Bible, they do not believe that all of the Bible is God's revealed Word. For them, the Quran is the highest, perfect, and final revelation of God to creation. According to the Quran, Allah said this to Muhammad:

Today the disbelievers have lost all hope that you will give up your religion. Do not fear them: fear Me. Today I have perfected your religion for you, completed My blessing upon you, and chosen as your religion Islam.[1]

Quran 5:3

For Muslims, the Quran is the holiest of all books and demands the highest respect and honor. It must never be placed on the floor or held any lower than a person's lap. It is often placed on a wooden stand while being read. When the Quran is placed on a shelf, it must be above all other books. In some Muslim schools, children must wash before touching the Quran. Then they kiss it three times before opening it. After reading

it, they must kiss it again and then touch their forehead with it before putting it away. When the Quran is not being read, it must be closed because Muslims believe that Satan might read it and bring dishonor to it by doing so.[2]

The Quran is about the length or size of the Christian New Testament. Muslims believe the Quran is an eternal book. They believe that even before the angel Gabriel spoke its words in Arabic to Muhammad, the Quran existed eternally on a well-guarded tablet in heaven. According to the Quran, Allah spoke these words to Muhammad:

[2] By the Scripture that makes things clear. [3] We have made it a Quran in Arabic so that you [people] may understand. [4] It is truly exalted in the Source of Scripture kept with Us, and full of wisdom.   Quran 43:2–4

[21] This is truly a glorious Quran [22] [written] on a preserved Tablet.   Quran 85:21–22

Arabic—The Pure Language of Islam: Because Gabriel is said to have spoken in Arabic so Muhammad could understand, many Muslims believe that the eternal Quran in heaven is also written in Arabic. For them, Arabic is the language of heaven. And because they believe Arabic is the language of Allah and heaven, the Arab people see themselves as God's unique and most favored people on Earth. The Arabic language is so central to the world of Islam that Muslims also believe the Quran is Allah's true revelation only when it is written or printed in Arabic. Even in countries where Muslims do not speak Arabic, like Indonesia, students must learn to read and recite the Quran in Arabic.

When the Quran is translated into any other language, such as English, Muslims believe that it is no longer the pure word of Allah. However, many Muslims and non-Muslims have translated the Quran into many languages, including English. Usually, when this is done, the Arabic Quran is printed next to the translation. In these lessons we will, of course, use English translations.

In Unit 2, most of the verses you will see quoted from the Quran were translated into English by Abdel Haleem. However, if a different translation is used, you will see the name of the person who translated the verse or verses into English after the reference. These names include Arabic translators such as Yusuf Ali, Shakir, and others as well as George Sale, a non-Arabic translator. The name of the translator after each reference is similar to the abbreviations you see after Bible references that tell you which translation you are reading, such as NLT (New Living Translation), NIV (New International Version), and others.

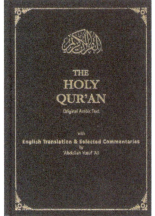

The Quran—A Perfect Book: For Muslims, the Quran contains the perfect words of God. They believe that not one word in the Quran is a mistake and nothing in the Quran contradicts itself. In other words, there is nothing false or "crooked" within its pages. In one revelation, Muhammad is said to have heard these words from Allah:

Praise be to God, who sent down the Scripture to His servant [Muhammad] and made it unerringly straight.   Quran 18:1

As Muhammad began to receive revelations, not everyone believed the words he spoke were really from Allah. People criticized him, saying the revelations he was supposedly receiving were full of contradictions. In response to this criticism, Muhammad said he received this new revelation from Allah:

Will they not think about this Quran? If it had been from anyone other than God, they would have found much inconsistency in it.   Quran 4:82

In other words, Muhammad said that because the Quran is from God it cannot possibly have any contradictions. Only if it were from someone other than God would it have contradictions.

As we will explore later, where verses in the Quran differ from or contradict the Bible, Muslims believe that the Bible is incorrect. They believe that over the years Christians and Jews have changed the Bible from the way God originally revealed it to them. They believe only the Quran has been preserved as Allah's perfect revelation to the world.

The Hadith—Islam's Second Most Important Source of Truth: Before we explore when, where, and how the Quran became Islam's most holy book, we must learn about another source of truth for Muslims. Like Christians, Muslims believe their worldview is based on revelation from God. Christians believe God's perfect revelation is recorded in the Bible, while Muslims believe God's perfect revelation is recorded in the Quran. Muslims, however, believe they have a second source of truth upon which to base their worldview. This source of truth includes the deeds, sayings, and commands of Muhammad that are not included in the Quran. Rather, they are recorded in books called *the Hadith*.

The word hadith means *a speech or saying*. However, the Hadith includes not only the sayings of Muhammad, but also his actions and his commands or decrees. Muslims do not believe the Hadith contains revelations from Allah. And they do not believe the Hadith is holy like the Quran. Nevertheless, the Hadith is second in importance only to the Quran. Muslims believe that the Hadith helps to explain the Quran and makes its teachings practical for everyday life. Today, there are several sets of books called *the Hadith* that have been compiled by Muslim scholars over the years.

One of the most respected collections was assembled by a man named *Muhammad al-Bukhari*, who lived from 810 to 870. For 16 years, he traveled and collected the sayings and deeds people reported were those of Muhammad. He collected about 600,000 hadiths. From this large number he chose only 7,300 that he believed were the most authentic or reliable. By the time al-Bukhari had completed his work, he had filled over nine books with the sayings, decrees, and deeds of Muhammad. Today, al-Bukhari's Hadith is one of the most respected among Muslims. Muslims believe that it is authentic. And because the Arabic word for authentic is *sahih*, Muhammad al-Bukhari's Hadith is simply entitled *Sahih al-Bukhari*.

> Prophet Muhammad (pbuh) said:
>
> *"If Allah wants to do good to somebody, He afflicts him with trials."*
>
> [Sahih al-Bukhari: 5640]

The Hadith has played an important role in shaping the worldview and behavior of Muslims and Islamic nations. For this reason, throughout the lessons on the Islamic worldview, we will include some of Muhammad's hadiths as recorded in al-Bukhari's collection.

Hadith
A speech or saying of Muhammad

Topic 2—The Revelation of the Quran

The Revelations in Mecca: In Lesson 3, you learned that when Muhammad was 25 years old, he married Khadijah, a wealthy caravan tradeswoman who lived in Mecca. For several years, Muhammad traveled with the caravans on their long journeys throughout Arabia. On these trips, Muhammad met tribes of Jews and Christians who did not follow the polytheism of most of the Arabic tribes. Many people believe that as Muhammad learned about the beliefs and behaviors of the Jews and Christians he met, he became troubled over the idolatry he found among the polytheistic tribes throughout Arabia. Perhaps for this reason among others, Muhammad began retreating to a cave in Mount Hira just outside Mecca where he would fast and pray, seeking wisdom and understanding. Then in the year 610, when he was 40 years old, Muhammad is said to have

MOUNT HIRA OUTSIDE MECCA, ALSO KNOWN AS JABAL AN-NOUR, MEANING "THE MOUNTAIN OF LIGHT" IN ARABIC

received his first revelation from Allah through the angel Gabriel. This first encounter frightened Muhammad so much that he thought he had been possessed by an evil spirit. But when he told his wife, Khadijah, she convinced him that the message was not from a demon, but from Allah himself.

Some time passed before Muhammad received another revelation. During this time, he became very depressed and even thought about killing himself. However, according to the Quran, Allah spoke again. This time he

MUSLIMS ENTERING THE CAVE OF MUHAMMAD'S REVELATIONS ON MOUNT HIRA

told Muhammad to go and preach to the people. Allah told him to warn the people to turn away from idolatry and to worship only Allah. Allah also told Muhammad to tell the people that he, Muhammad, was Allah's apostle or sent messenger.

You, wrapped in your cloak, arise and give warning!

Quran 74:1–2

I swear by the glorious Quran (that Muhammad is the Apostle of Allah).   Quran 50:1 Shakir

For the next 23 years, Muhammad continued to receive revelations from Allah. During the first 13 of these years, Muhammad lived and taught in Mecca. But as you learned earlier, most of the polytheists in Mecca did not like Muhammad's message. They became angry when he told them to stop worshipping their idols and to worship only Allah. They became so angry, in fact, that they began to persecute the new prophet and his followers. Yet, according to Muhammad, Allah told him not to fight back, but to simply turn away and bless them with peace.

[88] The Prophet has said, 'My Lord, truly these are people who do not believe, but turn away from them and say, 'Peace': they will come to know.   Quran 43:88–89

AN ANCIENT ILLUSTRATION OF MUHAMMAD TEACHING HIS DISCIPLES

Like the polytheists of Mecca, Jews and Christians also rejected Muhammad's message. Although they believed in only one true God, they knew that much of what Muhammad was teaching was not in harmony with God's Word in the Old and New Testaments. Yet, according to Muhammad, Allah revealed that Muhammed was not to argue with the Jews and Christians who believed that their Scriptures were revelation from God.

And do not dispute with the followers of the Book [Jews and Christians] except by what is best, except those of them who act unjustly, and say: We believe in that which has been revealed to us and revealed to you, and our Allah and your Allah is One, and to Him do we submit.   Quran 29:46

PROPHET MUHAMMAD

In other revelations Muhammad received while living in Mecca, he was told that both Jews and Christians who faithfully followed their Scriptures (the Bible) would receive a good reward from Allah.

The [Muslim] believers, the Jews, the Christians, and the Sabians- all those who believe in God and the Last Day and do good- will have their rewards with their Lord. No fear for them, nor will they grieve.   Quran 2:62

We learn from these kinds of revelations that in the early years of Islam, Muhammad believed he was being instructed to live at peace with those who did not agree with his message. He was to respect the Christians and Jews as well as their Scriptures, and he was to turn away from the unbelieving polytheists and bless them with peace. This message of peace and tolerance toward non-Muslims, however, was about to change. We'll explore these changes and why they occurred in the next section.

Muslim scholars believe that 86 of the 114 chapters, or surahs, of the Quran were revealed to Muhammad while he lived in Mecca.

The Revelations in Medina: The polytheists of Mecca continued to resist Muhammad's message. As their resistance increased, so did their persecution of Muslims. Finally, in 622, Muhammad and his small group of disciples fled Mecca and traveled north to the city of Medina. During the next 10 years, Muhammad reported more revelations he believed were from Allah. These new revelations, however, were not as friendly or tolerant toward polytheists, Jews, and Christians as those Muhammad had received in Mecca. For example, in one revelation Allah changed his command to live at peace with the polytheists who did not believe Muhammad. If the unbelieving polytheists did not desist or stop persecuting Muhammad, he was commanded to kill them.

[190] Fight in God's cause against those who fight you, but do not overstep the limits: God does not love those who overstep the limits.

MUHAMMAD AT MECCA BY ANDREAS MULLER, LATE 19TH CENTURY

[191] Kill them wherever you encounter them, and drive them out from where they drove you out, for persecution is more serious than killing. Do not fight them at the Sacred Mosque unless they fight you there. If they do fight you, kill them- this is what such disbelievers deserve-

[192] but if they stop, then God is most forgiving and merciful.

[193] Fight them until there is no more persecution, and worship is devoted to God. If they cease hostilities, there can be no [further] hostility, except towards aggressors.   Quran 2:190–193

AN ILLUSTRATION OF MUHAMMAD POSSIBLY DURING HIS FLIGHT TO MEDINA IN 622

According to the Quran, Allah also gave Muhammad new commands in Medina about how to treat and relate to Jews and Christians. In these commands, Muslims were no longer to be friends with Jews or Christians. Muslims were to fight them until they submitted to the teachings of Islam and paid a *jizyah*, or tax.

You who believe, do not take the Jews and Christians as allies: they are allies only to each other. Anyone who takes them as an ally becomes one of them- God does not guide such wrongdoers-   Quran 5:51

Fight those of the People of the Book [Jews and Christians] who do not [truly] believe in God and the Last Day, who do not forbid what God and His Messenger have forbidden, who do not obey the rule of justice, until they pay the tax and agree to submit.   Quran 9:29

After receiving these revelations and others like them, Muhammad believed Allah had given him permission to build an army of warriors to force the new religion of Islam on those who did not accept his message. In January 630, after eight years in Medina, Muhammad led an army of 10,000 men back to Mecca and conquered it. Islam was imposed on all the people in the city, and eventually on all people throughout Arabia.

INTERIOR OF MUHAMMAD'S TOMB
THE PROPHET MOSQUE, MEDINA, SAUDI ARABIA

The Final Revelations: Muslims believe that Muhammad received revelations from Allah until just nine days before his death on June 9, 632. Some believe that his last revelation was Quran 2:281.

Beware of a Day when you will be returned to God: every soul will be paid in full for what it has earned, and no one will be wronged.

Others believe that the message in Quran 5:3 was the last Muhammad received.

Today I have perfected your religion for you, completed My blessing upon you, and chosen as your religion Islam: [total devotion to God].

Muslim scholars believe that the longest surahs of the Quran were revealed to Muhammad while he lived in Medina. According to Islam, there have been no more revelations from Allah since Muhammad's death. Muslims believe that their religion is complete and perfect. They believe that the Quran is the last revelation people will ever need to receive from God. And they believe that Muhammad was the seal or last of all Allah's prophets.

Muhammad is not the father of any one of you men; he is God's Messenger and the seal of the prophets: God knows everything.   Quran 33:40

MUHAMMAD'S SWORDS INSIDE HIS TOMB
THE PROPHET'S MOSQUE, MEDINA, SAUDI ARABIA

Who Was Muhammad? Who Is Jesus? As we will study later in this lesson, there are many differences between God's revealed Word in the Bible and the words Muhammad is said to have received from Allah. One of the most important differences pertains to who Muhammad was and who Jesus is. Was Muhammad God's prophet? Did Muhammad receive God's final revelation to his creation? Is the Jesus spoken of in the Quran the same Jesus spoken of in the Bible?

The Quran teaches that Muhammad was only a man—God's messenger who lived and died. It also teaches that Jesus was only a man who lived and died. However, the Bible reveals that Jesus was not a mere man like Muhammad. Rather, Jesus is truly God in the flesh. And not only that, Jesus is the very living Word of God.

¹ In the beginning the Word already existed.
   The Word was with God, and the Word was God.
¹⁴ So the Word became human and made his home among us.   John 1:1, 14

As you will study later, the Quran teaches that Jesus was a prophet. But it also teaches that Muhammad was the last prophet to hear and speak God's word to creation. The Bible, however, reveals that God has spoken to us in these last days of earthly history through Jesus.

[1] Long ago God spoke many times and in many ways to our ancestors through the prophets. [2] And now in these final days, he has spoken to us through his Son.

Hebrews 1:1–2

Jesus himself revealed that he is the Beginning and the End. He is not only the First, he is also the Last. Creation owes its beginning to Jesus, the Word of God. And Jesus will bring this time of earthly history to an end when he returns and creates the new eternal heavens and earth.

"I am the Alpha and the Omega, the First and the Last, the Beginning and the End."

Revelation 22:13

Unlike Muhammad, who was born, died, and remains dead, Jesus is eternal. He existed before creation. He is the living God who was crucified for our sins, died, but now lives and will live forevermore.

I am the living one. I died, but look—I am alive forever and ever! And I hold the keys of death and the grave.

Revelation 1:18

The differences between who the Quran says Muhammad was and who the Bible says Jesus is are not minor differences. If Muhammad (who was only a man and is now dead) spoke God's final revelation, then this is the revelation we must follow. We must allow Muhammad's revelation to shape an Islamic worldview for our lives.

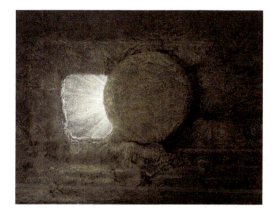

But if Jesus is the Living Word of God, the First and the Last, and God's final revelation in these last days, then we must follow Jesus. We must allow God's Word and his Son to shape a biblical Christian worldview for our life.

Topic 3—The Quran Becomes a Book

The Quran Before Muhammad's Death: Many Muslims believe Muhammad could neither read nor write. This belief is based on a verse in the Quran in which Muhammad is commanded to tell the people to believe that he is Allah's prophet and to follow him.

Say [Muhammad], 'People, I am the Messenger of God to you all, from Him who has control over the heavens and the earth. There is no God but Him; He gives life and death, so believe in God and His Messenger, the unlettered prophet who believes in God and His words, and follow him so that you may find guidance.'

Quran 7:158

A MUSLIM TEACHER INSTRUCTING HIS STUDENTS IN THE QURAN

Although some people reported seeing Muhammad read and write, most agree that he only spoke or recited the revelations he received. And if he did write down some of his revelations, he did not put them together in a book. If these traditions are true, how and when did the Quran become a book?

At first, as some people heard Muhammad recite his revelations, they began to memorize them. These memorized revelations were recited in public worship services at the mosque. Sometimes people memorized them so they could meditate on them privately. The Hadith of al-Bukhari reports that four Muslims actually memorized every revelation Muhammad ever received (Sahih al-Bukhari 5:155).

Other people began to write down Muhammad's revelations as they heard them. They wrote them on pieces of paper, on bark, stones, bones, leather, and almost anything they could find. But for many years these bits and pieces of written revelation were never organized. It was not until after Muhammad's death in 632 that the work of combining his revelations into a book began. This work began because of a battle that occurred after Muhammad died.

VERSES FROM THE QURAN
WRITTEN ON WOODEN TABLETS

The Quran After Muhammad's Death: In 633, some of the Arab tribes that Muhammad had conquered rebelled against Islam. Abu Bakr, Muhammad's successor and Islam's first caliph, set out with his army to bring the rebel tribes back into submission. During the battle, known as the *Battle of Yamama*, many people were killed. Among those who died were some of the men who had

memorized large portions of the Quran. One of the men who was killed was named *Salim*. It is written in the Hadith of al-Bukhari that Muhammad had declared Salim one of the four best reciters of the Quran. His death and the death of others who had memorized the Quran alarmed Abu Bakr and other Muslim leaders. They realized that the first generation of Muslims who had either memorized or written down parts of the Quran would not live forever. They also realized that unless something was done to collect and write down all of Allah's revelations to Muhammad, they would soon be lost to future generations.

As a result of the Battle of Yamama, Abu Bakr chose a man named *Zaid* to begin collecting all of Muhammad's revelations from Allah. Zaid had been one of Muhammad's most trusted scribes, and he had also memorized large portions of the Quran. According to the Hadith of al-Bukhari, Zaid told the story of his conversation with Abu Bakr.

Then Abu Bakr said (to me), "You are a wise young man and we do not have any suspicions about you, and you used to write the Divine Inspiration for Allah's Apostle. So you should search for (the fragmentary scripts of) the Quran and collect it (in one book)." So I started looking for the Quran and collecting it from (what was written on) palm-leaf, thin white stones, and also from the men who knew it by heart.

Sahih al-Bukhari 4978

After Zaid completed his version of the Quran, Abu Bakr decided to keep it private by hiding it. Umar the Great, Islam's second caliph, also kept Zaid's Quran hidden. But this version of the Quran would not be hidden forever. Unknown to Abu Bakr, while Zaid was collecting the bits and pieces of the Quran, other Muslims were also beginning to put together their own versions of the Quran. By the time Umar the Great became caliph, there were actually several versions of the Quran being used throughout the Islamic empire. These versions did not all agree. Finally, in order to keep the unity within the empire, the third caliph, a man named *Uthman*, ordered that all copies of the Quran be burned—all except one. The one Uthman chose to keep was the one Zaid had compiled several years earlier.

Uthman ordered three men from Muhammad's Quraysh tribe to work with Zaid to finalize the official copy of the Quran. This version and only this version was allowed to be copied and distributed throughout the Islamic empire.

Uthman's decision to force Zaid's version of the Quran on the empire made many Muslims angry. Others opposed Uthman because of the way he was leading the empire. This anger and opposition increased to such an extent that in 656 a group of rebels surrounded his house for several days. Finally, after setting fire to his door, a group of men forced their way into Uthman's house and killed him. He was killed while reading a copy of the Quran—the version he approved and had imposed on the empire.

Uthman's version of the Quran is the most accepted version today. Although some believe it has been changed, most Muslims believe it is the one true and perfect Quran as revealed to Muhammad from Allah. The original Uthman Quran is on display today in a museum in the city of Tashkent, the capital of Uzbekistan.

UTHMAN READING THE QURAN

UTHMAN'S QURAN ORIGINAL IN TASHKENT, UZBEKISTAN

ANCIENT TURKISH QURAN

Topic 4—Is the Quran a Perfect Book?

Is the Quran a Perfect Book? As we have learned, Muslims believe that Allah revealed absolute truth to Muhammad. Over 23 years of revelation, every word Muhammad heard and recited is believed to be without error. In one English translation of the Quran, Islam's holy book is said to be "unerringly straight" (without flaw). In another translation it is said to be without any "crookedness."

Praise be to God, who sent down the Scripture to His servant and made it unerringly straight.   Quran 18:1

(All) praise is due to Allah, Who revealed the Book to His servant and did not make in it any crookedness.

Quran 18:1 Shakir

Muslims believe that the words Allah revealed to Muhammad are not only flawless truth, but can't be changed.

There is no changing the words of Allah.   Quran 10:64 Shakir

There is none to change the words of Allah.   Quran 6:34 Shakir

Allah's words can never be changed because they are the same words that have existed forever on the tablet of the heavenly Quran. Like Allah, the words of the Quran are said to be eternal and immutable.

But is the Quran truly Allah's perfect, unchangeable revelation to Muhammad? As we look closer at other surahs, we find verses that tell us Allah cancels some revelations and replaces them with others. Other verses tell us Allah also causes some messages to be forgotten by those who hear them. Let's look at two translations of Quran 2:106.

Any revelation We cause to be superseded or forgotten, We replace with something better or similar. Do you [Prophet] not know that God has power over everything?
Quran 2:106

Whatever communications We abrogate or cause to be forgotten, We bring one better than it or like it. Do you not know that Allah has power over all things?
Quran 2:106 Shakir

Because Muhammad recited verses that sometimes contradicted verses he had recited earlier, some people began to accuse him of just making them up. They did not believe he had received true revelations from Allah. Then, according to Muhammad, Allah revealed that the people were saying these things only because they did not know or understand the truth. Of course, Muhammad recited this new revelation to those who had accused him of making up revelations that contradicted earlier revelations.

When We substitute one revelation for another- and God knows best what He reveals- they say, 'You are just making it up,' but most of them have no knowledge.
Quran 16:101

Why are these verses about cancelling and substituting Allah's revelations in the Quran? Doesn't the Quran say that Allah's words can never be changed? These verses exist because there are several contradictions within the Quran. Some verses say one thing, while other verses say something very different. To explain these contradictions, Muslims scholars and theologians have developed the theory of abrogation. This is an important concept to understand when studying Islam. To *abrogate* means *to annul or cancel something by legal authority*. With reference to the Quran, this means that Allah has the authority and power to cancel some of his revelations. It also means he can replace the canceled revelations with new ones. In other words, he can substitute a newer revelation or verse for an older one.

The concept of abrogation and substitution creates a problem for Islam. Remember that Muslims believe the Quran is eternal and unchangeable like Allah. It is uncreated. It is part of who Allah is supposed to be. If Allah abrogates (cancels by legal authority) or substitutes verses of the Quran, then Allah must not be immutable. And if Allah is not immutable, then the words of the Quran cannot be immutable.

Let's explore some of the abrogations and substitutions in the Quran.

1. How are non-Muslims to be treated? In some of Muhammad's revelations, he was told by Allah not to force Islam on the people. He was told to turn away from unbelievers and bless them with peace.

There is no compulsion in religion: true guidance has become distinct from error, so whoever rejects false gods and believes in God has grasped the firmest hand-hold, one that will never break. God is all hearing and all knowing.
Quran 2:256

In other revelations, however, Allah is said to have told Muhammad to kill unbelievers.

Wherever you encounter the idolaters, kill them, seize them, besiege them, wait for them at every lookout post; but if they turn [to God], maintain the prayer, and pay the prescribed alms, let them go on their way, for God is most forgiving and merciful.   Quran 9:5

2. Who was the first Muslim? According to the Quran, Muhammad was the first Muslim.

Say, 'I am commanded to be the first [of you] to devote myself [to Him—Allah].   Quran 6:14

162 Say, "Surely my prayer, and my rites, and my living, and my dying are for Allah, The Lord of the worlds." 163 No associate has He; and this I am commanded, and I am the first of the Muslims." (Literally: of the ones who have surrendered to Allah).   Quran 6:162–163 Ghali

ISLAMIC ARMIES DEFEATED IN ATTEMPT TO
CONQUER FRANCE
BATTLE OF TOURS, OCTOBER 25, 732
PAINTING BY CHARLES STEUBEN, 1788–1856

11 Say: "Verily, I am commanded to serve Allah with sincere devotion; 12 "And I am commanded to be the first of those who bow to Allah in Islam."

Quran 39:11–12 Yusuf Ali

In other verses of the Quran, however, we are told that there were Muslims living long before Muhammad was born. For example, the following verse from the Quran says that Abraham's sons and his grandson Jacob were Muslims.

And this was the legacy that Abraham left to his sons, and so did Jacob; "Oh my sons! Allah hath chosen the Faith for you; then die not except in the Faith of Islam."

Quran 2:132 Yusuf Ali

If these verses about Abraham and his sons and Jacob are true, we must ask this question: How did they become Muslims? Muhammad is supposed to be the first Muslim, and he did not live during the time of the Old Testament. He wasn't born until almost 2,700 years after Abraham. The only way Abraham and Jacob could have known the truth of the Quran would have been for Allah to reveal it to them before he revealed it to Muhammad.

Not only does the Quran state that some of the people in the Old Testament were Muslims, it also states that Jesus and his disciples were Muslims. According to the following verse, Jesus asked his disciples who would help him spread Allah's cause or Islam. All the disciples said they would help and declared that they were already Muslims.

When Jesus found Unbelief on their part He said: "Who will be My helpers to (the work of) Allah?" Said the disciples: "We are Allah's helpers: We believe in Allah, and do thou bear witness that we are Muslims."

Quran 3:52 Yusuf Ali

If, according to the Quran, Jesus and his disciples were Muslims, how did they become Muslims? Muhammad did not live during the time of Jesus and his disciples. He was not born until almost 600 years later. The only way Jesus and his disciples could have known the truth of the Quran would have been for Allah to reveal it to them before he revealed it to Muhammad.

3. Who will be blessed with eternal life with God? According to the Quran, it was revealed to Muhammad that God will reward all Muslims, Jews, and Christians who do good works and believe in God and the judgment day.

Surely those who believe, and those who are Jews, and the Christians, and the Sabians, whoever believes in Allah and the Last day and does good, they shall have their reward from their Lord, and there is no fear for them, nor shall they grieve.

Quran 2:62 Shakir

In other revelations that Muhammad recited, Islam is said to be the only path to follow in order to be accepted by God. People who follow any other religion will be one of the losers in the afterlife (on Judgment Day).

If anyone seeks a religion other than [Islam] complete devotion to God, it will not be accepted from him: he will be one of the losers in the Hereafter.

Quran 3:85

4. Did Jesus die and come back to life? According to the following verses from the Quran, Jesus clearly spoke about his birth, his death, and his resurrection.

31 [He has] made me blessed wherever I may be. He commanded me to pray, to give alms as long as I live, 32 to cherish my mother. He did not make me domineering or graceless. 33 Peace was on me the day I was born, and will be on me the day I die and the day I am raised to life again.' 34 Such was Jesus, son of Mary. [This is] a statement of the Truth about which they are in doubt.

Quran 19:31–34

In another surah of the Quran, Muhammad recited that Jesus had not been crucified. Rather, he said someone who looked like Jesus had been crucified and died in his place. In fact, Muhammad recited that Jesus never died at all. Instead, God [Allah] simply took his body and soul to heaven.

157 'We have killed the Messiah, Jesus, son of Mary, the Messenger of God.' (They did not kill him, nor did they crucify him, though it was made to appear like that to them; those that disagreed about him are full of doubt, with no knowledge to follow, only supposition: they certainly did not kill him-158 God raised him up to Himself. God is almighty and wise.

Quran 4:157–158

Muslims do not agree about the number of abrogations, or substitutions, in the Quran. Some believe there are as few as five. Others believe there are as many as 500. But whether there are five or 500, these changes have led people to doubt whether the Quran is truly a book without "any crookedness" (Quran 18:1). And these changes have led people to ask this and other questions: If the Quran has truly been sent from heaven by an unchangeable Allah through Gabriel, and if it is truly a perfect copy of the eternal uncreated Quran in heaven, then why are there so many changes and contradictions in it today?

Topic 5—Is the Quran in Harmony with the Bible?

The Bible as Seen through the Quran: As we discussed in Topic 4, the Quran teaches that Allah established the religion of Islam for people living during Old and New Testament times. The following verse explains that Allah established Islam for people like Noah, Abraham, Moses, and Jesus.

The same religion has He established for you as that which He enjoined on Noah. . . and that which We enjoined on Abraham, Moses, and Jesus. Quran 42:13 Yusuf Ali

The Quran also teaches that Muslims believe in the revelations that God gave to Jews and Christians as recorded in the Old and New Testaments.

Say, 'We believe in what was revealed to us and in what was revealed to you; our God and your God are one [and the same].' Quran 29:46

'We [Muslims] believe in God and in what has been sent down to us and to Abraham, Ishmael, Isaac, Jacob, and the Tribes. We believe in what has been given to Moses, Jesus, and the prophets from their Lord. We do not make a distinction between any of the [prophets].' Quran 3:84

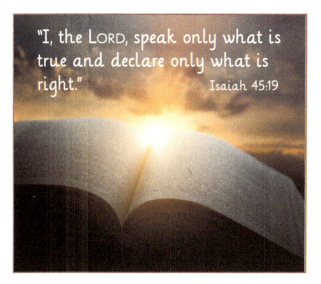

"I, the LORD, speak only what is true and declare only what is right." Isaiah 45:19

If, as Muslims believe, both the Bible and Quran are revelations from the same Allah, do you think the Bible and Quran should be in perfect harmony? Would you expect that what Allah says about Jesus in the Bible would be in harmony with his revelation about Jesus in the Quran? If indeed there is only one true Allah, and if he speaks only truth, then we should expect the Bible of Jews and Christians to be in perfect harmony with the Quran of Islam. This, however, is not the case. While the Quran contains some teachings about God and the creation that are in harmony with the Bible, it contains many teachings that are not. But why not? Why don't the Quran and the Bible agree in all teachings?

According to Islam, whenever there is a contradiction or difference between the Bible and the Quran, the Bible is wrong, not the holy Quran. But why? Didn't Allah reveal both books? Were some of Allah's revelations to Jews and Christians wrong? Did he abrogate or cancel them and then reveal a newer truth in the Quran? No, Muslims don't believe Allah did this. What they do believe is that some Jews and some Christians changed God's original revelation as recorded in the Bible. In other words, over many centuries, Jews and Christians corrupted or falsified God's words to people like Moses, David, and even Jesus. The verses on the next page from the Quran reveal this belief.

They distort the meaning of [revealed] words and have forgotten some of what they were told to remember.   Quran 5:13

There are some who twist the Scripture with their tongues to make you [people] think that what they say is part of the Scripture when it is not; they say it is from God when it is not; they attribute lies to God and they know it.   Quran 3:78

One verse in the Quran says that Jews and Christians changed the words of the Bible when they wrote or transcribed parts of it.

So woe to those who write something down with their own hands and then claim, 'This is from God.'   Quran 2:79

MOSES AND THE TEN COMMANDMENTS

THE TORAH

In future lessons as we explore the Islamic view of God, people, the universe, and values as they are presented in the Quran, we will compare the Islamic views with those revealed in the Bible. Occasionally these views will be in harmony, but as you will learn, the Quran is seldom in harmony with God's revealed Word in the Bible.

Let's examine a few examples of disharmony between the Bible and the Quran. As we do this, remember that Muslims believe where the Bible is not in harmony with the Quran, the Bible, not the Quran, is corrupted or wrong. Read the verses in the Bible and the Quran carefully in order to identify the contradictions.

1. Noah and the Flood

The Bible: ⁶ Noah was 600 years old when the flood covered the earth. ⁷ He went on board the boat to escape the flood—he and his wife and his sons and their wives.   Genesis 7:6–7

The Quran: ⁴² It [the ark] sailed with them on waves like mountains, and Noah called out to his son, who stayed behind, 'Come aboard with us, my son, do not stay with the disbelievers.' ⁴³ But he replied, 'I will seek refuge on a mountain to save me from the water.' Noah said, 'Today there is no refuge from God's command, except for those on whom He has mercy.' The waves cut them off from each other and he was among the drowned.   Quran 11:42–43

2. Moses and Pharaoh

The Bible: ⁵ Soon Pharaoh's daughter came down to bathe in the river, and her attendants walked along the riverbank. When the princess saw the basket among the reeds, she sent her maid to get it for her.

⁹ "Take this baby and nurse him for me," the princess told the baby's mother. "I will pay you for your help." So the woman took her baby home and nursed him.

¹⁰ Later, when the boy was older, his mother brought him back to Pharaoh's

daughter, who adopted him as her own son. The princess named him Moses, for she explained, "I lifted him out of the water."

Exodus 2:5, 9–10

The Quran: [8] Pharaoh's household picked him up––later to become an enemy and a source of grief for them: Pharaoh, Haman, and their armies were wrongdoers [sinners]––[9] and Pharaoh's wife said, 'Here is a joy to behold for me and for you! Do not kill him: he may be of use to us, or we may adopt him as a son.' They did not realize what they were doing.

Quran 28:8–9

3. The Crucifixion of Jesus

The Bible: [24] Then the soldiers nailed him to the cross. They divided his clothes and threw dice to decide who would get each piece. [25] It was nine o'clock in the morning when they crucified him. [26] A sign announced the charge against him. It read, "The King of the Jews." [27] Two revolutionaries were crucified with him, one on his right and one on his left.

Acts 12:22–24

The Quran: And [they] said, 'We have killed the Messiah, Jesus, son of Mary, the Messenger of God.' (They did not kill him, nor did they crucify him, though it was made to appear like that to them; those that disagreed about him are full of doubt, with no knowledge to follow, only supposition: they certainly did not kill him.

Quran 4:157

4. Jesus, the Son of God

The Bible: [13] When Jesus came to the region of Caesarea Philippi, he asked his disciples, "Who do people say that the Son of Man is?"

[16] Simon Peter answered, "You are the Messiah, the Son of the living God."

[17] Jesus replied, "You are blessed, Simon son of John, because my Father in heaven has revealed this to you. You did not learn this from any human being."

Matthew 16:13, 16–17

The Quran: The Jews said, 'Ezra is the son of God,' and the Christians said, 'The Messiah is the son of God': they said this with their own mouths, repeating what earlier disbelievers had said. May God confound them! How far astray they have been led!

Quran 9:30

5. God's Love

The Bible: [6] When we were utterly helpless, Christ came at just the right time and died for us sinners. [7] Now, most people would not be willing to die for an upright person, though someone might perhaps be willing to die for a person who is especially good. [8] But God showed his great love for us by sending Christ to die for us while we were still sinners.

Romans 5:6–8

The Quran: Surely He does not love the unjust [those who do wrong].

Quran 42:40 Shakir

The Quran: 'Do not seek to spread corruption in the land, for God does not love those who do this.'

Quran 28:77

ENDNOTES

1 Unless otherwise indicated, all Quran quotations are taken from *The Qur'an*, translated by Abdel Haleem, copyright© 2004 by Oxford University Press, Inc., New York.

2 Mateen Elass, *Understanding the Koran: A Quick Christian Guide to the Muslim Holy Book* (Grand Rapids: Zondervan, 2004), 8–9.

The Islamic View of God

Getting Started—Is Allah the Same as God?

Muslims view their world through the "eyes" of the Quran and the Hadith. They believe those books are the sources of truth for their lives and that within them they can find the truth about God, people, the universe, and right and wrong. In this lesson, we will explore what the Islamic worldview holds as truth about God. But before we study this important topic, we need to consider this question: Is Allah of the Quran and Islam the same as God of the Bible? This is not an easy question to answer. Considered one way, the answer is yes. Considered another way, the answer is no. Let's explain the "yes" answer first.

Topic 1—Who Is Allah? Who Is Yahweh?

THE ARABIC TEXT FOR ALLAH

Who Is Allah? The Arabic word for *God* is *Allah*. It is the word Muslims use when they refer to the one they believe is the supreme and only God. But Allah is also the word that Arabic-speaking Christians use for God. Allah is a contraction of the words *al-Ilah*, which literally mean *the Deity*. Both Muslims and Christians believe this supreme deity, or god, is the only true God—the Creator and ruler over all he created. Both Christians and Muslims worship only God. They believe they must submit to his laws. They believe that one day he will judge all creation and give eternal life to believers and eternal punishment to nonbelievers. Muslims, like Christians, believe Allah (God) is omnipotent, omniscient, eternal, and completely self-sufficient, having no needs. Based on this explanation, we can say, "Yes, Allah of the Quran and Islam and God of the Bible are the same."

Who Is Yahweh? Now we must consider the "no" answer to our question. The word *Allah* has a different meaning for Muslims than it does for Christians. For Muslims, Allah refers to the personal or proper name for God, similar to a person being named *Peter* or *Jane*. But for Arabic-speaking Christians and Jews, Allah is used only as a common noun or title for God; they would never use Allah as God's name. For them, God's (Allah's) name is *Yahweh*. Over time, the Jewish people came to see God's name as too holy to say out loud. When the Hebrew Scriptures were translated into Greek beginning in about 250 BC, the translators substituted the Greek word *Kurios* (Lord) for Yahweh, and most translators since then have followed the same practice. Where Yahweh is found in Hebrew, most Bibles now show the name as LORD. (Note: The Hebrew Scriptures in Greek, known as the *Septuagint*, were widely read in the first century AD, so when Jesus was called *Lord* in the New Testament, the readers knew that the apostles were saying that Jesus was Yahweh!) In the Hebrew language, Yahweh means I AM. God revealed this truth to Moses many centuries before Muhammad was born or Islam began. We can read about God's revelation to Moses in the Old Testament book of Exodus, where God chose Moses to lead the Israelites out of captivity in Egypt.

THE HEBREW TEXT FOR YAHWEH

God spoke miraculously to Moses from a burning bush to tell him of his special mission. Moses responded, "If I go to the people of Israel and tell them, 'The God of your ancestors has sent me to you,' they will ask me, 'What is his name?' Then what should I tell them?" (Exodus 3:13).

In response to Moses' question, God replied to Moses, "I AM WHO I AM. Say this to the people of Israel: I AM has sent me to you. Say this to the people of Israel: Yahweh, the God of your ancestors—the God of Abraham, the God of Isaac, and the God of Jacob—has sent me to you. This is my eternal name, my name to remember for all generations" (Exodus 3:14–15).

Yahweh is never mentioned in the Quran, and Muslims never use that term when they refer to God. For them, God's personal name is *Allah*.

As you study Islam in more depth, you will learn many other reasons why Allah of the Quran is not identical to God (Yahweh) of the Bible. For example, you already know that Muslims do not believe in the Trinity. They do not believe that Allah exists as one God in three Persons—Father, Son, and Holy Spirit. In Islam, Jesus is not God. For this reason alone, we must answer "no" to the question "Is Allah of the Quran and Islam the same as God (Yahweh) of the Bible?"

Do Muslims Worship a False God? As we explore the differences between Islam's Allah and Christianity's Yahweh, it is important to understand that the Muslim view of God is not completely wrong. Muslims do worship the deity they believe is the one and only true God. But their understanding of the one and only true God of biblical Christianity is incomplete and often wrong. This doesn't mean they worship a false god or an idol. It means they worship God without proper knowledge and understanding of who he really is.

In the early days of Christianity, the apostle Paul lived among Jews, who, like Muslims today, worshipped God, but rejected Jesus as God the Son and their Savior. In fact, the Jews persecuted the Christians for their beliefs. But in a letter that Paul wrote to Christians living in the city of Rome, he did not accuse the Jews of worshipping a false God. Rather, he said they were worshipping God whom they did not really know. And Paul's desire for the Jews was that they would come to know Jesus as their God and Savior.

¹ Dear brothers and sisters, the longing of my heart and my prayer to God is for the people of Israel to be saved. ² I know what enthusiasm they have for God, but it is misdirected zeal. ³ For they don't understand God's way of making people right with himself. Refusing to accept God's way, they cling to their own way of getting right with God by trying to keep the law.   Romans 10:1–3

Paul's words should guide our hearts and thoughts as we explore the Islamic view of God. Never look down on those who are sincere about their faith in God, even when their understanding of God is not in harmony with Scripture. Rather, pray with humility that they may come to know Jesus, not only as God the Son, but also as their Savior. Remember that the Bible says, If someone asks about your Christian hope, always be ready to explain it. But do this in a gentle and respectful way (1 Peter 3:15–16).

> **Yahweh**
> The personal name for God; from the
> Hebrew language, meaning I AM

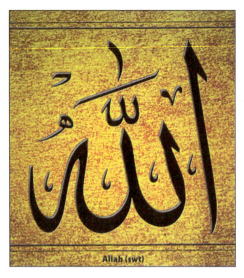

OLD MOSQUE WALL
INSCRIBED WITH "ALLAH"
IN EDIRNE, TURKEY

MAJOR MUSLIM NATIONS
OF THE MIDDLE EAST
AND AFRICA

Topic 2—Similarities between Allah and God

Before we look at some of the similarities between Allah and Yahweh, it is important to remember that being similar does not mean being the same. In this topic, we'll identify and explore four similarities. In Topic 3, we'll identify and explore five important differences.

Allah Is the Only God. Muslims do not believe in several gods. They believe only in Allah, and they worship only him. To worship anything or anyone other than God is idolatry, and idolatry is strictly forbidden in Islam. In Lesson 3, you learned that Muhammad's main message to the polytheists in Mecca was that there is only one god, Allah (Quran 2:255). You remember that the polytheists did not receive this radical message well, and they persecuted Muhammad and his small band of followers because of it.

A belief in the existence of only one true God is called *monotheism* (from the Greek words *mono*, meaning one, and *theos*, meaning God). Jews and Christians are also monotheists, and they, too, believe it is wrong to worship anything or anyone other than the only true and living God.

"For I alone am God! I am God, and there is none like me."   Isaiah 46:9

Allah Is the Creator. Muslims believe that Allah is the Creator of everything that exists and that he is sovereign over his creation. This means that he has complete, unlimited power and authority over all he has made. There is no one higher or greater than Allah. No one rules above or over him.

This is God, your Lord, there is no God but Him, the Creator of all things, so worship Him; He is in charge of everything.   Quran 6:102

The Bible likewise teaches that God is the sovereign Creator and that no one or anything in all creation compares with him.

"You alone are God of all the kingdoms of the earth. You alone created the heavens and the earth." 2 Kings 19:15

No pagan god is like you, O Lord. None can do what you do! Psalm 86:8

Allah Is All-Powerful and Eternal. Muslims believe that Allah is omnipotent, omniscient, omnipresent, and eternal. They believe he has no needs and that he exists eternally outside of the time he created when he made the world.

God: there is no god but Him, the Ever Living, the Ever Watchful. Neither slumber nor sleep overtakes Him. Quran 2:255

God knows everything that is in your hearts, whether you conceal or reveal it; He knows everything in the heavens and earth; God has power over all things. Quran 3:29

Christians and Jews also believe that God is omnipotent, omniscient, omnipresent, and eternal.

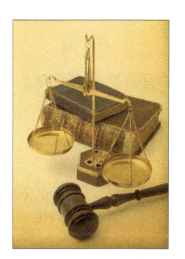

How great is our Lord! His power is absolute!
His understanding is beyond comprehension! Psalm 147:5

All honor and glory to God forever and ever! He is the eternal King, the unseen one who never dies; he alone is God. Amen. 1 Timothy 1:17

Allah Is Lawgiver and Judge. Muslims believe that Allah gave laws by which people should live. They believe that one day in the future he will judge all people according to what they have done. Those who obey Allah's laws will be saved from punishment and given eternal life in a place called *paradise*. Those who disobey Allah's laws will be punished eternally in hell.

In Lesson 6, we will study the Islamic view of salvation and punishment in more detail. For now, however, it's important to mention that the Islamic view is very different from the biblical Christian view. As you read these verses from the Quran about God's judgment, see if you can identify one of the important differences.

[101] On that Day when the Trumpet is blown, the ties between them will be as nothing and they will not ask about each other: [102] those whose good deeds weigh heavy will be successful, [103] but those whose balance is light will have lost their souls for ever and will stay in Hell- [104] the Fire will scorch their faces and their lips will be twisted in pain. Quran 23:101–104

What do you notice in these verses about the Islamic view of salvation? How is it different from the biblical Christian view? Reread verses 102 and 103. Notice that the Quran says a person's salvation depends on his or her good deeds or works. People who have done enough good deeds will be saved. But people who haven't done enough good deeds will live in hell as their eternal place of punishment. We'll explore this false teaching in more depth later.

Christians also believe that God gave laws and commands people are to live by and that one day in the future all people will have to stand before God as their judge.

¹¹ For the Scriptures say,

> "'As surely as I live,' says the LORD,
>   'every knee will bend to me,
>   and every tongue will declare allegiance to God.'"

¹² Yes, each of us will give a personal account to God.   Romans 14:11–12

These verses from the book of Romans tell us we will have to give an account of our lives to God. But our salvation is not based on our having to earn it by doing good deeds. No one could ever do enough good deeds to be saved. No matter how many good deeds we may do, just one sin is enough to keeps us separated from God. John's gospel tells us that we can be saved only because of God's grace and Jesus' sacrifice of his life on the cross for our sins (John 3:16–17). We'll also explore this important biblical truth in more depth in Lesson 6.

THE CRUCIFIXION OF CHRIST
WOODCUT BY GUSTAV DORÉ,
1832–1883

MUSLIMS BOW IN PRAYER TO ALLAH IN A
MOSQUE IN JAKARTA, INDONESIA
IN THE BACKGROUND, WOMEN IN WHITE
PRAY SEPARATELY BEHIND A SCREEN

Does It Matter? Because there are some similarities between Allah of the Quran and God of the Bible, many people believe they are the same. As Islam spreads throughout the world, more and more people believe that the god Muslims worship is identical to the God Christians worship. This belief is a serious mistake. Now that we have examined some of the similarities between Allah of Islam and God of biblical Christianity, we need to explore the great differences between them. Unless you understand these differences, you might think that it really doesn't matter whom you worship. But as you'll learn in Topic 3, it does make a difference—a very big, eternal difference!

Topic 3—Differences between Allah and God

Allah Cannot Be Known through a Personal Relationship. In Lesson 2, you studied some of God's unique attributes or characteristics. You learned that only God is omnipotent, eternal, and omnipresent. You also learned that God is transcendent, meaning he is beyond and above his creation. In other words, God cannot be contained within or by what he has made. If that were possible, he could certainly not be the sovereign ruler of all things.

> "But will God really live on earth among people? Why, even the highest heavens cannot contain you. How much less this Temple I [Solomon] have built!"
>   2 Chronicles 6:18

Scripture teaches that God is transcendent. It also teaches that God is with us. He lives with people who are contrite (grieving and sorrowful) and repentant for their sins.

> The high and lofty one who lives in eternity,
>   the Holy One, says this:
> "I live in the high and holy place
>   with those whose spirits are contrite and humble.
> I restore the crushed spirit of the humble
>   and revive the courage of those with repentant hearts."   Isaiah 57:15

The Bible also teaches that God gives us understanding so that we can know him—not just know about him, but actually know him as a Personal Being through the personal revelation of his Son, Jesus.

And we know that the Son of God has come, and he has given us understanding so that we can know the true God. And now we live in fellowship with the true God because we live in fellowship with his Son, Jesus Christ. He is the only true God, and he is eternal life.

1 John 5:20

If you have ever wondered whether you can really know God, remember that he came to Earth as Jesus Christ, the man. People saw him, touched him, and listened to him. In the new heavens and new earth, all his children will see him, touch him, listen to him, and know him personally for all eternity.

We proclaim to you the one who existed from the beginning, whom we have heard and seen. We saw him with our own eyes and touched him with our own hands. He is the Word of life.   1 John 1:1

Sadly, Muslims believe they cannot know Allah of the Quran personally like Christians believe they can know God of the Bible. Muslims believe Allah is so transcendent, so far above his creation, that no one can have a personal relationship with him. The following verse from the Quran tells Muslims that Allah is completely unlike the men and women (mates) he creates. This means people are not created in his image or likeness, and because they do not bear Allah's image, it is impossible for them to know or understand him. And if they can't know or understand him, it is impossible for them to have a personal relationship with him.

MUSLIM WOMEN
WEARING THE BURKA

'[He is] the Creator of the heavens and earth.' He made mates for you from among yourselves—and for the animals too—so that you may multiply. There is nothing like Him: He is the All Hearing, the All Seeing.   Quran 42:11

Muslims can know that Allah exists, and they can know about some of his activities. But the Quran does not teach that Allah can be known personally. The nature and attributes of Allah are far beyond what anyone can ever know. Allah does not reveal himself to people. He reveals only his will and commands.

Allah Is Not Love. The Quran says very little about Allah's love. In fact, Muslims do not believe that love is part of his nature. They would never say, as the Bible does about Yahweh, "God is love" (1 John 4:16). When the Quran speaks about Allah's love, it means that he approves of those who serve and follow him. Allah has no love at all for anyone who does not believe in him. The angel Gabriel is said to have told Muhammad to recite a message about this from Allah.

31 Say, 'If you love God, follow me, and God will love you and forgive you your sins; God is most forgiving, most merciful.' 32 Say, 'Obey God and the Messenger,' but if they turn away, [know that] God does not love those who ignore [His commands].

Quran 3:31–32

The belief that love is not part of who Allah is creates a problem for Muslims. As you just read, the Quran commands Muslims to love Allah. But loving Allah is difficult. How can they love Allah, who is so transcendent that they can't even know him? How can they love Allah, who is so completely unlike them? When the Quran speaks about Muslims' responsibility to love Allah, it is basically saying, "Obey Allah so you will be rewarded or saved."

The biblical Christian view of God's love is very different from Islam's view. First, the Scriptures tell us that God is love. Love is God's very nature.

We know how much God loves us, and we have put our trust in his love. God is love, and all who live in love live in God, and God lives in them.   1 John 4:16

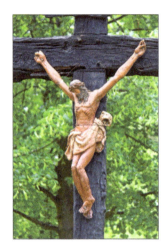

Second, God's love for us does not depend on our doing good deeds or our loving him. In fact, God loved us first—even before we turned from our sins or showed any love for him at all.

But God showed his great love for us by sending Christ to die for us while we were still sinners.   Romans 5:8

This is real love—not that we loved God, but that he loved us and sent his Son as a sacrifice to take away our sins.   1 John 4:10

Because God is love and because we are created in his image, we are able to respond in love to the love he showed us through Jesus. Because God, Yahweh, is knowable, we can know his love. And because we are created in his image with a heart to love and a will to choose, we can choose to love him, and we can express our love to him.

Allah Is Not a Father. The Bible tells us that when we believe in Jesus as our Savior, God gives us a new birth and we become his children. In his great love for us, God not only calls us his children, he allows us to call him *our Father*. The apostle John wrote about these wonderful blessings in his first letter to Christians of the early church.

Everyone who believes that Jesus is the Christ has become a child of God. And everyone who loves the Father loves his children, too.   1 John 5:1

See how very much our Father loves us, for he calls us his children, and that is what we are! But the people who belong to this world don't recognize that we are God's children because they don't know him.   1 John 3:1

Being born as a child of God is a wonderful blessing and privilege for Christians. As a loving Father, God invites us to come to him with our problems (1 Peter 5:7). As a loving father, God disciplines us for our good (Hebrews 12:5–6). And as a loving father, God invites us to call him Abba Father. In the Aramaic language spoken during the time Jesus lived on Earth, Abba was the intimate or personal word for *Father*. We would translate it in English as *Daddy* or *Papa*. Jesus used this word when he spoke to God, his Father. As God's children, we may use it also. By allowing us to call him *Daddy*, God makes it very clear that he wants us to know him and have a close

© ![logo] Walking in Truth Grade 7

relationship with him. In a letter to Christians living in the region of Galatia, the apostle Paul wrote about the blessing of being God's children.

And because we are his children, God has sent the Spirit of his Son into our hearts, prompting us to call out, "Abba, Father."

Galatians 4:6

Muslims do not understand or experience this wonderful Abba Father relationship with God as his children. The Quran teaches that just as Allah can never be known personally, neither can he be known as a father. No Muslim would ever dare to call Allah his or her father, much less Papa or Daddy. Muslims believe Allah is so transcendent, and so unlike anything he created, that no one can know him personally or have a close father-child relationship with him. According to the Quran, Allah never begets or gives birth to children, just as he was never begotten or born. In other words, Allah is father to no one. Let's read some verses from the Quran that Muslims believe Gabriel spoke to Muhammad on this topic.

The Jews and the Christians say, 'We are the children of God and His beloved ones.' Say, 'Then why does He punish you for your sins? You are merely human beings, part of his creation.'

Quran 5:18

[1] "Say, 'He is God the One, [2] God the eternal. [3] He begot no one nor was He begotten. [4] No one is comparable to Him."

Quran 112:2–4

It does not befit the Lord of Mercy [to have offspring].

Quran 19:92

Allah Is Not One God in Three Persons. In Scripture, God tells us that the Father is God, Jesus is God, and the Holy Spirit is God. This important truth is part of the foundation of the biblical Christian worldview. This truth is referred to as *the Trinity*. It means that God is a tri-unity, or one God in three Persons.

But for us, there is one God, the Father.

1 Corinthians 8:6

For in Christ lives all the fullness of God in a human body.

Colossians 2:9

No one can know God's thoughts except God's own Spirit.

1 Corinthians 2:11

Muslims do not accept the biblical truth of the Trinity. Allah is not one God in three Persons. The Quran warns Christians and Jews not to accept or even speak about the Trinity. If they do, they will experience the pain and suffering of hell.

Those people who say that God is the third of three are defying [the truth]: there is only One God. If they persist in what they are saying, a painful punishment will afflict those of them who persist.

Quran 5:73

It is also important to understand that Muslims do not believe that the Holy Spirit is one of the three Persons of the Trinity. Rather, Muslims believe that the Christian Trinity includes the Father (Allah), the Son (Jesus), and the mother (Mary). They believe that Christians worship Allah as God, Jesus as God, and Mary as God. In other words, Muslims believe that Christians are polytheists—that Christians worship three different gods.

When God says, 'Jesus, son of Mary, did you say to people, "Take me and my mother as two gods alongside God"?' he will say, 'May You be exalted! I would never say what I had no right to say- if I had said such a thing You would have known it: You know all that is within me, though I do not know what is within You, You alone have full knowledge of things unseen-

Quran 5:116

Not only does the Quran deny the Trinity, it also denies that Jesus is God's Son and God himself.

People of the Book [Jews and Christians], do not go to excess in your religion, and do not say anything about God except the truth: the Messiah, Jesus, son of Mary, was nothing more than a messenger of God, His word, directed to Mary, a spirit from Him. So believe in God and His messengers and do not speak of a 'Trinity'- stop [this], that is better for you- God is only one God, He is far above having a son, everything in the heavens and earth belongs to Him and He is the best one to trust.
Quran 4:171

Muslims' denial that Jesus is God the Son is one of the most serious differences between Islam and Christianity. Because this difference is so serious and so important, we will explore it in more detail in Topic 4.

Allah's Word Can Change. You've learned that Yahweh, the God of the Bible, is immutable. This means he does not change. His wisdom, holiness, righteousness, and love do not change.

"I am the LORD, and I do not change."
Malachi 3:6

Whatever is good and perfect is a gift coming down to us from God our Father, who created all the lights in the heavens. He never changes or casts a shifting shadow.
James 1:17

Not only does God himself not change, his Word does not change nor pass away. What God says we can trust as truth forever.

Your eternal word, O Lord,
    stands firm in heaven.
Psalm 119:89

"The grass withers and the flowers fade,
    but the word of our God stands forever."
Isaiah 40:8

Heaven and earth will disappear, but my words will never disappear.
Matthew 24:35

These Scriptures that assure us of the eternal and immutable nature of God and his Word are a great encouragement to us as his children. We do not have to worry about God changing his mind from one day to the next. He will do what he says he will do. What is true today will always be true. Even when we go through difficulties in our lives, we can trust God's Word that assures us we are his children, he loves us, and he will always care for us.

Muslims also claim that the words of Allah are immutable.

There is no changing the words of Allah.
Quran 10:64 Shakir

There is none that can alter the words (and decrees) of Allah.
Quran 6:34 Yusuf Ali

However, other verses in the Quran say that Allah cancels or abrogates his word or revelations. Then he replaces them with verses that are better or sometimes like the ones he abrogated.

Whatever communications We abrogate or cause to be forgotten, We bring one better than it or like it. Do you not know that Allah has power over all things?
Quran 2:106 Shakir

Muhammad often recited messages that contradicted earlier messages. This led people to accuse him of making them up. Because of the accusations people were making against him, one day he recited words that he claimed came directly from Allah.

When We substitute one revelation for another- and God knows best what He reveals- they say, 'You are just making it up,' but most of them have no knowledge.

Quran 16:101

As you can imagine, changes like these in Allah's words could confuse Muslims. If Allah abrogates his word, can he really be trusted? And if Allah changes or substitutes his word, can he, himself, really be immutable?

In contrast to the confusion brought about by Allah's changing messages, the Bible declares that God's Word does not change. It does not bring confusion, but rather peace.

"The word of the Lord remains forever."   1 Peter 1:25

For God is not a God of disorder but of peace.   1 Corinthians 14:33

Topic 4—Jesus of the Quran and Jesus of the Bible

IN THE VILLAGES THE SICK WERE BROUGHT UNTO HIM

Jesus of the Quran Is Not God. Islam teaches that Jesus was a real person. According to the Quran, he was a prophet or messenger of God. He was born of the virgin Mary, lived a sinless life, and even performed miracles, such as healing the sick. He is now living in heaven with God until the day he will return to Earth to rule as king. Muhammad recited messages about Jesus that he said he received from Allah.

He will send him as a messenger to the Children of Israel: "I have come to you with a sign from your Lord: I will . . . heal the blind and the leper, and bring the dead back to life with God's permission . . . There truly is a sign for you in this, if you are believers.   Quran 3:49

Does this Jesus of Islam sound like Jesus of the Bible? Certainly, he does, but be careful! A close look at other verses in the Quran reveals that the Jesus of Islam is quite different from the Jesus of biblical Christianity. We'll explore the most important difference first— Islam's strong denial that Jesus is God. The Quran says that anyone who believes that Jesus is God is an unbeliever to be cursed by God!

Those who say, 'God is the Messiah [Christ], the son of Mary,' are defying the truth.   Quran 5:17

The Christians said, 'The Messiah is the son of God': they said this with their own mouths, repeating what earlier disbelievers had said. May God confound them! How far astray they have been led!

Quran 9:30

Toward the end of Muhammad's life, he is said to have received revelations saying that Jesus was only a messenger, or apostle, like many who lived and died before him. Let's read two examples of this from the Quran.

The Messiah, son of Mary, was only a messenger; other messengers had come and gone before him.

Quran 5:75

People of the Book, do not go to excess in your religion, and do not say anything about God except the truth: the Messiah, Jesus, son of Mary, was nothing more than a messenger of God, His word, directed to Mary, a spirit from Him. So believe in God and His messengers and do not speak of a 'Trinity'- stop [this], that is better for you. God is only one God, He is far above having a son, everything in the heavens and earth belongs to Him and He is the best one to trust.

Quran 4:171

These and other Quranic verses that deny the Trinity leave no doubt that Islam rejects both Jesus as the Son of God and Jesus as God himself. Verses like these conflict with the teaching of Scripture as well as with God the Father's own words at Jesus' baptism.

16 After his baptism, as Jesus came up out of the water, the heavens were opened and he saw the Spirit of God descending like a dove and settling on him. 17 And a voice from heaven said, "This is my dearly loved Son, who brings me great joy."

Matthew 3:16–17

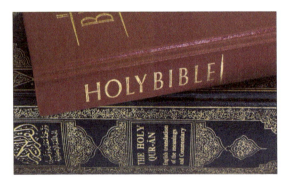

Is denying that Jesus is God really so serious? Absolutely! If Jesus is not God, then it makes no difference how many similarities there are between Jesus of the Quran and Jesus of the Bible. If Jesus is not God, then biblical Christianity is completely untrue. If Jesus is not God, then people who believe in him as God's Son and their Savior have no hope of eternal life with God. Paul wrote about this in a letter to Christians in Colosse, and John wrote about it in his gospel.

For in Christ lives all the fullness of God in a human body.

Colossians 2:9

16 "For this is how God loved the world: He gave his one and only Son, so that everyone who believes in him will not perish but have eternal life. 17 God sent his Son into the world not to judge the world, but to save the world through him.

18 "There is no judgment against anyone who believes in him. But anyone who does not believe in him has already been judged for not believing in God's one and only Son."

John 3:16–18

Although Muslims believe that Allah will judge people at the end of time and that some will be saved and others punished, they do not believe that salvation must come through Jesus.

Jesus of the Quran Was Not Crucified as Our Savior. Islam teaches that Jesus was a special, sinless prophet, but not the Son of God. Islam not only teaches that Jesus was not God, but also that he did not die on the cross for our sins. Muslims believe the Jews crucified someone who looked like Jesus. Instead of dying, Jesus was carried to heaven by Allah, where he lives today.

JESUS IS NAILED TO THE CROSS WOODCUT BY GUSTAV DORÉ, 1832–1883

157 [They] said, 'We have killed the Messiah, Jesus, son of Mary, the Messenger of God.' (They did not kill him, nor did they crucify him, though it was made to appear like that to them; those that disagreed about him are full of doubt, with no knowledge to follow, only supposition: they certainly did not kill him— 158 God raised him up to Himself. God is almighty and wise. Quran 4:157–158

Why do you think Islam so strongly denies the crucifixion and resurrection of Jesus? According to the Quran, it is impossible for anyone to bear punishment for someone else's sins. All people must bear their own sins. Muhammad is said to have received revelations about this that he taught his followers.

No burdened soul will bear the burden of another: even if a heavily laden soul should cry for help, none of its load will be carried, not even by a close relative. Quran 35:18

Whoever accepts guidance does so for his own good; whoever strays does so at his own peril. No soul will bear another's burden, nor do We punish until We have sent a messenger. Quran 17:15

For Muslims, the story of Jesus dying on the cross for the sins of the world is just that—a story made up by Christians. Muslims believe that no person could ever die for another person, much less for the sins of the world, not even Jesus, the sinless prophet of Islam. Muslims believe that the only way someone can receive forgiveness of sins and go to paradise is to do more good deeds than wrong deeds. If their good deeds weigh more than their sins, only then might they have the chance of receiving Allah's mercy.

The biblical Christian worldview rests upon the foundation that Jesus, God the Son, became sin for us. He took our sins and bore them on the cross. He took the punishment we deserve for our sins. The Quran and the teachings of Islam bear no such message.

For God made Christist, who never sinned, to be the offering for our sin, so that we could be made right with God through Christ. 2 Corinthians 5:21

He personally carried our sins
   in his body on the cross
so that we can be dead to sin
   and live for what is right.
By his wounds
   you are healed.   1 Peter 2:24

5 But he was pierced for our rebellion,
   crushed for our sins.
He was beaten so we could be whole.
   He was whipped so we could be healed.
12 . . . He bore the sins of many.
   Isaiah 53:5, 12

Topic 5—The Apocryphal Stories of Jesus in the Quran

What Are Apocryphal Stories? The word *apocrypha* comes from the late Latin word *apocryphus*, meaning *secret* or *hidden*. Apocryphal stories are stories that cannot be proven completely genuine or true. They are often based on legends and myths, although they may contain some truth.

As you learned earlier, Muhammad lived about 600 years after the time Jesus lived on Earth. By Muhammad's time, the early leaders of the Christian church had already carefully collected, studied, and approved the 27 books that make up the New Testament of the Bible we have today. These early church leaders believed these 27 books were authentic—that they had been inspired by God, who had carefully guided the writers of the book. However, during and after the time the approved books of the New Testament were written, other people also wrote books about Jesus. Those books included stories about Jesus that church leaders did not believe were genuine or completely true. For this reason, they were not included in the New Testament with the Gospels of Matthew, Mark, Luke, and John.

The apocryphal gospel stories and the true gospel stories were told among the people, including the people of Arabia where Muhammad lived. As Muhammad traveled with his wife's trade caravans north and south through Arabia and into Syria, he no doubt heard a mixture of both true and apocryphal gospel stories. Many non-Muslims, including Bible scholars, believe that the stories about Jesus in the Quran are based on both true and apocryphal gospel stories Muhammad heard during his travels. Muslims, however, do not believe any part of the Quran comes from stories Muhammad heard while traveling. They believe Allah revealed these stories to Muhammad, and therefore they are true. We'll explore three stories about Jesus that are in the Quran, but not in the Bible, and we'll explore some of the early apocryphal gospel writings that most likely influenced Muhammad's stories.

Jesus of the Quran Was Born under a Palm Tree. According to the Quran, Mary was told by angels that she would have a son. The Quran, like the Bible, teaches that Jesus' birth was a virgin birth. In other words, Jesus was not conceived in the normal way by a husband and wife, but by a special miracle of God. Let's read one of Muhammad's recitations on this subject.

45 The angels said, 'Mary, God gives you news of a Word from Him, whose name will be the Messiah, Jesus, son of Mary, who will be held in honour in this world and the next, who will be one of those brought near to God. 46 He will speak to people in his infancy and in his adulthood. He will be one of the righteous.'

Mary and Jesus Under the Palm
Central Asia or Near East Painting
12th–14th century

47 She said, 'My Lord, how can I have a son when no man has touched me?' [The angel] said, 'This is how God creates what He will: when He has ordained something, He only says, "Be", and it is.' Quran 3:45–47

Although the Quran's version of the announcement of Jesus' birth to Mary is similar to the biblical account, its account of Jesus' birth is very different from the accounts in Matthew's and Luke's gospels. In the Quran, Muhammad describes Jesus' birth as being in a faraway place. In this setting, Mary is by herself under a date palm tree. After giving birth, she is alone and ashamed, but the baby Jesus speaks to encourage her. He tells her that God has provided a stream of water for her and that if she will shake the palm tree, ripe dates will fall for food.

22 And so it was ordained: she conceived him. She withdrew to a distant place 23 and, when the pains of childbirth drove her to [cling to] the trunk of a palm tree, she exclaimed, 'I wish I had been dead and forgotten long before all this!'

²⁴ But a voice cried to her from below, 'Do not worry: your Lord has provided a stream at your feet ²⁵ and, if you shake the trunk of the palm tree towards you, it will deliver fresh ripe dates for you, ²⁶ so eat, drink, be glad.

Quran 19:22–26

Now let's compare the Quran's story of Jesus' birth with a story found in an old apocryphal book called *The History of the Nativity of Mary and the Infancy of the Savior*. This story has nothing to do with Jesus' birth. Rather, it is about Mary and Joseph's flight to Egypt to save Jesus from being killed by King Herod. According to *The History*, Mary, Joseph, and Jesus stop to rest under a palm tree in the desert. When they realize that the dates they need for food are too high to reach, and that they have no water, the infant Jesus speaks and performs a miracle.

> Then the child Jesus, who was sitting with a happy countenance in his mother's lap, said to the palm: "Bend down your branches, O tree, and refresh my mother with your fruit." And immediately at this command [voice] the palm bent down to the feet of the blessed Mary, and they gathered from its fruit and they all refreshed themselves . . . [Addressing the palm, Jesus says:] "And open beneath your roots a vein of water . . . and let the waters flow." . . . And when they saw the fountain of water, they greatly rejoiced and quenched their thirst.¹

Compare these accounts with the Bible. You can read Gabriel's announcement to Mary in Luke 1:26–38, the story of Jesus' birth in Luke 2:1–19, and the account of the flight to Egypt in Matthew 2:13–23. See how many differences you can find between the biblical accounts and the ones in the Quran and the apocryphal stories.

The Infant Jesus of the Quran Spoke from His Cradle. You read the passage in the Quran where Jesus spoke to Mary immediately after, or during, his birth to tell her where she could find food and water. The Quran tells another amazing story about the infant Jesus speaking.

The Quran says that after Mary gave birth to Jesus, she returned to her people, or family. When they saw her with the baby, they were amazed. They thought she had given birth to a baby without being married. They could not understand how she could have done such a thing, since both her father and mother were good people. Mary then pointed to the baby as if to say, "Ask him!" The people asked Mary how they could possibly converse with a baby in a cradle. To their surprise, the baby Jesus began to explain who he was and how he had come into existence.

THE NATIVITY
WOODCUT BY GUSTAV DORÉ,
1832–1883

²⁷ She went back to her people carrying the child, and they said, 'Mary! You have done something terrible! ²⁸ Sister of Aaron! Your father was not an evil man; your mother was not unchaste!' ²⁹ She pointed at him. They said, 'How can we converse with an infant?'

³⁰ [But] he said: 'I am a servant of God. He has granted me the Scripture; made me a prophet; ³¹ made me blessed wherever I may be. He commanded me to pray, to give alms as long as I live, ³² to cherish my mother. He did not make me domineering or graceless. ³³ Peace was on me the day I was born, and will be on me the day I die and the day I am raised to life again.'

³⁴ Such was Jesus, son of Mary. [This is] a statement of the Truth about which they are in doubt.

Quran 19:27–34

Do you notice something in this story that contradicts something else you read earlier in the Quran about Jesus' crucifixion and death? According to Quran 19:33, Jesus told the people that one day he would die

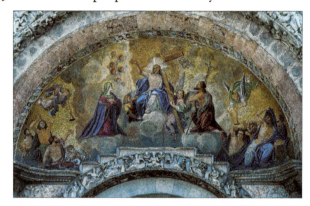

and then later he would be resurrected. But elsewhere, the Quran teaches that Jesus did not die. Instead, Allah took Jesus up to heaven; Jesus was not crucified; and the Jews killed someone who looked like Jesus (Quran 4:157–158). This is one of the examples of abrogation we explored in Lesson 4.

Like the story of Jesus speaking to Mary under the palm tree, the story of Jesus speaking from the cradle (Quran 19:27–34) is like a story in an apocryphal gospel. This is what *The Arabic Infancy Gospel* says:

> We have found it recorded in the book of Josephus the Chief Priest, who was in the time of Christ (and men say that he was Caiaphas), that this man said that Jesus spake when He was in the cradle, and said to Mary His Mother, "Verily I am Jesus, the Son of God, the Word which thou hast borne, according as the angel Gabriel gave thee the good news; and My Father hath sent Me for the salvation of the world."[2]

Although the Quranic story of Jesus speaking from the cradle is like this apocryphal story, do you notice something different in the two stories? Who does Jesus say he is in Quran 19:30? Now reread the passage from *The Arabic Infancy Gospel*. Whom does Jesus say he is in this apocryphal story?

According to the Quran, Jesus is a servant of God and a prophet, but according to *The Arabic Infancy Gospel*, Jesus is the Son of God and the Savior of the world. Why do you think Muhammad altered or changed the words that Jesus is supposed to have spoken? What problems would the words in *The Arabic Infancy Gospel* create for Muhammad? Wouldn't these words contradict Muhammad's message that Jesus was only a man, a servant or messenger of Allah, like Muhammad himself claimed to be?

We can see in this example that the Quran not only includes apocryphal gospel stories, but also that those stories were changed to deny that Jesus is God the Son and Savior of the world.

Jesus of the Quran Created a Clay Bird and Gave It Life. The Quran includes apocryphal stories of Jesus

speaking and performing miracles as an infant. It also includes apocryphal stories of miracles Jesus performed when he was older. One of the most popular stories—and one that people still tell today—is the miracle of the clay bird. In this story, Jesus promises that one day he will make a bird out of clay. Then he will breathe into it and make it become a real, living bird.

Muhammad recited the story of Jesus predicting he would perform this miracle:

[Then Jesus says to the children of Israel:] "I will make the shape of a bird for you out of clay, then breathe into it and, with God's permission, it will become a real bird."

Quran 3:49

In another chapter of the Quran, Muhammad recited words from Allah concerning Jesus having performed this miracle.

Then God will say, 'Jesus, son of Mary! Remember My favour to you and to your mother: how I strengthened you with the holy spirit, so that you spoke to people in your infancy and as a grown man; how I taught you the Scripture and wisdom, the Torah and the Gospel; how, by My leave, you fashioned the shape of a bird out of clay, breathed into it, and it became, by My leave, a bird; how, by My leave, you healed the blind person and the leper; how, by My leave, you brought the dead back to life.   Quran 5:110

Why do you think the Quran includes the story of the clay bird? Do you think Allah revealed it to Muhammad through the angel Gabriel? Or could Muhammad have heard the story on his caravan trade routes? As with other stories about Jesus in the Quran that are not in the Bible, we also find the story of the clay bird in one of the apocryphal gospels, *The Infancy Gospel of Thomas*.

> When this boy Jesus was five years old he was playing . . . He made soft clay and fashioned from it twelve sparrows. . . Jesus clapped his hands and cried to the sparrows: "Off with you!" And the sparrows took flight and went away chirping.[3]

Although the number of birds in this apocryphal gospel differs from the number in the Quran, the stories are so similar that many scholars believe Muhammad heard the story during his travels and included his version of it in the Quran.

ENDNOTES

1 "The History of the Nativity of Mary and the Infancy of the Savior" in Wilhelm Schneemelcher and R. Mcl. Wilson, *The New Testament Apocrypha, Vol. 1: Gospel and Related Writings* (Louisville, Kentucky: Westminster John Knox Press, 1990), 463.
2 William St. Clair Tisdall, *The Original Sources of the Qur'an* (London: Society for Promoting Christian Knowledge, 1911), 169–170.
3 "The Infancy Gospel of Thomas" in Wilhelm Schneemelcher and R. Mcl. Wilson, *The New Testament Apocrypha, Vol. 1: Gospel and Related Writings* (Louisville, Kentucky: Westminster John Knox Press, 1990), 444.

Getting Started—Allah Is the Creator

When a Muslim is asked the question "Where did the heavens and the earth and everything in them come from?" his or her answer is much like a Christian's answer—"Allah created them, of course!" Muslims and Christians believe the creation includes nonliving things such as the earth, sun, moon, stars, and planets. And they believe the creation also includes living things such as plants and animals and spiritual beings such as angels. Both Muslims and Christians also believe humans are the supreme created beings on Earth. However, even when Muslims and Christians  hold similar views, this does not mean their views are the same. Just as Allah of the Quran and Yahweh of the Bible are similar but not the same, so are Muslim and Christian beliefs about creation.

In this lesson, you will explore some of the similarities and differences between what the Quran and the Bible teach about the creation. Most importantly, you'll discover what the Quran teaches about people and their relationship with God. You'll learn that Muslims don't believe people are God's image-bearers, and they don't believe people are born with a sinful nature. This is why they don't believe people need Jesus to be their Savior.

 We'll begin our study of the Islamic view of the universe and people by looking at what the Quran teaches about the creation of the universe. Then we'll look at what the Quran teaches about the creation and nature of people. Next we'll investigate what Muslims believe about sin and the fall. We'll conclude the lesson by looking at the Islamic view of salvation and life after death. As we explore each of these topics, we'll evaluate or compare the Islamic view with what God reveals to us in his Word, the Bible.

Topic 1—The Islamic View of the Creation of the Heavens and the Earth

1. Allah Created the Heavens and the Earth and Rules Over and Sustains Them. Muslims live in a universe they believe Allah created. Most verses in the Quran about creation say that Allah created the heavens and the earth in six days.

It is God who created the heavens and the earth and everything between them in six Days.
Quran 32:4

This verse in the Quran is in agreement with God's revelation in the Bible: For in six days the LORD made the heavens, the earth, the sea, and everything in them (Exodus 20:11).

However, other verses in the Quran tell of Allah creating more than one heaven and more than one earth: It is God who created seven heavens and a similar [number] of earths (Quran 65:12).

The Bible does not say that God created seven heavens and seven earths. It says that In the beginning God created the heavens and the earth (Genesis 1:1). In this verse, the word *heavens* in this verse is plural because long ago, people thought heaven had three parts: The first heaven was the sky—Eath's atmosphere. The second heaven was space—where the sun, moon, and stars are found. The third heaven was where God and the angels dwell. But there is only one earth, and the LORD your God is the supreme God of the heavens above and the earth below (Joshua 10:11).

Not only does Islam teach that Allah created the heavens and the earth, it also teaches that he rules, controls, and holds his creation together.

Your Lord is God who created the heavens and earth in six Days, then established Himself on the Throne, governing everything.

Quran 10:3

God keeps the heavens and earth from vanishing.

Quran 35:41

Now let's compare the verses from the Quran about Allah's control of creation with the truths revealed in the Bible about God's control of creation.

15 Christ is the visible image of the invisible God. . . .16 for through him God created everything in the heavenly realms and on earth. . . .17 He existed before anything else, and he holds all creation together.

Colossians 1:15–17

The Son radiates God's own glory and expresses the very character of God, and he sustains everything by the mighty power of his command.

Hebrews 1:3

Again, we see that there is similarity between what Muslims believe about Allah's control and sustaining power and what Christians believe about God's control and sustaining power. However, reread the verses from the Quran and the Bible carefully to find an important difference. The Bible clearly teaches that Jesus is God. Jesus is the Person of the Trinity through whom God created everything and who holds everything together! The Quran, however, does not teach that Jesus is God, and it does not teach that Jesus is the Creator and the Sustainer of all things.

2. Allah Created the Land, Mountains, Rivers, and Oceans and Controls Them.
According to the Quran, Allah created the earth and its dry land, mountains, and rivers.

It is He who spread out the earth, placed firm mountains and rivers on it. Quran 13:3

Muslims believe that Allah created the saltwater oceans and freshwater rivers and the boundaries that separate them.

It is He who released the two bodies of flowing water, one sweet and fresh and the other salty and bitter, and put an insurmountable barrier between them. Quran 25:53

These statements from the Quran agree with statements in the Bible that tell us God created the mountains, the rivers, and the oceans and established boundaries for them. God established and maintains the boundaries for freshwater rivers and saltwater oceans.

⁹ Then God said, "Let the waters beneath the sky flow together into one place, so dry ground may appear." And that is what happened. ¹⁰ God called the dry ground "land" and the waters "seas." And God saw that it was good.

Genesis 1:9–10

¹⁰ A river flowed from the land of Eden, watering the garden and then dividing into four branches. ¹¹ The first branch, called the Pishon, flowed around the entire land of Havilah, where gold is found. ¹² The gold of that land is exceptionally pure; aromatic resin and onyx stone are also found there. ¹³ The second branch, called the Gihon, flowed around the entire land of Cush. ¹⁴ The third branch, called the Tigris, flowed east of the land of Asshur. The fourth branch is called the Euphrates.

Genesis 2:10–14

⁵ You placed the world on its foundation
     so it would never be moved.
⁶ You clothed the earth with floods of water,
     water that covered even the mountains.
⁷ At your command, the water fled;
     at the sound of your thunder, it hurried away.
⁸ Mountains rose and valleys sank
     to the levels you decreed.
⁹ Then you set a firm boundary for the seas,
     so they would never again cover the earth.   *Psalm 104:5–9*

3. Allah Created the Sun, Moon, and Stars and Night and Day and Controls Them. According to the Quran, Allah created the sun, moon, and stars.

Exalted is He who put constellations in the heavens, a radiant light, and an illuminating moon.

Quran 25:61

The Quran teaches that Allah created and controls the orbits for the sun and the moon, assuring day and night.

He has subjected the sun and the moon each to pursue its course for an appointed time; He regulates all things.

Quran 13:2

It is He who made the night and day follow each other.

Quran 25:62

If you were sharing your beliefs about God with a Muslim friend, would you agree or disagree with his or her views about who created the universe and who controls the orderly movements of the sun, moon, and stars? What Scriptures could you share with your friend to show that you agree? You could share verses from Genesis that reveal God not only created the sun, moon, and stars, but he also maintains the days and the nights that they rule.

¹⁴ Then God said, "Let lights appear in the sky to separate the day from the night. Let them be signs to mark the seasons, days, and years. ¹⁵ Let these lights in the sky shine down on the earth." And that is what happened. ¹⁶ God made two great lights—the larger one to govern the day, and the smaller one to govern the night. He

also made the stars. [17] God set these lights in the sky to light the earth, [18] to govern the day and night, and to separate the light from the darkness. And God saw that it was good. [19] And evening passed and morning came, marking the fourth day.

Genesis 1:14–19

"As long as the earth remains,
there will be planting and harvest,
cold and heat, summer and winter,
day and night."
Genesis 8:22

Topic 2—The Islamic View of the Creation of Plants, Animals, and Human Beings

1. Allah Created the Plants and Animals and Sustains Them. Not only do Muslims believe Allah created the heavens and the earth, they also believe he caused to grow therein (vegetation) of every noble kind (Quran 31:10 Shakir). This vegetation includes plants that can be used for food such as [11] fruits, its palm trees with sheathed clusters, [12] its husked grain, its fragrant plants. (Quran 55:11–12).

The Quran teaches that after Allah created the earth, He spread all kinds of animals around it (Quran 31:10), including cattle that were created especially for humans beings: And livestock–He created them too. You derive warmth and other benefits from them: you get food from them (Quran 16:5). In fact, Muslims believe that Allah created everything on the earth for the benefit of people: It was He who created all that is on the earth for you (Quran 2:29).

And just as Allah controls and sustains the heavens and the earth, the Quran teaches that he also sustains the life of plants, animals, and people through the rains he sends to Earth.

[48] It is He who sends the winds as heralds of good news before His Mercy. We send down pure water from the sky, [49] so that We can revive a dead land with it, and We give it as a drink to many animals and people We have created.

Quran 25:48–49

Again, if you were sharing your Christian beliefs about who created the plants and animals and who sustains them with your Muslim friend, would you and your friend agree? Of course! The story of creation in Genesis tells us clearly that God created and sustains all things. He created plants, many of which we use for food.

[11] Then God said, "Let the land sprout with vegetation—every sort of seed-bearing plant, and trees that grow seed-bearing fruit. These seeds will then produce the kinds of plants and trees from which they came." And that is what happened. . . .[29] Then God said, "Look! I have given you every seed-bearing plant throughout the earth and all the fruit trees for your food.

Genesis 1:11, 29

God created the wild animals; he also created the tame animals such as livestock, which we can use for work, food, and clothing.

[21] So God created great sea creatures and every living thing that scurries and swarms in the water, and every sort of bird—each producing offspring of the same kind. And God saw that it was good. [25] God made all sorts of wild animals, livestock, and small animals, each able to produce offspring of the same kind. And God saw that it was good.

Genesis 1:21, 25

Muslims believe Allah sustains the plants and animals just as Christians believe all plant and animal life is dependent upon God.

13 You send rain on the mountains from your heavenly home,
  and you fill the earth with the fruit of your labor.
14 You cause grass to grow for the livestock.

Psalm 104:13–14

"He never left them without evidence of himself and his goodness. For instance, he sends you rain and good crops and gives you food and joyful hearts."

Acts 14:17

2. Allah Created Human Beings and Sustains Them. The Quran teaches that human beings were created by Allah: He created man (Quran 55:3). The Quran also teaches that Allah displays his goodness, grace, and blessings by providing people with everything they need.

32 It is God who created the heavens and earth, who has sent down water from the sky and with it brought forth produce to nourish you; He has made ships useful to you, sailing the sea by His command, and the rivers too; 33 He has made the sun and the moon useful to you, steady on their paths; He has made the night and day useful to you 34 and given you some of everything you asked Him for. If you tried to count God's favours you could never calculate them.

Quran 14:32–34

And We have distributed the (water) amongst them, in order that they may celebrate (our) praises.

Quran 25:50 Yusuf Ali

These verses from the Quran about Allah creating and sustaining human life agree with truths in the Bible.

For in him we live and move and exist. As some of your own poets have said, 'We are his offspring.'

Acts 17:28

You cause grass to grow for the livestock and plants for people to use.

Psalm 104:14

"He [God] never left them without evidence of himself and his goodness. For instance, he sends you rain and good crops and gives you food and joyful hearts."

Acts 14:17

As these Scriptures tell us, Yahweh, the God of the Bible, created us and gives us life. He displays his kindness to us by providing us with everything we need for life. Muslims would agree with these truths, as you can see by reading the verses above from the Quran.

However, there is a major difference between what the Quran teaches about the creation of people and what the Bible teaches. To find out what this difference is, reread Quran 55:3 on this page and Genesis 1:27 below.

So God created human beings in his own image.
  In the image of God he created them;
  male and female he created them.

Genesis 1:27

What important phrase is missing in the Quran's description of the creation of human beings? The Quran says that Allah created man, but it does not say that he created man "in his own image" as we read in the Bible. We'll explore this major difference again in Topic 3 as we look at the Islamic view of people in more detail.

3. Allah Created All Things for His Glory. The Quran teaches that creation exists to declare Allah's glory.

The seven heavens and the earth and everyone in them glorify Him. There is not a single thing that does not celebrate His praise, though you do not understand their praise: He is most forbearing, most forgiving.

Quran 17:44

The plants and the trees submit to His designs. Quran 55:6

The Bible and the Quran agree that all creation declares God's glory.

The heavens proclaim the glory of God.
    The skies display his craftsmanship. Psalm 19:1

Not only do the nonliving parts of the creation declare God's glory, but everything that has breath is commanded to praise him.

Let everything that breathes sing praises to the LORD! Psalm 150:6

And most important, as God's image-bearers, we are commanded to bring glory to God.

[1] Honor the LORD, you heavenly beings;
    honor the LORD for his glory and strength.
[2] Honor the LORD for the glory of his name.
    Worship the LORD in the splendor of his holiness. Psalm 29:1–2

In spite of this agreement, there are two important differences between Islam's understanding of Allah's glory and the biblical Christian understanding of Yahweh's glory. As you learned in the last lesson, Allah of Islam is so transcendent that there is no way people can see or understand his greatness and majesty. The Bible, however, tells us clearly that God has shown us his glory in the Person of his Son, Jesus Christ. John wrote about this truth in his gospel:

The Word [Jesus] became human and made his home among us. He was full of unfailing love and faithfulness. And we have seen his glory, the glory of the Father's one and only Son. John 1:14

John witnessed Jesus' glory firsthand. On that occasion, Jesus took John along with Peter and James up on a mountain. While they were there, Jesus' appearance was transformed (transfigured) so that his face and clothes shone like the sun. Then God spoke from a bright cloud telling the three apostles that Jesus was, indeed, his Son.

[1] Six days later Jesus took Peter and the two brothers, James and John, and led them up a high mountain to be alone. [2] As the men watched, Jesus' appearance was transformed so that his face shone like the sun, and his clothes became as white as light. [3] Suddenly, Moses and Elijah appeared and began talking with Jesus.

⁴ Peter exclaimed, "Lord, it's wonderful for us to be here! If you want, I'll make three shelters as memorials—one for you, one for Moses, and one for Elijah."

⁵ But even as he spoke, a bright cloud overshadowed them, and a voice from the cloud said, "This is my dearly loved Son, who brings me great joy. Listen to him." ⁶ The disciples were terrified and fell face down on the ground.

⁷ Then Jesus came over and touched them. "Get up," he said. "Don't be afraid." ⁸ And when they looked up, Moses and Elijah were gone, and they saw only Jesus.   Matthew 17:1–8

The second important difference between the Islamic and Christian understanding of God's glory also stems from the Islamic belief that Allah did not create people in his image. Since people do not bear Allah's image,

it is impossible for them to reflect or bear the image of Allah's glory in their own lives. In contrast, the Bible tells us that when we become God's children through faith in Jesus, he begins to change us. And how does he change us? He begins to make us more and more like his glorious image. How is this possible? It's possible because God created us as his image-bearers. Our ability to show God's glory grows little by little while we live on this Earth. But when Jesus returns to the earth, this change will be complete. At that time, all God's children will share in all his glory.

And the Lord—who is the Spirit—makes us more and more like him as we are changed into his glorious image.   2 Corinthians 3:18

And when Christ, who is your life, is revealed to the whole world, you will share in all his glory. Colossians 3:4

Sadly, the Quran does not teach that people can bear God's glory in their lives here on Earth. It does not teach that Jesus showed us God's glory. And it does not accept or teach the biblical view that all believers will one day share in all God's glory.

4. The Creation Reveals the Existence of Allah. Muslims believe the creation reveals the existence of Allah just as Christians believe the creation reveals the existence of God. The Quran says that the heavens and the earth and everything Allah created are signs that prove he exists and that he is the creator. However, the Quran adds that the creation and the works of Allah are signs only for those who can understand them.

In the creation of the heavens and earth; in the alternation of night and day; in the ships that sail the seas with goods for people; in the water which God sends down from the sky to give life to the earth when it has been barren, scattering all kinds of creatures over it; in the changing of the winds and clouds that run their appointed courses between the sky and earth: there are signs in all these for those who use their minds.
                                        Quran 2:164

The Bible not only teaches that the creation reveals the existence of God, it also teaches that creation reveals his power and divine nature. In fact, the Bible says the creation reveals the existence of God so clearly that no person has an excuse for not knowing him. This means that God's creation is a revelation of his existence for everyone, not, as the Quran teaches, for just the few who can understand it.

Topic 3—The Islamic View of Human Beings and Their Responsibilities

1. The Islamic View of the Creation of Adam and Eve: As we explored in Topic 2, the Quran teaches that Allah created all things, including human beings. According to the Quran, Allah created Adam from clay or mud from the earth. Allah shaped Adam's body, giving him eyes for seeing, ears for hearing, and a brain for thinking. Then Allah breathed life into him from his own spirit.

We created man out of dried clay formed from dark mud.

Quran 15:26

Then He moulded him; He breathed from His Spirit into him; He gave you hearing, sight, and minds. How seldom you are grateful!

Quran 32:9

Some translations of the Quran say that Allah gave Adam a heart, meaning he created him with emotions or feelings. Then after Allah had created Adam, he told all the angels to bow down and worship him.

We created you, We gave you shape, and then We said to the angels, 'Bow down before Adam,' and they did. But not Iblis [Satan]: he was not one of those who bowed down.   Quran 7:11

The Quran tells us that Allah then created *Hawwa* (Eve) from Adam to be Adam's wife.

It is He who created you all from one soul, and from it made its mate so that he might find comfort in her: when one [of them] lies with his wife and she conceives a light burden, going about freely, then grows heavy, they both pray to God, their Lord, 'If You give us a good child we shall certainly be grateful.'   Quran 7:189

The Quran clearly states that Allah created Adam and Eve as mates (husband and wife), but it does not clearly state that Allah created them in his image. Furthermore, Muslims deny that any person can bear Allah's image.

The Originator of the heavens and the earth; He made mates for you from among yourselves, and mates of the cattle too, multiplying you thereby; nothing like a likeness of Him; and He is the Hearing, the Seeing.

Quran 42:11 Shakir

Muslims not only deny that Allah created people in his image (as you learned in Topic 2), Muhammad also taught that Allah created women as less intelligent than men. Because of this, according to Muhammad, more women will be in hell than men. The al-Bukhari's Hadith explains Muhammad's belief about this difference between men and women.

[Muhammad said], "O women! Give to charity, for I have seen that the majority of the dwellers of Hell-Fire were women." The women asked, "O Allah's Apostle! What is the reason for it?" He said: "O women! You curse frequently, and are ungrateful to your husbands. I have not seen anyone more deficient in intelligence and religion than you."

Sahih al-Bukhari 1462

As you learned in Lesson 4, the hadiths are books that contain the words and deeds of Muhammad. Even though they are not part of the Quran, Muslims believe they are true. Thus, they play an important role in shaping the Islamic worldview.

The Quran tells us that after Allah created the first man and woman, he placed them in a garden filled with plenty of things to eat. Then Allah said to Adam,: "Adam, live with your wife in this garden. Both of you eat freely there as you will, but do not go near this tree, or you will both become wrongdoers." Quran 2:35

Muslims do not believe Adam and Eve's garden was on Earth. They believe the garden where Adam and Eve lived was in heaven and that in the beginning they lived in heaven with Allah. Allah did not send them

to Earth to live until after Satan tempted them and they sinned. You'll learn more about this in Topic 4. The Quran tells us that after Adam and Eve were sent to live on Earth, they began to have children. And from this first family, Allah formed all the tribes and nations of the earth.

People, We created you all from a single man and a single woman, and made you into races and tribes. Quran 49:13

2. The Biblical Christian View of the Creation of Adam and Eve: Does the story of the creation of Adam and Eve in the Quran sound similar to the story in the Bible? Let's examine the story of the creation of Adam and Eve in the Bible to see how many similarities and differences there are between the two.

⁷ Then the LORD God formed the man from the dust of the ground. He breathed the breath of life into the man's nostrils, and the man became a living person. ⁸ Then the LORD God planted a garden in Eden in the east, and there he placed the man he had made.

¹⁸ Then the LORD God said, "It is not good for the man to be alone. I will make a helper who is just right for him."

²¹ So the LORD God caused the man to fall into a deep sleep. While the man slept, the LORD God took out one of the man's ribs and closed up the opening. ²² Then the LORD God made a woman from the rib, and he brought her to the man. Genesis 2:7–8, 18, 21–22

From one man he created all the nations throughout the whole earth. He decided beforehand when they should rise and fall, and he determined their boundaries. Acts 17:26

As you can see, both the Quran and the Bible say Adam and Eve were created by the almighty Deity, Allah or God. Both books tell us that God breathed life into Adam after creating him from the dust or clay of the earth. Both books tell us that Eve was created from Adam to be his wife, although the Quran does not say

Allah created Eve from one of Adam's ribs. The Quran and the Bible both say Adam and Eve were placed in a garden that provided them food to eat. However, as you read earlier in this topic, the Quran says the garden was in heaven, not on Earth. And finally, both the Quran and the Bible teach that God created all the nations of the earth from the first family of Adam and Eve.

Now, let's look at the important differences in the Quran's account and the Bible's account. First, do you remember what Allah told the angels to do after he created Adam? He told them to bow down and worship Adam. Do you think this command is in harmony or disharmony with the Bible? Luke recorded these words of Jesus in his Gospel that show us such a command is clearly not in harmony with Scripture:

Jesus replied, "The Scriptures say, 'You must worship the LORD your God and serve only him.'"   Luke 4:8

Now let's look at the two accounts of the creation of Adam and Eve again. Do you notice another important difference? The Quran says that Allah created Adam and Eve with eyes for seeing, ears for hearing, and a brain for knowing (or a heart for feeling). However, as you learned earlier, the Quran does not say that Allah created Adam and Eve in his image. Muslims do not believe that people have any godlikeness within them. As you learned in Lesson 5, Allah is so transcendent over his creation that there is nothing like Him (Quran 42:11). And as you just learned in Topic 2, this means people cannot have a personal relationship with Allah and they will never be able to reflect or display any of Allah's glory. This, of course, is not in harmony with what the Bible says. Because all people are God's image-bearers, he calls us [Christians] his children, and that is what we are! And because people are God's image-bearers, God makes us more and more like him as we are changed into his glorious image (2 Corinthians 3:18).

These similarities and differences between the Quran's and the Bible's accounts of the creation of human beings provide more examples of what we mean when we say that although the Quran teaches some things that are similar to what the Bible teaches, it does not teach the same thing. Two books can be similar, but they are not the same. Adam and Eve described in the Quran are not the same Adam and Eve described in the Bible as God's image-bearers. Furthermore, Adam and Eve of the Bible were not created to be worshipped by angels or by any other human beings.

3. The Islamic View of the Responsibilities of Adam and Eve:
The Quran says that Allah created human beings in a position higher than the earth's animals.

We have honoured the children of Adam. . . .We have provided good sustenance for them and favoured them specially above many of those We have created.   Quran 17:70

People were created to serve Allah as stewards or vicegerents of the earth. The Quran explains that Allah announced this part of his plan to the angels.

Behold, thy Lord said to the angels: "I will create a vicegerent on earth."   Quran 2:30

The Quran teaches that Allah gave human beings the authority to be the earth's stewards and made all the animals submit to their authority.

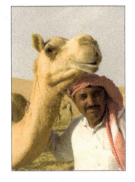

We established you [people] on the earth and provided you with a means of livelihood there.   Quran 7:10

We made animals subject to you, that ye [you] may be grateful.   Quran 22:36

The Quran says that Allah taught Adam the names for everything he had created. Then because the angels did not know these names, Allah commanded Adam to teach the names to them.

He taught Adam all the names [of things], then He showed them to the angels and said, 'Tell me the names of these if you truly [think you can].' They [angels] said, 'May You be glorified! We have knowledge only of what You have taught us. You are the All Knowing and All Wise.' Then He said, 'Adam, tell them the names of these.'   Quran 2:31–33

4. The Biblical Christian View of the Responsibilities of Adam and Eve: Again, let's compare these statements in the Quran with what God revealed to us in the Bible. As you read the Scriptures below, look for the similarities as well as the differences between them and the verses from the Quran above.

Then God blessed them and said, "Be fruitful and multiply. Fill the earth and govern it. Reign over the fish in the sea, the birds in the sky, and all the animals that scurry along the ground."   Genesis 1:28

[3] When I look at the night sky and see the work of your fingers—
   the moon and the stars you set in place–
[4] what are mere mortals that you should think about them,
   human beings that you should care for them?
[5] Yet you made them only a little lower than God
   and crowned them with glory and honor.
[6] You gave them charge of everything you made,
   putting all things under their authority—
[7] the flocks and the herds
   and all the wild animals,
[8] the birds in the sky, the fish in the sea, and everything that swims the ocean currents.   Psalm 8:3–8

[19] So the LORD God formed from the ground all the wild animals and all the birds of the sky. He brought them to the man to see what he would call them, and the man chose a name for each one. [20] He gave names to all the livestock, all the birds of the sky, and all the wild animals. But still there was no helper just right for him. Genesis 2:19–20

First, let's look at the similarities. The Bible reveals that God created people to rule over, care for, and fill the earth. The Bible says people are created just a little lower than heavenly beings and above the animals we are to care for. In these two truths, the teachings of the Quran are similar to those of the Bible.

However, did you notice the important difference in the responsibility given to Adam in the Bible and in the Quran? In the book of Genesis, God gave Adam the responsibility for naming the animals. God had given Adam, as his image-bearer, a creative mind for carrying out such a task. But the Quran says that Allah named the animals for Adam and then told Adam to teach the names to the angels.

How do we explain these similarities and great differences in the nature of Adam and Eve and their role as God's stewards or vicegerents of creation? Muslims believe the Quran tells the true story and that Christians and Jews have changed the words of the Bible from its original truth. But as you learned in earlier lessons, much of what Muhammad is said to have recited as truth from Allah he probably heard from Christian and Jewish tribes during his travels along the caravan trade routes of Arabia. No doubt parts of the stories he heard were true, but much of what he heard was probably a mixture of truth and untruth. Do you remember some of the apocryphal stories of Jesus you read about in Lesson 5 that eventually found their way into the Quran?

For Christians, God's revealed Word, the Bible, is the primary source of truth. Everything that people believe is truth from Allah must be carefully evaluated and compared with what the Bible says. If it is not in harmony with the Bible, then we must reject it as untrue. Remember the words Jesus prayed for his disciples about God's words, saying, "Teach them your word, which is truth" (John 17:17).

Topic 4—The Fall

1. The Islamic View of the Fall of Satan: In Topic 3, you learned that Allah created Adam and then told the angels to fall down and worship Adam. But that is only part of the story. The Quran continues the story by telling us that one angel did not obey Allah's command. This angel was *Iblis* or Satan. For his disobedience, Allah cast him out of heaven.

ANGELS HONORING ADAM (CIRCA 1560)

[11] And We created you, [your father Adam] then We shaped you, then We said to the Angels: "Submit to Adam;" so they submitted except for Satan, he was not of those who submitted. [12] God said, 'What prevented you from bowing down as I commanded you?'

(Satan) said, 'I am better than him: You created me from fire and him from clay.'

[13] God said, 'Get down from here! This is no place [heaven] for your arrogance. Get out! You are contemptible!'   Quran 7:11–13

After Allah commanded Satan to leave heaven, Satan promised to attack Adam and Eve from all sides. This meant he would tempt them to disobey Allah. In return, Allah told Satan that he and any who followed him would be sent into hell.

[16] And then Iblis said, "Because You have put me in the wrong, I will lie in wait for them all on Your straight path: [17] I will come at them- from their front and their back, from their right and their left."

¹⁸ God said, 'Get out! You are disgraced and banished! I swear I shall fill Hell with you and all who follow you!

Quran 7:16–18

2. The Biblical Christian View of the Fall of Satan: The story about Satan refusing to bow down to Adam is not in the Bible. In fact, the Bible says very little about the origin of Satan except that he is a spiritual being whom God cast out of heaven because of his pride. Some Bible scholars believe that the fall of Satan from heaven is described in the Old Testament in Isaiah 14:12–14 and Ezekiel 28:11–19. Although not all Christians interpret these Scriptures in this way, all Christians do believe that Satan is the evil one (1 John 5:19) and that he is an enemy of both God and his children. Christians also believe that when Jesus returns to Earth, Satan and his army of fallen angels, known as *demons*, will be defeated. They will be punished forever in the lake of fire (Revelation 20:10).

ADAM AND EVE COVER
THEMSELVES WITH LEAVES

3. The Islamic View of the Fall of Adam and Eve: The Quran includes a story about Satan's temptation of Adam and Eve and their disobedience. It is similar to the story of the fall in the Bible, but there are some important differences. As you read the story from the Quran, look for the differences. The story begins with Allah warning Adam not to eat from one particular tree of the garden.

¹⁹ But you and your wife, Adam, live in the Garden. Both of you eat whatever you like, but do not go near this tree or you will become wrongdoers.'

²⁰ Satan whispered to them . . . 'Your Lord only forbade you this tree to prevent you becoming angels or immortals,' ²¹ and he swore to them, 'I am giving you sincere advice'- ²² he lured them with lies. Their nakedness became exposed to them when they had eaten from the tree: they began to put together leaves from the Garden to cover themselves. Their Lord called to them, 'Did I not forbid you to approach that tree? Did I not warn you that Satan was your sworn enemy?'

²³ They replied, 'Our Lord, we have wronged our souls: if You do not forgive us and have mercy, we shall be lost.'

²⁴ He said, 'All of you get out! You are each other's enemies. On earth you will have a place to stay and livelihood- for a time.'

²⁵ He said, 'There you will live; there you will die; from there you will be brought out.'

Quran 7:19–25

In another surah (chapter) of the Quran, we read that Adam repented of his disobedience and Allah, the Merciful, forgave him.

Then Adam received some words from his Lord and He accepted his repentance: He is the Ever Relenting, the Most Merciful.

Quran 2:37

Most Muslims believe that Adam repented of his disobedience before Allah sent him and Eve to live on the earth. Allah did not send them to the earth as punishment. He simply sent them to earth so they could begin caring for it as his stewards.

Muslims believe that all people are born innocent. They do not believe as Christians do that all people since the fall of Adam are born with a sinful nature. According to the Quran, Allah told Muhammad that he and all people were created or framed with an upright or sinless nature. And because all people are created or framed with an upright or sinless heart, they are commanded and are able to make the religion of Islam the purpose or goal of their life.

Then set your face upright for religion in the right state-- the nature made by Allah in which He has made men.　　　　Quran 30:30 Shakir

The Quran also teaches that all people have chosen to sin and are therefore no longer innocent like they were at birth. "Man is truly unjust and ungrateful." (Quran 14:34). However, people sin by choice, not because they

have an inborn sinful nature. According to the Quran, if people will repent and practice what is good, they will be rewarded greatly. And if they avoid "great" sins, Allah will forgive their "minor" sins and allow them to enter paradise.

But if you avoid the great sins you have been forbidden, We shall wipe out your minor misdeeds and let you in through the entrance of honour [paradise].　　Quran 4:31

4. The Biblical Christian View of the Fall of Adam and Eve: Now let's look at the story of the fall in the Bible and compare it to the story in the Quran. The complete story of the fall is found in Genesis 3:1–24; however, let's look at certain verses and compare them with similar verses from the Quran.

You remember from the Genesis story that after God placed Adam and Eve in the garden, he named a specific tree—the Tree of the Knowledge of Good and Evil—and commanded them not to eat from it. Then he clearly told them the consequence they would suffer if they disobeyed his command.

15 "The Lord God placed the man in the Garden of Eden to tend and watch over it. 16 But the Lord God warned him, "You may freely eat the fruit of every tree in the garden— 17 except the tree of the knowledge of good and evil. If you eat its fruit, you are sure to die."　　Genesis 2:15–17

The Quran does not name the tree from which Adam and Eve were forbidden to eat. And it does not state a consequence for disobedience. It states only that if Adam and Eve were to eat the fruit, they would fall into sin.

According to the Bible, Satan asked Eve a question.

"Did God really say you must not eat the fruit from any of the trees in the garden?"　　Genesis 3:1

Eve answered Satan's question.

2 "Of course we may eat fruit from the trees in the garden," the woman replied. 3 "It's only the fruit from the tree in the middle of the garden that we are not allowed to eat. God said, 'You must not eat it or even touch it; if you do, you will die.'"　　Genesis 3:2–3

According to the Quran, Satan did not ask Eve a question. He simply told her that Allah had not forbidden them to eat from the tree. In the Bible, Satan asked Eve a question designed to make her doubt God's command. Then Eve clearly answered the question and told Satan the consequences she and Adam would suffer if they disobeyed.

In the Bible's account of the fall, Satan told Eve that she and Adam would not die for eating the fruit. Instead, he told her they would become wise like God.

4 "You won't die!" the serpent replied to the woman. 5 "God knows that your eyes will be opened as soon as you eat it, and you will be like God, knowing both good and evil."   Genesis 3:4–5

In the Quran's story of the fall, Satan did not mention the consequence of death for disobedience. He simply told Adam and Eve that if they ate the fruit, they would become like angels and live forever.

Now let's explore a major difference between the story of the fall in the Quran and the Bible. In the Genesis account, God spoke to the serpent (Satan) and condemned him to crawl on his belly all the days of his life. Then God announced his great plan of salvation for his image-bearers. God said that one day a Savior would be born from one of Eve's descendants. The Savior God promised was Jesus, his Son, who would strike Satan and his works. Yes, Satan would strike Jesus' heel, meaning that Jesus would die on the cross for our sins. But as you know, God raised Jesus to life again and gives eternal life to all who place their faith in him as their Savior.

14 Then the LORD God said to the serpent,

"Because you have done this, you are cursed
    more than all animals, domestic and wild.
You will crawl on your belly,
    groveling in the dust as long as you live.
15 And I will cause hostility between you and the woman,
    and between your offspring and her offspring.
He will strike your head,
    and you will strike his heel."

Genesis 3:14–15

Why do you suppose this good news is not mentioned in the Quran? This is because according to the Quran, people do not need a Savior and a burdened soul cannot bear the burden of another (Quran 35:18 Shakir).

In the narrative of the fall found in the Bible, after Adam and Eve disobeyed, God announced the consequences for their disobedience—pain in childbirth, a cursed earth, hard work, and finally, death.

16 Then he said to the woman,

"I will sharpen the pain of your pregnancy,
    and in pain you will give birth.
And you will desire to control your husband,
    but he will rule over you."

¹⁷ And to the man he said,

"Since you listened to your wife and ate from the tree
    whose fruit I commanded you not to eat,
the ground is cursed because of you.

¹⁹ By the sweat of your brow
    will you have food to eat
until you return to the ground
    from which you were made.
For you were made from dust,
    and to dust you will return."   Genesis 3:16–17, 19

The Quran does not mention these consequences. In the Quran, after Adam and Eve repent for their disobedience, Allah simply forgives them and sends them to the earth.

According to the biblical account of the fall, God did not send Adam and Eve out of a garden in heaven down to Earth. Rather, he made clothes for them and then drove them out of the earthly garden of Eden. From that day on, they were no longer stewards of the garden, but of the entire earth.

²¹ And the LORD God made clothing from animal skins for Adam and his wife.

²² Then the LORD God said, "Look, the human beings have become like us, knowing both good and evil. What if they reach out, take fruit from the tree of life, and eat it? Then they will live forever!" ²³ So the LORD God banished them from the Garden of Eden, and he sent Adam out to cultivate the ground from which he had been made. ²⁴ After sending them out, the LORD God stationed mighty cherubim to the east of the Garden of Eden. And he placed a flaming sword that flashed back and forth to guard the way to the tree of life.   Genesis 3:21–24

The story of the fall in the Quran does not say anything about this consequence for Adam and Eve. As you read earlier in Quran 2 and 7, Allah simply forgave Adam and Eve and sent them down to Earth to be its stewards.

Topic 5—Salvation

1. The Islamic View of Salvation: The Quran teaches that time and history began when Allah created the seven heavens and earths. It also teaches that time and history will end on the day of resurrection. On that day, Muslims believe all people will be judged according to their belief in Allah and Islam and according to their deeds or works. If they have done enough good deeds and if Allah is merciful, they will be saved from the fires of hell and enter paradise. But if they have not believed in Allah and Islam and not done enough good deeds, they will be lost.

Every soul will taste death and you will be paid in full only on the Day of Resurrection. Whoever is kept away from the Fire and admitted to the Garden will have triumphed.   Quran 3:185

¹⁰¹ On that Day when the Trumpet is blown. . . ¹⁰² those whose good deeds weigh heavy will be successful, ¹⁰³ but those whose balance is light will have lost their souls forever and will stay in Hell.   Quran 23:101–103

⁹ God has promised forgiveness and a rich reward to those who have faith [in Allah and Islam] and do good works; ¹⁰ those who reject faith and deny Our [Allah's] revelations will inhabit the blazing Fire.   Quran 5:9–10

As you can see from these verses above, the Quran teaches that salvation from hell comes through believing in Islam and doing good works. Muslims, as you learned, do not believe that they need a Savior to be redeemed. Each person is responsible for his or her own salvation. Muslims do not believe that anyone, not even a close relative, can bear another person's sins.

No burdened soul will bear the burden of another: even if a heavily laden soul should cry for help, none of its load will be carried, not even by a close relative. But you [Prophet] can only warn those who fear their Lord, though they cannot see Him, and keep up the prayer- whoever purifies himself does so for his own benefit.   Quran 35:18

No one will suffer for the sins of others.   Quran 17:15 Sarwar

For Muslims, heaven, or paradise, will be filled with wonderful delights. There will be big mansions, gardens, and rivers. Men will have many wives, and people will be served by boys who will remain young forever. They will eat delicious foods and drink flowing wine.

¹⁵ They will recline on jewelled couches ¹⁶ facing one another.. ¹⁷ Immortal youths will serve them ¹⁸ with goblets, jugs and cups of crystal clear wine ¹⁹ which will not cause them any intoxication or illness. ²⁰ Also, they will be served with the fruits of their choice ²¹ and the flesh of birds, as they desire. ²² They will have maidens with large, lovely black and white eyes.   Quran 56:15–22 Sarwar

God has promised the believers, both men and women, Gardens graced with flowing streams where they will remain; good, peaceful homes in Gardens of lasting bliss; and- greatest of all- God's good pleasure. That is the supreme triumph.   Quran 9:72

However, no one will actually see Allah in paradise.

No vision can take Him in.   Quran 6:103

No mortal eyes can see Him.   Quran 6:103 Sarwar

Allah cannot be seen because he is transcendent. As you learned, people can never have a personal relationship with him. Though people may praise Allah in paradise, he is not obviously present or living with those who have been saved.

2. The Biblical Christian View of Salvation: From what you just read from the Quran and from what you learned earlier, do you see any differences between the way Muslims view salvation and the way Christians view salvation? Let's explore God's Word to find out what these differences are.

First, unlike the Quran, the Bible teaches clearly that all people since the fall of Adam and Eve are born with a sinful nature or sinful heart.

When Adam sinned, sin entered the world. Adam's sin brought death, so death spread to everyone, for everyone sinned.   Romans 5:12

4 Against you, and you alone, have I sinned;
    I have done what is evil in your sight.
You will be proved right in what you say,
    and your judgment against me is just.
5 For I was born a sinner—
    yes, from the moment my mother conceived me.   Psalm 51:4–5

Second, unlike the Quran, the Bible teaches that our sin nature and our sins separate us from God. We cannot simply repent and do good works and be restored to fellowship with God. Neither can we earn God's forgiveness for "small" sins by avoiding "great" sins, as Islam teaches. Any sin separates us from God and eternal life with him.

It's your sins that have cut you off from God.
    Because of your sins, he has turned away
        and will not listen anymore.   Isaiah 59:2

4 When people work, their wages are not a gift, but something they have earned. 5 But people are counted as righteous, not because of their work, but because of their faith in God who forgives sinners.   Romans 4:4–5

According to God's Word, the only way our sins can be forgiven is through faith in Jesus as God's Son and our Savior.

9 For God chose to save us through our Lord Jesus Christ, not to pour out his anger on us. 10 Christ died for us so that, whether we are dead or alive when he returns, we can live with him forever.   1 Thessalonians 5:9–10

I no longer count on my own righteousness through obeying the law; rather, I become righteous through faith in Christ. For God's way of making us right with himself depends on faith.   Philippians 3:9

But according to the Quran, sins are forgiven through belief in Allah, Muhammad, and Islam and by doing good deeds.

Third, unlike the Quran's teaching that no one can carry the sins of another person (Quran 35:18), the Bible teaches that someone must bear or carry our sins for us in order for them to be forgiven. And the sin-bearer must be without sin. The only Person capable of fulfilling this demand of God is Jesus.

He personally carried our sins in his body on the cross so that we can be dead to sin and live for what is right.   1 Peter 2:24

When we place our faith in Jesus as our Savior and, yes, repent of our sins, God brings us back into fellowship with himself. Only people who refuse to believe in God's Son and refuse to accept his wonderful gift will be condemned or lost.

16 "For this is how God loved the world: He gave his one and only Son, so that everyone who believes in him will not perish but have eternal life. 17 God sent his Son into the world not to judge the world, but to save the world through him.

18 "There is no judgment against anyone who believes in him. But anyone who does not believe in him has already been judged for not believing in God's one and only Son."

John 3:16–18

Matthew wrote Jesus' words that describe the eternal homes of the righteous and the condemned. In this account, Jesus refers to the righteous and saved as sheep. He refers to the unrighteous and condemned as goats.

31 "But when the Son of Man comes in his glory, and all the angels with him, then he will sit upon his glorious throne. 32 All the nations will be gathered in his presence, and he will separate the people as a shepherd separates the sheep from the goats. 33 He will place the sheep at his right hand and the goats at his left.

34 "Then the King will say to those on his right, 'Come, you who are blessed by my Father, inherit the Kingdom prepared for you from the creation of the world. . . . 41 "Then the King will turn to those on the left and say, 'Away with you, you cursed ones, into the eternal fire prepared for the devil and his demons'."

Matthew 25:31–34, 41

While the condemned will spend eternity in hell, the righteous will spend eternity in God's kingdom. They will see Jesus when he returns to earth. And they will live with him forever in the new Jerusalem, which God will send down out of heaven to the new earth. The apostle John first wrote about these events in a letter to Christians and, later, in the book of Revelation.

Dear friends, we are already God's children, but he has not yet shown us what we will be like when Christ appears. But we do know that we will be like him, for we will see him as he really is.

1 John 3:2

Look! He comes with the clouds of heaven.
    And everyone will see him—
even those who pierced him.

Revelation 1:7

1 Then I saw a new heaven and a new earth, for the old heaven and the old earth had disappeared. And the sea was also gone. 2 And I saw the holy city, the new Jerusalem, coming down from God out of heaven like a bride beautifully dressed for her husband.

3 I heard a loud shout from the throne, saying, "Look, God's home is now among his people! He will live with them, and they will be his people. God himself will be with them.

Revelation 21:1–3

Does It Matter? Some people believe the Christian and Muslim view of salvation are the same because there are some similarities between them. But remember, just because two views are similar does not mean they are the same. So, does it really matter if the way of salvation in the Quran is not the same as the way of salvation in the Bible? Don't both worldviews lead their followers to eternal life, but just along slightly different paths? God's Word answers this question for us very clearly.

Jesus told him, "I am the way, the truth, and the life. No one can come to the Father except through me." John 14:6

Does it matter which path of salvation you follow? Yes, it does! It makes an eternal difference!

The Islamic View of Moral Laws and Values

Getting Started—Good and Evil Are Not Alike

So far in our exploration of the Islamic worldview, we've learned what Muslims believe is true about God, truth, people, and the universe. In this final lesson about Islam, we'll learn what Muslims believe is true about right and wrong and the moral laws and values that determine how they live within their families and communities. Like Christians, Muslims believe that good and evil cannot be equal (Quran 41:34). Certain behaviors are right, while others are wrong. For example, both Muslims and Christians believe stealing is wrong. Both believe having a sexual relationship with another person's husband or wife (adultery) is wrong. Both Muslims and Christians believe being honest, practicing hospitality, giving to the poor, and helping orphans are good. But do similarities like these mean the Islamic view of moral laws and values is the same as the biblical Christian view? As you learned in previous lessons, having similarities does not mean the two worldviews are the same. This truth also applies to the Islamic and biblical Christian views of moral laws and value. While there are similarities between them, we will discover that many Islamic beliefs are not in harmony with the truth of the Bible.

In this lesson, we'll explore the foundations of Islamic moral laws and values. We'll identify the five pillars of Islam—the most important moral responsibilities Muslims must fulfill. We'll also study the different ways Muslims define and practice a moral duty called *jihad*, which is sometimes included as a sixth pillar of Islam. And we'll learn about *shariah*, the unique system of laws that governs everything Muslims must do in worship and in their families, communities, and nations. As we've done in previous lessons, we'll compare and contrast the Islamic view of moral laws and values with the truth of God's Word revealed in the Bible.

Topic 1—The Christian Foundation of Moral Laws and Values

The study of right and wrong is called ethics. Before we explore the Islamic view of ethics—which includes their moral laws and values—let's examine the biblical Christian view so that we can identify how they are similar and how they are different.

Moral Awareness, Moral Laws, and Moral Values: Everyone is created possessing *moral awareness*. This means God creates us with the ability to know the difference between what is moral (right) and immoral (wrong). God does this by writing his *moral laws* within our heart and conscience. All people, including Christians and Muslims, have an awareness that murder and stealing are immoral. Likewise, they are aware that being honest and being faithful in marriage are moral behaviors. They also understand that right behaviors such as honesty and faithfulness are good and valuable not only for themselves but also for their communities. For this reason, we refer to right behaviors as *moral values*. Moral values become an important foundation for the lives of individuals, communities, and nations. Sadly, since the fall, our moral awareness is imperfect. And if people reject God's moral laws and create their own set of values for living, their values are no longer moral. Rather, they are immoral.

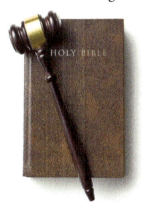

The Biblical Christian Foundation of Moral Awareness, Moral Laws, and Moral Values: The biblical Christian foundation of moral awareness, moral laws, and moral values is God himself. God is perfectly moral in everything he says and does. He is absolutely holy, and he can say and do only what is sinless and perfectly right. Because God is perfectly moral, he expects his image-bearers to be perfectly moral. To help us understand what he means when he commands us to "be holy, because I am holy" (Leviticus 11:44), God has revealed his perfect moral character and laws to us in three unique ways throughout history.

Ethics
The study of right and wrong

1. Conscience: According to the Bible, God has written his moral laws on our hearts. This gift from God makes us morally aware, which is one of the ways that all people bear the image of God. Although we are born with a sinful nature because of the fall, God still places within us (and all people) an awareness of what is right and wrong. He writes his moral laws on our hearts and the Holy Spirit guides us through our conscience to tell us when we have obeyed or disobeyed one of his moral laws.

In the apostle Paul's letter to the Romans, he explained that Gentiles knew right from wrong even without God's written laws such as the Ten Commandments. They had this knowledge because God had already written his moral laws on their hearts. He also gave them a conscience that told them when they obeyed or disobeyed his laws.

14 Even Gentiles, who do not have God's written law, show that they know his law when they instinctively obey it, even without having heard it. 15 They demonstrate that God's law is written in their hearts, for their own conscience and thoughts either accuse them or tell them they are doing right. Romans 2:14–15

2. Scripture: Although the Bible teaches that God writes his moral laws on the hearts of all people, it also teaches that since the fall, everyone's conscience is imperfect. People don't perfectly know right from wrong, and often they don't listen to their conscience. Some people completely reject God and define for themselves what is moral and immoral. However, God also chose to reveal his holy character and laws in writing through Scripture so that even as fallen image-bearers, we would know them clearly. Paul wrote a letter to Timothy, a young pastor of the early church, explaining this very important truth.

¹⁶All Scripture is inspired by God and is useful to teach us what is true and to make us realize what is wrong in our lives. It corrects us when we are wrong and teaches us to do what is right. ¹⁷God uses it to prepare and equip his people to do every good work.

2 Timothy 3:16–17

3. Jesus Christ: God not only revealed his perfect moral character and laws through conscience and in writing through Scripture, he also showed his character and laws to people through the sinless life of Jesus. People have the example of his perfect moral life to follow.

²¹ For God called you to do good, even if it means suffering, just as Christ suffered for you. He is your example, and you must follow in his steps. ²² He never sinned, nor ever deceived anyone.

1 Peter 2:21–22

Now, as we begin to explore the Islamic foundation of moral laws and values, remember these very important truths. First, the foundation for the biblical Christian view of moral laws and values is the absolutely good and holy nature of God himself. And second, God revealed his perfect moral nature and laws to all people in three ways—through the Holy Spirit guiding our conscience, through Scripture, and through Jesus, God the Son.

Topic 2—The Islamic Foundation of Moral Laws and Values

The Islamic Foundation of Moral Laws and Values: Like Christians, Muslims have a foundation or basis for moral laws and values. Unlike biblical Christianity, however, this foundation is not the character and moral nature of Allah. For Muslims, the character and moral nature of Allah are largely unknowable because Allah himself is unknowable. Allah is above and beyond everything he created. And Allah is completely unlike anything he created. (Remember, Islam teaches that Allah did not create people in his image). Any ideas human beings have about personal character traits, such as loyalty or honesty, cannot and must not be applied to Allah because Allah is totally unlike human beings.

For Muslims, Yahweh's command to "be holy, because I am holy" (Leviticus 11:44) is impossible to obey. If Allah had issued that command, it would be impossible to obey because Muslims do not believe they can know or understand Allah's moral nature. And if they cannot know or understand what Allah's holiness is like, they cannot ever hope to be holy like he is, and they shouldn't even try.

So, what is the Islamic foundation for moral laws and values if it is not the perfectly moral nature of Allah? For Muslims, behaviors are either right or wrong simply because Allah (the Almighty) says they are. Allah did not command Muslims to be holy because he is holy. He simply said they must obey his words and the words of Muhammad, stating "Obey Allah and His Messenger": But if they turn back, Allah loveth not those who reject Faith (Quran 3:32 Yusuf Ali).

1. Conscience: Like Christians, Muslims believe that part of the foundation for Islamic moral laws and values is the moral awareness found in the heart or conscience of all people. The Quran teaches that after Allah created the soul of each person, he inspired it to understand what is right and wrong for it (Quran 91:8 Shakir). In other words, Allah gives each person enlightenment as to its wrong and its right (Quran 91:8 Yusuf Ali).

This belief about conscience is similar to the biblical Christian view, but it is not exactly the same. The Bible teaches that people are morally aware because God created them in his moral image.

Muslims don't believe Allah creates people in his image. Remember that according to the Quran, Allah is so transcendent, or above, human beings that he created nothing like Him (Quran 42:11). So, when Allah gave people a conscience for knowing right from wrong, it is not because they bear his moral image. He gave them this ability only so they could know, accept, and obey his laws.

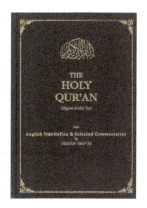

2. The Quran: Just as Christians believe their moral laws and values are founded on written revelation from God in the Bible, Muslims believe their moral laws and values are founded on written revelation from Allah in the Quran. Muslims believe that Allah revealed his moral laws and values for their personal lives and for Islamic communities around the world within the pages of the Quran.

Now let's consider this question: Why would Muslims need a book to tell them how to live? Islam teaches that Allah creates all people by nature upright—the nature (framed) of Allah, in which He hath created man. (Quran 30:30 Pickthall). If Allah creates people upright by nature and sinless when they are born, why do they need the Quran to teach them moral laws? Why don't they follow their conscience and always do right? The answer to these questions is found in the Islamic belief that all people are created with a will. Even though they are born sinless, they choose to sin. By choosing to sin, all people become inept [sinful] and foolish (Quran 33:72). They are unjust, ignorant (Quran 33:72 Shakir). And even though the Quran says Allah gives people more blessings than they can count, they are given up to injustice and ingratitude (Quran 14:34 Yusuf Ali).

Because all people are sinful, foolish, ignorant, and unthankful, Muslims believe Allah is merciful in choosing to reveal his moral laws to them in the Quran. Through his prophet Muhammad, Allah gives all people every moral law they need to know to live perfect lives. Islam teaches that people can purify themselves from their sins and live perfect lives simply by obeying Allah's moral laws found in the Quran.

⁹ The one who purifies his soul succeeds [obeys and performs all that Allah ordered] ¹⁰ and the one who corrupts it fails [disobeys what Allah ordered].   Quran 91:9–10

MUSLIM WOMAN WEARING WHITE HIJAB ISLAMIC SYMBOL OF PURITY AND LIGHT

Later in this lesson, we will explore in more detail the laws Muslims must obey and the deeds they must carry out in order to purify themselves.

3. The Hadith: When we studied the Islamic view of truth, we learned that Muslims believe their worldview is based on truth found in two written documents—the Quran and the Hadith. Muslims believe the Quran is the perfect revealed word of Allah for all people for all times. It is their most trusted book of truth. The Hadith, which includes several books, contains the sayings and deeds of the prophet Muhammad. It is Muslims' second most trusted source of truth. In fact, many Muslims believe that the Quran and the Hadith are equally true.

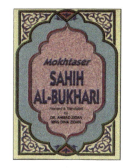

Like the words of Allah in the Quran, the sayings and deeds of Muhammad in the Hadith are an important part of the foundation of Islamic moral laws and values. For most Muslims, what Muhammad said and did are as important and truthful as Allah's words in the Quran. If Muhammad said a behavior was right or wrong, it is right or wrong, even if the Quran says nothing about the behavior at all.

Now let's ask some important questions. Read each question and think about how you would answer it before you read the rest of Topic 2.

1. Why do you think the words and deeds of Muhammad are such an important part of the foundation of Islamic moral laws and values?

2. Do you think Muhammad was sinless and holy in everything he said and did just as Jesus was? Why or why not?

3. If Muhammad's words and deeds are part of the foundation of Islamic moral laws and values, do you think Islam's prophet should have lived a perfect, sinless life? Why or why not?

Although some Muslims believe Muhammad had minor faults and made small mistakes, most believe he was sinless. They believe that everything he said and everything he did was without sin. This is why the Hadith is an important part of the foundation for Islamic moral laws and values. Muslims believe they can become morally perfect and one day go to paradise by following the words and actions of a sinless prophet. However, there is a problem with this belief about Muhammad. According to the Quran, Muhammad was not sinless. Muhammad only received these verses from Allah through the angel Gabriel; he did not claim to have been the author of the verses.

So [Prophet], bear in mind that there is no god but God, and ask forgiveness for your sins and for the sins of believing men and women. God knows whenever any of you move, and whenever any of you stay still. *Quran 47:19*

So be patient, Prophet, for what God has promised is sure to come. Ask forgiveness for your sins; praise your Lord morning and evening. *Quran 40:55*

We learn from the Quran that Muhammad was a sinner, and Muhammad asked Allah to forgive his sins. Al-Bukhari recorded one of Muhammad's prayers for forgiveness in his Hadith. The prayer was heard one night by Ibn Abbas (*Ibn* means *son of* in Arabic), who related it to al-Bukhari:

Oh Allah! Forgive me my sins that I did in the past or will do in the future, and also the sins I did in secret or in public. You are my only God and there is no other God for me. *Sahih al-Bukhari 7371*

Similar but Not the Same: Do you see the similarities between the Islamic foundation of moral laws and values and the biblical Christian foundation? The moral beliefs of both worldviews are based on moral laws found in the heart and conscience of every person created by God/Allah. Both Christians and Muslims believe God/Allah revealed his moral laws in books—the Bible for Christians and the Quran for Muslims. And both worldviews base their moral beliefs and practices on the words and deeds of a person they consider to be holy—Jesus for Christians and Muhammad for Muslims.

MOSES AND THE TEN COMMANDMENTS
WOODCUT BY GUSTAVE DORÉ, 1832–1883

However, ideas that are similar are not exactly the same. The true foundation for biblical Christianity's moral laws and values is the nature and character of God. The moral laws God places in the hearts of his image-bearers reflect who he is. This is why God commands us to "be holy, because I am holy" (Leviticus 11:44). The moral laws that God reveals in written Scripture reflect who he is. And the moral laws and values perfectly lived out by Jesus, God the Son, show that everything about God's holiness we know about in our hearts and read about in Scripture is absolutely true.

The Islamic foundation for moral laws and values is not based on the nature and character of Allah because his nature and character cannot be fully known. Allah is unlike anything he created. Allah would never command Muslims to be holy because he is holy, since they cannot know him. And if they cannot know him personally, they could never know how he is holy.

Jesus Enters Jerusalem on a Donkey
Woodcut by Gustave Doré, 1832–1883

Muhammad enters Mecca

The Islamic foundation of moral laws and values is based on what Allah says, not on who he is. Something is right because Allah says it is. And something is wrong because Allah says it is. Therefore, Allah's laws and commands in the Quran are considered good because Allah says they are good, not because they reflect his holiness, as no one can know it.

The foundation for Islamic moral laws and values is also based on what Muhammad said and did as recorded in the Hadith. Unlike Jesus, Muhammad was not holy. He was a human being who sinned like all people sin. Should a foundation of moral laws and values be built on the words and deeds of anyone who is less than perfectly moral, or righteous? Shouldn't it be built on someone who is perfectly sinless and righteous? Only Jesus, God the Son, is that Person.

Topic 3—The Five Pillars of Islam

The Five Most Important Duties of Islam: Muslims are expected to faithfully obey many moral laws and duties. However, five moral duties are considered the most important, and all Muslims must fulfill them. These five duties or responsibilities are called the Five Pillars of Islam. They include confession of faith, prayer, fasting, giving, and pilgrimage. We'll explore the first two pillars in Part 1 of Topic 3.

The Five Pillars of Islam
The five moral responsibilities of all Muslims

1. Shahada (The Confession of Faith): The first pillar of the Islamic faith and worldview is the confession of faith or *shahada*. All Muslims are required to fulfill this moral duty by reciting these words: There is no god but Allah, and Muhammad is the prophet (messenger) of Allah. To become a Muslim, all a person needs to do is believe and make this confession. The moment a person says these words, he or she becomes one who is in submission (Islam) to Allah. By making this confession, Muslims are saying that they will obey everything Allah and Muhammad require. In Topic 2, you learned that Islamic moral laws and values are based, or founded, on Allah's words to Muhammad and Muhammad's words, deeds, and sayings.

The exact words of the shahada are not found in the Quran. However, they are pieced together into one confession from two verses that are found in the Quran.

But they were commanded to serve only one God: there is no god but Him.   Quran 9:31

Muhammad is not the father of any of your men, but (he is) the Messenger of Allah, and the Seal of the Prophets: and Allah has full knowledge of all things.   Quran 33:40 Yusuf Ali

The shahada is the most important statement a Muslim can make. It is written above entrances to mosques, on stationery, posters, jewelry, and other objects. Many years ago, an American missionary to Muslims described just how important the shahada is to the Islamic view of moral laws and values. He said, "On these two phrases ("There is no god but Allah and Muhammad is his prophet"), hang all the laws and teaching and morals of Islam."[1]

The first words newborn Muslim babies hear are the words of the shahada whispered in their ears. Just before Muslims die, they are encouraged to repeat the shahada. Many Muslims believe that just by saying and believing the shahada, they will go to paradise when they die.

Since the birth of Christianity almost 2,000 years ago, Christians have also made statements or confessions of their faith. Some of these confessions come directly from the New Testament. On the right is one such confession, revealed by the Holy Spirit and written by the apostle Paul in one of his letters to the young pastor, Timothy.

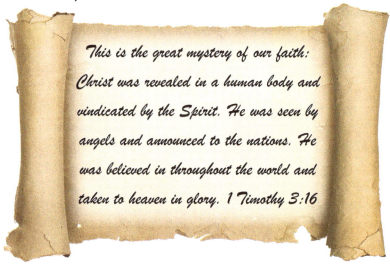

This is the great mystery of our faith: Christ was revealed in a human body and vindicated by the Spirit. He was seen by angels and announced to the nations. He was believed in throughout the world and taken to heaven in glory. 1 Timothy 3:16

By the time all the books of the New Testament had been written and assembled together, church leaders wrote creeds, or confessions, of what all Christians believe. They did this first by searching the Scriptures and then by writing down the essential beliefs of their faith. One such creed that many Christians memorize and recite today is called *the Apostles' Creed.*

We believe in God, the Father almighty, creator of heaven and earth.

We believe in Jesus Christ, God's only Son, our Lord, who was conceived by the Holy Spirit, born of the Virgin Mary, suffered under Pontius Pilate, was crucified, died, and was buried; he descended to the dead. On the third day he rose again; he ascended into heaven, he is seated at the right hand of the Father, and he will come again to judge the living and the dead.

We believe in the Holy Spirit, the holy catholic [universal] church, the communion of saints, the forgiveness of sins, the resurrection of the body, and the life everlasting. AMEN

Let's think about how the confessions of faith made by Christians differ from the confession of faith made by Muslims. First, the Allah of the shahada is not God the Father, God the Son, and God the Holy Spirit. Second, Christians do not consider Muhammad to be one of God's prophets. And third, whereas just reciting and believing the shahada makes a person a Muslim, just reciting and believing a Christian confession of faith does not make a person a Christian. Yes, believing or having faith in Jesus as God's Son and our Savior is necessary. But repentance and turning away from sin are also required. Then we must receive God's free gift of salvation.

2. Salat (Prayer): The second pillar of the Islamic faith and worldview is *salat* (the letter *t* is silent) and refers to prayers. All Muslims, both men and women, are expected to offer salat five times a day. Although Muslims may pray anywhere, they are encouraged to pray in a mosque. On Fridays, prayers are mandatory for all Muslim men and must be offered in a mosque.

High above many mosques stand towers called *minarets*. In some Muslim communities, men called *muezzin* stand on a platform around the minaret and call people to prayer five times a day. The muezzin always faces the city of Mecca, no matter in what country the mosque is located. In larger modern Muslim communities, the call to prayer is made through loudspeakers located inside the minaret.

Inside the mosque, both men and women may pray, but they may not stand or pray next to each other. In some mosques, women pray in rows behind the men. In others they pray behind a small screen or wall to one side of the men. Muslims say this separation is necessary for modesty so that men and women will not be thinking about or looking at someone of the opposite sex while they are praying. Both men and women pray facing the direction of Mecca, which is in Saudi Arabia. Special markers in each mosque show worshippers the direction of Mecca.

The Quran says Muslims must wash their bodies before they go to the mosque to pray, and it gives specific instructions about what parts of the body to wash. This washing is a ritual that Muslims believe makes them outwardly clean so they can approach Allah in prayer.

You who believe, when you are about to pray, wash your faces and your hands up to the elbows, wipe your heads, wash your feet up to the ankles and, if required, wash your whole body.

Quran 5:6

In the same verse, the Quran says people can "take some clean sand and wipe your face and hands with it" if water is not available. Notice, though, that this requirement to wash before prayers has nothing to do with spiritually purifying the heart. It is a ritual that appears religious, but it cleans only outward parts of the body, not the heart.

Once inside the mosque, Muslims are led in prayer by a religious leader called the *imam*. The imam leads the congregation to pray simple and exact prayers. During prayers, Muslims assume different positions. They begin by standing, then they bow, lie prostrate, and then sit. In between the different positions, Muslims say specific Arabic words that are considered prayers: "Allah is most great;" "praise be to Allah;" "there is no god but Allah;" and "may Allah be glorified." Muslims are not allowed to depart from these words during required prayers. They say them rigidly five times every day, day after day. They believe these words help them remember Allah. In addition to the required prayers, Muslims are permitted to pray personal prayers to ask Allah for his blessings and help. Although Muslims pray to Allah for personal needs, they cannot have an intimate personal relationship with him because of his transcendence.

Of course, Christians pray to God too. However, Christians pray to God their Father in a personal and relational way through Jesus. Although Christians pray to ask God to meet their needs, they also pray to thank and praise him. For Christians, prayer provides a way to grow in their personal relationship with their *Abba* (daddy) Father. The apostle Paul wrote about this truth in a letter to Christians in the region of Galatia. Today, Galatia is part of the Islamic nation of Turkey where there are few Christians.

And because we are his children, God has sent the Spirit of his Son into our hearts, prompting us to call out, "Abba, Father." Galatians 4:6

Because as Christians we are God's children, we don't have to pray in certain body positions and repeat specific words over and over to make sure God hears and answers our prayers. The Bible tells us he knows what we need even before we ask. The apostle Matthew recorded Jesus' teaching on prayer in his gospel.

7 "When you pray, don't babble on and on as the Gentiles do. They think their prayers are answered merely by repeating their words again and again. 8 Don't be like them, for your Father knows exactly what you need even before you ask him!"

Matthew 6:7–8

Perhaps the greatest difference between the Islamic and Christian views of prayer is that Christians believe the Holy Spirit lives within their hearts and prays for them. As Christians, we don't have to worry about saying everything just right. God knows our hearts and prayers, and his Holy Spirit prays for us, especially when we can't express our hurts or needs. Paul wrote about how the Holy Spirit helps us pray in a letter to early Christians in Rome.

²⁶And the Holy Spirit helps us in our weakness. For example, we don't know what God wants us to pray for. But the Holy Spirit prays for us with groanings that cannot be expressed in words. ²⁷And the Father who knows all hearts knows what the Spirit is saying, for the Spirit pleads for us believers in harmony with God's own will.

Romans 8:26–27

MUSLIMS MUST WASH BEFORE SALAT

MUSLIMS MUST REMOVE THEIR SHOES BEFORE SALAT

Part 2—Giving and Fasting

3. Zakat (Giving): The third pillar of the Islamic faith and worldview is the *zakat* (the letter *t* is silent). This moral duty refers to giving money, food, clothing, and other items. Muslims are required to give two and one-half percent of their wealth each year. This money is collected within each Islamic nation and is used to help the poor and those who are in debt. It is also used to convert people to Islam. It is even used to help Muslims fight wars for Islam that help spread the Islamic worldview to other countries. Muhammad recited Allah's teaching about the zakat.

Alms are meant only for the poor, the needy, those who administer them, those whose hearts need winning over, to free slaves and help those in debt, for God's cause, and for travellers in need. This is ordained by God; God is all knowing and wise.

Quran 9:60

Islam teaches that giving alms purifies a person's soul. In fact, the word *zakat* comes from a root word that means *to be pure*. Thus, the zakat is seen as a duty that if practiced faithfully will purify a person and help him or her enter paradise. Muhammad recited Allah's teaching that those who do not give would burn in hell.

Tell those who hoard gold and silver instead of giving in God's cause that they will have a grievous punishment: on the Day it is heated up in Hell's Fire and used to brand their foreheads, sides, and backs, they will be told, 'This is what you hoarded up for yourselves! Now feel the pain of what you hoarded!'

Quran 9:34–35

Christians, of course, also give. They are not to give because of outside pressure or a fear of burning in hell. Christians give because of their love and honor for God, and they decide in their hearts how much to give. Paul explained to Christians in the city of Corinth how they should give.

⁷You must each decide in your heart how much to give. And don't give reluctantly or in response to pressure. "For God loves a person who gives cheerfully." ⁸And God will generously provide all you need. Then you will always have everything you need and plenty left over to share with others.

2 Corinthians 9:7–8

Muslims use the zakat to help only Muslims, but the Bible instructs Christians to give to all who are in need, including strangers. Jesus illustrated this truth in his parable of the Good Samaritan. You can read the parable in Luke 10:25–37.

Paul used Jesus' words to instruct the Roman Christians about giving in his letter to them. "If your enemies are hungry, feed them; if they are thirsty, give them something to drink" (Romans 12:20).

While Muslims practice the duty of zakat to help themselves get into paradise, Christians know they are not saved by doing good works. Rather, they are saved by their faith in Jesus.

> But people are counted as righteous, not because of their work, but because of their faith in God who forgives sinners.
>
> Romans 4:5

Christians give and do other good works that God has already prepared for them to do. They do these works out of gratitude and out of love for God and others. And they do them as evidence that God has saved them by his grace. Paul wrote to the believers in the early church in Ephesus:

> [8] God saved you by his grace when you believed. And you can't take credit for this; it is a gift from God. [9] Salvation is not a reward for the good things we have done, so none of us can boast about it. [10] For we are God's masterpiece. He has created us anew in Christ Jesus, so we can do the good things he planned for us long ago.
>
> Ephesians 2:8–10

4. Sawm (Fasting): The fourth pillar of the Islamic faith and worldview is the *sawm*. This moral duty refers to fasting—abstaining from or doing without food, drink, and all sexual relations during a specified time. Muslims must observe this fast from sunrise to sunset for 30 days during the ninth month of the Islamic calendar. This special month is called *Ramadan*. During the fast Muslims are to pray to Allah more often, asking for forgiveness of sins and trying not to commit new sins.

Muslims believe Ramadan is the month Allah first sent down the message of the Quran to Muhammad. For this reason, Muslims are required to read the entire Quran at least once during the sawm. In some Islamic nations, it is a crime not to participate in the sawm of Ramadan, and people who refuse to fast are often punished.

Every Muslim—except those who are ill, on a long journey, pregnant, breast-feeding, or under 10 years old—is required to observe the sawm of Ramadan. The purpose of this long fast is to help Muslims obtain their salvation and show their gratitude to Allah for all he has done for them. At the end of each fast day (sunset), Muslims traditionally eat foods such as fresh dates, sponge cakes filled with cheese, and drink hot tea.

> [183] You who believe, fasting is prescribed for you, as it was prescribed for those before you, so that you may be mindful of God. [184] Fast for a specific number of days, but if one of you is ill, or on a journey, on other days later. For those who can fast only with extreme difficulty, there is a way to compensate—feed a needy person. But if anyone does good of his own accord, it is better for him, and fasting is better for you, if only you knew. [185] It was in the month of Ramadan that the Quran was revealed as guidance for mankind, clear messages giving guidance and distinguishing between right and wrong. So any one of you

who is present that month should fast, and anyone who is ill or on a journey should make up for the lost days by fasting on other days later. God wants ease for you, not hardship. He wants you to complete the prescribed period and to glorify Him for having guided you, so that you may be thankful. *Quran 2:183–185*

Christians also fast. However, for Christians fasting is a personal choice that should be done privately. The gospel of Matthew records Jesus' instructions about fasting.

[16] "And when you fast, don't make it obvious, as the hypocrites do, for they try to look miserable and disheveled so people will admire them for their fasting. I tell you the truth, that is the only reward they will ever get. [17] But when you fast, comb your hair and wash your face. [18] Then no one will notice that you are fasting, except your Father, who knows what you do in private. And your Father, who sees everything, will reward you. *Matthew 6:16–18*

For Christians, fasting can be a sign of true repentance (Joel 2:12–13). Many Christians fast to help them resist temptations as Jesus did (Matthew 4:1–11). Fasting helps Christians focus on prayer and their relationship with God instead of focusing on their physical needs. Biblical Christianity rejects the Islamic teaching that fasting helps a person earn salvation.

Part 3—Pilgrimage to Mecca

The Five Most Important Duties of Islam: In Part 1 of Topic 3, we explored two of the five moral duties or pillars of Islam that all Muslims must fulfill—the shahada, or confession of faith, and salat, or prayer. All Muslims must confess their faith by reciting the words: "There is no god but Allah, and Muhammad is the prophet (messenger) of Allah." The moment someone makes this confession, Muslims teach that he or she is in submission to Allah and will obey everything Allah and Muhammad require.

All Muslims are required to offer salat, or pray, five times a day. They may pray anywhere; however, it is encouraged to pray in a mosque. Muslims must wash their bodies—heads, hands, arms, and feet—before they pray. This ritual washing is called *wudhu*.

In Part 2, we learned about the third and fourth moral duties—zakat, or the giving of alms, and sawm, or fasting. Remember that Muslims are required to give two and one-half percent of their wealth every year. This money is used to help Muslims who are poor or in debt. It is also used to help fight wars and spread the Islamic worldview.

Recall that sawm is a special type of fasting that is done during the month of Ramadan. Muslims abstain from eating, drinking and sexual relations from sunrise to sunset for 30 days. They are also required to pray to Allah more often and read the entire Quran at least once during Ramadan. Now we've reached the last of the five pillars.

5. The Hajj (Pilgrimage to Mecca): The fifth pillar of the Islamic faith and worldview is the *hajj*. This moral duty refers to a pilgrimage or journey to a sacred place. This sacred place, as you learned in Lesson 3, is the black shrine, or Ka'aba, located in the Saudi Arabian city of Mecca.

The hajj is required of every Muslim once in his or her lifetime. Only those who are ill or poor and cannot afford to make such a long pilgrimage may be excused.

Pilgrimage to the House [the Ka'aba] is a duty owed to God by people who are able to undertake it. Those who reject this [should know that] God has no need of anyone.   Quran 3:97

Proclaim the Pilgrimage to all people. They will come to you on foot and on every kind of swift mount, emerging from every deep mountain pass.   Quran 22:27

The hajj takes place over a period of three to five days during the last month of the Islamic calendar. This special month is called *Zu'l-Hijjah*. Each year, millions of Muslims participate in this religious duty.

The Hajj—Day 1: Before the pilgrims enter Mecca, they meet outside the city where they wash and put on special white robes. As the people walk toward Mecca they recite, "Here I come, O Allah, here I come." Once they arrive at the large mosque complex inside the city, they enter a very large outdoor arena. In the center stands the large Ka'aba shrine with its famous black stone mounted into its southeast corner. Muslim tradition says that Abraham and his son Ishmael built the Ka'aba. They believe the black stone was sent from heaven and was originally crystal clear. As people came to the shrine and kissed the stone, it became black as it took on the sins of those who kissed it. All pilgrims walk around the Ka'aba seven times and kiss the black stone each time they circle it. Muslims believe that the heavens above the Ka'aba are directly open to Allah. Any prayers they offer there will go to him without delay, and he will answer them.

PILGRIMS ENCIRCLE THE KA'ABA

PILGRIMS CLIMB THE HILLS
OF SAFA AND MARWA

Next the pilgrims run back and forth seven times between two small hills enclosed inside a large tunnel within the grounds of the huge mosque complex. This ritual is in memory of Hagar, the servant of Abraham's wife, Sarah, and the mother of Abraham's son Ishmael. After Isaac was born, Sarah and Abraham sent Hagar and Ishmael away into the desert (Genesis 21:8–21). Once their water was gone, Hagar went in search of water to save her son, and the ritual commemorates this search. According to Islamic tradition, Hagar ran back and forth between the two small hills of *Safa* and *Marwa*, looking for water. According to legend, she found the well that Muslims call *Zamzam*. It is also located within the mosque area, and Muslims often drink its water, believing it is holy and that it will cure illness.

PILGRIMS DRINK FROM
ZAMZAM WELL

At the end of the first day of the hajj, the pilgrims travel to Mina, an open field three miles east of Mecca. After saying more prayers, the pilgrims sleep in white air-conditioned tents provided by the Saudi Arabian government.

MOUNT ARAFAT COVERED
WITH PILGRIMS

The Hajj—Day 2: On this day, the pilgrims walk nine miles east from Mina to Mount Arafat, the place where Muhammad preached his last sermon. People pray and may listen to a special hajj sermon. From afternoon to sunset, all the pilgrims stand facing Mecca, meditating on Muhammad and Islam. That evening, they walk another six miles to an open area where they sleep without tents. Here each pilgrim collects seven stones that he or she will use the next day to "stone the devil." Before sunrise, the pilgrims walk back to Mina.

The Hajj—Day 3: In Mina, every Muslim throws seven small stones at very large pillars that represent Satan. After stoning the pillars, an animal is sacrificed. This sacrifice symbolizes the ram God provided for Abraham to sacrifice instead of his son Isaac (Genesis 22). Muslims, however, believe the son God spared was Ishmael, not Isaac.

THROWING STONES AT ONE
OF THE PILLARS OF SATAN

As a final sacrifice, men shave their heads and women cut off a lock of hair. The people then return to Mecca and walk around the Ka'aba seven more times. After these ceremonies, the pilgrims change back into their regular clothing and begin the journey home. Many pilgrims will also travel to Medina where Muhammad is buried in the Prophet's Mosque along with his successors, Caliph Abu Bakr and Caliph Umar, or Omar. By fulfilling the moral duty of the hajj, Muslims hope to win Allah's favor. They believe the hajj will wipe away past sins.

Christians also worship and pray to God. They perform good deeds, and they resist Satan and his temptations. They sacrifice their time, money, and talents to help build God's kingdom. Jesus said:

"Let your good deeds shine out for all to see, so that everyone will praise your heavenly Father." Matthew 5:16

But Christians don't do good deeds to earn salvation or to get God to love them more. God showed his love to us before we were saved and before we had done any good works for his glory.

But God showed his great love for us by sending Christ to die for us while we were still sinners. Romans 5:8

Christians' works are a demonstration of gratitude and love for God, and they demonstrate the saving faith we have in Jesus.

¹⁷ So you see, faith by itself isn't enough. Unless it produces good deeds, it is dead and useless.

¹⁸ Now someone may argue, "Some people have faith; others have good deeds." But I say, "How can you show me your faith if you don't have good deeds? I will show you my faith by my good deeds." James 2:17–18

Topic 4–A Sixth Pillar

A Sixth Pillar of Islam: All Muslims believe the five pillars of Islam are the most important moral laws or duties they must perform, but many Muslims add a sixth pillar. This pillar is called *jihad*, which means *to strive*, *struggle*, or *exert effort*. Most Muslims believe that when the Quran speaks about jihad, it is referring to each person's own struggle against sin in their lives. They believe that each person should battle against temptation and sin.

Other Muslims, however, believe that jihad also refers to actual wars or battles against people and nations that resist or do not believe in Islam. According to the Quran, Allah's plan for creation is to make Islam victorious over every other religion in the world.

It is He who has sent His Messenger with guidance and the religion of truth, to show that it is above all [other] religions, however much the idolaters may hate this. Quran 9:33

In this view of jihad, Allah has commanded all Muslims to participate in holy fighting for his cause so that Islam will one day conquer all other religions.

Fighting [jihad] is ordained for you, though you dislike it. You may dislike something although it is good for you, or like something although it is bad for you: God knows and you do not. Quran 2:216

According to the Quran, Allah commanded Muhammad and his armies to attack and capture people who would not convert to Islam. The Quran calls these people *disbelievers*.

When you meet the disbelievers in battle, strike them in the neck, and once they are defeated, bind any captives firmly. Quran 47:4

The Quran also commands Islamic armies to carry out jihad against Jews and Christians. If they submit peacefully, their lives can be spared. However, they must pay a high *jizyah*, or tax, to their Islamic conquerors.

Fight those of the People of the Book [Jews and Christians] who do not [truly] believe in God {Allah} and the Last Day, who do not forbid what God and His Messenger have forbidden, who do not obey the rule of justice, until they pay the tax and agree to submit. Quran 9:29

Shariah law includes strict rules about how jihad is conducted. It includes prohibitions against starting the conflict and against harming innocent people. The Quran advocates ending jihad once the enemy asks for peace.

But if they [enemies of the state] incline towards peace, you [Prophet] must also incline towards it, and put your trust in God: He is the All Hearing, the All Knowing. Quran 8:61

Although Christians and Jews today are allowed to live in Muslim countries, they are often persecuted. In countries like Saudi Arabia, they are not permitted to build churches or synagogues or worship in public. They can only meet privately in their homes, and they may not talk about their faith with a Muslim. In most Islamic nations it is illegal for a Muslim to become a Christian. In some countries, the penalty for leaving Islam and converting to another religion is death.

The Biblical Christian Response to Jihad: Does God call Christians to fight for his kingdom? Are Christians called to strive and battle for God? Yes! But God does not call Christians to fight his battle with swords or the weapons of modern warfare such as guns and bombs.

On the night Jesus was arrested before his crucifixion, he was praying in the garden of Gethsemane. When Judas, the disciple who betrayed him, arrived with the soldiers, one of Jesus' disciples drew his sword and cut off the ear of the high priest's servant. But Jesus made it very clear that his kingdom was not to be built by violence or warfare. Matthew wrote about this event in his gospel.

⁴⁸ The traitor, Judas, had given them a prearranged signal: "You will know which one to arrest when I greet him with a kiss." ⁴⁹ So Judas came straight to Jesus. "Greetings, Rabbi!" he exclaimed and gave him the kiss.

⁵⁰ Jesus said, "My friend, go ahead and do what you have come for."

Then the others grabbed Jesus and arrested him. ⁵¹ But one of the men with Jesus pulled out his sword and struck the high priest's slave, slashing off his ear.

⁵² "Put away your sword," Jesus told him. "Those who use the sword will die by the sword. ⁵³ Don't you realize that I could ask my Father for thousands of angels to protect us, and he would send them instantly? ⁵⁴ But if I did, how would the Scriptures be fulfilled that describe what must happen now?"

Matthew 26:48–54

In Paul's letter to Christians in Corinth, he also taught very clearly that Christian warfare is spiritual, not physical.

³ We are human, but we don't wage war as humans do. ⁴ We use God's mighty weapons, not worldly weapons, to knock down the strongholds of human reasoning and to destroy false arguments. ⁵ We destroy every proud obstacle that keeps people from knowing God. We capture their rebellious thoughts and teach them to obey Christ.

2 Corinthians 10:3–5

So, what are the weapons Christians are to use to fight against sin in their own lives and to build God's kingdom in the world? Again, Paul describes the weapons God tells us to use. See how many pieces of armor you can identify in Paul's letter to Christians in the city of Ephesus.

¹¹ Put on all of God's armor so that you will be able to stand firm against all strategies of the devil. ¹² For we are not fighting against flesh-and-blood enemies, but against evil rulers and authorities of the unseen world, against mighty powers in this dark world, and against evil spirits in the heavenly places.

¹³ Therefore, put on every piece of God's armor so you will be able to resist the enemy in the time of evil. Then after the battle you will still be standing firm. ¹⁴ Stand your ground, putting on the belt of truth and the body armor of God's righteousness. ¹⁵ For shoes, put on the peace that comes from the Good News so that you will be fully prepared. ¹⁶ In addition to all of these, hold up the shield of faith to stop the fiery arrows of the devil. ¹⁷ Put on salvation as your helmet, and take the sword of the Spirit, which is the word of God.

Ephesians 6:11–17

Topic 5—Shariah: The Islamic Laws

Islam—More Than Just a Religion: Muslims do not separate their religious life from their everyday life. For them, all of life is religious. Muslims believe that the revelations of Allah in the Quran and the sayings and deeds of Muhammad in the Hadith are the foundations for their moral duties and acts of worship. Muslims believe that the Quran and the Hadith are the foundations for all the laws regarding everything they do in their personal lives, families, communities, and nations.

There are special Islamic laws for the family regarding marriage, divorce, and raising children. There are detailed laws for how businesses are to operate. There are Islamic laws that say what actions are crimes and the punishments they deserve. There are laws about how the government should operate. There are tax laws, and there are laws for how people must behave in every social situation. Of course, all nations have many laws. But Islamic laws are not based on decisions by government leaders or by the votes of the citizens. Islamic laws are instead based on the words of Allah revealed in the Quran and the words and commands of Muhammad recorded in the Hadith. Because Muslims believe the words of Allah and Muhammad are without error, they also believe that the Islamic laws based on Allah's and Muhammad's words are perfect. Muslims believe that Islamic laws are not only perfect, but also absolute and unchangeable.

The Shariah: The complete union of Islamic religious laws with all the other laws that govern everything Muslims do is known as *shariah*. This word means *way* or *right path*. There is only one verse in the Quran that speaks of this kind of law. In the English translation of the Quran by Yusuf Ali, Allah tells Muhammad that he has been put on the right way (*shariah* in Arabic), and he is to follow it. In the English translation by Sale, Allah tells Muhammad that he has been appointed to proclaim these laws to the people and to follow them.

Then We put thee on the (right) Way of Religion: so follow thou that (Way), and follow not the desires of those who know not.   Quran 45:18 Yusuf Ali

Afterwards We appointed thee, O Mohammed [sic], to promulgate a law concerning the business of religion: Wherefore follow the same, and follow not the desires of those who are ignorant.   Quran 45:18 Sale

From these two translations of the Quran, we can understand more clearly the meaning of the Arabic word *shariah*. It refers to the *right way* or the *way of religion* that every Muslim must follow. This right way, or shariah, governs all parts of Islamic life. Shariah law tells people how to worship and how to operate a business. It prescribes how people must dress and the foods they can and cannot eat. It declares that any child born into a Muslim family is automatically a Muslim, and he or she may not leave Islam without serious consequences.

The purpose of shariah law is to bring Islamic nations and all other nations into complete submission to Allah. This submission is to Allah's will by obeying his laws. Muslims believe that by obeying shariah law, they can create the perfect Islamic world for Allah's glory. Islam teaches that such a perfect world is possible to achieve because, as you learned earlier, Muslims do not believe that people are fallen or have a sinful nature. Muslims believe only that people are weak and make mistakes. Therefore, through strict obedience to the Quran and the Hadith and through enforcement of such obedience with punishment for disobedience, people can overcome their weaknesses and build the perfect Islamic world. And through perfect obedience to shariah, Muslims believe they will have a better chance of living in paradise after they die.

Five Kinds of Behavior: According to the shariah, there are five categories of human actions or behaviors.

1. Commanded: Certain behaviors or acts are required or commanded. These include the five pillars of Islam. Disobedience results in punishment now and in eternity. Obedience will be rewarded in eternity.

2. Recommended: Other behaviors are not commanded but are highly recommended. Such acts include hospitality, giving more than the two and one-half percent zakat, offering more prayers, and performing other good deeds. These recommended acts earn more rewards in paradise. However, there is no punishment now or in eternity if they are not done.

NINETEENTH-CENTURY
SHARIAH LAW JUDGE,
SUDAN

3. Discouraged or Disapproved: Some behaviors, such as divorce, are only discouraged, not forbidden. Discouraged or disapproved behaviors do not result in punishment now or in eternity.

4. Forbidden: Some actions are definitely forbidden by shariah law. These include stealing, drinking alcoholic beverages, eating pork, leaving the Islamic faith, and taking part in idolatry or adultery. These behaviors often result in punishment in this life and are always punished in eternity. Muslims earn rewards in paradise by avoiding forbidden acts.

5. Neutral or Silent: Some behaviors are permitted because they are neither commanded, recommended, discouraged, nor forbidden. Such acts include showing kindness to animals. There is neither punishment nor reward for these behaviors either now or in eternity.

In order to live according to shariah law, Muslims must know both the Quran and the Hadith. They must know which behaviors are commanded, recommended, discouraged, forbidden, or neutral. By doing the commanded actions and avoiding the forbidden ones, Muslims believe they can bring their lives into harmony with Allah's will. And Muslims hope they will spend eternity in paradise by bringing their lives into harmony with Allah's laws.

Topic 6—Shariah Law and Biblical Christian Moral Laws and Values

What's the Difference? Let's conclude our study of the Islamic worldview by looking at the important differences between Islamic shariah law and biblical Christian moral laws and values. Do both Islam and Christianity tell people what's right and what's wrong? Do they both teach that God's/Allah's moral laws and values must guide everything people do, not just their worship? Again, we do see similarities between the two worldviews, but as you've learned, having similarities does not mean they are the same.

1. Shariah Law Is Not Based on the Righteous and Holy Character of God. According to the Quran, Allah cannot be known personally. All Muslims can know is what Allah commands. Shariah law exists to make people submit to Allah. Muslims submit to Allah's will by obeying his laws.

In contrast, biblical Christian moral laws and values are based on God's holy character. Christians follow the Ten Commandments as well as the two commandments that Jesus emphasized: You must love the Lord your God with all your heart, all your soul, and all your mind and love your neighbor as yourself (Matthew 22:37–39). God wants us to know what he is like, and he shows us his holy character not only in his just and righteous laws but also in the perfect, sinless life of Jesus. God wants us to submit to him and obey his laws because he loves us and wants what's best for us. As we love God with all our heart, soul, and mind, we get to know him better. And God wants us to become image-bearers who become more and more like him. In fact, God commands us to be holy because he is holy. Moses recorded God's command in the book of Leviticus.

¹ The LORD also said to Moses, ² "Give the following instructions to the entire community of Israel. You must be holy because I, the LORD your God, am holy."

Leviticus 19:1–2

Holiness should not only be evident in our actions, but also in our attitudes. The Old Testament prophet Micah described holiness in how we think and view other people.

The LORD has told you what is good,
    and this is what he requires of you:
to do what is right, to love mercy,
    and to walk humbly with your God.   Micah 6:8

A psalmist also tells us what holiness should be like.

³ "Give justice to the poor and the orphan;
    uphold the rights of the oppressed and the destitute.
⁴ Rescue the poor and helpless,
    deliver them from the grasp of evil people."

Psalm 82:3–4

2. Shariah Law Is Not Based on the Belief that All People Are Born with a Sinful Nature. Islam teaches that people sin only because they are weak or forgetful. Therefore, the purpose of shariah law is to show people Allah's perfect will so they can obey it and overcome their weaknesses. By affirming that there is no true god but Allah and Muhammad is his prophet, and by obeying the Islamic laws (and there are many) people automatically become Muslims. They also become a part of a worldwide community of individuals and nations completely submitted to Allah. Obeying and submitting to Allah's laws is what Muslims believe to be all that Allah requires of them. They believe that their obedience and submission will help them go to paradise after they die. Sadly, however, Islam teaches that there is no guarantee that Muslims will go to paradise, even if they follow shariah law very carefully. They will go only if it is Allah's will.

Unlike Islam, biblical Christian moral laws and values are based on the truth that because of the fall, all people are born with a sinful nature that separates them from God. We are not just weak and forgetful people who can make ourselves acceptable to God by obeying a set of laws. In fact, one of the reasons God revealed his moral laws was to show us just how sinful and helpless we really are. Paul explained this truth in his letter to the Romans.

It was the law that showed me my sin. I would never have known that coveting is wrong if the law had not said, "You must not covet."

Romans 7:7

God also revealed his laws to correct and teach us (2 Timothy 3:16–17). However, just knowing God's laws and trying to obey them does not make us righteous. No one can obey God's laws perfectly, and any sin keeps us separated from God. We cannot become Christians by creating and carefully obeying some form of "Christian shariah law." The only way we can be made righteous and be restored in fellowship with God is through faith in Jesus as God's Son and our Savior. This is true because only Jesus is righteous and kept God's moral law perfectly. And only a perfectly righteous and holy Jesus could fulfill God's requirement of a sinless sacrifice for sin. As the sinless, sacrificed Lamb of God, Jesus took the punishment we deserve for not being able to keep God's moral law. And when we believe in Jesus and his sacrifice for us, his righteousness becomes our righteousness. Paul explained these truths in letters to Christians in the cities of Rome, Philippi, and Corinth.

3 The law of Moses was unable to save us because of the weakness of our sinful nature. So God did what the law could not do. He sent his own Son in a body like the bodies we sinners have. And in that body God declared an end to sin's control over us by giving his Son as a sacrifice for our sins. 4 He did this so that the just requirement of the law would be fully satisfied for us, who no longer follow our sinful nature but instead follow the Spirit.

Romans 8:3–4

I no longer count on my own righteousness through obeying the law; rather, I become righteous through faith in Christ. For God's way of making us right with himself depends on faith.

Philippians 3:9

God has united you with Christ Jesus. For our benefit God made him to be wisdom itself. Christ made us right with God; he made us pure and holy, and he freed us from sin.

1 Corinthians 1:30

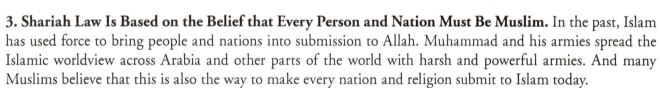

3. Shariah Law Is Based on the Belief that Every Person and Nation Must Be Muslim. In the past, Islam has used force to bring people and nations into submission to Allah. Muhammad and his armies spread the Islamic worldview across Arabia and other parts of the world with harsh and powerful armies. And many Muslims believe that this is also the way to make every nation and religion submit to Islam today.

Shariah law does not separate religious laws from the laws of national governments. Shariah insists that religion and government be woven together. Shariah declares that the government has the right to enforce obedience to Islamic religious laws. This is why Muslims who do not participate in daily prayers (salat) or who choose to leave Islam are often punished by their government.

Shariah law does not always respect the rights God gives each of his image-bearers—the right to life, the right to freedom, and the right to choose. In nations that practice strict shariah law, people's personal freedoms are often very limited. In some nations, women cannot attend school or work outside their homes. Women are required to wear clothing that covers every part of their body, including most of their face. Citizens are not allowed to speak out against injustice in the government because they would be speaking against the laws of Allah and the words of Muhammad—laws and words that are believed to be perfect and unchangeable.

In contrast to the Islamic view of moral laws and values, the biblical Christian view is not based on the belief that every person and nation should be forced to become Christian. Jesus did not come with an army and swords (as Muhammad did) to build an earthly Christian kingdom in every nation to rule by force with strict laws and punishments for disobedience. At Jesus' trial before his crucifixion, he revealed this truth to the Roman governor, Pilate.

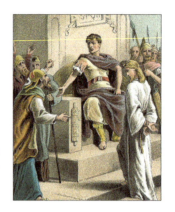

Jesus answered, "My Kingdom is not an earthly kingdom. If it were, my followers would fight to keep me from being handed over to the Jewish leaders. But my Kingdom is not of this world."

John 18:36

Jesus also revealed this truth about his kingdom to the Jewish leaders when he lived on Earth. They were expecting him to create a kingdom with physical land (Israel), borders, government officials, buildings, and armies. But Jesus told them that God's kingdom is a spiritual kingdom found within the hearts of people. Luke recorded Jesus' words in his gospel:

[20] One day the Pharisees asked Jesus, "When will the Kingdom of God come?" Jesus replied, "The Kingdom of God can't be detected by visible signs. [21] You won't be able to say, 'Here it is!' or 'It's over there!' For the Kingdom of God is already among you."

Luke 17:20–21

Although God does not build his kingdom in nations by the force of armies, he has established human governments in the nations of the earth to control human sinfulness. Governments must protect human life, the innocent, and the helpless. They are required to do this because every person has been created by God and bears his image. Governments must protect property and a person's right to own property. They must protect the freedom of God's image-bearers to make personal choices. But they must not allow people to make choices that harm the life, property and freedom of others. Because some people do harm or deny the rights of others, God has also given governments the authority to punish people who do wrong. Paul explained these truths in his letter to the Romans.

[1] Everyone must submit to governing authorities. For all authority comes from God, and those in positions of authority have been placed there by God. [2] So anyone who rebels against authority is rebelling against what God has instituted, and they will be punished. [3] For the authorities do not strike fear in people who are doing right, but in those who are doing wrong. Would you like to live without fear of the authorities? Do what is right, and they will honor you. [4] The authorities are God's servants, sent for your good. But if you are doing wrong, of course you should be afraid, for they have the power to punish you. They are God's servants, sent for the very purpose of punishing those who do what is wrong. [5] So you must submit to them, not only to avoid punishment, but also to keep a clear conscience.

[6] Pay your taxes, too, for these same reasons. For government workers need to be paid. They are serving God in what they do. [7] Give to everyone what you owe them: Pay your taxes and government fees to those who collect them and give respect and honor to those who are in authority.

Romans 13:1–7

When governments make laws to control human sinfulness, the laws must be based on God's holy character. They must be righteous and just even as God is righteous and just. They must never be written based on what a few people feel or think is right or wrong. Laws must exist to protect the life, property, and human liberties that God has given to all people. And laws must never exist to force people to become Christians or to punish them for refusing to do so.

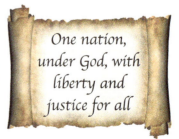

One nation, under God, with liberty and justice for all

ENDNOTES

1 Samuel M. Zwemer, *The Moslem Doctrine of God* (New York: American Tract Society, 1905), 15.

Naturalism
An Unbiblical View of the World without God

Getting Started—What Is Naturalism?

So far in our study of *Competing Worldviews*, we've explored biblical Christianity and Islam, two of the three major monotheistic worldviews and religions of history. (The third, Judaism, the worldview and religion of the Jewish people, is not included in this study.) Now we're ready to study a worldview called naturalism. Notice the root word *nature*. This worldview holds that only things that can be observed or proved to exist in the natural world are real. Naturalism is an atheistic worldview based on the belief that our senses, science, and reason prove that the natural or physical universe is all that exists. The supernatural—immaterial things that are *super* or above nature—simply does not exist. Included in the supernatural are God, spiritual beings such as angels and demons, and the Spirit that God placed in each image-bearer. Most naturalists, therefore, are atheistic, meaning God is not a part of what they believe is true about the world. However, some naturalists are *agnostic*—meaning they are unsure if God exists. They do not feel that the existence of God (or gods) is an important matter to be concerned with.

Like all worldviews, naturalism is based on what naturalists believe is true about truth itself. Since naturalists believe that truth is limited to what can be proved to exist in the natural world, they deny the truth that God reveals through creation, through the Bible, and through Jesus Christ and the Holy Spirit. As we explore the naturalist views of God and truth, we'll contrast them with the biblical Christian view as we did with Islam. In Lesson 9, we'll explore the naturalist view of people and the universe, and in Lesson 10, we'll explore the naturalist view of moral laws and values.

> **Naturalism**
> An atheistic worldview based on
> the belief that our senses, science,
> and reason prove that the natural or
> physical universe is all that exists

Topic 1—A Universe without God

Who Are the Highest Beings? Now let's explore this question: In a universe without God or any other supernatural beings, who are the highest beings? If your answer is humans, you're right. Naturalists believe there are no higher living beings than humans. This way of thinking is called *humanism*, and people who hold this belief are known as *humanists*.

In 1933, a group of humanists wrote and signed a manifesto or document that listed 15 beliefs they held about God, the universe, and human beings. This document was called the *Humanist Manifesto I*. The writers expressed their disbelief in God in these words: "We are convinced that the time has passed for theism."[1] In other words, these humanists believed that the time for believing in God was over. The time had come for people to believe that humans are the highest beings or forms of life, not God.

Forty years later, another group of humanists published the *Humanist Manifesto II*. Like the writers of the first manifesto, they also expressed their disbelief in God. These humanists wrote, "We find insufficient evidence for belief in the existence of a supernatural. As non-theists, we begin with humans, not God . . . ."[2]

Humanists continue to write manifestos or documents declaring their disbelief in God. In 2000, another group of humanists expressed their disbelief in God with these words: "As humanists, we urge today, as in the past, that humans not look beyond themselves for salvation. We alone are responsible for our own destiny."[3]

By destiny, humanists do not mean heaven or hell because they do not believe in either. When humanists say they are responsible for their own destiny, they mean they are in charge of planning and directing their lives. In other words, they are their own highest authority. Since God doesn't exist, they have the right to take complete charge of their own lives.

The Biblical Christian View: The naturalist belief that people are the highest beings in the universe is not in harmony with the biblical Christian view of God and people. The Bible declares that God exists and that he is the supreme authority over all people and the earth. He is the one who determines everything that happens in the world. He is the one who rules over the lives of all his image-bearers. God clearly revealed this truth to the prophet Daniel.

[20] He said,

"Praise the name of God forever and ever,
    for he has all wisdom and power.
[21] He controls the course of world events;
    he removes kings and sets up other kings.
He gives wisdom to the wise
    and knowledge to the scholars.   Daniel 2:20–21

In one of his psalms, King David described the folly of people who refuse to believe in God.

Only fools say in their hearts, "There is no God."   Psalm 53:1

The prophet Jeremiah described God's judgment against people who set themselves up as the highest authority in their lives.

5 This is what the LORD says:
"Cursed are those who put their trust in mere humans,
   who rely on human strength
   and turn their hearts away from the LORD.
6 They are like stunted shrubs in the desert,
   with no hope for the future.
They will live in the barren wilderness,
   in an uninhabited salty land.   Jeremiah 17:5–6

In contrast to the judgment that God promises will come to people who trust only in themselves, Jeremiah also told of the great blessings God promises to people who believe and trust in him.

7 "But blessed are those who trust in the LORD
   and have made the LORD their hope and confidence.
8 They are like trees planted along a riverbank,
   with roots that reach deep into the water.
Such trees are not bothered by the heat
   or worried by long months of drought.
Their leaves stay green,
   and they never stop producing fruit.   Jeremiah 17:7–8

Topic 2—Can God's Existence Be Proved?

The Bible Doesn't Try to Prove that God Exists. While humanist manifestos deny that God exists, the Bible declares his eternal existence in its very first sentence: In the beginning God created the heavens and the earth (Genesis 1:1). Notice that the Bible does not begin with a list of 10 ways to prove that God exists. It simply tells us that he exists and that he is the one who created everything. In fact, the biblical Christian worldview begins with faith in God rather than proof that he exists. God revealed this important truth to the writer of the New Testament book of Hebrews.

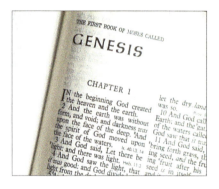

And it is impossible to please God without faith. Anyone who wants to come to him must believe that God exists and that he rewards those who sincerely seek him.   Hebrews 11:6

This Scripture does not mean that we should ignore the evidence for God's existence. But it does say that we must believe by faith that God exists. Then God will reveal himself and truths about himself to those who earnestly seek to know him. Do you remember what Jesus said to Thomas, his disciple who said he wouldn't believe Jesus had been raised from the dead unless he saw him in person?

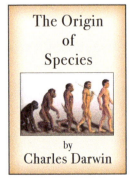

The Origin of Species

by Charles Darwin

Then Jesus told him, "You believe because you have seen me. Blessed are those who believe without seeing me."   John 20:29

Evidence for God's Existence: There are many ways naturalists communicate their belief that God does not exist. Some write science textbooks stating that the universe and everything in it have evolved accidentally from eternal matter. Some communicate their beliefs through songs or literature. Some communicate their message through movies and television dramas. Because the naturalist message that God does not exist is so powerful and common today, it's important to remember three strong evidences for God's existence.

1. Everything that Exists or Happens Has a Cause. Think about what you ate for breakfast this morning. Did the cereal, milk, toast, eggs, bacon, or other foods just appear on your table from nothing? How did these foods get into your kitchen in the first place? How did they get into the grocery store? How were the cereal, bread, eggs, and bacon made before they arrived at the market? If you follow the chain of events further back, you realize that a cause exists for every step it takes to grow, prepare, market, buy, cook, and place food on your table.

This example, of course, is only one illustration of the truth that everything that exists or happens has a cause—everything, that is, except God himself. God is uncaused. If he were caused, there would be someone or something more powerful than God that caused him to exist. But the Bible tells us that God is eternal. He has no cause. He has no beginning or end. He has always been and always will be. In fact, the eternal, uncaused God is the cause for the heavens and Earth and everything in them. This truth was revealed to Moses, who wrote the oldest psalm in the book of Psalms.

Before the mountains were born,
    before you gave birth to the earth and the world,
    from beginning to end, you are God.   Psalm 90:2

The very existence of the heavens and Earth is powerful evidence of God's eternal existence. Paul wrote in a letter to Christians in Rome that creation clearly reveals to all people that its cause is the eternal, all-powerful God. Creation reveals its cause so clearly, in fact, that people have no excuse for not giving God glory and thanks for it.

For ever since the world was created, people have seen the earth and sky. Through everything God made, they can clearly see his invisible qualities—his eternal power and divine nature. So they have no excuse for not knowing God.   Romans 1:20

2. The Universe that Exists Has Perfect Design and Order. People not only believe in God because they know the universe must have a cause, they also believe in God because they see perfect design in everything that exists. By God's inspiration, King David described the incredible design of the earth, including its stability in space, its land and water forms, and the permanent boundaries of the oceans.

5 You placed the world on its foundation
    so it would never be moved.
6 You clothed the earth with floods of water,
    water that covered even the mountains.
7 At your command, the water fled;
    at the sound of your thunder, it hurried away.
8 Mountains rose and valleys sank
    to the levels you decreed.
9 Then you set a firm boundary for the seas,
    so they would never again cover the earth.
          Psalm 104:5–9

God made a promise to Noah after the flood that revealed his design and control of night and day and the seasons.

"As long as the earth remains, there will be planting and harvest, cold and heat, summer and winter, day and night." Genesis 8:22

But is all this order and design really evidence that God exists? To find out, let's think about these questions: Could a computer exist without a hardware and software engineer? Could it work if each of its pieces were not perfectly designed and fit together with other perfectly designed pieces? Could a skyscraper exist without an architect? Could it provide safe and comfortable apartments and offices if its elevators, plumbing, electricity, and heating

and cooling systems were not perfectly designed to work in harmony with all the other parts and systems? Could the earth continue to exist without its perfect design and balance of air and water, plants and animals, seasons, and exact distance from the sun? Of course not. Computers and skyscrapers reveal careful design. So does the earth. This evidence from design and purpose leads people to acknowledge the existence of a supremely wise engineer or architect, who is much greater than the universe itself. For people who hold a theistic worldview, such as biblical Christianity, the engineer or architect is God.

3. All People Possess an Inner Sense of Right and Wrong. Although people with different worldviews hold many different beliefs about God, almost all people share similar beliefs about things that are right to do and things that are wrong to do. For example, most people agree that it is good and right to help someone who is in danger or someone who is suffering. Most people agree that it is bad and wrong to lie and steal. Most people agree that it is wrong to murder, kidnap, or abuse another person. And most people, even with very different worldviews, agree that it is wrong for a married person to be unfaithful by having a relationship with someone who is not his or her spouse.

Most people also have an inborn sense of responsibility to do what they believe is right and to avoid doing what they believe is wrong. This inner light that guides people to do right and avoid doing wrong is called *conscience*. Every human being born since the creation of the world has this inner light or conscience. Of course, since the fall, people's consciences are imperfect. Unfortunately, people don't always follow their conscience even when it clearly tells them something is wrong or right to do. When people don't listen to and follow the leading of their conscience, they experience guilt feelings and fears of being caught and punished for doing what they know

is wrong or failing to do what they know is right. Conscience works like an alarm system in a car that sounds off to remind us we haven't fastened our seat belts.

This fact that all people, even those with different worldviews, believe that certain things are right and certain things are wrong is another evidence that God exists. People don't need to be taught that certain behaviors are wrong. They know. And their knowing has a cause. The cause is God. God is the great Lawgiver, who created people with a built-in awareness of right and wrong.

In the book of Romans, Paul describes the inner light or conscience that all people possess.

¹⁴ Even Gentiles, who do not have God's written law, show that they know his law when they instinctively obey it, even without having heard it. ¹⁵ They demonstrate that God's law is written in their hearts, for their own conscience and thoughts either accuse them or tell them they are doing right. Romans 2:14–15

Topic 3—The Naturalist View of Truth

What Is Truth? You've learned that worldviews are based upon what people believe is true about God, people, the universe, moral laws and values, and even truth itself. Whether people are Christians or Muslims or naturalists, they believe only in ideas or things they think are true. They never intentionally include beliefs in their worldview that they know are false (even though some of their beliefs may be false). So how do people arrive at the beliefs in their worldview that they hold as true? Before answering this important question, let's review the meaning of truth.

Truth is *that which agrees with and accurately describes and explains reality*. For example, 2 + 2 = 5 is not true because it does not agree with the reality that 2 + 2 = 4. And to say that a round object is square is also untrue. This is because such a statement does not agree with the reality that no object can be two shapes at the same time. The minute you force something square into another shape, it is no longer square.

Truth is always objective. This means that it exists as a reality independently of what people think or feel. The fact that someone may believe or feel that the world is flat does not change the objective truth that the world is round. Objective truth also applies to morals. The fact that someone thinks or feels it is not wrong to cheat and steal does not change the objective truth that such behavior is morally wrong.

How Do We Know Truth? So how do people decide whether something is true or not? If someone tells you it's 100 degrees outside, the sun is shining, and it's snowing, how do you know if he or she is telling the truth? You could go outside and let your senses tell you. You might feel that the temperature is 100 degrees and you might see that the sun is shining. But you wouldn't see or feel any snow. Of course, there's another way you could tell whether the person was telling the truth or not. You wouldn't need to go outside and feel or see anything. Based on what you've learned about weather and seasons, you could very well reason with your mind that such a statement could not be true.

We can come to know many things that are true through our senses and reason. A Christian, a Muslim, a naturalist, and all other people can determine either through reason or their senses that the statement about a snowstorm on a hot summer day is not true.

But we also know that our senses and reason don't always lead us to truth. Our eyes can play tricks on us as they do when we look at the lines in Figure 1. Sometimes we fail to reason correctly because we don't have all the facts. Then we reach conclusions that are simply not true.

There is another way many people believe they can come to know truth. As you learned, Christians and Muslim believe some truth can be known only by revelation from God. For example, Islam and biblical Christianity declare that God reveals

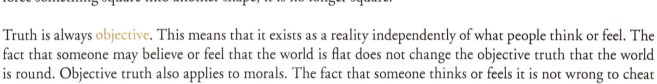

Figure 1

moral truth through conscience. Christianity and Islam are also based on the belief that God reveals truth about his existence through his creation. And both Christians and Muslims believe some truth can be known only through God's written revelation, either in the Bible or in the Quran. Of course, this does not mean that everything Muslims believe is revealed truth from Allah is actually truth. But it does mean that both Christians and Muslims believe there is some truth that can be known only through revelation.

> **Objective**
> Existing as a reality independently of
> what we may think or feel

The Naturalist View of Truth: Now let's apply what you know about truth to naturalism. First, most (but not all) naturalists believe there is such a thing as objective truth. For example, they would agree that the existence of the physical universe is an objective truth. They believe its existence is real or true because they can observe it with their senses. Naturalists also believe that through their senses, reason, and science they can discover many objective truths about the universe. For example, you probably would never hear a naturalist

deny the objective truth of the law of gravity. They know the truth of this law because they can observe things being held in place on the earth's surface. And they know the truth of this law because they can observe things in the earth's atmosphere returning back to Earth. No naturalist would ever jump off a skyscraper thinking he or she could defy the law of gravity. He knows the law of gravity is an objective truth, whether he likes it or not. And no naturalist scientists would ever design and launch a space shuttle without confidence in the laws of gravity and other laws of the universe. They design rockets powerful enough to launch the shuttle against the forces of gravity. And they design the shuttle with wings and rockets to safely return to Earth in harmony with the forces of gravity. If they could not count on the truth and reliability of the law of gravity as well as other laws of the universe, there could be no space program.

While naturalists believe they can discover truth through their senses, they also know that their senses don't always show or tell them the truth. Years ago, many people believed the earth was flat because that's what their eyes showed them. They believed that ships would eventually sail over the edge of the planet when they reached the far horizon. But scientific exploration later disproved this belief, and it had to be rejected.

Naturalists also know that reason doesn't always lead to truth. They know that sometimes the things they believe are untrue because they seem unreasonable later turn out to be true. This happens as their reasoning changes or as they discover more facts and other objective truths. Of course, the opposite is also true. Sometimes naturalists discover that things they once believed were true are not true. This happens as they discover other objective truths through their senses, through science, and through reason.

How Does the Naturalist View of Truth Differ from the Biblical Christian View? Now let's ask ourselves some questions: If both naturalists and Christians believe there is objective truth that can be discovered through the senses, science, and reason, is there any difference then in how each views truth? If they both agree that the law of gravity is an objective truth they can prove through scientific investigation, is there really any difference in the way they search for truth? To answer these questions, let's review our earlier definition of naturalism. You learned that naturalism is an atheistic worldview based on the belief that our senses, science, and reason prove that the natural or physical universe is all that exists. From this definition, can you identify how the naturalist view of truth differs from the biblical Christian or even the Islamic view? Let's explore some of these differences.

First, naturalism denies the truth of God's existence. Remember, naturalists don't believe in the supernatural. That's because they can't see, touch, or prove through science that invisible, spiritual beings, such as angels and God, exist. In 1963, the Russian cosmonaut Valery Bykovsky told newspeople that no Soviet cosmonaut believed in God. And he said that none of them had seen anything to change their minds during their space flights. In other words, because they hadn't seen God, he doesn't exist.

Second, because naturalists don't believe that God exists, they don't believe truth can be known through revelation from God. Naturalists, therefore, do not believe that God reveals the truth of his existence through creation. This is not in harmony with the biblical truth that "The heavens proclaim the glory of God. The skies display his craftsmanship" (Psalm 19:1). As we will explore in Lesson 9, naturalists believe the universe came into existence by itself from materials that have always existed. In other words, matter is eternal, not God. And one day, without any help from God, that eternal matter accidentally began to interact in ways that eventually produced the universe, including life on Earth.

Naturalists not only reject the idea that God reveals truth through creation, they also reject the idea that God reveals his moral laws in the hearts of people. They reject the truth that God places a moral compass in our heart that tells us if our thoughts or actions are right or wrong. This belief is also not in harmony with the biblical truth that even Gentiles, who do not have God's written law . . . demonstrate that God's law is written in their hearts (Romans 2:14–15). Although many naturalists believe that some things are right and some things are wrong, they do not believe that God has revealed any absolute moral laws. They believe instead that people determine their own moral values. And they believe that these moral values can and do change as people's beliefs and feelings change.

If naturalists reject God's revelation of truth through creation and through the heart or conscience, they most certainly reject his revelation of truth in Scripture. They believe the Bible is only a collection of stories and beliefs written by people. They might agree that some of the stories describe real historical events. And they might even agree that some of the moral teachings of the Bible are good for people. But they would never agree that the Bible is truthful revelation from God. Therefore, the naturalist belief that God did not reveal his truth through Scripture is not in harmony with the biblical truth that all Scripture is inspired by God and is useful to teach us what is true (2 Timothy 3:16).

Topic 4—Problems with the Naturalist View of Truth

What Is Wrong with the Naturalist View of Truth? When naturalists reject God's existence, they also reject the one who is Truth. Jesus said, "I am the way, the truth, and the life" (John 14:6). By rejecting God and his truth, naturalists are left completely on their own to discover truth. But as you know, all people are imperfect. And some things they think are true simply are not. For example, because naturalists deny that God created the universe, they try to discover through science and reason just how the universe came into existence. They know that the material that makes up the universe could not have created itself out of nothing. That's not reasonable. Therefore, the only explanation that naturalists can give for its existence is that it has always existed. In other words, since there is no God to create it, it must be eternal. They have no way of proving this belief. They simply accept it by faith.

Once naturalists believe that matter is eternal, they must try to discover how it all came together to produce the universe and life. Now here there is a real problem. Because naturalists are intelligent, they can see through reason and science that the universe is extremely orderly. Everywhere they look, they see how well designed it is. They also know that there must be a cause for every event. For example, seasons come and go every year in exactly the same way. Naturalists know that the seasons are caused because a slightly tilted Earth rotates each year around the sun. They see that plants and animals always reproduce after their kind. They know that apple trees are always caused by apple seeds that contain all the special genetic material that reproduces only apple trees. However, because naturalists see the order of the universe and because they understand there must be a cause for every event in the universe, they are faced with a big problem. Let's briefly explore this problem.

According to naturalism, the material that makes up the orderly universe has no cause. It is eternal. And according to naturalism, the universe itself has no outside cause or reason such as God for its existence. It's simply an accident. That's the only way it can exist if there is no Creator God.

The problem, therefore, is this: How can uncaused eternal material accidentally produce the perfectly ordered and designed universe? How can an accident produce humans who can think, choose, discover, and create? Accidents just don't produce such perfect order, design, and intelligence. Not only that, accidents can't produce people with moral awareness of right and wrong. There is no right or wrong in an accident. Only a holy and omnipotent God could ever design and create an orderly universe and fill it with his image-bearers who think, feel, choose, know right from wrong, and create. But because naturalists reject God, the only explanation they can offer for the existence of such an amazingly designed universe populated with intelligent human beings is that it just happened accidentally. That's as far as their reasoning and science can lead them.

No naturalist would ever believe that a computer or airplane could create itself accidentally out of eternal matter. They would say believing such a thing is totally unreasonable and therefore untrue. They know computers and airplanes and works of art and music cannot possibly create themselves accidentally. But when naturalists look at the world and reject its Designer and Creator, they are left only with one explanation for its existence—it's all an accident. What naturalists are saying then is this: It's unreasonable to think that a computer or airplane could create itself. However, it's not unreasonable to think that the universe could create itself. Now you decide. Is this kind of thinking among naturalists reasonable or unreasonable?

ENDNOTES
1 John Dewey, Paul Kurtz, and Edwin H. Wilson, *Humanist Manifesto I* (Buffalo, NY: Prometheus Books, 1933), 8.
2 Paul Kurtz and Edwin H. Wilson, *Humanist Manifesto II* (Buffalo, NY: Prometheus Books, 1973), 16.
3 Paul Kurtz, *Humanist Manifesto 2000: A Call for a New Planetary Humanism* (Amherst, NY: Prometheus Books, 2000), 63.

The Naturalist View of People and the Universe

Getting Started—Same Questions, Different Answers

In Lesson 8, you learned that the naturalist belief about God is clearly opposite the belief of theists such as Christians and Muslims. Naturalists say simply, "There is no God!" They believe God does not exist because they cannot prove his existence through scientific experiments or through their senses. You also learned that naturalists believe the only things that exist and are true are those things that can be proved by science or known through the senses. On the other hand, naturalists believe in their own existence. Like all humans, naturalists are aware of, or conscious of, their own lives. Their senses tell them that their physical bodies are real. And their thoughts, feelings, and choices are constant reminders that they are indeed alive and real. They also believe the universe exists because they can prove it through their senses and through science. But naturalist beliefs about people and the universe are quite different from Christian beliefs. Remember—the naturalist view of people and the universe does not begin with or include God. Instead of believing In the beginning God . . . (Genesis 1:1), naturalists believe "In the beginning matter. . . ."

Because naturalists exclude God from their worldview, their beliefs about truth, people, the universe, and right and wrong cannot agree with biblical Christian beliefs. In this lesson, we'll explore the naturalist view of people and the universe. First, we'll explore the naturalist view of people by asking and answering the same questions

all people ask about themselves: Where did I come from? Who am I? Why am I here? and Where am I going? Next, we'll explore very similar questions related to the naturalist view of the universe: Where did the universe come from? Why is the universe here? What is the universe like? What is my relationship with the universe? and What will happen to the universe in the future? As we have done before, we will compare and contrast the answers in a naturalist worldview with those in a biblical Christian worldview.

Topic 1—Where Did I Come From?

When naturalists answer the question, *Where did I come from?*, they begin with matter, not God. As you learned in Lesson 8, many (but not all) naturalists believe the materials that produced the universe and everything in it, including human beings, have always existed. Naturalists say this material must be eternal because there is no

God who could have created it. And it must be eternal because it could not have created itself out of nothing. To believe that nothing can create something is just not reasonable. Instead, many naturalists believe that over billions and billions of years this eternal matter moved about accidentally or by chance to produce the universe and life we know today. Naturalists do not believe this matter was ever living or had any ability to reason and plan the universe. This means that naturalists believe people are simply amazing accidents.

I Evolved from Spontaneously Generated Life. *The Humanist Manifesto I* states, "Humanism believes that man is part of nature and that he has emerged as the result of a continuous process."[1] Naturalists call this continuous process *evolution*. Evolution is *the theory that the first life on earth was accidentally produced by nonliving matter and over billions of years changed into all the different kinds of organisms that have ever lived*. Naturalists call the process that generated (produced) the first life spontaneously (accidentally) *spontaneous generation*, or *abiogenesis*. Although science has proved that nonliving material cannot produce living material, many naturalists hold this belief anyway. If they did not, they would have to admit that a supernatural force such as God caused the first life on Earth.

Naturalists believe that the primitive life caused by spontaneous generation slowly evolved or changed into higher forms of life. Fish eventually evolved into amphibians such as frogs, which can live in water and on land. Later, amphibians evolved into reptiles with scales. Next, reptiles with scales evolved into birds with feathers. Birds with feathers eventually evolved into mammals with hair such as bears and apes. And finally, naturalists believe, higher mammals evolved into human beings. Of course, they do not believe that any supernatural Being such as God planned or designed any stage of evolution. What they do believe is that the universe and all living things, including human beings, are the result of chance or accident.

> **Evolution**
> The theory that the first life on Earth was accidentally produced by nonliving matter and changed over billions of years into all the different organisms that have ever lived

The Biblical Christian View of Where People Come From: In stark contrast to the naturalist view of where people come from, the biblical Christian worldview states clearly that people are not the result of spontaneous generation and evolution. Rather, people are created by God.

> Acknowledge that the LORD is God!
> He made us. . . . We are his people.   Psalm 100:3

In contrast to the naturalist view that people are the result of an unplanned accident of nonliving matter, the biblical Christian view affirms that people are part of God's eternal plan for creation.

> Even before he made the world, God loved us and chose us in Christ to be holy and without fault in his eyes.
> Ephesians 1:4

And in stark contrast to the naturalist view that there is no God who creates and gives life to people, the biblical Christian view affirms that God forms the life of each individual in his or her mother's body and gives each individual the breath of life.

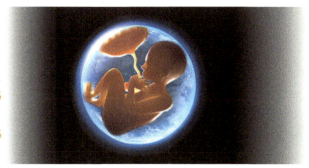

¹³ You made all the delicate, inner parts of my body
and knit me together in my mother's womb.
¹⁴ Thank you for making me so wonderfully complex!
Your workmanship is marvelous—how well I know it.

Psalm 139:14–15

He himself gives life and breath to everything.   Acts 17:25

Topic 2—Who Am I?

I'm an Accident. When naturalists ask the question, *Who am I?*, their answer would be like most people's answer: "Why, I'm a human being, of course." While this answer may be correct, in the naturalist worldview there are other parts to the answer that most naturalists would hesitate to admit. If naturalists answer the *Who am I?* question honestly, they would have to say, "I am a human being, but I am also an accident. I am a being who evolved from the accidental moving and changing of eternal matter. I am not here because I was planned, designed, and created by any supernatural Being. I and all other human beings are accidents of nature." Of course, such an answer doesn't seem at all reasonable when we look at the design and complexity of the universe and human life. Nevertheless, this answer is the only one naturalists can give to the question, *Who am I?* if they are to remain true to the beliefs of their worldview.

I'm the Highest-Evolved Accident. Although naturalists believe all life is an accident, most describe humans as the highest form of animal life on Earth. This doesn't mean naturalists believe people are image-bearers of God. They still believe people are only animals. But perhaps to give themselves some dignity above lower animals, many naturalists emphasize the characteristics of humans that set them above other animals.

Although naturalists believe that people are highly evolved, physical animals, they don't believe that we have a nonphysical spirit that continues to live after we die. Many naturalists believe that invisible things

like thoughts, feelings, and conscience are only the result of chemical and electrical processes inside the brain. Some naturalists even believe that people have such an animal nature that they have no freedom to make choices. They believe our actions or behaviors are controlled by instincts, much like the instinct that tells a bear when to hibernate in the winter. These naturalists believe that people's behavior is so influenced by the environment around them that they can't help but act in certain ways. And they believe that people inherit certain behaviors from their parents over which they have no control. In other words, some naturalists view people as accidental machines whose behaviors are programmed (like a computer) either at birth or later by their environment.

Not all naturalists believe that people are only biological and chemical machines. While they admit that life is an accident, they don't like to think of themselves as living robots or machines. These naturalists suggest that people have a nonphysical part that allows them to think, feel, and make choices on their own. They believe that human beings are not like lower animals because they can choose to think about themselves. People are not merely aware of their environment like lower animals. People can actually think about their own nature

and behavior. They can reason and make choices about how they will behave. These abilities, naturalists believe, make people more than automatons! However, they still do not believe this nonphysical side of humans that allows them to think about thinking, feel, and make choices is a soul or a spirit from God. All naturalists believe that life ends with death. There is no possibility that a soul or mind or any kind of awareness of being a person can exist after death.

I'm a Valuable Accident. People sometimes say they learn valuable lessons from accidents. Let's say your father had an automobile accident because he was talking on his cell phone and not paying enough attention to the road. He might say afterward, "That accident taught me

a valuable lesson—I'll never use my cell phone while I'm driving again because it distracts my attention away from my driving." But does an accident have any value within itself? Can something not planned or created for a purpose have any value on its own? We may give it value by saying it taught us a valuable lesson. But an accident in itself has no value.

In a similar way, naturalists must admit that if their lives really are accidents, they cannot possibly have any value. But naturalists, like all people, want and need to feel valuable. Because they don't believe in a God who gives them value, naturalists try to create or determine their value or worth in different ways. They may try to create their value by their outward appearance and dress. They may think that having many friends or accumulating great wealth gives them value. Some may try to find their value in their athletic ability or in their intelligence. Still others may look for their value in their race or nationality, while some seek to create their value by having authority over others.

Interestingly, some naturalists believe that human beings have no more value than the lowest animal. How can they believe this? It is the logical conclusion of believing that naturalism is true. Think about it this way. Can one unplanned accident be any more valuable than another? Does an automobile accident have more value, in itself, than when someone accidentally hits his thumb with a hammer? No. An accident is an

accident. If people are accidents of evolution, and so are all other living creatures, even cockroaches, how can anyone say that any one accident is more valuable than another? Of course, most people, including naturalists, would assert that human beings are much more valuable than cockroaches, which is quite true. But according to naturalism, everything that exists is an accident. So, some naturalists come to the conclusion that they cannot assign value to people or the universe or anything in it. How can they?

I'm a Good Accident. Whether naturalists believe their lives have value or not, they believe they are born with a good or sinless nature. Sin is not a word naturalists use because it refers to disobedience to God or to some higher being in whom they don't believe. However, as you will study in Lesson 10, some naturalists admit there are such things as right and wrong and good and evil. But they believe people, not God, decide which behaviors are good and morally right and which are bad and morally wrong.

When some naturalists try to explain why good people do bad things, they blame such behavior on the influence of others instead of the individual person. They believe that when people do bad things, it's not really their fault. People behave badly because of bad influences around them or because they inherited bad behaviors from their parents. In other words, people aren't directly responsible for the wrong things they do. Therefore, when people do wrong things, they should not be

punished. They should be retrained or reeducated and taken away from bad influences. Then they will make right choices. Of course, those naturalists who believe people are free to make their own decisions do believe people are responsible for the wrong things they do and should be punished for them.

Some naturalists don't even believe right and wrong exist. Again, this is because if God does not exist, there are no objective moral laws either in writing or in our hearts to tell us what is right and wrong. And if everything is an accident and accidents are neither right nor wrong, accidents cannot have the ability to decide what is right and wrong. We'll study more about the naturalist view of moral values in Lesson 10.

The Biblical Christian View of Who We Are: The biblical Christian worldview rejects the naturalist belief that people are the result of an accident. God reveals to us that he planned our creation long before he created the world. And how long ago was that? Well, there never was a time when God did not have a plan to create people and the universe! That's because God is eternal, and if he is eternal, his plan to create people is also eternal—before time began.

⁴ Even before he made the world, God loved us and chose us in Christ to be holy and without fault in his eyes. ⁵ God decided in advance to adopt us into his own family by bringing us to himself through Jesus Christ.   Ephesians 1:4–5

Scripture also assures us that people and the creation are no accident because everything God created, he created with wisdom.

O Lord, what a variety of things you have made!
    In wisdom you have made them all.
    The earth is full of your creatures.   Psalm 104:24

To create the earth and all its creatures, including us, with wisdom means that God intelligently and carefully designed us. God didn't leave our existence to the chance of nonliving matter moving around in space until one day it produced organisms that eventually gave rise to human beings.

Naturalists believe that people must create or find their own meaning and value for their lives. But God tells us that our value is found in one thing, and one thing only—that we are his creations who bear his image.

Then God said, "Let us make human beings in our image, to be like us.   Genesis 1:26

Our appearance, our intelligence, our friends, our family, or the things we own do not give us value. These ideas about who we are and what makes us valuable are false and will not last.

Charm is deceptive, and beauty does not last.   Proverbs 31:30

Trust in your money and down you go!   Proverbs 11:28

The biblical Christian answer to the question, *Who am I?*, affirms God created us in his image with the ability to think, to feel, to make choices, to create, and to know right from wrong. He also created us with a spirit that allows us to have fellowship with God, who is Spirit. Being God's image-bearers means that we are not highly evolved animals as naturalists believe. Rather, we are special creatures whom God made just a little lower than himself. He crowned his image-bearers with special glory and honor as stewards and rulers over all the animals and everything else on the earth. King David wrote about the special position of honor God created for human beings within his creation.

³ When I look at the night sky and see the work of your fingers—the moon and the stars you set in place—
⁴ what are people that you should think about them, mere mortals that you should care for them?
⁵ Yet you made them only a little lower than God and crowned them with glory and honor.
⁶ You gave them charge of everything you made, putting all things under their authority—
⁷ the flocks and the herds and all the wild animals,
⁸ the birds in the sky, the fish in the sea, and everything that swims the ocean currents.   Psalm 8:3–8

Finally, Christians do not agree with the naturalist belief that people are not sinners. The apostle Paul wrote about the sin nature that every person since Adam has been born with.

When Adam sinned, sin entered the world. Adam's sin brought death, so death spread to everyone, for everyone sinned.   Romans 5:12

Paul agreed completely with the truth about sin that God revealed to him. He explained his personal struggle with sin in a letter to early Christians in Rome.

¹⁹ I want to do what is good, but I don't. I don't want to do what is wrong, but I do it anyway. . . . ²¹ I have discovered this principle of life—that when I want to do what is right, I inevitably do what is wrong. ²² I love God's law with all my heart. ²³ But there is another power within me that is at war with my mind. This power makes me a slave to the sin that is still within me. ²⁴ Oh, what a miserable person I am!   Romans 7:19, 21–24

Although we are sinful by nature, it is important for us to remember that our sin nature does not mean that we do not bear God's image. Rather, it means that we bear it imperfectly. And it does not mean that we have no value or that God has abandoned his eternal plan to adopt us into his own family by bringing us to himself through Jesus Christ (Ephesians 1:5). God planned and created us in his love, and he saved us for eternal life with him in his love.

Topic 3—Why Am I Here?

I Am an Accident with a Purpose. Accidents have causes, but they are not planned or created to happen for any purpose. If they were planned, they would not be called *accidents*. In Topic 2, we learned that if naturalists answer the *Who am I?* question honestly according to their worldview, they would say that all life is an unplanned accident. They would have to answer, "Since I am not created by God, then I am an accident. And since I am an accident, I cannot have a purpose." However, this answer creates a problem for naturalists. Accidents don't search for their meaning and purpose. But people do search for meaning and purpose for their lives. They make plans. They set goals. They make choices. Even though naturalists understand that accidents are not planned and have no purpose within themselves, they, like all people, still want to find meaning and purpose for living. But they are faced with a question that has no reasonable answer: If I am an accident, and if accidents are unplanned and have no purpose in themselves, how then can my life have any purpose?

Some naturalists believe that because humans now have such a highly developed brain and mind, they have the ability to control or greatly influence the evolution of the human race. In other words, they believe they have the ability to use the "tools" of reason and science to control their own future and much of the future of all people. These naturalists believe that human beings don't have to be completely controlled by their environment or by behaviors they inherit from their parents. These naturalists set goals, and they declare their own value. They decide for themselves the purposes or goals for their lives and then make their own plans in

order to reach them. For most naturalists, their main purpose or goal in life is to become happy and fulfilled individuals and to improve human life on Earth. Because they believe life ends at death, their main purpose is to make life on Earth the best it can possibly be. In order to reach their goals, naturalists believe people must work hard to get rid of all the evil that has been forced on them by others and the environment. Naturalists believe that if all people do this together, the world will become a wonderful place to live and work. This perfect world many naturalists work hard to create is called *utopia*.

The Biblical Christian View of Why We Are Here: The biblical Christian answer to the question, *Why am I here?*, is not in harmony with the naturalist answer. Naturalists believe they must find their own reasons for being here. They must make their own plans for their lives and for the world. And they have great hope in the ability of human beings to create utopia on Earth. But God warns people that the plans and purposes they create for themselves and the world without him will not succeed. They will simply die.

³ Don't put your confidence in powerful people;
there is no help for you there.
⁴ When they breathe their last,
they return to the earth,
and all their plans die with them.   Psalm 146:3–4

On the other hand, the biblical Christian worldview declares that God made his plans for our lives even before we were born. And the main plan or purpose for our lives is not to live for ourselves. Rather, we are to live for God and praise his glory in all we do.

You saw me before I was born.
    Every day of my life was recorded in your book.
Every moment was laid out
    before a single day had passed.   Psalm 139:16

God's purpose was that we Jews who were the first to trust in Christ would bring praise and glory to God.
                    Ephesians 1:12

This does not mean God created people as robots without the ability to choose or make plans. But it does mean that God created us to do good works that he planned for us even before we were born. Paul wrote about God's plan for people in a letter to Christians in Ephesus.

For we are God's masterpiece. He has created us anew in Christ Jesus, so we can do the good things he planned for us long ago.   Ephesians 2:10

A Very Serious Question: Regardless of their worldview, all people ask this important question sometime during their life: *Where am I going?* They don't mean where am I going after school or on vacation. They mean is there life after death? If there is, where will I be, and what will that place be like? While all theistic worldviews provide several answers to this question, naturalism answers it with only one word: Nowhere!

As shocking as this answer may be, it is the only answer possible for the naturalist. According to the naturalist worldview, human beings are only biological and chemical machines without souls. When the machine wears out and stops working, it dies. That's it—no more life. Simply put, death is the end, and we go nowhere except to the grave.

A Future with No Hope or Plan: The naturalist view of human destiny is depressing for many people. If death is our end forever, then what's the use of living at all? Why should people work so hard to find meaning

and purpose in their lives and in the world if death is the end of everything they work for? To overcome the depression this kind of thinking causes, most naturalists believe they must do everything they can to enjoy life now. They are like some of the early Christians in the city of Corinth, Greece who did not believe in life after death. Paul wrote to correct their belief, telling these mistaken Christians that if there is no resurrection, "Let's feast and drink, for tomorrow we die!" (1 Corinthians 15:32). Sadly, most people who do not believe in God or life after death live their lives this way. Naturalists believe they must do everything they can to be the person they want to be now. Today is everything because there is no tomorrow after death.

A Hopeless Dream for the Future: Naturalists not only believe that people are going nowhere after they die, many also believe that history has no real purpose or direction. Dreaming about a happy, perfect future is hopeless. Naturalists believe this because they believe that history, like people's individual lives, is also an accident. It is not the result of a Creator God. However, some naturalists believe they have the ability to

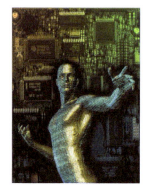

change the future direction of human history. They believe that as they control their own evolution through science, they will be able to perfect human beings. In fact, some naturalists believe that people will continue to evolve until a new animal even higher than human beings will be produced. And then this perfect superhuman being will be able to create a perfect world where all people will live together in harmony and peace. As you learned earlier, this future perfect world to be created by perfect human beings is often called *utopia*. Yet even with their dream of superhumans living on a perfect, utopian earth, naturalists know that all people eventually die. And no naturalist hopes for anything after death. Death is the end. All human efforts to make a perfect people and a perfect earth will have no eternal purpose beyond the grave.

The Biblical Christian View of Where We Are Going: The biblical Christian answer to the question, *Where am I going?*, is not in harmony with the naturalist answer. God reveals through Scripture that we have hope after death. Death is not our end. Life goes on after we return to the dust of the earth in our graves. People who believe in Jesus as God's Son and their Savior have the hope of eternal life in the presence of God. But people who reject God will spend their eternal life of punishment separated from him. Let's look at some of the truths about life after death Jesus taught while he lived on Earth.

[25] Jesus told her, "I am the resurrection and the life. Anyone who believes in me will live, even after dying. [26] Everyone who lives in me and believes in me will never ever die."   John 11:25–26

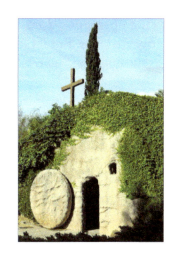

²⁴ "I tell you the truth, those who listen to my message and believe in God who sent me have eternal life. They will never be condemned for their sins, but they have already passed from death into life. . . .²⁸ Don't be so surprised! Indeed, the time is coming when all the dead in their graves will hear the voice of God's Son, ²⁹ and they will rise again. Those who have done good will rise to experience eternal life, and those who have continued in evil will rise to experience judgment.
John 5:24, 28–29

Naturalists' only hope is that science will help human beings evolve into perfect superhumans. Biblical Christians, however, have God's promise that one day God himself will create new and perfect bodies for his children. Paul explained what happens when God's children die and what they have to look forward to afterward.

¹ For we know that when this earthly tent we live in is taken down (that is, when we die and leave this earthly body), we will have a house in heaven, an eternal body made for us by God himself and not by human hands. ² We grow weary in our present bodies, and we long to put on our heavenly bodies like new clothing. ³ For we will put on heavenly bodies; we will not be spirits without bodies. ⁴ While we live in these earthly bodies, we groan and sigh, but it's not that we want to die and get rid of these bodies that clothe us. Rather, we want to put on our new bodies so that these dying bodies will be swallowed up by life.
2 Corinthians 5:1–4

John explained that in this new eternal life, God's children will not only have perfect bodies, they will also perfectly bear God's image.

Dear friends, we are already God's children, but he has not yet shown us what we will be like when Christ appears. But we do know that we will be like him, for we will see him as he really is.
1 John 3:2

All God's perfected children will live on a new earth created by him to be his home and the home of his children throughout eternity, not a naturalist utopian earth that people will never be able to create. Peter explained part of what the new earth will be like.

But we are looking forward to the new heavens and new earth he has promised, a world filled with God's righteousness.
2 Peter 3:13

Topic 5—The Naturalist View of the Universe

To understand the naturalist view of the universe, let's explore how they would answer four basic questions that people of every worldview ask: Where did the universe come from? Why does it exist? What is my relationship to the universe? and What will happen to the universe in the future? As you can see, these questions about the universe are similar to the questions all people ask and try to answer about themselves.

Where Did the Universe Come From? Before naturalists or people holding other worldviews can answer this question, they must first answer the big

"God question"—*Does God exist?* If God exists, then questions about his relationship to the universe must be answered first. But if God does not exist, as naturalists believe, then they must begin to look for other answers to the question, *Where did the universe come from?*

If you ask how the universe could exist without a Creator, there are only two possible answers. Neither answer can be proved, and therefore must be accepted by faith. The first answer states that the universe came into existence out of nothing and by nothing. In other words, there was a time when absolutely nothing existed, not even lifeless matter. Then one day out of this nothingness and without a Creator, matter just suddenly appeared. Then slowly, like sand taking billions of years to flow through an hourglass, this matter that appeared from nothing began to form gases and other nonliving material that formed the universe. After billions more years, this nonliving material changed into living material that evolved into the life on Earth we see today. In this view, the universe is not eternal. It has a beginning.

However, naturalists don't believe that nothing can produce something. They don't believe that matter that doesn't exist can produce matter that does exist. They say this is unreasonable, and it is. Therefore, naturalists suggest another answer to the question, *Where did the universe come from?* Like the first answer, it also requires faith, since it can't be proved. These naturalists say that the universe, or at least the energy and materials that

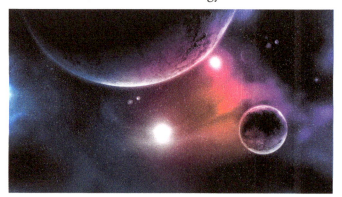

make up the universe, have always existed. They say the energy and matter is not caused—it's always been there. They say this because if it has not always been there, and if it did not create itself out of nothing, then it must have been created by a Creator. And as you know, naturalists don't believe (or want to believe) in a supernatural Creator. Remember, for naturalists, nature is all that exists. In the words of the naturalist Carl Sagan, "The cosmos is all there is or ever was or ever will be."[2]

We can summarize both of these naturalist views of where the universe and life in it came from this way:

1. The energy and material that produced the universe is either eternal or self-created out of nothing. If it is eternal, it has no beginning or end. If it is self-created out of nothing, it is not eternal because it has a beginning.

2. The nonliving material of the universe spontaneously or automatically generated or produced the first simple life. This process is called *spontaneous generation*.

3. People and all living things on Earth evolved from the first unicellular lifeforms.

Why Does the Universe Exist? Because naturalists deny the existence of a designer Creator God, there is only one way to answer this question—the universe has no purpose. Without a Creator, the universe can exist only because of chance. In other words, it's an accident. And, as you learned earlier, accidents have no planned purpose. They are simply accidents of nature. It's true that something causes all accidents. But the cause cannot give an accident a purpose. If an accident were planned for some purpose, could you still call it an accident? Of course not.

Naturalists cannot say that the purpose of the universe is to show the power and glory of a creative designer God because they don't believe in a Creator. In fact, naturalists are very careful not to admit that the universe is filled with order and design. Although they see examples of order and design everywhere they look, they know that admitting it moves them too close to admitting the existence of an omniscient Designer. Therefore, naturalists choose to ignore the obvious complex design of things like the human eye, or the order of the seasons, or the fact that the universe supports life on Earth. It's all an accident, they say. It was never planned and has no purpose.

What Is My Relationship to the Universe? For the naturalist, human beings are simply matter in motion. They believe they have no soul that lives eternally after they die. Although people do have a relationship with the earth, it is not a planned relationship because their existence is an accident. This means that people must discover the kind of relationship they have with the earth. Then they must learn what their responsibilities are in that relationship.

Like most people who live on planet earth, naturalists understand they have a dependent relationship with the earth. They must depend on the earth to provide everything they need for life. For this reason, naturalists know they have a responsibility to care for the earth. They know they should not abuse it or misuse its natural resources such as oil, forests, coal, and water. They believe that because human beings are the most intelligent of all living beings, they have the ability and responsibility to care for the earth's living and nonliving things.

Some naturalists work to conserve clean water supplies or reduce air pollution. Others work to preserve various kinds of plant and animal life. Many scientists work to find cures for diseases, while others work to invent machines that can help improve the quality of life on Earth. But naturalists don't take responsibility for the earth because they believe God commands them to. Rather, they believe that even if there is no life after death, they must take care of the planet that supports their life now. They understand that without proper care, the length and quality of all life on the planet will be decreased.

What Will Happen to the Universe in the Future? People ask not only about their own personal future, many wonder what the future holds for the universe itself. Will it burn up and disappear? Will it continue as it is? If it continues, how will it change? Will it always support life on planet Earth as we experience it now? Naturalists can only guess about the future or destiny of the universe. This is because they reject God's existence. And by rejecting God's existence, they reject the truth that God has revealed about the future of people and the universe. So what are some naturalist guesses or predictions about the universe of tomorrow?

Naturalists who believe that matter is eternal also believe the universe will always exist. Some naturalist scientists believe that the universe may grow larger and larger until one day it collapses. But when that happens, they believe the matter of the collapsed universe will produce another universe. They don't know what the new universe will be like or if it will produce new life. But what they do believe is that because matter is eternal, having no beginning or end, some kind of universe will always exist. These naturalist scientists believe the universe will go through these growing and collapsing cycles over and over again for eternity.

Other naturalist scientists believe the universe is not eternal. They believe it began long ago when noneternal matter came together and exploded with a big bang. Since then, this matter has grown and expanded into the universe we know today. However, these scientists have proved that the universe is actually slowing down. They believe that one day it will simply wear out or burn up. But this belief creates another problem for

naturalists. If the universe began from noneternal matter, then something had to cause the matter that caused the universe. But because naturalists reject God as the cause, they are left with no explanation for how anything began. These scientists who believe matter and the universe had a beginning can only say, "They just began somehow from nothing." They make this statement by faith because they cannot prove it by science or reason.

Although naturalists don't agree with each other about how the universe began or how or if it will end, most agree they must work hard to make life better. In fact, many naturalists are very optimistic about the future of the earth and the people who live on it. They believe that it is their responsibility to create a world of peace and harmony. Many believe this is possible through science and reason. And many believe that as human beings evolve into even more intelligent beings, they will be able to fulfill their responsibility to create the utopia many dream about. Even if the universe may end one day, they must work to make the world a better place to live now.

The Biblical Christian View of the Universe: Now let's go through the same questions about the universe and see how the naturalist view differs from the biblical Christian view.

Where Did the Universe Come From? The biblical Christian view of the existence of the universe, is, of course, quite different from the naturalist view. God revealed to us in Scripture that the universe is not eternal. It had a beginning.

In the beginning God created the heavens and the earth. Genesis 1:1

Before the universe began, there was no eternal matter just waiting to suddenly come together and make a universe. Nor did the matter of the universe just create itself out of nothing. The various materials that God used to make the universe were themselves created by him. They were not eternally in existence just waiting for God to shape them into the heavens and the earth. God, through Jesus, created everything that exists.

[15] Christ is the visible image of the invisible God. He existed before anything was created and is supreme over all creation, [16] for through him God created everything in the heavenly realms and on earth. He made the things we can see and the things we can't see—such as thrones, kingdoms, rulers, and authorities in the unseen world. Everything was created through him and for him. [17] He existed before anything else, and he holds all creation together. Colossians 1:15–17

Why Does the Universe Exist? While naturalists believe the universe and everything in it exist for no reason, the biblical Christian worldview declares very clearly that the universe exists for the glory of God and his pleasure.

"You are worthy, O Lord our God,
    to receive glory and honor and power.
For you created all things,
    and they exist because you created what you pleased."
                                        Revelation 4:11

The heavens proclaim the glory of God.
    The skies display his craftsmanship.   Psalm 19:1

What Is My Relationship to the Universe? The biblical Christian view of our relationship with the earth both agrees and disagrees with the naturalist view. Both views agree that people have a responsibility to care for the earth and its natural resources that support life. They agree that when people abuse and harm the earth and its resources, they harm and sometimes even destroy life. But the naturalist and biblical Christian views are not in agreement regarding where our responsibility to care for the earth comes from. Naturalists believe that people determine their responsibility through reason. They say it's only reasonable to care for the earth that provides the things people need to survive. Christians also say it's reasonable to care for the earth, but they declare our responsibility to care for the earth is given to us by God.

"Then God blessed them and said, "Be fruitful and multiply. Fill the earth and govern it. Reign over the fish in the sea, the birds in the sky, and all the animals that scurry along the ground." Genesis 1:28

Naturalists believe they have the responsibility to care for the earth because they are the only evolved animals with enough intelligence to do so. Christians believe that human beings fulfill their responsibilities for the earth as God's image-bearers. People are not just "matter in motion" with more intelligence than lower forms of life.

So God created human beings in his own image.
In the image of God he created them;
male and female he created them. Genesis 1:27

The biblical Christian worldview declares that human beings fulfill their responsibilities for the earth as its stewards. People do not own the earth. It was created by God, and it belongs to him. But he made people stewards over everything on Earth.

The earth is the LORD's, and everything in it. Psalm 24:1

You gave them charge of everything you made, putting all things under their authority. Psalm 8:6

What Will Happen to the Universe in the Future? You learned that naturalists do not agree with each other about the future of the universe. Some believe it will continue forever in some form, but others believe that some day it will burn out and possibly disappear altogether. God, however, revealed the truth about the future of the universe. The biblical Christian worldview affirms that God will make the present universe new. There will be a new heaven and a new earth that will last for eternity. It will be the home of God and those he has saved through their faith in Jesus as his Son and their Savior. Peter described the new universe in his second letter to early Christians.

But we are looking forward to the new heavens and new earth he has promised, a world filled with God's righteousness. 2 Peter 3:13

God revealed a vision of the new heaven and earth to the apostle John, who described his vision in the book of Revelation.

[1] Then I saw a new heaven and a new earth, for the old heaven and the old earth had disappeared. And the sea was also gone. [2] And I saw the holy city, the new Jerusalem, coming down from God out of heaven like a bride beautifully dressed for her husband.

[3] I heard a loud shout from the throne, saying, "Look, God's home is now among his people! He will live with them, and they will be his people. God himself will be with them.

Revelation 21:1–3

ENDNOTES

1 John Dewey, Paul Kurtz, and Edwin H. Wilson, *Humanist Manifesto I* (Buffalo, NY: Prometheus Books, 1933), 8.
2 Carl Sagan, *Cosmos* (New York: Random House, 1980), 1.

The Naturalist View of Moral Laws and Values

Getting Started—Some Important Questions

In our study of the naturalist worldview so far, we have explored what naturalists believe about God, truth, people, and the universe. Now it's time to explore what naturalists believe about moral laws and values. As we have done before, we'll ask and answer questions that people of all worldviews seek to understand.

1. Do right and wrong exist?

2. If moral laws exist, where do they come from?

3. If moral laws exist, what are their characteristics?

Because naturalists deny the existence of God and his Word revealed in Scripture, they must search for answers to these questions within themselves. As you will discover in this lesson, their answers are seldom if ever in harmony with the biblical Christian worldview. As we've done in previous lessons, we'll compare and contrast naturalists' answers to these questions with the truths of the Bible.

Topic 1—Do Right and Wrong Exist?

The Naturalist View of Right and Wrong: Naturalists don't all agree with each other about right and wrong. Some believe that right and wrong do exist. However, they also believe that it's impossible to know for sure if something is right or wrong. They say that because God doesn't exist, people can't possibly have his moral laws written in their hearts or in a book such as the Bible. They believe that because there are no absolute moral laws from God, people are on their own to decide what's right and wrong. Naturalists believe these laws are relative—they are determined in relation to each situation. And they understand that when different people try to decide what's right and wrong, there will be different opinions. In fact, what some people call good, others may call evil. And what some call wrong, others may call right. Therefore, naturalists believe moral laws are subjective. This means that moral laws must be determined by what people think and how they feel.

Relative	**Subjective**
Determined in relation to each situation	Existing only in the mind based on what we may feel or think is true

Other naturalists believe that right and wrong don't even exist. Although it's hard to imagine how anyone could really believe right and wrong don't exist, let's stop and think for just a minute. Naturalists who believe this are being quite honest—at least according to their worldview. This is because naturalists believe people and everything else that exist are simply accidents of nature. And as you learned earlier, accidents are neither good nor bad in themselves. How can an accident have any moral value in itself? An accident is something that occurs with no planning or purpose. It's just an accident that is neither moral nor immoral. If it were planned with a purpose, it wouldn't be an accident.

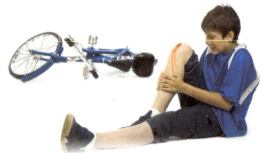

Of course, most naturalists do say that some things are right and some things are wrong. They know it in their hearts even though they don't believe this knowledge comes from God. These naturalists believe that human beings can tell from reasoning that some acts are evil and

some acts are good. But even these naturalists would never admit that the reason evil exists is because people are born with a sinful heart. Remember, naturalists don't believe in creation or the fall. They believe that human beings evolved from lower forms of life and that all people are born with a good heart or nature. They don't believe people are born with instincts or drives to hear, see, speak, or do evil. Rather, they believe people actually want to do good. In fact, many naturalists believe that as human beings continue to evolve, one day they will be able to perfect themselves. Then they will do only the good that is already within them.

Some Difficult Questions: Naturalists who believe in the existence of good and evil must answer a difficult question: If people are born with a good nature, why do they ever do bad things? In other words, why do good people do bad things? Some naturalists answer this question by saying that people aren't really responsible for the wrong things they do. Instead, people's environment or the world in which they live makes them do bad things. Thus, naturalists might give the following reasons for their behavior: "It's not my fault I stole the money. My parents are to blame because they're selfish and don't give me what I want." Or "It's not my fault I got into a fight. People are always picking on me." Or "It's not my fault I failed the test. My teacher doesn't like me."

If the environment or other people are to blame for evil, naturalists have another difficult question to answer: If everyone is born with a good nature, how did the evil in the environment originate? How did the world we live in become evil if all people are basically good? As you can easily see, blaming others for evil is not even reasonable. If people really are born with good hearts, there would be no evil or wrong doing in the world to make people do bad things in the first place!

The Biblical Christian View of Right and Wrong: The biblical Christian worldview is based on the truth that right and wrong do exist. Some things are good and moral, while other things are evil and immoral. Before God created Adam and Eve, Satan and his angels had already rebelled against God in heaven. Satan and evil were already a reality when God warned Adam not to eat from the Tree of the Knowledge of Good and Evil in the garden of Eden.

¹⁶ But the LORD God warned him, "You may freely eat the fruit of every tree in the garden—¹⁷ except the tree of the knowledge of good and evil. If you eat its fruit, you are sure to die." Genesis 2:17–18

As you know, Adam and Eve disobeyed God and ate the forbidden fruit. And when they did, they not only became sinners, they also became aware that evil was present in God's good creation. In fact, they became participants in that evil, along with Satan and the other fallen angels.

Then the LORD God said, "Look, the human beings have become like us, knowing both good and evil.

Genesis 3:22

The biblical Christian worldview is also based on the truth that there is a definite difference between good and evil. Good and evil are not determined by what people think or believe. If this were the case, what some people think is good, others would think is bad. And what some people believe is evil, others might believe is right. The prophet Isaiah warned against people deciding what is right and wrong for themselves because he knew that very often they could not tell the difference.

What sorrow for those who say that evil is good and good is evil.

Isaiah 5:20

In a letter to the early church in the city of Rome, Paul told Christians they must hate what is wrong and hold tightly to what is good (Romans 12:9). He also told them to be wise in doing right and to stay innocent of any wrong (Romans 16:19). Paul would not have given these instructions if there were no difference between good and evil.

Not only is the biblical Christian worldview based on acknowledging the existence of good and evil, it is also based on the truth that all people are born with a sinful nature. Since the fall, all people are born into the world with their hearts turned away from God and with a desire to do what is wrong.

For I was born a sinner—
yes, from the moment my mother conceived me.

Psalm 51:5

10 As the Scriptures say,
  "No one is righteous—
    not even one.
11 No one is truly wise;
  no one is seeking God.
12 All have turned away;
  all have become useless.
  No one does good,
    not a single one."

Romans 3:10–12

While naturalism blames people's environment for evil, biblical Christianity teaches that each person is responsible for the wrong he or she commits. Though other people may influence our behavior, each one of us is accountable to God for the good or bad things we do. God revealed this truth to Paul, who wrote to Christians living in Rome that each of us will give a personal account to God (Romans 14:12).

God also revealed to the prophet Ezekiel that each person will bear his or her guilt alone. No one will be able to blame someone else for the evil he or she commits.

Topic 2—If Moral Laws Exist, Where Do They Come From?

Who Makes the Rules? As you learned in Topic 1, most naturalists believe that some behaviors are good or moral and some behaviors are wrong or immoral. But because naturalists don't believe in God, they would never say that the moral laws people follow come from God. In other words, naturalists don't believe that their knowledge of right and wrong is placed in their hearts by God. And they certainly don't believe that moral awareness, moral laws, and moral values are based on written revelation from God in the Bible. So just where do naturalists believe moral awareness, moral laws, and moral values come from? Most naturalists believe that people are responsible for creating them. This belief is stated very clearly in the *Humanist Manifesto I*: "We affirm that moral values derive their source from human experience."[1]

Because naturalists don't believe God or his moral laws exist, they don't feel they are doing wrong in creating their own moral laws. In other words, if God does not exist, then people are completely free to decide for themselves what is right and what is wrong. People make these laws based on what they think or how they feel about certain behaviors. If they think or feel something is right, then it's right. If they think or feel something is wrong, then it's wrong.

Laws for Meeting Our Needs: Now let's ask ourselves this question: If naturalists believe that God and his moral laws and values don't exist, why do they attempt to determine their own set of moral laws and values?

Through their own reasoning, naturalists understand they must have certain moral laws and values in order to meet their own needs. For example, they reason that stealing is wrong because it takes things away from people that they need in order to survive. If everyone were to steal from others, no one would be able to meet his or her basic needs for food, clothing, and shelter. In other words, naturalists would say that respecting the property of others is morally right because it allows people to have and keep the things they need in order to survive. Therefore, naturalists would say it is morally right to make laws against stealing and laws that protect the property of others.

Laws for Fulfilling Our Wants: Most naturalists also believe that people create their own moral laws to satisfy their wants, not just their needs. For example, people have created laws that make it legal to kill or

abort unwanted babies before they are born. They've made these laws because some people want freedom from the responsibility of bringing an unwanted child into the world and having to raise it. People have also created their own moral laws making it legal for two people of the same sex to marry one another. They have made these laws because this is what some people want. And people have created laws making it legal to end the lives of very ill people who no longer want to go on living. Why? Because this is what many people want.

The Biblical Christian View of the Origin of Moral Laws and Values: The biblical Christian worldview declares that moral laws are given to people by God, not created by human beings. These moral laws are based on the absolutely holy character of God. Because God's moral laws are based on his holy and good character, we can always trust them to be good for us. King David described some of the blessings or benefits of God's perfect laws in one of his psalms.

> [7] The instructions of the LORD are perfect, reviving the soul. The decrees of the LORD are trustworthy, making wise the simple. [8] The commandments of the LORD are right, bringing joy to the heart.
>
> The commands of the LORD are clear, giving insight for living. [9] Reverence for the LORD is pure, lasting forever. The laws of the LORD are true; each one is fair.
>
> Psalm 19:7–9

God reveals his moral laws in the hearts of all people so that no one has an excuse for not understanding right from wrong. Paul wrote about this truth in a letter to the early church in the city of Rome. He wrote that people demonstrate that God's law is written in their hearts, for their own conscience and thoughts either accuse them or tell them they are doing right (Romans 2:15).

God has also revealed his moral laws through his written Word, the Bible. Again, the apostle Paul explained this truth in one of his letters to Timothy.

[16] All Scripture is inspired by God and is useful to teach us what is true and to make us realize what is wrong in our lives. It corrects us when we are wrong and teaches us to do what is right. [17] God uses it to prepare and equip his people to do every good work.　　　　　　　　　　　　　　　　　　　　　　2 Timothy 3:16–17

Topic 3—If Moral Laws Exist, What Are Their Characteristics?

Are Moral Laws Objective or Subjective? You learned previously that God's moral laws are always objective. This means that they exist and are truthful regardless of what people may think or feel. Human beings play no role in creating God's laws. He did not ask us what kind of laws we prefer. God did not ask us whether we approve of the laws he made. In fact, his laws are eternal, existing long before we were created.

Naturalists, however, do not accept the truth that God's moral laws are objective. How can they? They don't even believe God exists. For naturalists, moral laws are subjective. If people think or feel a certain moral law is true, then it is. If they don't, then it isn't. Of course, moral laws based on human reasoning and feelings are not always based on truth. Just "feeling" or "thinking" something is true does not guarantee that it is.

Are Moral Laws Absolute or Relative? You have also learned that God's moral laws are absolute. This means that his laws are always perfect, pure, unquestionable, and unchangeable. God's moral laws against murder, stealing, and adultery are as true and perfect today as they were the day God gave the Ten Commandments to Moses at Mount Sinai. Naturalists, of course, reject God and his moral absolutes. They say there are no moral absolutes. But wait a minute! What about the moral laws and values naturalists create for themselves? Don't naturalists believe they are absolute? Absolutely not!

Naturalists believe that the moral laws and values they create can easily be changed. They can be changed as people's needs and desires change. They can be changed as people's ideas about right and wrong change. Instead of believing that moral laws and values are absolute or unchangeable, naturalists believe that moral laws and values can change. These changes are always related to the situation in which people find themselves. In other words, in some situations, naturalists believe it may not be wrong to steal or commit adultery or even to commit murder. In other situations, naturalists believe such behaviors are wrong. Because naturalists believe moral laws and values can be changed in relation to each situation, they say that moral laws and values are relative rather than absolute.

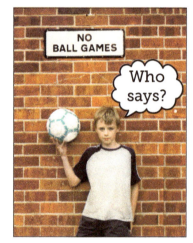

You can probably see some problems with this relative view of moral values. Behaviors that some people believe are morally wrong, other people believe are morally right. This is why you may hear someone say, "Who are you to tell me what's right or wrong? I'll decide for myself!" However, if naturalists are honest, they know that people cannot be completely free to decide for themselves what is morally right or morally wrong. They know that people will not always act responsibly toward others. Although someone may believe it's right to steal, naturalists know that such behavior cannot be tolerated. That's why naturalists believe there must be laws against many behaviors that harm others. If such laws did not exist, naturalists know that life in their families, communities, and nations would be dangerous and unbearable.

Do you see a contradiction in the illustration about stealing that naturalists must live with? On the one hand, naturalists may say that stealing is not always wrong. They say this because they believe that moral values are relative to the situation and personal choice of each individual. On the other hand, however, most naturalists believe it is absolutely necessary to make laws against stealing. This is because most naturalists believe stealing is harmful to others, and harming others, they say, is absolutely wrong! Do you think something can be relative and absolute at the same time? Of course not! That's a contradiction.

Are Moral Laws Universal or Local? God's moral laws are universal. This means that his laws are for all people in all places at all times. In contrast, we say that God's moral laws are not local. This means they are not just for some people in some locations at certain times. For example, when God gave the Ten Commandments, his law against lying was not given just for the Hebrew people who lived in the land of Israel thousands of years ago. It was given for all times and for all people from every nation on Earth. Many naturalists, however, do not accept the truth that moral laws are universal. They believe that moral laws for people in one location and time do not necessarily apply to people living in another location or time.

Naturalists do not always live their lives as if they believe that moral laws are not universal. Consider this example. A seventh-grade teacher taught her students that each of them must personally decide which behaviors

were morally right and which were morally wrong. She explained that she could not tell them what was right and what was wrong. She encouraged her students to make their own decisions and then behave accordingly. One day, this teacher gave her class a test. Before the test, the students announced that they had all decided cheating was morally right. It was a moral value each student had chosen to accept for his or her life. Now, how do you think the teacher responded to her students' announcement? Do you think her actions were consistent with her teaching about their personal freedom to choose their own moral values? Do you think she allowed her students to cheat on the test? Or do you think her actions were inconsistent with her teaching, and she refused to let her students cheat?

As you can imagine, the teacher was quite surprised. She told her students that cheating was not a moral value she had chosen for herself. Then she told them that they were not allowed to cheat in her class. They could cheat in other situations if allowed, but not in her class. In other words, she made her moral choice not to cheat a universal moral absolute at least for her students while they were in her class. Do you see the contradiction? Naturalists may say moral laws and values are not universal and do not apply to all people. They may say people should choose their own values and then live by them. But in reality, naturalists face situations every day where they feel they must impose their moral values on others. In this true story, the teacher made her moral value of honesty universal for all the students in her class.

The Biblical Christian View of Moral Laws and Values: The biblical Christian worldview declares that God's moral laws are objective, not subjective. They are truth, and they exist regardless of whether we think they do or not. God himself revealed these laws directly to people. In the Old Testament book of Exodus, Moses wrote about the time when God gave the Ten Commandments to the Israelites at Mount Sinai. Notice that God both spoke and wrote his laws.

And the LORD said to Moses, "Say this to the people of Israel: You saw for yourselves that I spoke to you from heaven." Exodus 20:22

"These are the regulations you must present to Israel." Exodus 21:1

[15] Then Moses turned and went down the mountain. He held in his hands the two stone tablets inscribed with the terms of the covenant. They were inscribed on both sides, front and back. [16] These tablets were God's work; the words on them were written by God himself. Exodus 32:15–16

Throughout history God has spoken or revealed his objective truths to people. These truths have been recorded by the writers of the Bible, and they have been spoken in Person to us through God's Son, Jesus. The writer of the book of Hebrews wrote about this truth.

[1] Long ago God spoke many times and in many ways to our ancestors through the prophets. [2] And now in these final days, he has spoken to us through his Son. Hebrews 1:1–2

God's moral laws are not only objective, they are also absolute, not relative. They are perfect, pure, unquestionable, unchangeable, and eternal. They do not change in relation to different situations or according to what people believe or prefer. The writers of the books of Psalms and Proverbs often wrote about the absolute nature of God's words, which includes his moral laws.

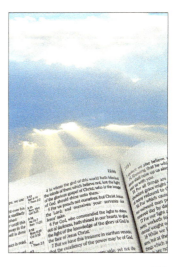

The instructions of the LORD are perfect. Psalm 19:7

Your eternal word, O LORD,
stands firm in heaven. Psalm 119:89

5 Every word of God proves true.
   He is a shield to all who come to him for protection.
6 Do not add to his words,
   or he may rebuke you and expose you as a liar.

Proverbs 30:5–6

Jesus himself declared the absolute, unchanging nature of God's moral laws.

"I tell you the truth, until heaven and earth disappear, not even the smallest detail of God's law will disappear until its purpose is achieved."

Matthew 5:18

God's moral laws are not only objective and absolute, they are also universal, not local.

Paul wrote about this truth in his letter to the early church in Rome. He explained that all people at all times and in all places are responsible for either accepting or rejecting God and his universal moral laws. Because God and his laws can be known by all people, there is no excuse for rejecting God or disobeying his laws.

18 But God shows his anger from heaven against all sinful, wicked people who suppress the truth by their wickedness. 19 They know the truth about God because he has made it obvious to them. 20 For ever since the world was created, people have seen the earth and sky. Through everything God made, they can clearly see his invisible qualities—his eternal power and divine nature. So they have no excuse for not knowing God.

21 Yes, they knew God, but they wouldn't worship him as God or even give him thanks. And they began to think up foolish ideas of what God was like. As a result, their minds became dark and confused. 22 Claiming to be wise, they instead became utter fools.

28 Since they thought it foolish to acknowledge God, he abandoned them to their foolish thinking and let them do things that should never be done. . . . 32 They know God's justice requires that those who do these things deserve to die, yet they do them anyway. Worse yet, they encourage others to do them, too.

Romans 1:18–22; 28, 32

Further on in his letter to the Roman Christians, Paul again made it very clear that God's moral laws are universal. All people in every nation and at all times know God's laws are universal because they demonstrate that God's law is written in their hearts, for their own conscience and thoughts either accuse them or tell them they are doing right (Romans 2:15).

Jesus clearly declared the objective, absolute, and universal nature of God's moral laws and truth when he made this claim: "I am the way, the truth, and the life. No one can come to the Father except through me" (John 14:6).

Notice that Jesus did not say, "I am a way and a truth and a life."

God's Word clearly warns naturalists and all people who reject his moral laws, values, and truths as revealed in Jesus and who instead trust in their own ideas of what is morally right and what is morally wrong.

There is a path before each person that seems right,
   but it ends in death.

Proverbs 14:12

ENDNOTES:
1 *Humanist Manifesto I* (Buffalo, NY: Prometheus Books), 1933.

New Spirituality
An Unbiblical View of the World as God

Getting Started—What Is the New Spirituality Worldview?

A Quick Review: In your exploration of Walking in Truth, you have already studied three of today's dominant worldviews. You began by studying biblical Christianity, the view of God and the world we believe is true. You learned that it is a monotheistic worldview because it is based on a belief in the existence of the one true and almighty creator God.

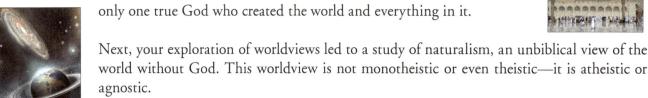

The second worldview you explored was Islam, an unbiblical view of God and the world. You learned that Islam is also a monotheistic worldview because Muslims believe there is only one true God who created the world and everything in it.

Next, your exploration of worldviews led to a study of naturalism, an unbiblical view of the world without God. This worldview is not monotheistic or even theistic—it is atheistic or agnostic.

A Pantheistic Worldview: Now you are about to investigate a fourth kind of worldview, an unbiblical view of the world as god. It is called new spirituality (formerly known as *the New Age movement*), and people who hold this worldview believe that everything that exists is God. The word pantheism is often used to describe the new spirituality worldview. The term *pantheism* is formed by two Greek words: *pan*, meaning *all*, and *theos*, meaning *God*. Thus, pantheism is a worldview that includes the belief that *all things are god*, and this includes you and this book and everything else in the universe. New spiritualists do not see God as a personal being, but rather as an impersonal force, spirit, or energy. Everything that exists is part of this impersonal spiritual energy they call *god*. In other words, the earth is god, I am god, and you are god. Everything that exists is part of this one impersonal "god force."

You might think from its name that new spirituality is a new worldview. Actually, it is a very old worldview, held in some form by people since ancient times. It was originally called *New Age* because people who hold

this worldview believe that one day a time of peace and harmony will come on Earth. This time will begin when enough people understand that everything that exists is part of the spiritual energy force called *god*. Like all worldviews, new spirituality includes beliefs about God, the universe, people, truth, and right and wrong. You will explore these beliefs, and as you did with Islam and naturalism, you will compare and contrast them with the biblical Christian worldview.

> **New Spirituality**
> A primarily pantheistic worldview based on mystical beliefs that god and everything in the universe are one impersonal spiritual being or energy force

Topic 1—The New Spirituality View of God

The God of Star Wars: In the science fiction movie *Star Wars*, the Jedi Master Obi-Wan Kenobi says, "The force is what gives a Jedi his power. It is an energy field created by all living things. It surrounds us, penetrates us, and binds the galaxy together." *Star Wars—Episode IV, A New Hope*

In the *Star Wars* comic book series, *The Tales of the Jedi*, Jedi Master Ood Bnar says, "The force is our power and our ally. The force has always been with us. That is its nature. It surrounds us and penetrates. It binds the universe together. Those who become sensitive to its presence can learn how to use it for good or evil." *Star Wars—The Tales of the Jedi: The Saga of Nomi Sunrider*

Today, it is not uncommon to hear people say, "May the force be with you!" But what does this mean? Who or what is this force made so popular by the *Star Wars* movies, books, and comics? To the writers who created *Star Wars*, the force is not a person. Rather, as they describe it through the words of Obi-Wan Kenobi, the force is an "energy field." And in the words of Ood Bnar, the force is a power that "penetrates" and "binds the universe together."

Now let's ask three questions:

(1) Could this power and energy called *the force* be similar to a god character?

(2) Is the god character of *Star Wars* found only in science fiction books and movies?

(3) Is there a worldview that actually believes that god is only a penetrating, binding energy field like Ood Bnar says? If so, what is it called?

GEORGE LUCAS, PRODUCER OF *STAR WARS*

Let's answer the three questions. The answer to the first question is a definite yes. The producer of the *Star Wars* film, George Lucas, said that in making the film he was "telling an old myth in a new way."[1] The old myth he was referring to is pantheism, the belief that god is everything and everything is god.

The answer to the second question is no. The belief that everything is god is not found only in science fiction. It is a belief held by millions of people living in the nonfiction world of today.

Finally, the answer to the third question is yes. There is a worldview based on the belief that god is a penetrating, binding energy field. The name of that worldview is *new spirituality*.

The God of New Spirituality: Like other worldviews, the new spirituality worldview includes a certain view of God. However, that view is not based on monotheism, as are biblical Christianity and Islam. And it is not based on atheism or agnosticism, as is naturalism. Rather, the new spirituality worldview is based on pantheism, the belief that god is an impersonal energy force that fills the entire universe. New spiritualists believe that god is not only a force that fills the entire universe, this force is the universe. Everything that exists is god. Stars are god, water is god, plants are god, trees are god, the earth is god, whales and dolphins are god, and of course, people are god. New spiritualists believe that everything that exists has divine power within it. Therefore, they say the entire universe is sacred. When new spiritualists worship, they worship the creation, and that includes themselves. They do not worship the biblical God of creation.

One new spiritualist author named *Etan Boritzer* wrote a children's book entitled *What Is God?* that became very popular. Boritzer says this in his book:

> There are many ways to talk about God. Does that mean that everything that everybody ever says about God is right? Does that mean that God is everything? Yes! God is everything great and small! God is everything far away and near! God is everything bright and dark! And God is everything in between! If everything is God, God is the last leaf on a tree. If everything is God, God is an elephant crashing through the jungle.[2]

What do you notice about the title of Boritzer's book that sets the stage for his description of God? Did you notice that he doesn't ask *who* God is, but rather *what* God is? He uses the word *what* because that allows him to describe God as many things, such as a leaf or an elephant. He doesn't use *who* because that would imply that God is a personal Being, something new spiritualists do not believe.

Who Is Jesus? New spiritualists believe that Jesus Christ once lived on Earth. They don't believe, however, that Jesus is the God of the Bible or the Son of God the Father. Rather, they believe that Jesus was a human just like everyone else. However, they believe that Jesus was special. New spiritualists believe that during Jesus' life on Earth, he came to realize that he was God. They believe that somehow Jesus came to understand that he was one with, and the same as, the universal "god force," and that this realization enabled him to do miracles and even rise from the dead. In one new spirituality publication entitled *Science of Mind*, John White explains the new spirituality belief this way: "The significance of [the] resurrection is not that Jesus was a human like us but rather that we are gods like him."[3]

Topic 2—The New Spirituality View of Truth

Bonfires and Marshmallows: New spiritualists know that Christians believe God has revealed truth through the Bible. They know that Muslims believe Allah has spoken truth to them through the Quran. And they know that many people believe they can find truth in other books written by great teachers throughout history. However, new spiritualists do not believe that any such book is more important than any other. In fact, one new spiritualist author thinks the Bible, the Quran, and all other "books of truth" are not worth anything except as fuel for a bonfire.

David Spangler writes in his book *Reflections on the Christ*, "We can take all the scriptures, and all the teachings, and all the tablets, and all the laws, and all the marshmallows and have a jolly good bonfire and marshmallow roast, because that is all they are worth."[4]

Where Do New Spiritualists Look for Truth? If Spangler and other new spiritualists reject the authority of the Bible as well as all the books of other worldviews, where do you think they look for truth? Do you think that, like naturalists who also reject the Bible, new spiritualists look to science and reason? No. To answer this question, let's look again at what new spiritualists believe about God. They believe that everything is god—that everything is part of one invisible spiritual energy force throughout the cosmos. In other words, many of them believe that the things we can see and feel are not actually real. What is ultimately real is the invisible spiritual energy force they call *god*. This means that new spiritualists disagree with the ideas found in naturalism, which, as you learned, state that only nature or matter is real. In fact, many new spiritualists believe just the opposite. They say that only the immaterial, or spiritual, is real. For this reason, they reject trying to find truth in the scientific study of the natural world.

So where do new spiritualists look for truth? They look within themselves, or their own consciousness. Because they believe that everyone is part of the one universal energy force or god, new spiritualists teach that all

people must get in touch with the god within themselves if they want to find truth. Once people get in contact with their own inner god—that is, when they realize they are god—they will suddenly know all truth. Many new spiritualists believe that there are no limits to the truth people can discover within themselves. They believe that what people must stop doing is looking for truth outside of themselves because that distracts people from realizing they are themselves god. New spiritualists believe that people must stop looking to things like the Bible or the Quran or other books of wisdom written over the centuries.

This interesting pathway to finding truth does not mean that new spiritualists define truth the same as biblical Christians do. You have learned that truth is that which agrees with, accurately describes, and accurately

explains what is real. Truth about God and the universe is not based on what any one person feels or thinks is true, but on what is real. But Christians do not deny that people have subjective experiences and feelings. Truth about an individual's feelings and perspective is subjective and relative to them. Christians take care not to confuse subjective and relative truth from their own limited experiences with the objective and absolute truth about God and the universe. They do this with the Holy Spirit's help and the study of God's Word.

For new spiritualists, truth is completely subjective. They believe that each person creates his or her own truth. This belief is often expressed in the statement "If it feels like truth to you, it's true." Truth, therefore, becomes only a feeling or an experience, and no one is free to judge another person's view of truth.

The Power of the Truth Within: New spiritualists not only believe that people have the ability to find truth within themselves, they also believe that there is mystical power in the truth they do find. One new spiritualist named *Jack Underhill* thinks the power within people is so great it can actually turn the sun off and on. And he believes this power can do even more than that. In an article entitled "My Goal in Life," Underhill explains what would happen if everyone in the world could connect with his or her inner godhood: "They can turn off the sun and turn it back on. They can freeze oceans into ice, turn the air into gold, talk as one with no

movement or sound. They can fly without wings and love without pain, cure with no more than a thought or a smile. They can make the earth go backwards or bounce up and down, crack it in half or shift it around. . . There is nothing they cannot do."[5]

New spiritualists look for truth within themselves. They often search for truth in the ancient writings of philosophers and magicians. They may use fortune-tellers, spirit boards, or tarot cards in order to learn about their future. Many new spiritualists search for truth through crystal therapy, channeling, meditation, and astrologers—people who study the position and movement of stars in order to determine a person's future. Astrologers use special charts called *horoscopes* that describe the position of the planets on the day and time a person was born. Many new spiritualists believe that their horoscope determines all the events in their life, and that they have no power to change them.

New spiritualists believe that because they are sincere about their quest for truth, they will know truth when they see it. But they also see their own limitations. They may feel that their bodies trap them from roaming the universe searching for answers, or that they are distracted too much by past emotional pain or by desire and ambition. So, they pay close attention to those who seem to have secret knowledge that may help them on their spiritual quest for truth.

Topic 3—The Biblical Christian View of God and Truth

The Biblical Christian View of God: Many people today are confused about who God is, and multitudes believe that he is like the god of new spirituality. Some of this confusion comes from misunderstanding the biblical truths that God is an invisible Spirit and that he is omnipresent. Recall that new spiritualists believe that god is an invisible spiritual reality and that he is everywhere in the universe. Although these biblical Christian and new spiritualist beliefs sound similar, a closer look reveals how different they are.

First, the God of biblical Christianity is not an invisible energy force. Yes, God is Spirit, and he is invisible, but he is also a personal Being. From the beginning of creation, God has spoken to his image-bearers. A personal Being can communicate, but a force cannot. Because all people are God's image-bearers, they can understand and respond to God's personal communication.

God spoke to Adam and Eve and told them to fill the earth and care for it. God told Noah to build an ark because he was going to destroy the earth and all its wicked people. God told Abraham, Isaac, and Jacob that he was going to make their descendants into a great nation through whom all people on Earth would be blessed. After Jacob's descendants had multiplied greatly and were slaves in Egypt, God told Moses to lead them to freedom. Moses wrote about his conversation with God in Exodus. In this conversation, God revealed himself in an audible voice from a burning bush and told Moses his name.

God replied to Moses, "I AM WHO I AM. Say this to the people of Israel: I AM has sent me to you."   Exodus 3:14

Christians use the name *Yahweh* for God because it comes from the words *I AM* in the Hebrew language. A name identifies a person. A name and speech from a person tell us he or she is not an unknowable force. A person reveals his or her name to others in order to be known by them. By revealing his name to Moses, God was saying that he is capable of being known intimately. He was inviting Moses, and us, to address or speak to him personally. Real persons have names and relationships. They communicate. God, whose name is *Yahweh*, is a personal Being.

Although God is an invisible personal Being, he has revealed himself physically through Jesus, God the Son. Though Jesus is eternal like God the Father, he became visible in a physical body. Many people saw him when he lived on Earth, and everyone will see him when he returns to Earth. Jesus is not an invisible energy force like the god of the new spiritualist.

Christ is the visible image of the invisible God. He existed before anything was created and is supreme over all creation.
Colossians 1:15

So the Word became human and made his home among us. He was full of unfailing love and faithfulness. And we have seen his glory, the glory of the Father's one and only Son.
John 1:14

But we do know that we will be like him, for we will see him as he really is.
1 John 3:2

Look! He comes with the clouds of heaven. And everyone will see him—even those who pierced him.
Revelation 1:7

Second, although God is omnipresent throughout his creation, the Bible clearly reveals that God is not equal to or the same thing as everything in creation. Although God is present everywhere throughout his creation, and although his Holy Spirit lives or dwells within his children, God is not the same thing as his creation. He is separate from what he created. Remember, he is the Creator! People and the heavens and the earth are the creation.

When we explain this truth about God, we say that God is transcendent. The word *transcendent* comes from two Latin words—*trans*, meaning *beyond*, and *escendo*, meaning *to ascend*. In other words, God ascends beyond or is above his creation even though he is everywhere within it.

Solomon, King David's son and Israel's third king, built the first temple for God in Jerusalem. King Solomon acknowledged God's transcendence in a prayer at the dedication ceremony for the temple.

"Even the highest heavens cannot contain you. How much less this Temple I have built!
2 Chronicles 6:18

Solomon knew that God was greater than his creation. He knew that God could never be contained within it or by it.

God also spoke of his transcendence to the prophet Isaiah when he revealed that all his thoughts and all his ways are far above the thoughts and ways of his image-bearers.

8 "My thoughts are nothing like your thoughts," says the LORD.
"And my ways are far beyond anything you could imagine.
9 For just as the heavens are higher than the earth,
so my ways are higher than your ways
and my thoughts higher than your thoughts."
Isaiah 55:8–9

When you hear people say things like, "God is everything," or "Everything is God," remember that this is not the biblical Christian view of God. It is, however, very much the new spiritualist view of god!

The Biblical Christian View of Truth: While new spiritualists look within themselves to find truth, the biblical Christian worldview declares that people do not create truth or find it by suddenly getting in touch with their own godhood. Rather, truth is found in the only God who is himself Truth. Jesus explained to his disciples that he is the Truth when he told them, "'I am the way, the truth, and the life'" (John 14:6). And when Jesus prayed to his Father on behalf of his disciples, he declared the truthfulness of God's word when he said "your word, which is truth" (John 17:17).

While new spiritualists look inside themselves to find truth, Scripture tells us that God's truth is revealed to us in four primary ways. First, God's truth is revealed through creation.

¹⁹ They know the truth about God because he has made it obvious to them. ²⁰ For ever since the world was created, people have seen the earth and sky. Through everything God made, they can clearly see his invisible qualities—his eternal power and divine nature. So they have no excuse for not knowing God.   Romans 1:19–20

Second, God's truth is revealed through Scripture.

¹⁶ All Scripture is inspired by God and is useful to teach us what is true and to make us realize what is wrong in our lives. It corrects us when we are wrong and teaches us to do what is right. ¹⁷ God uses it to prepare and equip his people to do every good work.
                                        2 Timothy 3:16–17

Third, God's truth is revealed through the life and teaching of his Son, Jesus.

¹ Long ago God spoke many times and in many ways to our ancestors through the prophets. ² And now in these final days, he has spoken to us through his Son. God promised everything to the Son as an inheritance, and through the Son he created the universe.   Hebrews 1:1–2

Fourth, God reveals truth to us through the Holy Spirit.

¹⁷ He is the Holy Spirit, who leads into all truth.   John 14:17

When we say that people do not create or find truth within themselves as new spiritualists do, this does not mean that people do not discover truth. People are always discovering truth! We discover it by studying God's creation. And we discover it from God's Word, his Son, and the Holy Spirit. Biblical Christianity emphasizes that what people discover is truth about God and the universe. People do not create the truth or find it by looking to some inner "god force."

Scripture tell us where we can find truth. It also tells us where we must not look for truth. While many new spiritualists search for truth through fortune-telling and magic, God warns us not to use such people or methods. God revealed this rule to the Israelites through Moses.

¹⁰ And do not let your people practice fortune-telling, or use sorcery, or interpret omens, or engage in witchcraft, ¹¹ or cast spells, or function as mediums or psychics, or call forth the spirits of the dead.
                                        Deuteronomy 18:10–11

God made it very clear that those who practice the magic arts, and who do not repent, will never enter the kingdom of heaven. Instead, they will be punished forever apart from God. John recorded this truth in the book of Revelation, the last book of the Bible.

[6] And [Jesus] also said, "It is finished! I am the Alpha and the Omega—the Beginning and the End. To all who are thirsty I will give freely from the springs of the water of life. [7] All who are victorious will inherit all these blessings, and I will be their God, and they will be my children.

[8] "But cowards, unbelievers, the corrupt, murderers, the immoral, those who practice witchcraft, idol worshipers, and all liars—their fate is in the fiery lake of burning sulfur. This is the second death."   Revelation 21:6–8

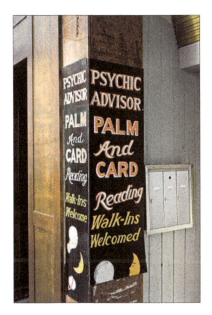

A FORTUNE-TELLER'S SIGN

TAROT CARDS

SPIRIT BOARD

OUIJA BOARD

ENDNOTES

1 "Of Myth and Men: A Conversation Between Bill Moyers and George Lucas on the Meaning of the Force and the True Theology of Star Wars." *Time*, April 26, 1999, p. 92.

2 Etan Boritzer. *What Is God?* (Willowdale, CA: Firefly Books, 1990), p. 26.

3 John White, "A Course in Miracles: Spiritual Wisdom for the New Spiritualist." *Science of Mind*, March 1986.

Getting Started—Who Was I? Who Am I? Who Will I Be?

Am I Really Me? Do you remember who you were before you were born to the life you now live? Do you know if you were a Persian princess during the 1800s? Can you remember if you were a Spanish sea captain searching for the New World? Do you remember ever being a Roman soldier, an Egyptian slave, or even a butterfly? If you can't remember being someone or something else in your previous lives, do you know who you are now? And do you have any idea who you might become in your next life?

So how do you answer these questions? Do they make sense to you? Why or why not? Do you think some people actually believe they have lived as many different people or even as other creatures over thousands of years? Do you think some people believe they will die and come back to life as someone or something else? Believe it or not, there are many people that do!

BUDDHIST WHEEL OF LIFE—A REPRESENTATION
OF THE CYCLE OF BIRTH AND REBIRTH

In this lesson, you'll explore the new spirituality view of people, which includes the belief that people live and die over and over again. You'll also explore the new spirituality view of the universe, which includes the belief that the universe gives life to all things, from the Milky Way to a newborn baby. And you'll discover why some people who hold a new spirituality worldview refer to our planet as "Mother Earth."

Topic 1—The New Spirituality View of People

Who Am I? In Lesson 11, you learned that the new spirituality worldview is basically a pantheistic worldview. Pantheism is *a worldview based on the belief that all things are god*. God is no different from planets in space or trees in a garden. God and people are not separate, distinct beings. All things are god, and god is all things. The new spirituality god is seen as a living force or energy that gives birth and life to all things. It is often described as the *universal mind*. Although new spiritualists believe this god force is a living force, they do not believe it is a personal Being like the God of biblical Christianity.

So, if everything is god, who are people? According to the new spirituality worldview, each individual is a part of and the same as this universal mind called *god*. One new spirituality philosopher named *Gary Zukav* explains each person's oneness with this universal god force like this: "Consider that the ocean is God. It has always been. Now reach in and grab a cup full of water. In that instant, the cup [of water] becomes individual, but it has always been, has it not? This is the case with your soul. There was the instant when you became a cup of energy, but it was of an immortal original Being. You have always been because what it is that you are is God."[1]

For new spiritualists, the most real thing that exists is the spiritual dimension of the universe—the universal mind or god force. This does not necessarily mean that new spiritualists deny the existence of the natural or physical dimension. You and other people, the earth, the planets, and the stars are real. But new spiritualists say these material things are not the most real things. They exist only because they are a part of the spiritual, universal god force. Therefore, people have real bones and muscles. People can see and interact with the world and with others through their senses. However, people's physical existence is not really the most important aspect of who they are. The most real and most important fact about people is their spiritual oneness with the god force. People are God! People are one with the universal mind!

Where Did I Come from and Come from and Come from?

According to the new spirituality worldview, everything flows from the universal mind or god force. Imagine a large lake with several rivers that flow from it. You are like one of the rivers. You are an individual, but you are the same water that flows from the lake into a riverbed. There is no difference between you and other rivers of people that flow from the lake. Your origin is the lake, or in new spirituality terms, you flow from the universal mind or god force.

Imagine again that you are one of the rivers flowing from a lake or one of the cups of water dipped from the ocean. You are an individual river or cup of water. However, you did not come from the lake as a river or from the ocean as a cup of water only once. Rather, you have been many rivers flowing from the lake, or

many cups of water dipped from the ocean. In other words, you have lived many lives before now. You have lived, died, and come back to life as part of the universal god force many times, perhaps over thousands of years. One new spiritualist, a Hollywood actress named *Shirley MacLaine*, says she knows she has lived thousands of lives before now. She remembers having been "a Spanish infant wearing diamond earrings . . . a monk meditating in a cave . . . a ballet dancer in Russia . . . [and] an Inca youth in Peru."[2] MacLaine also believes she was once a "princess of the elephants" in India and saved a village from being destroyed.[3]

The new spirituality belief that people are reborn over and over again is called reincarnation. This word is made from the prefix *re*, meaning *again* and the word *incarnation*, meaning *the act of becoming flesh*. In other words, new spiritualists believe that people are born over and over again into a new body or other living form. Yet as many times as they are reborn, they are still part of the god force—of which everything that exists is a part.

Reincarnation
The belief that the human soul is reborn
into a new body or form over and over again

Why Am I Here Over and Over Again? So, why do you think new spiritualists believe in reincarnation? They believe that the reason people are born over and over again is because people do not fully realize that they are divine or god. New spiritualists believe that people are ignorant of the fact that everything in the universe is united together as one reality. Until people finally grasp what it means to be one with the universal mind or god force, they will have to be born over and over again. Reincarnation is a consequence of being ignorant of the "most real" and important truth about all that exists. Reincarnation is also a consequence of the way people live and treat others. However, new spiritualists don't call mistreatment of others *sin* because they don't believe people have a sinful nature. Reincarnation is the result of being ignorant of who we are and how we should live in harmony with other people and the earth.

Where Am I Going? New spiritualists believe that people and the universe are evolving and moving in an forward direction. This forward direction is toward a new age or time on planet Earth when people will no longer be ignorant of their divinity and oneness with all things. They imagine what it would be like to be aware of their godhood, to cure diseases with their minds, end war and poverty with a thought, or imagine themselves into a state of wealth and popularity. That's what perfection looks like to new spiritualists. When this perfection occurs, reincarnation will no longer be necessary.

Topic 2—The New Spirituality View of the Universe

Around and Around: New spiritualists not only believe that people are god and part of the one universal mind, they also believe that the earth and all other parts of the universe are god. Remember that according to the new spirituality worldview, everything is god and god is everything.

Not only do new spiritualists believe the universe is god, they also believe that it must be reborn over and over again like people. The universe cycles around and around, from birth through life to death to birth through life to death. New spiritualists believe that after billions of years the cosmos dies, but then somehow it gives birth to itself all over again. Just how this rebirth takes place is not explained or understood. They believe the universal god force just gives itself a new life. Some believe the universe begins and grows like a seed. But whatever explanation is offered, the new spirituality view does not include the Creator God of biblical Christianity. New spiritualists say that somehow the universal mind or god force just recreates the universe and life by itself. And everything that is created is simply one and the same with the god force that created it.

Is It Real or Not? What would you say if someone told you the book you are now reading doesn't really exist? Or what if someone told you everything you see, touch, smell, and hear doesn't really exist? In other words, everything you think is real isn't. As strange as these questions may sound, there are some new spiritualists who truly believe the physical world is only an illusion. According to them, the reason most people think the universe and everything in it are real is because they are ignorant. They are ignorant of the truth that they are god and everything is god. These new spiritualists believe that when

people finally realize their deity and oneness with the god force, their illusions about a physical universe will disappear. This belief is widely held in religions like Hinduism and Buddhism, and these religions have greatly influenced the beliefs of many new spiritualists.

The Physical Universe: Other new spiritualists believe the physical universe is real. This doesn't mean they think the physical universe is separate from the god force any more than people are. They just acknowledge that it's real. However, these new spiritualists believe there are two dimensions of the real universe—a physical dimension (which is visible) and a spiritual dimension (which is invisible). And they also believe there are two ways to look at this very real universe.

The first way is through the ordinary senses. This way is used to look at the physical universe. By touching, seeing, smelling, tasting, and hearing the physical dimension around us, we can come to understand much about it. Most new spiritualists believe that our senses tell us that the physical dimension is orderly. It follows certain laws of nature such as the law of gravity. Time moves in one direction, meaning yesterday is over and we are now living in the present. A person cannot be in two places at one time, and two people cannot occupy the same space at the same time. Most new spiritualists agree about these and other truths about the physical dimension and how it works.

The Spiritual Universe: New spiritualists use a very different method to look at the spiritual dimension of the universe. This way does not use the ordinary senses. Rather, it way requires a mystical use of the mind. In this process, the mind opens itself to a higher way of thinking that allows it to get in touch with the god force. New spiritualists believe they can explore the spiritual dimension of the universe through meditation, chanting, yoga, spiritual guides, channelers, various forms of magic, fasting, and even drugs.

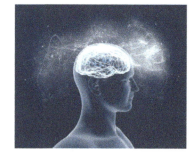

So what does the spiritual dimension look or feel like to a new spiritualist? What truths about the universal mind or god force do new spiritualists find? Some say they learn that they will live forever. They learn that

they are actually one with the universe and that they really are god. Many report that they have seen the universe in very different ways. Sometimes they see it as a colorful light show. They may feel it as electrical sensations. Some say they feel their soul lifting out of their body and traveling into the endless universe. Others say they have experienced going beyond time and even space itself. Some report being changed into various kinds of animals or having the ability to fly between planets. Whatever they are experiencing, new spiritualists believe they have truly seen a spiritual dimension of the universe that cannot be known through ordinary senses.

As you learned in Lesson 11, new spiritualists believe that once they get in touch with the mystical power of god, they can use it to control the order and form of the universe.

The Living Universe: Think about some of the things you see every day. Can you distinguish or tell the difference between things that are living and those that are nonliving? For example, is a tree full of green leaves and fruit a living or nonliving organism? Why? Is a rock living or nonliving? Why? What other examples of living and nonliving things within the universe can you think of?

New spiritualists see things differently. They believe that everything in the universe is part of one gigantic living system. This living system includes the stars and planets. They believe the earth, for example, is not just a sphere made of rock and soil and water that supports life. New spiritualists see the earth as a living organism that actually gives birth to all living things from plants to animals to people. This belief in the earth as a living organism is why new spiritualists often refer to the earth as *Mother Earth* and to the natural environment as *Mother Nature*. They believe that the earth is god and deserving of worship. This belief has led many people away from the worship of the one true God to the worship of nature, or the environment. New spiritualists also believe that the sun, the moon, and the stars, and all of nature are to be worshipped as god.

Not only do many new spiritualists believe the earth is alive, they believe that everything on the earth has a living spirit within it. This includes not only trees, but also whales, rocks, oceans, and volcanoes. What is most important, however, is that new spiritualists believe that everything on the earth and in the universe comes from and is part of the one, living, god force. You also learned that new spiritualists don't believe one living thing is any different than any other living thing. Therefore, no part of the universe is any more important than any other part. This is why many new spiritualists believe that animals have the same rights as humans. A baby whale, for example, is equally as important as a baby human being. In fact, some new spiritualists are more concerned about preserving the life of a beached whale than they are about preserving the life of an unborn child.

While Christians believe it is important to care for God's Earth, new spiritualists believe that in order to bring about the time of peace and harmony on Earth, they must first save our planet from all its environmental problems as well as realize their own divinity and oneness with the god force. Once this utopian new age comes, the earth and everyone living on it will experience the peace and harmony we all long for.

Topic 3—The Biblical Christian View of People

God Is a Personal Being and Separate from His Creation. As you have been learning in Unit 4, the new spirituality worldview is neither a theistic nor an atheistic worldview. It is best described as *pantheistic*. Pantheists believe that everything is god and god is the same as everything that exists. This means that God is no different from people or anything else in the universe. You've also learned that this god of the new spirituality worldview is not a personal being, but a god force, or energy, flowing through everything that exists. Biblical Christianity denies both of these false beliefs and instead affirms that God is a personal Being who is transcendent, or separate, from everything he created.

You've learned that God revealed to Moses that he is a personal Being when he said to Moses, "'I AM WHO I AM'" (Exodus 3:14).

King Solomon knew that God is a transcendent personal Being. On the day he dedicated the first temple in Jerusalem, he prayed directly to God as a Person, not to some impersonal universal energy force. In his prayer, Solomon acknowledged God's transcendence by saying that neither heaven nor earth could possibly contain or hold God. After Solomon prayed, God's glory filled the temple, but God himself was separate from and not the same as the temple.

When Solomon finished praying . . . the glorious presence of the LORD filled the Temple.   2 Chronicles 7:1

King David wrote about God's transcendence in many of his psalms. Notice the underlined words that tell us God is separate from and above all he created.

For the LORD is <u>high above</u> the nations; his glory is <u>higher than</u> the heavens.

Psalm 113:4

People Are Not God. The new spirituality worldview makes no distinction between God and people. "I am god," is a common statement made by many new spiritualists. However, God has spoken to many writers of the Bible, implying that no one and no thing is equal to him. For example, God asked the prophet Isaiah the following question, a question that answers itself.

"To whom will you compare me? Who is my equal?" asks the Holy One.   Isaiah 40:25

The writer of Psalm 113 posed the same question.

⁵ Who can be compared with the LORD our God,
     who is enthroned on high?
⁶ He stoops to look down
     on heaven and on earth.   Psalm 113:5–6

These Bible passages make clear that God cannot be compared to anyone within his creation. He is separate from and high above everything he created. No person exists who is equal to God as new spiritualists believe.

People Are Created by God. You've learned that people who hold the new spirituality worldview believe that no one knows or can know how people evolved from the universal god force. But God revealed to Moses that the origin of our lives is really no mystery at all. People are created living beings. God created people in his image. Moses recorded God's words in the book of Genesis.

Then God said, "Let us make human beings in our image, to be like us.   Genesis 1:26

In the Old Testament, Job also understood and explained the difference between the Creator and the image-bearers he created.

⁸ "'You formed me with your hands; you made me . . .
⁹ Remember that you made me from dust . . .
¹⁰ You . . . formed me in the womb.
¹¹ You clothed me with skin and flesh,
     and you knit my bones and sinews together.
¹² You gave me life and showed me your unfailing love.
     My life was preserved by your care.   Job 10:8–12

King David also understood that God and people are not one and the same. He clearly acknowledged that people are created by God and crowned with glory and honor by God. David knew that people are not the result of a universal god force giving birth to everything from a magical cosmic seed or big bang.

³ When I look at the night sky and see the work of your fingers—
     the moon and the stars you set in place—
⁴ what are mere mortals that you should think about them,
     human beings that you should care for them?
⁵ Yet you made them only a little lower than God
     and crowned them with glory and honor.   Psalm 8:3–5

People Have a Sin Nature. You've learned that people who hold the new spirituality worldview do not believe that people have a sin nature. New spiritualists believe that people are just ignorant of their deity or godhood. Biblical Christianity, however, affirms that each individual born since the fall is sinful by nature at birth. This is why all people desperately need a Savior. They aren't just ignorant as new spiritualists believe. And they don't need to meditate, practice yoga, or contact the spirit of a dead person to find out that they are god. They do need the power of God's Word and his Holy Spirit to show them their sinful nature, to convict them of their sin, and to confirm their desperate need for a Savior.

Paul described people's sinful nature in a letter to early Christians living in the city of Ephesus.

² You used to live in sin, just like the rest of the world, obeying the devil—the commander of the powers in the unseen world. He is the spirit at work in the hearts of those who refuse to obey God. ³ All of us used to live that way, following the passionate desires and inclinations of our sinful nature. By our very nature we were subject to God's anger, just like everyone else.   Ephesians 2:2–3

Do you remember the first sin on Earth? What was Satan's temptation to Adam and Eve? It wasn't just to taste a delicious fruit that God had forbidden them to eat. Satan's temptation appealed to their pride. Satan promised God's first image-bearers that the fruit they were forbidden to eat would make them wise like God. Do you see a connection between Satan's temptation, Adam and Eve's sin, and the new spirituality worldview? What makes the new spirituality worldview so attractive to people? Just as Satan promised Adam and Eve they would be like God, the new spirituality worldview promises people that they already are god! And when they get in touch with the god force within themselves, they'll understand the real truth about God and the universe. And what truth do new spiritualists believe—a belief that is actually not a truth, but a lie? It's the lie that people *are* god.

After Eve told Satan that they would die if they ate the forbidden fruit from the Tree of the Knowledge of Good and Evil, this is the lie Satan told her—and you know what happened next.

⁴ "You won't die!" the serpent replied to the woman. ⁵ "God knows that your eyes will be opened as soon as you eat it, and you will be like God, knowing both good and evil."

⁶ The woman was convinced. She saw that the tree was beautiful, and its fruit looked delicious, and she wanted the wisdom it would give her. So she took some of the fruit and ate it. Then she gave some to her husband, who was with her, and he ate it, too.   Genesis 3:4–6

Since the very beginning of history, people have wanted to be like God or to be God themselves. This temptation and desire lie at the very heart of the new spirituality worldview.

People Do Not Go through Cycles of Reincarnation. New spiritualists believe each life in the universe is like an individual drop or cup of water in a huge cosmic ocean. When that life dies, new spiritualists believe it is absorbed back into the god force until it reincarnates again as a new, individual life. This cycle of reincarnation occurs over and over again until the person realizes he or she is actually god and one with god. Again, biblical Christianity denies this false belief. God revealed to the writer of the New Testament book of Hebrews that people are born and die physically only once in this world. And a time will come when all people who have died will be resurrected to life and stand before God to be judged by him.

27 And just as each person is destined to die once and after that comes judgment, 28 so also Christ was offered once for all time as a sacrifice to take away the sins of many people. He will come again, not to deal with our sins, but to bring salvation to all who are eagerly waiting for him.

Hebrews 9:27–28

For people who believe in Jesus as God's Son and their Savior, their reward is eternal life. But for people who deny Jesus is God and reject him as their Savior and instead live evil lives, their punishment is eternal condemnation apart from God. The apostle John recorded Jesus' words about these truths in his gospel.

24 "I tell you the truth, those who listen to my message and believe in God who sent me have eternal life. They will never be condemned for their sins, but they have already passed from death into life.

28 Don't be so surprised! Indeed, the time is coming when all the dead in their graves will hear the voice of God's Son, 29 and they will rise again. Those who have done good will rise to experience eternal life, and those who have continued in evil will rise to experience judgment. John 5:24, 28–29

At the resurrection and final judgment, people will not be reincarnated and come back as different people. Rather, people who have received Jesus as God's Son and their Savior will be resurrected as the same people they are now. However, they will be given a new eternal body with a new heart and mind completely conformed to the character and image of Jesus—a transformation that begins when a person accepts Jesus as his or her Savior. God's image-bearers will never become God, but they will one day bear his holiness and righteousness as his perfected image-bearers!

God also revealed this wonderful truth about resurrection life after death to Paul, who explained it in his second letter to the Christians in Corinth.

1 For we know that when this earthly tent we live in is taken down (that is, when we die and leave this earthly body), we will have a house in heaven, an eternal body made for us by God himself and not by human hands. 2 We grow weary in our present bodies, and we long to put on our heavenly bodies like new clothing. 3 For we will put on heavenly bodies; we will not be spirits without bodies. 4 While we live in these earthly bodies, we groan and sigh, but it's not that we want to die and get rid of these bodies that clothe us. Rather, we want to put on our new bodies so that these dying bodies will be swallowed up by life. 2 Corinthians 5:1–4

Topic 4—The Biblical Christian View of the Universe

The Universe Is Not God. Just as people are not the same as God, neither is the earth or any other part of the universe the same as God. God has revealed to many writers of the Bible that he alone is the Creator. Isaiah, inspired by God, explained this truth to the people of his day.

For the LORD is God,
 and he created the heavens and earth
 and put everything in place.
He made the world to be lived in,

not to be a place of empty chaos.
"I am the LORD," he says,
 "and there is no other."   Isaiah 45:18

This is what the LORD says—
 your Redeemer and Creator:
"I am the LORD, who made all things.
 I alone stretched out the heavens.
Who was with me
 when I made the earth?   Isaiah 44:24

The new spirituality worldview denies that the God of Scripture is the transcendent Creator of all things. Instead, new spiritualists believe that they and everything in the universe are one and the same with the impersonal universal energy they call *the god force*. Therefore, instead of worshipping the only true and living God, they worship themselves and all of nature as god. Paul wrote about this ancient sin in a letter to early Christians living in Rome. In this letter, Paul describes very clearly what people who hold the new spirituality worldview are doing.

They traded the truth about God for a lie. So they worshiped and served the things God created instead of the Creator himself, who is worthy of eternal praise! Amen   Romans 1:25

Biblical Christianity declares that people are to worship only the transcendent Creator God, not themselves or anything else. Matthew recorded Jesus' words to Satan after Satan tempted Jesus to worship him.

"Get out of here, Satan," Jesus told him. "For the Scriptures say, 'You must worship the LORD your God and serve only him.'"   Matthew 4:10

The Universe Does Not Go through Cycles of Reincarnation. You learned in this lesson that people who hold the new spirituality worldview believe that the universe is somehow born over and over again, perhaps from a cosmic seed. This view of the universe means that new spiritualists believe history is cyclical, always going in circles with no real beginning or end. However, the Bible tells us that history does not go in circles. It tells us that God planned the history of creation to move in a straight line. The original creation has a definite beginning and will have a definite end, just like our present lives.

The first verse of the Bible tells us that in the beginning God created the heavens and the earth (Genesis 1:1), revealing clearly that the history of the universe and everything in it had a beginning.

Likewise, Jesus taught that this present age of history will end one day. It will end after the gospel has been preached to the whole world, and those who remain faithful until the end of time will be saved. Matthew recorded Jesus' words about these truths in his gospel.

12 Sin will be rampant everywhere, and the love of many will grow cold. 13 But the one who endures to the end will be saved. 14 And the Good News about the Kingdom will be preached throughout the whole world, so that all nations will hear it; and then the end will come.   Matthew 24:12–14

New Spiritualists Cannot Create a Utopian Universe. People who hold the new spirituality worldview believe that the universe has been going through cycles of rebirth for millions of years. However, the biblical Christian worldview declares that at the end of this present age of history, God will create a new heavens and a new earth that will last for all eternity. The new heavens and new earth that God will create will not be the utopian world new spiritualists dream about creating. It will be a perfect world, that will be God's eternal kingdom where all God's children will live eternally in their new resurrection bodies.

John wrote down the vision he received from God of the new heaven and new earth in the last book of the Bible, the book of Revelation.

[1] Then I saw a new heaven and a new earth, for the old heaven and the old earth had disappeared. And the sea was also gone. [2] And I saw the holy city, the new Jerusalem, coming down from God out of heaven like a bride beautifully dressed for her husband.

[3] I heard a loud shout from the throne, saying, "Look, God's home is now among his people! He will live with them, and they will be his people. God himself will be with them. [4] He will wipe every tear from their eyes, and there will be no more death or sorrow or crying or pain. All these things are gone forever."

[5] And the one sitting on the throne said, "Look, I am making everything new!" And then he said to me, "Write this down, for what I tell you is trustworthy and true." Revelation 21:1–5

ENDNOTES
1 Gary Zukav, *The Seat of the Soul* (New York: Simon and Schuster), 85–86.
2 Shirley MacLaine, *Dancing in the Light* (New York: Bantam), 353–359.

The New Spirituality View of Moral Laws and Values

Getting Started—Do Good and Evil Really Exist?

Good or Evil? On September 11, 2001, Islamic terrorists hijacked two commercial airplanes and flew them into the World Trade Center towers in New York City. On the same day, other terrorists took over a third passenger plane and crashed it into the Pentagon in Washington, DC. A fourth hijacked plane was meant to strike either the US Capitol building or the White House, but it crashed in Pennsylvania before reaching its target. On that September day, almost 3,000 Americans lost their lives.

Now think for just a moment. What words would you use to describe this day in American history?

THE WORLD TRADE CENTER TOWERS IMMEDIATELY AFTER TERRORIST ATTACK SEPTEMBER 11, 2001

THE RUINS OF THE SOUTH TOWER WORLD TRADE CENTER

You and your classmates very likely described the September 11th attacks on America with words like *terrible, horrible, sad, cruel, unbelievable, bad, tragic,* and *evil*. Certainly no one described the events of that day with words like *wonderful, happy, good,* or *kind*. But why? Why do people choose negative words and not positive words to describe that day? It is because of the moral awareness that God placed in the heart of each of his image-bearers. This awareness tells us that certain acts are wrong or evil, and others are right or good. Even people who do not believe in God agree that the acts committed on that day were wrong. To take the lives of thousands of innocent people as they worked and traveled was unquestionably an evil act.

Would it surprise you to learn, however, that not all people believed the attacks of September 11th were evil? We are not talking about the men who carried out the attacks. They believed their actions were good because they were carrying out a holy war, or *jihad*, in the name of Allah. But other people did not believe the attacks were evil because those people claim there is no difference between good and evil. To them, the attacks of September 11th were neither moral nor immoral. As unbelievable as this may sound, the new spirituality worldview includes such beliefs. In this lesson, we'll explore the answer to this question and others related to the new spirituality view of moral laws and values. As always, we'll compare and contrast the new spirituality view with God's Word and the biblical Christian worldview.

Topic 1—Why New Spiritualists Deny the Existence of Good and Evil

Before you can possibly understand how new spiritualists can deny the existence of good and evil and the difference between them, you must remember what they believe is true about God, people, and the universe.

As you learned earlier, new spiritualists believe God is an impersonal energy or "god force" that fills the entire universe and beyond. Not only is god a force that *fills* the universe, but everything that exists is god—including people, plants, animals, and nonliving things. In other words, according to the new spirituality worldview, everything is god and god is everything. Everything that exists is part of and equal to the one universal god force. They believe everything is interconnected in the universe and there is no difference between anything or anyone. Everything is the same.

MARILYN FERGUSON
NEW SPIRITUALITY AUTHOR

New spirituality author Marilyn Ferguson explains how new spiritualists understand the unity of all things. She says that because everything is united as part of the one universal god force, things that we believe are different or opposite from each other are actually not. Rather, everything is one with and the same as everything else. For this reason, she believes, " . . . there is neither good nor evil."[1] In other words, she would say that the September 11th attacks on America were neither good nor evil. They were just attacks.

New spirituality author David Spangler also believes there is no difference between any one thing that exists or happens and another. He believes, for example, that "Christ is the same force as Lucifer [Satan]."[2] For Spangler and other new spiritualists there is no difference between kindness and cruelty, right and wrong, or good and evil.

DAVID SPANGLER
NEW SPIRITUALITY AUTHOR

Some new spiritualists believe that when people understand that they are one with the god force, nothing they do can be considered good or evil. If people are one with everything and everything is one, then there can be no differences among them. You and the god force are the same. Right and wrong are the same. You and God and right and wrong are all the same. This means that it would not be wrong for you to rob a bank. But, of course, it wouldn't be right either. It would just be robbing a bank. Some new spiritualists even go so far as to believe that if someone robs you, it shouldn't matter at all. Why should it matter? You, the robber, and good and evil are one and the same with the god force. There is no difference. If there is no difference, then no wrong has been committed. And so, if no wrong has been committed, then the robbery shouldn't matter.

Does all of this sound confusing and perhaps crazy? If it doesn't, it should—because this kind of thinking does not line up with reality. As you will explore in Topic 2, new spiritualists do know right and wrong exist even if their worldview says there is no difference between them.

THE YIN-YANG SYMBOL REPRESENTS
THE NEW SPIRITUALIST BELIEF THAT
EVERYTHING IS ONE—THERE IS A
LITTLE LIGHT IN DARKNESS AND A
LITTLE DARKNESS IN LIGHT.

The Reality of Evil in the World: While new spiritualists may say they believe there is no difference between good and evil, do you think they actually live their daily lives as if there were no difference? Is it realistic to do so? Why or why not? Think about how a new spiritualist might respond to the following situation:

Suppose someone breaks into a new spiritualist's house and begins attacking his family. How do you think he would react? Would he just smile and allow the attack to continue, or do you think he would try to stop it?

Probably, he would try to protect his family. But why? He would do so because, deep inside, he knows there is a difference between good and evil and he doesn't want harm to come to his family. The moral awareness God placed within him shouts out that what is happening is evil and must be stopped. New spiritualists face situations every day that show them there is a definite difference between good and evil. When evil is happening to someone else, they might be able to ignore it and say there is no such thing as evil. But when it happens to them personally, or to someone they know and love, it is difficult, if not impossible, for them to continue denying that evil exists.

New Spirituality Contradictions: Let's test your ability to find an inconsistency in what new spiritualists *say* they believe and what they *actually* believe. In Lesson 12, you read about new spirituality Hollywood actress Shirley MacLaine, who believes that she has lived many reincarnated lives. In one of her books, entitled *Dancing in the Light*, she makes this comment about good and evil: "Until mankind realizes there is, in truth, no good and there is, in truth, no evil—there will be no peace."[3] She means that as long as people believe that good and evil exist as two separate things, people will not have peace within themselves or with others. But in another of her books titled *Out on a Limb*, MacLaine writes these words: "For every act, for every indifference, for every misuse of life, we are finally held accountable."[4] She means that if people are indifferent (fail to do good when there is a need) and misuse their lives (use their lives for evil instead of good), they will be held accountable for these actions in their next life.

SHIRLEY MACLAINE, ACTRESS

Now, let's examine these two statements. Do you see any contradiction between them? In *Dancing in the Light*, Ms. MacLaine says good and evil do not exist. In *Out on a Limb*, she says that acts of indifference do exist, and they are wrong. She also says that people can misuse their lives, and this is also wrong. But if good and evil do not exist, then indifference and misuse of a life cannot be wrong. But neither can they be right. Of

course, MacLaine does believe indifference and misuse of life are evil and not good. She plainly says people will be held accountable for these wrongs in their next life. So, do you see the contradiction and the inconsistency in her beliefs?

Let's look at another inconsistency. New spiritualists call the total of good and bad actions in a person's life karma. They believe a person's karma results in good or bad consequences for him or her, either in this life or in a reincarnated life. For example, if a person treats others cruelly or even murders someone, new spiritualists believe he or she accumulates bad karma. As a consequence, this person might be treated cruelly by others or murdered either in this life or after a reincarnation. New spiritualists believe reincarnation allows people to learn from their mistakes in one life and hopefully become better people in their next life. New spiritualists believe that the cycles of reincarnation will end only when people realize that they are god and that god is everything that exists.

If new spiritualists believe there is no difference between good and evil, how can they believe in karma? If karma is true and really happens as they say, then the behavior choices people make must be either good or bad. Not only that, but how does karma decide if what a person does is good or evil?

The truth is that most new spiritualists cannot and do not live their lives as if good and evil do not exist. They know in their hearts that good and evil do exist, and every day they make moral judgments about different actions. Neither they nor Shirley MacLaine can make the real world of good and evil go away.

> **Karma**
> The total of a person's good and bad actions
> that results in good or bad consequences in
> this life or in a reincarnated life

Topic 3—How New Spiritualists Determine Right and Wrong

"What Feels Right for You?" Even though most new spiritualists believe there is no difference between good and evil or right and wrong, they must still make the right kinds of choices to receive good karma. If they make bad choices, they will receive bad karma. So how do you think new spiritualists determine what is right and what is wrong? Do they look in the Bible to see what God says? Do they look in the Quran or in books written by religious leaders? The answer to these questions is a resounding no!

New spiritualists believe that they themselves are god. This means that there is no higher authority in their lives than themselves. They believe that people must look within themselves to find out what is true. And remember that what one person believes is true for herself doesn't have to agree with what another person believes is true for himself. One person's truth is not necessarily another person's truth! To a new spiritualist, truth is always local (just for some people in some locations at certain times) rather than universal. It is always subjective rather than objective. And it is always relative rather than absolute. In the same way, new spiritualists look within themselves to determine what is right or wrong, good or evil, just or unjust, and kind or cruel.

New spiritualists believe that no one should be controlled by another person's beliefs about truth or moral values. They believe that when this happens people are no longer free to get in touch with their inner godhood. And if people can't contact their inner higher consciousness or godhood, then they'll continue going through cycles of reincarnation. As long as people let others "set the rules" about moral values, the birth of the new spirituality utopia will be delayed. New spirituality author Shakti Gawain believes that when we let others set the rules for us "we give our personal power away."[5] And without our personal power, we'll never realize that we are God.

Just as new spiritualists believe that people have the right to create their own moral values, they also believe people can change their values. As people change and grow, what once felt wrong may no longer feel wrong. When this happens, new spiritualists believe people are as free to change their moral values as they are to change their clothes each day. A professor who is a new spiritualist put it this way, "I always tell my students [to] go where your body and soul want to go. When you have the feeling, then stay with it, and don't let anyone throw you off."[6] New spiritualists believe that having freedom to follow their changing feelings about truth and values will help them finally reach a state of higher consciousness and oneness with the universal god force.

No Right or Wrong: As you can see, the new spirituality view of moral values is full of contradictions. New spiritualists claim that because all is one, there is no difference between right and wrong. But most of them would admit that some things really are right and some things really are wrong. Remember that Shirley MacLaine says that being indifferent to others or misusing your life are wrong.

New spiritualists believe that people must look inside themselves to decide what is right and what is wrong for them. Yet almost all new spiritualists say that it is wrong to judge other people's moral beliefs and actions. So, if I decide it is right to judge someone else's moral beliefs and values, how can someone else tell me it is wrong? I've discovered my own moral values, and according to the new spirituality worldview, this is what each person must do.

You are probably beginning to see that new spirituality thinking about truth and moral values goes around and around in circles. Eventually the real differences between right and wrong, good and evil, justice and injustice, and kindness and cruelty become very blurred. Nothing is really right, and nothing is really wrong. Nevertheless, new spiritualists continually declare that some things are good and some things are evil. But this kind of declaration is useless. If people are supposed to find truth and values within themselves, then who can really say what's good and what's evil? And how does karma know the difference, especially since karma is not a person who can make decisions?

Topic 4—The Biblical Christian View of Moral Laws and Values

Moral Laws and Values Come from God, Not People. The biblical Christian worldview declares that our moral awareness does not come from within ourselves, as new spiritualists believe. Rather, it comes from God, the perfect moral Being, who blesses us with moral awareness in two primary ways. First, he reveals his moral laws in the hearts of all people, so that no one has an excuse for not understanding right from wrong. Paul wrote about this truth in a letter to the early church in Rome.

[People] demonstrate that God's law is written in their hearts, for their own conscience and thoughts either accuse them or tell them they are doing right.   Romans 2:15

Second, God revealed his moral laws through his written Word, the Bible. Again, Paul explained this truth in his second letter to Timothy.

¹⁶ All Scripture is inspired by God and is useful to teach us what is true and to make us realize what is wrong in our lives. It corrects us when we are wrong and teaches us to do what is right. ¹⁷ God uses it to prepare and equip his people to do every good work.

2 Timothy 3:16–17

Not only do moral laws come from God rather than from people, they are also always based on God's perfect and absolutely holy character, not on the sinful and changing character of human beings. John wrote about God's holiness in the book of Revelation.

"Who will not fear you, Lord, and glorify your name? For you alone are holy." Revelation 15:4

Because God is holy and perfect, his laws are also holy and perfect. It is impossible for a holy God to make any law that is not perfect and good in every way. Moses wrote about the perfection of God's works and ways in the book of Deuteronomy.

He is the Rock; his deeds are perfect.
Everything he does is just and fair.
He is a faithful God who does no wrong;
how just and upright he is! Deuteronomy 32:4

God's Moral Laws Are Objective, Absolute, and Universal. When we say that God's moral laws are objective, we mean that they are real and that they exist apart from or independently of us. Regardless of whether we or any new spiritualist thinks they exist or not, they still exist. We play no role in creating God's laws. He did not consult us to ask what kinds of laws we prefer. God did not ask us whether we approve of the laws he made. In fact, his laws are eternal, existing long before people were even created. If we or others deny that God's laws exist, the truth that they do exist does not change. God made this truth clear to Moses when he gave the Ten Commandments.

And the LORD said to Moses, "Say this to the people of Israel: You saw for yourselves that I spoke to you from heaven." Exodus 20:22

"These are the regulations you must present to Israel." Exodus 21:1

¹⁵ Then Moses turned and went down the mountain. He held in his hands the two stone tablets inscribed with the terms of the covenant. They were inscribed on both sides, front and back. ¹⁶ These tablets were God's work; the words on them were written by God himself.

Exodus 32:15–16

In contrast to human laws that are often imperfect and changeable, God's moral laws are absolute. This means they are absolutely perfect in every way, and they never change. They are not true one day and untrue the next. We do not have the right, as new spiritualists believe, to change moral laws and values just like we change our clothes. When we say that God's moral laws are absolute, we mean that they are true for all times and for all situations. Murdering someone or taking someone else's money is not wrong one day or in one situation and right another day or in another situation.

Saying that God's moral laws are absolute also means that some things are absolutely right, and some things are absolutely wrong. Right and wrong and good and evil are not, as new spiritualists believe, one and the same thing. They are also not part of the same universal god force as everything else is in the new spirituality worldview. God used the prophet Isaiah to warn people against the foolishness of saying that good is evil and evil is good.

[20] What sorrow for those who say that evil is good and good is evil,
    that dark is light and light is dark,
    that bitter is sweet and sweet is bitter.
[21] What sorrow for those who are wise in their own eyes
    and think themselves so clever.

Isaiah 5:20–21

The writer of the book of Hebrews describes mature Christians as people who through training have the skill to recognize the difference between right and wrong (Hebrews 5:14).

Finally, in stark contrast to the new spirituality view that right and wrong is determined by what feels right to each individual, the Bible declares that God's moral laws are universal. They apply to everyone, wherever and whenever they live on the earth. Lying is just as wrong for someone who lives on the island of Tahiti as it is for someone who lives in Iceland.

In his letter to the Christians in Rome, Paul made it very clear that God's moral laws are universal. All people in every nation and at all times know God's laws are universal because they demonstrate that God's law is written in their hearts, for their own conscience and thoughts either accuse them or tell them they are doing right (Romans 2:15).

God's Word clearly warns those who trust in their own ideas of what is morally right and wrong.

There is a path before each person that seems right,
    but it ends in death.

Proverbs 14:12

Likewise, God lovingly tells his image-bearers that there is a way that leads to life and freedom. As you have learned in the lessons of Walking in Truth, only God's Word can lead us from confusion to truth that gives us life and sets us free from sin and death. God's truth also sets us free from the false "truths" of all the unbiblical worldviews you have studied this year, including Islam, naturalism, and most recently, the new spirituality worldview.

Hide these words of Jesus in your heart because they are true words that lead to life and freedom.

[31] Jesus said to the people who believed in him, "You are truly my disciples if you remain faithful to my teachings. [32] And you will know the truth, and the truth will set you free."

John 8:31–32

ENDNOTES

1 Marilyn Ferguson, *The Aquarian Conspiracy* (Los Angeles: J. P. Tarcher, 1980), 381.
2 David Spangler, *Reflections of the Christ* (Forres, Scotland: Findhorn, 1977), 40–44.
3 Shirley MacLaine, *Dancing in the Light* (New York: Bantam, 1985), 341–342.
4 Shirley MacLaine, *Out on a Limb* (New York: Bantam, 1984), 96, 111.
5 Shakti Gawain, *Living in the Light* (San Rafael, CA: New World Library, 1986), 37.
6 Mark Satin, *New Age Politics* (New York: Dell Publishing, 1978), 103.

Unit 5
Bible Survey

Getting Started—The Main Ideas

Paul's letter to the Romans is the longest letter in the New Testament. Paul began the letter by telling the Christians in Rome how much he longed to meet them because he had heard about their congregation, but he didn't know them personally. Paul wanted to visit them and encourage their faith as they encouraged his.

The book of Romans contains the basic teachings of Christianity. Paul first proclaimed the good news of the power of salvation to set believers free from sin and into a restored relationship with God. Paul commended the believers for their changed hearts, but he also reminded them that a changed heart must result in a changed life. Christians, both Gentiles and Jews, cannot continue to willfully sin against God and think they will escape his righteous judgment.

The doctrines concerning sin and righteousness outlined by Paul in his letter to the Romans are the foundations of the biblical Christian worldview. Muslims, naturalists, and new spiritualists also have views about right and wrong behavior, although these views may be deeply personal and not the same for all followers of each faith.

Topic 1—God's Good News

Introduction: The book of Romans is more accurately titled *Paul's Epistle to the Romans* because the book is really a letter, or an *epistle*. The apostle Paul wrote this letter while staying with a fellow believer, Gaius, who lived in Corinth. Paul addressed the letter to the church in Rome—a congregation made up of both Jewish converts to Christianity and Gentile believers. Bible scholars believe that Paul wrote the epistle during his third missionary journey at the time he stayed in Corinth (Acts 20:2–3). This would place the date of the letter at about AD 55–56. Phoebe, a woman who lived in Cenchrea, near Corinth, probably took the letter to Rome. The letter was then circulated among the churches and copied by hand. The picture to the right is an early copy of Romans 1:1–16 in the original Greek.

ROMANS 1:1–16 ON PAPYRUS

Part 1—Introduction to Romans

The church in Rome was made up of both Jewish converts to Christianity and Gentile believers. It probably included many slaves. (A third of Rome's population was enslaved.) So Paul began his letter by identifying himself as *a slave*, or *servant*, of Christ Jesus and an apostle sent to preach the good news.

Paul added that he was writing to all in Rome who are loved by God and are called to be his own holy people (Romans 1:7). This designation was a wonderful reminder to a church made up of Jewish and Gentile believers, free and slave, rich and poor, and citizens and foreigners. Paul began to teach both Paul began to teach both Jews and Gentiles the essential doctrines of the Christian faith, those teachings that are important for believers to learn in order to live as God's holy people. The word *doctrine* comes from the Latin *doctrina*, which means *teaching*.

> **Doctrines**
> The principle teachings or system of beliefs of a religious faith

Part 2—A Letter from Paul

In addition to greeting the Roman church, Paul stated that Jesus' coming to Earth was foretold by the prophets. As a descendant of David, Jesus was truly human. Yet Jesus rose from the dead, showing himself to be truly God the Son. A major theme of the book of Romans is the power of salvation through faith in Christ's resurrection. Through Christ, Paul and the other apostles were granted authority to reach the Gentiles with the good news of salvation so that God would be glorified.

[1] This letter is from Paul, a slave of Christ Jesus, chosen by God to be an apostle and sent out to preach his Good News. [2] God promised this Good News long ago through his prophets in the holy Scriptures. [3] The Good News is about his Son. In his earthly life he was born into King David's family line, [4] and he was shown to be the Son of God when he was raised from the dead by the power of the Holy Spirit. He is Jesus Christ our Lord. [5] Through Christ, God has given us the privilege and authority as apostles to tell Gentiles everywhere what God has done for them, so that they will believe and obey him, bringing glory to his name.

[6] And you are included among those Gentiles who have been called to belong to Jesus Christ. [7] I am writing to all of you in Rome who are loved by God and are called to be his own holy people. May God our Father and the Lord Jesus Christ give you grace and peace.

Romans 1:1–7

Topic 2—God's Power for Salvation

Introduction: The Greek word Paul used for salvation (*soteria*) is the noun form of a verb meaning *to rescue, deliver*, or *set free*. Paul explained to the Roman church that not only are they saved *from* something, but they are also saved *to do* something. Paul wrote that not only have the Roman Christians been set free, or delivered, from eternal separation from God, but they had also been called to belong to Christ and to obey him, bringing glory to his name.

The Greek word for *power*—when discussing God's salvation power—is *dunamis*. (This is the same word from which the English words *dynamic*, *dynamo*, and *dynamite* come from.) God's power to save changes lives, yet it is important to remember that this power is God's; it is not under human control. The good news that Paul proclaimed to the Romans begins with the fact that no one is able to save himself or herself. It is as if a drowning person calls out for help, saying, "Somebody help me!" And God says, "I will help you." The good news proclaims that Jesus did what human beings could never do. Salvation is both rescue and restoration; believers are delivered from sin and restored to harmony with God, within themselves, with others, and with creation.

Paul wanted not only to remind the Roman Christians of their salvation and restoration but also to strengthen their faith and to impart a spiritual gift. The love and respect that Paul had for the believers is evident throughout the letter. Though he desired to see them personally and to help them grow spiritually, he had been prevented from visiting them so far.

Paul emphasized that he was not ashamed of the gospel, the good news. The word *ashamed* comes from two Greek words. The first word (*epi*) acts to make the second word stronger. The second word (*aischunomai*), means *to be humiliated*. When Paul said he was not ashamed of the good news, he meant he was not humiliated. He was not embarrassed by the message he boldly proclaimed.

8 Let me say first that I thank my God through Jesus Christ for all of you, because your faith in him is being talked about all over the world. 9 God knows how often I pray for you. Day and night I bring you and your needs in prayer to God, whom I serve with all my heart by spreading the Good News about his Son.

10 One of the things I always pray for is the opportunity, God willing, to come at last to see you. 11 For I long to visit you so I can bring you some spiritual gift that will help you grow strong in the Lord. 12 When we get together, I want to encourage you in your faith, but I also want to be encouraged by yours.

13 I want you to know, dear brothers and sisters, that I planned many times to visit you, but I was prevented until now. I want to work among you and see spiritual fruit, just as I have seen among other Gentiles. 14 For I have a great sense of obligation to people in both the civilized world and the rest of the world, to the educated and uneducated alike. 15 So I am eager to come to you in Rome, too, to preach the Good News.

16 For I am not ashamed of this Good News about Christ. It is the power of God at work, saving everyone who believes—the Jew first and also the Gentile. 17 This Good News tells us how God makes us right in his sight. This is accomplished from start to finish by faith. As the Scriptures say, "It is through faith that a righteous person has life."

Romans 1:8–17

Topic 3—God's Anger at Sin

Introduction: The Roman Christians lived in the capital of the most influential culture of the time. The empire gave them many advantages that previous cultures did not have, including rights for citizens. However, it was also a culture that practiced slavery, idolatry, and all kinds of evil. Divorce was common, and fathers had the right to put their children to death for any reason they wished. The sad truth is that people in the first century suppressed the truth of their own sinful nature. Instead of crying out to God for rescue, they denied that they were drowning in sin. From the time of Adam and Eve, to today, sinful human beings do not want God in their business. They will do anything to get away from God. If they even acknowledge God's existence, they say, "Get lost, God. I can live my own way and rely on myself." They want nothing to do with God's law or knowledge of him. Everyone on Earth is guilty of sin.

Some versions of the Bible call this irreverent attitude toward God *unrighteousness*. Sin always begins with an unrighteous or ungodly attitude. God's anger, or wrath, is revealed from heaven toward all unrighteousness— both sinful deeds and sinful attitudes. Even people who have never heard of God are guilty and subject to God's wrath, because God reveals himself through the natural world and through all human beings' innate understanding of right and wrong. This is called general revelation.

[18] But God shows his anger from heaven against all sinful, wicked people who suppress the truth by their wickedness. [19] They know the truth about God because he has made it obvious to them. [20] For ever since the world was created, people have seen the earth and sky. Through everything God made, they can clearly see his invisible qualities—his eternal power and divine nature. So they have no excuse for not knowing God.

[21] Yes, they knew God, but they wouldn't worship him as God or even give him thanks. And they began to think up foolish ideas of what God was like. As a result, their minds became dark and confused. [22] Claiming to be wise, they instead became utter fools. [23] And instead of worshiping the glorious, ever-living God, they worshiped idols made to look like mere people and birds and animals and reptiles.   Romans 1:18–23

The people Paul described thought it was a good idea to abandon God. However, Paul argued that this was not a very good idea at all, and it had bad consequences.

General Revelation
The knowledge of God through
creation and through our conscience

[28] Since they thought it foolish to acknowledge God, he abandoned them to their foolish thinking and let them do things that should never be done. [29] Their lives became full of every kind of wickedness, sin, greed, hate, envy, murder, quarreling, deception, malicious behavior, and gossip. [30] They are backstabbers, haters of God, insolent, proud, and boastful. They invent new ways of sinning, and they disobey their parents. [31] They refuse to understand, break their promises, are heartless, and have no mercy. [32] They know God's justice requires that those who do these things deserve to die, yet they do them anyway. Worse yet, they encourage others to do them, too.
                    Romans 1:28–32

This final passage in Romans 1 marks a very low point in the history of human beings. After reading it, no one would ever be tempted to yell, "Hooray for humankind!" Ever since the fall, all people have been born with a sinful nature. Not only do people continue to practice all sorts of sin, but they encourage others to do so too. Human beings constantly fail in doing what is right and good.

Topic 4—God's Judgment

Introduction: Many of the Roman Christians had been Gentiles who previously engaged in pagan practices (Romans 1:5–6). But Paul told the Roman Christians who had a Jewish background that they were guilty of many of the same sins. Jewish believers felt that because they had the Law and were circumcised, they would escape God's judgment and wrath for their evil deeds. Paul's assertion that it is impossible to sin and still maintain a relationship of harmony with God must have shaken their faulty beliefs. Christians today cannot continue in willful disobedience to God and expect to escape his judgment.

Part 1—Sin's Consequences

[1] You may think you can condemn such people, but you are just as bad, and you have no excuse! When you say they are wicked and should be punished, you are condemning yourself, for you who judge others do these very same things. [2] And we know that God, in his justice, will punish anyone who does such things. [3] Since you judge others for doing these things, why do you think you can avoid God's judgment when you do the same things? [4] Don't you see how wonderfully kind, tolerant, and patient God is with you? Does this mean nothing to you? Can't you see that his kindness is intended to turn you from your sin?

[5] But because you are stubborn and refuse to turn from your sin, you are storing up terrible punishment for yourself. For a day of anger is coming, when God's righteous judgment will be revealed. [6] He will judge everyone according to what they have done. [7] He will give eternal life to those who keep on doing good, seeking after the glory and honor and immortality that God offers. [8] But he will pour out his anger and wrath on those who live for themselves, who refuse to obey the truth and instead live lives of wickedness. [9] There will be trouble and calamity for everyone who keeps on doing what is evil—for the Jew first and also for the Gentile. [10] But there will be glory and honor and peace from God for all who do good—for the Jew first and also for the Gentile. [11] For God does not show favoritism.   Romans 2:1–11

Paul made it clear that God's judgment falls on all those who live self-centered, wicked lives. Gentiles, who do not have the written Law, are judged according to their good or evil thoughts and and actions. Do they respect their parents? Do they steal, murder, bear false witness, or covet what belongs to others? Even though Gentiles might not know the Law, they are judged by their obedience to its principles. The law's principles were written on their hearts, and their consciences either approve or condemn them. Jews who do have the written Law are judged according to their obedience to it.

[12] When the Gentiles sin, they will be destroyed, even though they never had God's written law. And the Jews, who do have God's law, will be judged by that law when they fail to obey it. [13] For merely

listening to the law doesn't make us right with God. It is obeying the law that makes us right in his sight. [14] Even Gentiles, who do not have God's written law, show that they know his law when they instinctively obey it, even without having heard it. [15] They demonstrate that God's law is written in their hearts, for their own conscience and thoughts either accuse them or tell them they are doing right. [16] And this is the message I proclaim—that the day is coming when God, through Christ Jesus, will judge everyone's secret life.

Romans 2:12–16

Part 2—The Law and Sinners

Because God will judge all people without showing favoritism, Paul warned Jewish believers against hypocrisy. The Jews felt comfortable and secure, boasting in their superior knowledge of God's written law, his special revelation. And because the Jewish Christians had God's special revelation as well as the covenant of circumcision, they felt it unnecessary to turn from their sinful attitudes. They were, after all, God's chosen people! But Paul stripped away their boasting and revealed them to be just as sinful as the Gentiles. He encouraged the Jewish believers to be "true Jews," those with hearts that are right toward God through the indwelling of the Holy Spirit.

> **Special Revelation**
> The unique knowledge of God through
> the Scriptures and through Jesus Christ

[17] You who call yourselves Jews are relying on God's law, and you boast about your special relationship with him. [18] You know what he wants; you know what is right because you have been taught his law. [19] You are convinced that you are a guide for the blind and a light for people who are lost in darkness. [20] You think you can instruct the ignorant and teach children the ways of God. For you are certain that God's law gives you complete knowledge and truth.

[21] Well then, if you teach others, why don't you teach yourself? You tell others not to steal, but do you steal? [22] You say it is wrong to commit adultery, but do you commit adultery? You condemn idolatry, but do you use items stolen from pagan temples? [23] You are so proud of knowing the law, but you dishonor God by breaking it. [24] No wonder the Scriptures say, "The Gentiles blaspheme the name of God because of you."

[25] The Jewish ceremony of circumcision has value only if you obey God's law. But if you don't obey God's law, you are no better off than an uncircumcised Gentile. [26] And if the Gentiles obey God's law, won't God declare them to be his own people? [27] In fact, uncircumcised Gentiles who keep God's law will condemn you Jews who are circumcised and possess God's law but don't obey it.

[28] For you are not a true Jew just because you were born of Jewish parents or because you have gone through the ceremony of circumcision. [29] No, a true Jew is one whose heart is right with God. And true circumcision

is not merely obeying the letter of the law; rather, it is a change of heart produced by the Spirit. And a person with a changed heart seeks praise from God, not from people.

Romans 2:17–29

Topic 5—God's Faithfulness

Introduction: Have you ever heard a foolish question such as "Could God make a rock so heavy that he couldn't lift it?" or "How many angels can dance on the head of a pin?" Questions like these have no answers and really don't make sense. One foolish thought some of the Roman believers may have held was that their sinfulness was actually a good thing, because it provided a contrast to God's nature, showing him to be righteous. If sinfulness was actually a good thing, then God would have been wrong to punish them for their sins. Paul showed them the foolishness of this type of thinking.

Part 1—God Is Fair

¹ Then what's the advantage of being a Jew? Is there any value in the ceremony of circumcision? ² Yes, there are great benefits! First of all, the Jews were entrusted with the whole revelation of God.

³ True, some of them were unfaithful; but just because they were unfaithful, does that mean God will be unfaithful? ⁴ Of course not! Even if everyone else is a liar, God is true. As the Scriptures say about him,

"You will be proved right in what you say,
  and you will win your case in court."

⁵ "But," some might say, "our sinfulness serves a good purpose, for it helps people see how righteous God is. Isn't it unfair, then, for him to punish us?" (This is merely a human point of view.) ⁶ Of course not! If God were not entirely fair, how would he be qualified to judge the world? ⁷ "But," someone might still argue, "how can God condemn me as a sinner if my dishonesty highlights his truthfulness and brings him more glory?" ⁸ And some people even slander us by claiming that we say, "The more we sin, the better it is!" Those who say such things deserve to be condemned.

Romans 3:1–8

Notice that Paul anticipated the Jewish believers' questions about the value of Jewish traditions, especially circumcision. When Jesus was asked about keeping the Law, he said, "Don't misunderstand why I have come. I did not come to abolish the law of Moses or the writings of the prophets. No, I came to accomplish their purpose" (Matthew 5:17). Both Jesus and Paul upheld the value of the Law as an absolute standard (a perfect measure) to show people how sinful they are. The argument that sin is actually a good thing, because it gives God a chance to show how good he is, is completely ridiculous!

Part 2—No One Is Righteous

After condemning both Gentiles and Jews, Paul went on to address the question of who is righteous (morally perfect) before God. Righteousness would have been understood by the Gentiles as living a decent life. The Jewish believers would have defined righteousness as right standing before God fulfilled by keeping the Law. Both Gentiles and Jews saw righteousness as the ticket to eternal life.

Jesus was asked about eternal life by a rich young man. In Mark 10, this young man asked Jesus what he needed to do to inherit eternal life. The youth knew that righteousness came through obedience to the Law because he bragged that he had followed the commandments all his life. However, he flinched when Jesus told him that he lacked one thing—he needed to sell his possessions and give the money to the poor. Jesus

wasn't adding the requirement of monetary poverty to be righteous with God; he was pointing out the young man's breaking of the second greatest commandment of the Law—to love one's neighbor as oneself. Paul reminded the Roman Christians, both Jews and Gentiles, that no one can attain righteousness through one's own efforts.

> **Righteousness**
> The state of moral perfection required by God

9 Well then, should we conclude that we Jews are better than others? No, not at all, for we have already shown that all people, whether Jews or Gentiles, are under the power of sin. 10 As the Scriptures say,

"No one is righteous—
  not even one.
11 No one is truly wise;
  no one is seeking God.
12 All have turned away;
  all have become useless.
No one does good,
  not a single one."
13 "Their talk is foul, like the stench from an open grave.
  Their tongues are filled with lies."
"Snake venom drips from their lips."
14 "Their mouths are full of cursing and bitterness."
15 "They rush to commit murder.
16 Destruction and misery always follow them.
17 They don't know where to find peace."
18 "They have no fear of God at all."

19 Obviously, the law applies to those to whom it was given, for its purpose is to keep people from having excuses, and to show that the entire world is guilty before God. 20 For no one can ever be made right with God by doing what the law commands. The law simply shows us how sinful we are.   Romans 3:9–20

Topic 6—Comparing Views about Sin

Introduction: The doctrines of sin and righteousness outlined by Paul in the early chapters of Romans represent the Christian worldview regarding sin. Other worldviews also have beliefs about sin or unrighteous behavior. The apostles Paul and Peter instructed Christians to speak to non-Christians on the topic of sin (or any other topic) with the love of Christ—never belligerently or defensively. Recall that Muslims believe there is one true God. But their understanding of the one and only true God of biblical Christianity is incomplete, as are their views on sin. When discussing sin with a person of a different faith, remember Paul's advice to live wisely among those who are not believers, and make the most of every opportunity. Let your conversation be gracious and attractive so that you will have the right response for everyone (Colossians 4:5–6).

Part 1—The Islamic View of Sin

Recall that the Allah of Islam is not the God of the Bible. Although the existence of evil, individual accountability, and judgment for sin are included within Islamic teaching, its idea of sin is different from the biblical Christian worldview that says sin is sin, regardless of whether it is small or great by human standards. Paul states in Romans 3:23 that all people are guilty of sin.

Muslims agree that people are sinful. The Quran states that if Allah were to punish men for their wrongdoing, he would not leave any living creature on the earth (Quran 16:61). Yet Muslims believe that there are small sins that Allah may forgive, or overlook.

But if you avoid the great sins you have been forbidden, We shall wipe out your minor misdeeds and let you in through the entrance of honour. — Quran 4:31

Muslims do not see the fall in the same way as Christians see it. The fall did not result in a death sentence for all human beings; it was merely a mistake. Death is not a punishment for sin, but it is simply a natural process. Adam was created as God's *kalifa* (vicegerent) on Earth, yet he was not created in God's image, and neither was Eve. Satan deceived Adam and Eve into eating forbidden fruit; but this act of blatant disobedience did not separate them from God. When Adam and Eve repented, Allah accepted their repentance because he is a merciful and forgiving God (Quran 2:37). People became sinful because they learned to sin from those around them. Sin, according to the Muslim worldview, involves only actions. If a Muslim has a sinful thought, but does not act on it, it is not considered a sin.

Below are some of the numerous sins that many Muslim scholars agree are major sins:

1. *shirk* (idolatry; worshipping other gods instead of or in addition to Allah)
2. magic
3. murder (killing those who oppose Islam in jihad is not considered murder)
4. usury (lending money at unfair interest rates)
5. taking advantage of orphans
6. fleeing from a battle
7. false charges of adultery
8. disobedience to parents

Biblical Christianity asserts that sin is willful disobedience against God. Unlike Islam, Christianity teaches that people commit sins by their thoughts, not just their actions. Any sin, no matter how small, separates us from God. No amount of good deeds can fix this problem, because even our most righteous deeds are as filthy rags when compared with the absolute holiness of God (Isaiah 64:6). But Jesus, who was sinless, died and rose again to redeem us from our sins. Through faith in him we can have forgiveness and be made new to live eternally with him.

Part 2—The Naturalist View of Sin

The idea of God's judgment for sin after the death of an individual is foreign to the naturalist because he or she does not believe in an afterlife. Sin, therefore, does not result in eternal separation from God. Naturalists do not usually use the term *sin* because it is a religious term, and they do not believe in God or any religion.

They admit that some deeds are inherently "bad" because they hurt others, provoke revenge, or cause people to hold grudges. These deeds may also produce feelings of guilt and a desire to be forgiven. Selfish and destructive acts turn people against one another, resulting in the destruction of human relationships. Naturalists also say that some deeds are "bad" because they go against the norms, or laws, of society. Such deeds, or illegal acts, can result in judicial punishment.

Naturalists do not believe that God exists, which means there is no God that reinforces their "good" behavior or punishes their "bad" behavior. They rely on other people for correction as well as their own feelings. Since there is no God to make the rules, it is up to people to make the rules. Whether an action is good or bad is a matter of individual decision and one's own moral code or the laws of one's government. However, if people make the rules, then the rules can change at any time. They can also change from person to person or from country to country.

Contrary to the naturalist viewpoint, Christians believe that God has written his laws on human hearts and given every human being a conscience. The Holy Spirit convicts people of their sin. Christians believe that God, who knows everything, will judge all human beings justly—whether or not they recognize their sins or believe in Jesus (Romans 2:14–16).

Part 3—The New Spirituality View of Sin

Though followers of new spirituality do not believe people have a sinful nature, they do have various views about what is right and wrong, good and bad. Many new spiritualists believe there is neither good nor bad. Right and wrong are the same.

Many new spiritualists believe in reincarnation. They believe that individuals are required to go through numerous cycles of death and birth in which they continue their quest for godhood in other bodies. Cycles of reincarnation will end only when people realize that they are god and that god is everything that exists. Once people understand they are god, nothing they can do is good or evil. They and god are the same. New spiritualists also believe in karma—the total of a person's good and bad actions that results in good or bad consequences in this life or in a reincarnated life. Therefore, if someone has accumulated bad karma, it will affect him or her either in this life or a reincarnation. However, there is no deity to judge which actions are good or bad. So, who decides what actions are right and wrong? This is difficult for the new spiritualist to answer.

The new spirituality view of God, people, and karma is opposed to Christian teaching. For Christians, salvation does not depend on how hard you work to progress toward higher consciousness. No amount of meditation will make you divine. Biblical Christianity teaches that a person is cleansed from sin only through repentance and sincere faith in Jesus' sacrifice. As Paul put it when he greeted the Roman Christians:

[16] For I am not ashamed of this Good News about Christ. It is the power of God at work, saving everyone who believes. . . . [17] This Good News tells us how God makes us right in his sight. This is accomplished from start to finish by faith. As the Scriptures say, "It is through faith that a righteous person has life."   Romans 1:16–17

Getting Started—The Main Ideas

In the first two chapters of Romans, Paul discussed the sinfulness of all people, both Gentiles and Jews. He taught that God would judge people for their sin. In the next two chapters, Paul supported his argument by quoting the Hebrew Scriptures. He then stated that Christ took the punishment for our sins and that everyone who believes in him is made right before God. Using the patriarch Abraham's life as an example, Paul showed that God counted Abraham righteous because of his faith.

Paul's writing continued to develop the essential doctrines of the Christian faith. One concept that is key to understanding the teaching of Christianity is redemption—the act of delievering us from the penalty we deserve for our sin. The noun *redemption* is related to the verb *redeem*, which means *to regain possession of something through payment*. Christ died on the cross in order to redeem us from the judgment we deserve because of our sin. His death brings us back into a relationship of harmony with God. A second key concept is justification. That term is related to the words *just* and *justice*. God, who is just, declares that we are "not guilty" when we have faith in his Son, accepting Christ's sacrifice on our behalf. Therefore, justification is the state of being made righteous before God.

Redemption
The act of delivering us from the penalty we deserve for our sin

Justification
The state of being made righteous before God

Topic 1—Redemption through Christ

Introduction: In the first two chapters of his letter to the church in Rome, Paul described human sin and the need for redemption, or salvation. He showed that even though people are aware that God exists, they sin anyway. They do it on purpose, and they do it despite being aware of God's general revelation—what he has taught us about who he is, and what he is like, through nature and through our conscience.

The church in Rome was made up of both Jews and Gentiles. Everyone who heard Paul's letter read out loud agreed that sin is bad. They condemned the sins he listed: pride, disobedience, hate, worshipping all kinds of idols, and much more. But the Jews thought Paul was talking about other people, because the sins he listed included pagan practices like making idols. In the second chapter of his letter, however, Paul reminded the Jews that they had sinned, too, and that God would judge them just as he would judge the Gentiles.

Can you image how the people in Paul's audience felt about what he said? The Gentile believers might have felt singled out by the long list of sins that Paul described. The Jewish believers might have been feeling proud that they, as God's chosen people, at least had the Law (part of God's special revelation). But Paul reminded them that they were no better than the Gentiles in living according to God's will.

Faith Is the Key: Paul continued his letter to the believers in Rome by reminding them, both Jews and Gentiles, that redemption is through faith in Jesus Christ.

21 But now God has shown us a way to be made right with him without keeping the requirements of the law, as was promised in the writings of Moses and the prophets long ago. 22 We are made right with God by placing our faith in Jesus Christ. And this is true for everyone who believes, no matter who we are.

23 For everyone has sinned; we all fall short of God's glorious standard. 24 Yet God, in his grace, freely makes us right in his sight. He did this through Christ Jesus when he freed us from the penalty for our sins. 25 For God presented Jesus as the sacrifice for sin. People are made right with God when they believe that Jesus sacrificed his life, shedding his blood. This sacrifice shows that God was being fair when he held back and did not punish those who sinned in times past, 26 for he was looking ahead and including them in what he would do in this present time. God did this to demonstrate his righteousness, for he himself is fair and just, and he makes sinners right in his sight when they believe in Jesus.   Romans 3:21–26

Paul emphasized that God's plan to save everyone was fair. He continued:

27 Can we boast, then, that we have done anything to be accepted by God? No, because our acquittal is not based on obeying the law. It is based on faith. 28 So we are made right with God through faith and not by obeying the law.

29 After all, is God the God of the Jews only? Isn't he also the God of the Gentiles? Of course he is. 30 There is only one God, and he makes people right with himself only by faith, whether they are Jews or Gentiles. 31 Well then, if we emphasize faith, does this mean that we can forget about the law? Of course not! In fact, only when we have faith do we truly fulfill the law.   Romans 3:27–31

Having faith in Christ is a true shift in focus from what we do (follow rules) to what God does (grant us forgiveness and reconciliation with him). It doesn't cancel out the need to follow God's rules. When we put God's Law in its proper place (obedience out of love and respect for God), we glorify him.

Topic 2—Abraham's Faith

Introduction: Recall that Paul's audience was made up of both Jewish believers and Gentile converts who had been learning about the Law, the patriarchs, and the history of the Jewish nation. Jewish believers in Jesus studied the Scriptures that foretold the Messiah in order to understand what God had promised. Gentiles wanted to know more about who Jesus was, and this included learning about the culture and traditions he observed as he grew up. Therefore, Paul thought it was very important to explain how faith fit in with the history of Israel.

Paul started with Abraham, but he also mentioned David. Both Abraham and David were heroes to his listeners, and both were ancestors of the Lord Jesus Christ. Paul quoted the Scriptures so that his listeners could confirm that he was telling the truth and could even study for themselves what God had said.

Part 1—Justified by Faith

[1] Abraham was, humanly speaking, the founder of our Jewish nation. What did he discover about being made right with God? [2] If his good deeds had made him acceptable to God, he would have had something to boast about. But that was not God's way. [3] For the Scriptures tell us, "Abraham believed God, and God counted him as righteous because of his faith."

[4] When people work, their wages are not a gift, but something they have earned. [5] But people are counted as righteous, not because of their work, but because of their faith in God who forgives sinners. [6] David also spoke of this when he described the happiness of those who are declared righteous without working for it:

[7] "Oh, what joy for those
  whose disobedience is forgiven,
  whose sins are put out of sight.
[8] Yes, what joy for those
  whose record the LORD has cleared of sin."

Romans 4:1–8

Notice that Paul made it a point to say that salvation is not earned. It is a result of faith in God, who forgives sinners. Paul said as much on another occasion, when he was writing to the believers in Ephesus:

[8] God saved you by his grace when you believed. And you can't take credit for this; it is a gift from God. [9] Salvation is not a reward for the good things we have done, so none of us can boast about it.

Ephesians 2:8–9

Now you can imagine that some of Paul's listeners might have asked, "If faith was all that was needed, why was Abraham circumcised?" And it wasn't just Abraham who was circumcised, but also his son Ishmael and all the male servants (Genesis 17:23). So, Paul explained that Abraham's circumcision was an outward sign of an inward faith.

[9] Now, is this blessing [of salvation] only for the Jews, or is it also for uncircumcised Gentiles? Well, we have been saying that Abraham was counted as righteous by God because of his faith. [10] But how did this happen? Was he counted as righteous only after he was circumcised, or was it before he was circumcised? Clearly, God accepted Abraham before he was circumcised!

[11] Circumcision was a sign that Abraham already had faith and that God had already accepted him and declared him to be righteous—even before he was circumcised. So Abraham is the spiritual father of those who have faith but

have not been circumcised. They are counted as righteous because of their faith. ¹² And Abraham is also the spiritual father of those who have been circumcised, but only if they have the same kind of faith Abraham had before he was circumcised.

Romans 4:9–12

Part 2—God's Promise to Abraham

Paul continued explaining how important faith is for salvation. He discussed how faith relates to the promises that God made to Abraham long ago, so that both Jewish and Gentile believers might understand the value of believing God's promises. He wanted them to see that faith is essential to a right relationship with God.

¹³ Clearly, God's promise to give the whole earth to Abraham and his descendants was based not on his obedience to God's law, but on a right relationship with God that comes by faith. ¹⁴ If God's promise is only for those who obey the law, then faith is not necessary and the promise is pointless. ¹⁵ For the law always brings punishment on those who try to obey it. (The only way to avoid breaking the law is to have no law to break!)

¹⁶ So the promise is received by faith. It is given as a free gift. And we are all certain to receive it, whether or not we live according to the law of Moses, if we have faith like Abraham's. For Abraham is the father of all who believe. ¹⁷ That is what the Scriptures mean when God told him, "I have made you the father of many nations." This happened because Abraham believed in the God who brings the dead back to life and who creates new things out of nothing.

¹⁸ Even when there was no reason for hope, Abraham kept hoping—believing that he would become the father of many nations. For God had said to him, "That's how many descendants you will have!" ¹⁹ And Abraham's faith did not weaken, even though, at about 100 years of age, he figured his body was as good as dead—and so was Sarah's womb.

²⁰ Abraham never wavered in believing God's promise. In fact, his faith grew stronger, and in this he brought glory to God. ²¹ He was fully convinced that God is able to do whatever he promises. ²² And because of Abraham's faith, God counted him as righteous. ²³ And when God counted him as righteous, it wasn't just for Abraham's benefit. It was recorded ²⁴ for our benefit, too, assuring us that God will also count us as righteous if we believe in him, the one who raised Jesus our Lord from the dead. ²⁵ He was handed over to die because of our sins, and he was raised to life to make us right with God.

Romans 4:13–25

What united the Jewish and Gentile believers? Their faith. Paul wanted all believers in the church in Rome to know that in trusting God, they were following Abraham's example and able to receive God's gift of being counted righteous in his sight. Paul reminded the church that God is able to keep his promises. He reminded them that Jesus is God's promised Messiah, that he died on the cross for sins, and that he rose again.

Topic 3—Comparing Views of Justification

Introduction: As Christians, we rejoice in the redemption and justification we have through Jesus Christ, our Lord. But people who do not share our faith view these things differently. Because Muslims believe that God exists, they are interested in being made righteous before God. Naturalists' disbelief in God means that they don't think that justification is necessary. And for people who follow new spirituality beliefs, their views about the nature of God and the role of karma affect how they think about justification.

Part 1—The Islamic View of Justification

Muslims teach that a believer must confess faith in Allah, and in Muhammad as his prophet. This is the first pillar of Islam, the shahada. Muslims consider that such faith is necessary to be saved:

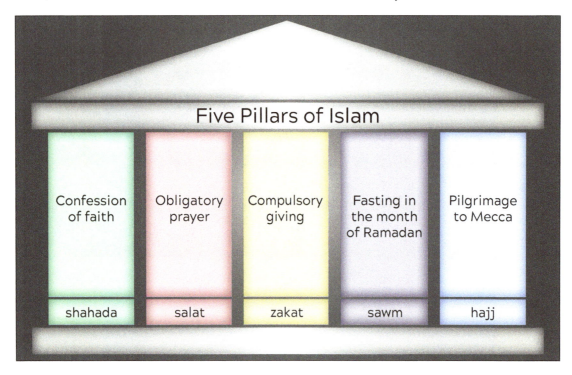

Five Pillars of Islam

Confession of faith	Obligatory prayer	Compulsory giving	Fasting in the month of Ramadan	Pilgrimage to Mecca
shahada	salat	zakat	sawm	hajj

If anyone seeks a religion other than [Islam] complete devotion to God, it will not be accepted from him: he will be one of the losers in the Hereafter.

Quran 3:85

But faith is not enough. A Muslim must also fulfill the four other pillars of Islam: prayer (*salat*), alms (*zakat*), fasting (*sawm*), and a pilgrimage to Mecca (*hajj*):

Those who believe, do good deeds, keep up the prayer, and pay the prescribed alms will have their reward with their Lord: no fear for them, nor will they grieve.

Quran 2:277

In Islam, receiving God's love and forgiveness ultimately depends on one's actions. A Muslim must do good works, but only God decides whether someone has done enough to be saved:

Those whose good deeds weigh heavy will be successful, but those whose balance is light will have lost their souls for ever and will stay in Hell-

Quran 23:102–103

Do you think that anyone can ever do enough to satisfy God, who is infinite, eternal, holy, and perfect? Christians do not think this is possible. We are limited creatures; God is not. In Romans, Paul teaches that people are not made righteous because of their work, good deeds, prayers, or charity, but because of their faith in God (Romans 3:5). That is what Jesus told his disciples:

"This is the only work God wants from you: Believe in the one he has sent."   John 6:29

This does not mean that God does not want us to do good deeds. Rather, Christians believe that faith is a gift from God, who loves us and redeems us from our sin, in order that we may do good works. Because we have been justified, we do good works because we are glad, grateful, and love God and one another.

Part 2—The Naturalist View of Justification

Justification is the state of being made righteous before God. Because naturalists do not believe God exists, they do not believe God will judge them for their sins or that they need justification before him. Stephen Hawking, a British physicist and atheist, put it this way: "We are each free to believe what we want, and it's my view that the simplest explanation is that there is no God. No one created the universe and no one directs our fate."[1]

Even though naturalists deny that God is real, they do not deny that evil is real. They know that people can be mean, short-sighted, or even criminal. George Bernard Shaw, a British playwright and atheist, wrote: "If the atheist steals, he . . . is a thief and knows that he is a thief. Nothing can rub that off him. He may try to soothe his shame by some sort of restitution or equivalent act of benevolence; but that does not alter the fact that he did steal; and his conscience will not be easy until he has conquered his will to steal and changed himself into an honest man." Shaw wrote that "the drive of evolution" motivates people to change themselves for the better.[2]

Naturalists believe that people need to accept and forgive themselves for all the sins and evil they commit. André Comte-Sponville, author of *The Little Book of Atheist Spirituality*, explained it this way: "We must forgive humanity, and ourselves, for being what we are. . . . No other animal species could have achieved humanity's best—or its worst."[3] To naturalists, people are only exceptional animals, not beloved image-bearers of God.

Naturalists believe forgiveness (toward themselves and others) is only needed when they break their own moral code or harm other people. The need for this sort of "justification" varies from one day to the next and from one situation to another. Because of this, justification is never finished. In contrast, for Christians justification is complete. We can be fully forgiven, and therefore justified before God, because Christ's work on the cross was finished. The Holy Spirit shows us our sins so that we might confess them, repent, and be healed. God accepts us and considers us righteous when we put our faith in him. Even when we sin and fall short of the holy life that God desires, we know that Jesus is our Advocate and that the Holy Spirit is working within us to transform us so that we can become like Jesus.

Part 3—The New Spirituality View of Justification

New spirituality teaches that there is no personal God who judges human beings for their sin, so there is no need to be justified before him. People who believe in new spirituality feel that everyone and everything is divine and part of the god force that is the universe, so they trust their feelings and intuitions above everything else. Because of this, when they feel guilt or sadness, they may seek forgiveness from within themselves.

New spiritualists may also assert that there is no distinction between good and evil. Deepak Chopra, a leading figure in new spirituality, wrote: "The universe has no fixed agenda. Once you make any decision, it [the universe] works around that decision. There is no right or wrong, only a series of possibilities that shift with each thought, feeling, and action that you experience."[4]

But believers in new spirituality also affirm that people reap the consequences of their actions. Chopra put it this way, "Karma keeps good and evil in balance. . . . One misdeed alters a person's destiny."[5] But these statements contradict each other. How are good and evil kept in balance if right and wrong don't exist? How can anything be considered a misdeed?

In new spirituality, explaining such contradictions isn't important. Whether good and evil really exist or not is not important because everything is one and part of the universal god force. Justice and justification are somehow taken care of automatically through karma—if not in this life, then in a future reincarnation.

In contrast, the Bible teaches that God is a personal Being, not a force. He is holy, perfect, good, and without sin or darkness. Good, evil, and judgment are all real. Each person lives only once and then faces judgment. There is no forgiveness or mercy in karma, but God offers forgiveness and justification to every person who trusts in Christ.

ENDNOTES

1 Stephen Hawking, *Brief Answers to the Big Questions* (New York: Bantam, 2018), 38.
2 George Bernard Shaw, *Androcles and the Lion* (London: Constable & Company Ltd., 1920), civ.
3 André Comte-Sponville, *The Little Book of Atheist Spirituality* (New York: Viking Penguin, 2007), 120–121.
4 Deepak Chopra, *The Book of Secrets: Unlocking the Hidden Dimensions of Your Life* (New York: Harmony Books, 2004), 92.
5 Deepak Chopra and Joshua Dysart, *Buddha: A Story of Enlightenment* (Runnemede, NJ: Dynamite Entertainment, 2010), 201.

Freedom in Christ

Getting Started—The Main Ideas

Lesson 16 continues Paul's letter to the church at Rome. Paul further instructed believers on the concept of justification—the state of being made righteous with God. He explained that we are made right with God because of Christ's sacrificial death on the cross.

Paul stated that the fall, the first sin, was the cause of the human condition. He contrasted one man's (Adam's) sin with one Man's (Christ's) deliverance. Because of Christ's atonement for our sin, we are no longer slaves to sin, and we are free to become slaves to righteousness.

Paul continued to speak of the Law—a topic of specific importance to the Jewish believers who felt justified with God through their obedience to the Law. Paul's argument was that no one can be justified by the Law because no one can keep it. Despite our inability to keep the Law, the Law itself is still good because it shows us how sinful we are and how much we need a Savior.

Paul wrote about the personal disharmony he experienced as a result of realizing that he was a sinner. He came to the conclusion that the only way out of his sinful condition was through trust in Christ and reliance on the Holy Spirit. He went on to tell the believers in the church in Rome, and all who would read his letter, that one day we will finally be free from our sinful natures at the return of Christ. In the meantime, we can be assured that nothing can separate us from God's love.

Topic 1—Freedom from Wrath

Introduction: It is reasonable to wonder why God took the trouble to make people at all. His foreknowledge of human history showed him that his children would willfully disobey his laws, harm, and even kill other image-bearers, and fail to thank him or even acknowledge his existence. No one is righteous in God's eyes, and no one can become righteous through his or her own effort. God, who is perfectly holy, cannot stand sin. His attitude toward sin is described as anger, or wrath. And because God is just, he judges people fairly for their sins. Since all people sin, all deserve the same punishment.

Yet, for Christians, there is the promise of eternal life through faith. At the end of Romans 4, Paul explained to the Romans that God is not only holy and fair, but also merciful and gracious. God's covenant relationship with Abraham was not based on Abraham's sinlessness (because Abraham was a sinner) but rather on God's grace and Abraham's enduring faith. Abraham believed God's promise of a son even though he had plenty of reasons to doubt God. His faith in God made him righteous, and even though he lived long before Jesus, he trusted God's promises (Hebrews 11:10, 13). By faith, God counts us as righteous, too, if we believe and trust in Christ.

Part 1—Christ Died for Sinners

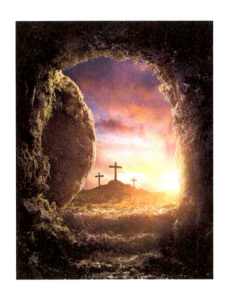

After explaining that Abraham was saved and made right with God because of his faith, Paul concluded that peace with God, an undeserved privilege, is available to all people. Paul did not deny that living the Christian life would have its problems, but he promised that God's peace would allow Christ-followers to rejoice and praise God despite trials, knowing that even difficulties help believers to grow in patient endurance. Paul added that we are not alone in trials, because the Holy Spirit is with us to fill our hearts with his love, no matter what we may be going through.

[1] Therefore, since we have been made right in God's sight by faith, we have peace with God because of what Jesus Christ our Lord has done for us. [2] Because of our faith, Christ has brought us into this place of undeserved privilege where we now stand, and we confidently and joyfully look forward to sharing God's glory.

[3] We can rejoice, too, when we run into problems and trials, for we know that they help us develop endurance. [4] And endurance develops strength of character, and character strengthens our confident hope of salvation. [5] And this hope will not lead to disappointment. For we know how dearly God loves us, because he has given us the Holy Spirit to fill our hearts with his love.

Romans 5:1–5

God did not wait for human beings to "get their act together" before sending his Son to redeem us. At the time of Christ's death, people were just as sinful as they had ever been. All sinners then and now are subject to God's eternal condemnation. God showed enormous love to all people by dying for us when we were totally estranged from him.

[6] When we were utterly helpless, Christ came at just the right time and died for us sinners. [7] Now, most people would not be willing to die for an upright person, though someone might perhaps be willing to die for a person who is especially good. [8] But God showed his great love for us by sending Christ to die for us while we were still sinners. [9] And since we have been made right in God's sight by the blood of Christ, he will certainly save us from God's condemnation. [10] For since our friendship with God was restored by the death of his Son while we were still his enemies, we will certainly be saved through the life of his Son. [11] So now we can rejoice in our wonderful new relationship with God because our Lord Jesus Christ has made us friends of God.

Romans 5:6–11

Condemnation
The state of eternal separation from God
because of his righteous judgment for sin

After reminding the Roman Christians that they were saved from God's righteous condemnation by faith in Christ's atoning work on the cross, Paul went into greater detail about how people are freed from bondage to sin and death. He contrasted Adam and Jesus, reminding us that just as one man's disobedience got all people

© **Walking in Truth Grade 7**

into trouble, one Man's obedience got us out of trouble and into a brand-new life.

Later in Romans 5, Paul used the term *rule* to describe the human condition and its relationship to both Adam and Christ. Those who have not placed their faith in Christ still live in sin's domain and under the rule, or reign, of sin. However, those who have placed their faith and trust in Christ live under God's rule of grace in his kingdom.

Part 2—Adam's Sin and God's Grace

¹² When Adam sinned, sin entered the world. Adam's sin brought death, so death spread to everyone, for everyone sinned. ¹³ Yes, people sinned even before the law was given. But it was not counted as sin because there was not yet any law to break. ¹⁴ Still, everyone died—from the time of Adam to the time of Moses—even those who did not disobey an explicit commandment of God, as Adam did. Now Adam is a symbol, a representation of Christ, who was yet to come. ¹⁵ But there is a great difference between Adam's sin and God's gracious gift. For the sin of this one man, Adam, brought death to many. But even greater is God's wonderful grace and his gift of forgiveness to many through this other man, Jesus Christ. ¹⁶ And the result of God's gracious gift is very different from the result of that one man's sin. For Adam's sin led to condemnation, but God's free gift leads to our being made right with God, even though we are guilty of many sins. ¹⁷ For the sin of this one man, Adam, caused death to rule over many. But even greater is God's wonderful grace and his gift of righteousness, for all who receive it will live in triumph over sin and death through this one man, Jesus Christ.

¹⁸ Yes, Adam's one sin brings condemnation for everyone, but Christ's one act of righteousness brings a right relationship with God and new life for everyone. ¹⁹ Because one person disobeyed God, many became sinners. But because one other person obeyed God, many will be made righteous.

²⁰ God's law was given so that all people could see how sinful they were. But as people sinned more and more, God's wonderful grace became more abundant. ²¹ So just as sin ruled over all people and brought them to death, now God's wonderful grace rules instead, giving us right standing with God and resulting in eternal life through Jesus Christ our Lord.

Romans 5:12–21

Topic 2—Freedom from Sin

Introduction: Recall that in Romans 3, Paul dealt with the foolish argument that sin is actually a good thing because it highlights God's righteousness (Romans 3:5–8). Paul taught that freedom from sin is not permission to do whatever we want to do; it's the power to do what God wants us to do.

Paul made an analogy of our sinful, corrupt selves being crucified with Christ. The power that sin used to have over our lives is dead! Now we can live to glorify God in Christ. Through Christ, God showed everyone his grace, which is his mercy and forgiveness that we do not deserve.

Part 1—Dead to Sin, Alive in Christ

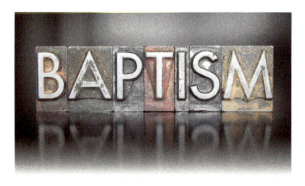

¹ Well then, should we keep on sinning so that God can show us more and more of his wonderful grace? ² Of course not! Since we have died to sin, how can we continue to live in it? ³ Or have you forgotten that when we were joined with Christ Jesus in baptism, we joined him in his death? ⁴ For we died and were buried with Christ by baptism. And just as Christ was raised from the dead by the glorious power of the Father, now we also may live new lives.

⁵ Since we have been united with him in his death, we will also be raised to life as he was. ⁶ We know that our old sinful selves were crucified with Christ so that sin might lose its power in our lives. We are no longer slaves to sin. ⁷ For when we died with Christ, we were set free from the power of sin. ⁸ And since we died with Christ, we know we will also live with him. ⁹ We are sure of this because Christ was raised from the dead, and he will never die again. Death no longer has any power over him. ¹⁰ When he died, he died once to break the power of sin. But now that he lives, he lives for the glory of God. ¹¹ So you also should consider yourselves to be dead to the power of sin and alive to God through Christ Jesus.

¹² Do not let sin control the way you live; do not give in to sinful desires. ¹³ Do not let any part of your body become an instrument of evil to serve sin. Instead, give yourselves completely to God, for you were dead, but now you have new life. So use your whole body as an instrument to do what is right for the glory of God. ¹⁴ Sin is no longer your master, for you no longer live under the requirements of the law. Instead, you live under the freedom of God's grace.　　Romans 6:1–14

Part 2—Slaves to Righteousness

Slavery was common in the Roman Empire. During the time the book of Romans was written, about a third of all Romans were slaves. Slaves were treated as property and had no rights, yet they could be freed if a benevolent master willed it or if someone paid for their freedom. So, in Paul's analogy of being a slave to sin, his audience would have understood the hard life of a slave.

Although it was rare in the ancient world, free persons could sell themselves into slavery in order to pay a debt or some other obligation. Paul used a similar analogy when he talked about becoming a slave to righteousness. Becoming a slave to righteousness is a voluntary act of obedience and submission to Christ that results in reconciliation with God and a joyful life. It is an act that shows our love for God, in the same way that loving children submit to the authority of their parents.

¹⁵ Well then, since God's grace has set us free from the law, does that mean we can go on sinning? Of course not! ¹⁶ Don't you realize that you become the slave of whatever you choose to obey? You can be a slave to sin, which leads to death, or you can choose to obey God, which leads to righteous living. ¹⁷ Thank God! Once you were slaves of sin, but now you wholeheartedly obey this teaching we have given you. ¹⁸ Now you are free from your slavery to sin, and you have become slaves to righteous living.

[19] Because of the weakness of your human nature, I am using the illustration of slavery to help you understand all this. Previously, you let yourselves be slaves to impurity and lawlessness, which led ever deeper into sin. Now you must give yourselves to be slaves to righteous living so that you will become holy.

[20] When you were slaves to sin, you were free from the obligation to do right. [21] And what was the result? You are now ashamed of the things you used to do, things that end in eternal doom. [22] But now you are free from the power of sin and have become slaves of God. Now you do those things that lead to holiness and result in eternal life. [23] For the wages of sin is death, but the free gift of God is eternal life through Christ Jesus our Lord.

Romans 6:15–23

> **Reconciliation**
> The state of being brought back into fellowship with God

Topic 3—Freedom from the Law

Introduction: Devout Jews would have obeyed hundreds of *mitzvot* (commandments). The commandments governed every aspect of Jewish life, including what a Jew could eat, wear, or do on the Sabbath. Some mitzvot were for the community at large and not just for individuals.

In discussing the Law, Paul told the Roman believers, both Jews and Gentiles, that they were free from the obligation to obey the Law, just as a widow is freed from her marriage obligation when her husband dies. She can remain single or she can remarry without committing adultery.

Recall that in Romans 6, Paul told the Roman believers that being free from slavery to sin did not mean that they were free to do whatever they wanted. Instead, they were free to serve a new master—Jesus Christ. Paul again reminded believers that they must not be controlled by their old, sinful lifestyles, but instead use their freedom in Christ to live in a new way—serving God through the power of the Holy Spirit.

Part 1—Dead to the Law

IN MEMORY OF MY HUSBAND

[1] Now, dear brothers and sisters—you who are familiar with the law—don't you know that the law applies only while a person is living? [2] For example, when a woman marries, the law binds her to her husband as long as he is alive. But if he dies, the laws of marriage no longer apply to her. [3] So while her husband is alive, she would be committing adultery if she married another man. But if her husband dies, she is free from that law and does not commit adultery when she remarries.

[4] So, my dear brothers and sisters, this is the point: You died to the power of the law when you died with Christ. And now you are united with the one who was raised from the dead. As a result, we can produce a harvest of good deeds for God. [5] When we were controlled by our old nature, sinful desires were at work within us, and the law aroused these evil desires that produced a harvest of sinful deeds, resulting in death. [6] But now we have

been released from the law, for we died to it and are no longer captive to its power. Now we can serve God, not in the old way of obeying the letter of the law, but in the new way of living in the Spirit.   Romans 7:1–6

Part 2—The Law Reveals Sin

Paul never said that the Old Testament Law was sinful. In fact, he told the Romans that the Law was holy and good. Jesus, too, affirmed the goodness of God's Law when he said that not even the smallest detail of the Law will disappear until its purpose is achieved (Matthew 5:18). What Paul did say is that when we know the Law and do not follow it, we are guilty of sin. The Law is like a mirror that shows our sinfulness. We may look into a mirror and not like what we see, but the mirror is not to blame! The Law, too, is not to blame for our sin; it simply proves that we are sinners.

7 Well then, am I suggesting that the law of God is sinful? Of course not! In fact, it was the law that showed me my sin. I would never have known that coveting is wrong if the law had not said, "You must not covet." 8 But sin used this command to arouse all kinds of covetous desires within me! If there were no law, sin would not have that power. 9 At one time I lived without understanding the law. But when I learned the command not to covet, for instance, the power of sin came to life, 10 and I died. So I discovered that the law's commands, which were supposed to bring life, brought spiritual death instead. 11 Sin took advantage of those commands and deceived me; it used the commands to kill me. 12 But still, the law itself is holy, and its commands are holy and right and good.

13 But how can that be? Did the law, which is good, cause my death? Of course not! Sin used what was good to bring about my condemnation to death. So we can see how terrible sin really is. It uses God's good commands for its own evil purposes.   Romans 7:7–13

Part 3—Sin Causes Personal Disharmony

Paul continued his message about the Law as something God-given and good. Yet, he found himself doing things that he knew were wrong. Because Paul really didn't want to do things that violate God's law, his own conscience made him realize that there was something hostile to God inside his heart—sin.

One way to think about Paul's internal struggle is to understand that sin causes personal disharmony in our hearts. Guilt, fear, shame, and self-hatred are some negative emotions associated with sin. Sometimes people try to ignore these feelings, or even deny that they are sinners. However, sin always shows up in our actions, attitudes, and in the way we think about ourselves. Paul described his feelings:

14 So the trouble is not with the law, for it is spiritual and good. The trouble is with me, for I am all too human, a slave to sin. 15 I don't really understand myself, for I want to do what is right, but I don't do it. Instead, I do what I hate. 16 But if I know that what I am doing is wrong, this shows that I agree that the law is good. 17 So I am not the one doing wrong; it is sin living in me that does it.

¹⁸ And I know that nothing good lives in me, that is, in my sinful nature. I want to do what is right, but I can't. ¹⁹ I want to do what is good, but I don't. I don't want to do what is wrong, but I do it anyway. ²⁰ But if I do what I don't want to do, I am not really the one doing wrong; it is sin living in me that does it. ²¹ I have discovered this principle of life—that when I want to do what is right, I inevitably do what is wrong. ²² I love God's law with all my heart. ²³ But there is another power within me that is at war with my mind. This power makes me a slave to the sin that is still within me. ²⁴ Oh, what a miserable person I am! Who will free me from this life that is dominated by sin and death? Romans 7:14–24

We have all shared in Paul's misery. No matter how hard we try to be good, at the end of the day we realize that we've done or said something we didn't mean or that we failed to do something we should have said or done. We simply cannot trust ourselves to do what we know is right. What is the solution for our problem? Who can take control of our heart and life so that we are rescued from our own sinful nature? Paul tells us the answer: Jesus Christ.

²⁵ Thank God! The answer is in Jesus Christ our Lord. So you see how it is: In my mind I really want to obey God's law, but because of my sinful nature I am a slave to sin. Romans 7:25

Topic 4—Freedom from Death

Introduction: Because no one could stop sinning or could become righteous in God's eyes through obedience to the Law, God stepped in and provided a solution where we had none. In Old Testament times, this solution was the annual sacrifice of animals on the Day of Atonement (Yom Kippur). However, this sacrifice had to be repeated over and over; it did nothing to permanently pardon the sins of the people. It was only when God gave his Son Jesus to die on the cross that we could be truly freed from condemnation for sin.

The power of the Holy Spirit living in our hearts frees us from being controlled by our sinful nature. Because God's Spirit lives in those who belong to Christ, we can now be led by the Spirit and not by our selfish and rebellious nature.

Part 1—God in Us

¹ So now there is no condemnation for those who belong to Christ Jesus. ² And because you belong to him, the power of the life-giving Spirit has freed you from the power of sin that leads to death. ³ The law of Moses was unable to save us because of the weakness of our sinful nature. So God did what the law could not do. He sent

his own Son in a body like the bodies we sinners have. And in that body God declared an end to sin's control over us by giving his Son as a sacrifice for our sins. [4] He did this so that the just requirement of the law would be fully satisfied for us, who no longer follow our sinful nature but instead follow the Spirit.

[5] Those who are dominated by the sinful nature think about sinful things, but those who are controlled by the Holy Spirit think about things that please the Spirit. [6] So letting your sinful nature control your mind leads to death. But letting the Spirit control your mind leads to life and peace. [7] For the sinful nature is always hostile to God. It never did obey God's laws, and it never will. [8] That's why those who are still under the control of their sinful nature can never please God.

Romans 8:1–8

How can we allow the Spirit to control our minds? We can change the way we think. In another letter, Paul wrote, "Fix your thoughts on what is true, and honorable, and right, and pure, and lovely, and admirable. Think about things that are excellent and worthy of praise" (Philippians 4:8). This is why daily quiet time spent in prayer and Bible reading is so important for us as Christians. These are times to connect with God.

[9] But you are not controlled by your sinful nature. You are controlled by the Spirit if you have the Spirit of God living in you. (And remember that those who do not have the Spirit of Christ living in them do not belong to him at all.) [10] And Christ lives within you, so even though your body will die because of sin, the Spirit gives you life because you have been made right with God. [11] The Spirit of God, who raised Jesus from the dead, lives in you. And just as God raised Christ Jesus from the dead, he will give life to your mortal bodies by this same Spirit living within you.

[12] Therefore, dear brothers and sisters, you have no obligation to do what your sinful nature urges you to do. [13] For if you live by its dictates, you will die. But if through the power of the Spirit you put to death the deeds of your sinful nature, you will live. [14] For all who are led by the Spirit of God are children of God.

Romans 8:9–14

Part 2—A New Hope

Paul reminded the believers in Rome that they were God's adopted children. Remember that the church in Rome was, for the most part, made up of poor people, servants, slaves, and immigrants. A few believers were wealthy and educated, but many were not. Some had a Jewish heritage, but many were Gentiles who had come to faith in Christ. Yet God had made this diverse group of people one great family.

[15] So you have not received a spirit that makes you fearful slaves. Instead, you received God's Spirit when he adopted you as his own children. Now we call him, "Abba, Father." [16] For his Spirit joins with our spirit to affirm that we are God's children. [17] And since we are his children, we are his heirs. In fact, together with Christ we are heirs of God's glory. But if we are to share his glory, we must also share his suffering.

Romans 8:15–17

What was Christ's suffering that Paul spoke about? Well, Jesus was rejected by his own people. He proclaimed the good news of God's kingdom, but the religious leaders did not want to listen to him. They even arranged for him to be killed. Paul knew that the believers he wrote to in Rome might face similar opposition; he had himself experienced beatings, shipwrecks, and imprisonment.

But Jesus knew more than the suffering that comes from persecution. He understood the sufferings of human existence. He was despised and rejected—a man of sorrows, acquainted with deepest grief (Isaiah 53:3). Jesus understands what it feels like to be treated unfairly, to have your heart broken, to be ignored, and to be in pain. And Paul knew that the Christians he was writing to, despite living in the richest, most powerful city of the Roman empire, experienced many hardships. Paul told them that a glorious future in God's presence far outweighed the trials, sorrow, and strife they were experiencing then, and that all believers experience from time to time. We are not immune from painful circumstances in our lives, no matter how much we would like the inheritance of glory without the suffering.

18 Yet what we suffer now is nothing compared to the glory he will reveal to us later. 19 For all creation is waiting eagerly for that future day when God will reveal who his children really are. 20 Against its will, all creation was subjected to God's curse. But with eager hope, 21 the creation looks forward to the day when it will join God's children in glorious freedom from death and decay. 22 For we know that all creation has been groaning as in the pains of childbirth right up to the present time.

23 And we believers also groan, even though we have the Holy Spirit within us as a foretaste of future glory, for we long for our bodies to be released from sin and suffering. We, too, wait with eager hope for the day when God will give us our full rights as his adopted children, including the new bodies he has promised us. 24 We were given this hope when we were saved. (If we already have something, we don't need to hope for it. 25 But if we look forward to something we don't yet have, we must wait patiently and confidently.)   Romans 8:18–25

Part 3—The Spirit Prays for Us

There are times when we simply don't know what to say to God. We want to please God and ask rightly for what we need, but we may not have the words. Here, Paul said, the Holy Spirit helps us in our weakness by praying for us.

26 And the Holy Spirit helps us in our weakness. For example, we don't know what God wants us to pray for. But the Holy Spirit prays for us with groanings that cannot be expressed in words. 27 And the Father who knows all hearts knows what the Spirit is saying, for the Spirit pleads for us believers in harmony with God's own will.   Romans 8:26–27

God knows us far better than we know ourselves. He knows what is best for us, even when we doubt that our trials or problems are doing us any good at all. We can be sure that God knows the details of our lives and that he is at work for our good even in difficult times.

²⁸ And we know that God causes everything to work together for the good of those who love God and are called according to his purpose for them. ²⁹ For God knew his people in advance, and he chose them to become like his Son, so that his Son would be the firstborn among many brothers and sisters. ³⁰ And having chosen them, he called them to come to him. And having called them, he gave them right standing with himself. And having given them right standing, he gave them his glory.

Romans 8:28–30

Part 4—Nothing Can Separate Us

Paul concluded Romans 8 by making several undeniable points. First, it is clear that God is on our side. We can't lose! Next, we have God the Son, Jesus Christ, sticking up for us. And it's impossible for anyone or anything to separate us from Christ, not even death!

³¹ What shall we say about such wonderful things as these? If God is for us, who can ever be against us? ³² Since he did not spare even his own Son but gave him up for us all, won't he also give us everything else? ³³ Who dares accuse us whom God has chosen for his own? No one—for God himself has given us right standing with himself. ³⁴ Who then will condemn us? No one—for Christ Jesus died for us and was raised to life for us, and he is sitting in the place of honor at God's right hand, pleading for us.

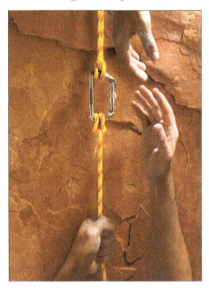

³⁵ Can anything ever separate us from Christ's love? Does it mean he no longer loves us if we have trouble or calamity, or are persecuted, or hungry, or destitute, or in danger, or threatened with death? ³⁶ (As the Scriptures say, "For your sake we are killed every day; we are being slaughtered like sheep.") ³⁷ No, despite all these things, overwhelming victory is ours through Christ, who loved us.

³⁸ And I am convinced that nothing can ever separate us from God's love. Neither death nor life, neither angels nor demons, neither our fears for today nor our worries about tomorrow—not even the powers of hell can separate us from God's love. ³⁹ No power in the sky above or in the earth below—indeed, nothing in all creation will ever be able to separate us from the love of God that is revealed in Christ Jesus our Lord.   Romans 8:31–39

Getting Started—The Main Ideas

In the previous chapters in Romans, Paul provided the congregation with basic instructions in living the Christian life. The believers knew they were saved through faith in the atoning work of Christ on the cross. They also knew that they no longer had to strictly adhere to the Law or do good deeds to obtain salvation. But they still needed to hear that they were free to serve God and other people out of love. This is what Paul emphasized next, in chapters 10 to 15 of Romans. The message Paul wrote to the Roman believers is just as relevant to us today.

As living sacrifices, we give up our self-centered ambitions in order to live new lives for Christ. We live to glorify God, and he helps us do exactly that by giving us spiritual gifts. When we use the spiritual gifts given to us by the Holy Spirit, we feel joy and are encouraged by knowing God is present and active in our lives. The church is at its most effective when believers use their various gifts.

The Roman Christians did not spend all their time just with other believers. They often interacted with people who disagreed with their beliefs, including those who persecuted and mistreated them. Paul understood persecution because he had been subject to it himself. Yet, he advised the Romans to submit to authority because civic officials are God's servants.

In Paul's letter to this church, he emphasized edification, which is *the act of being uplifted or encouraged in one's faith.* The word *edification* comes from *aedificare*, a Latin term meaning *to build.* Therefore, edifying is building others up in their faith. Paul wanted the Roman believers to be like construction workers. God builds our faith by listening to us, ministering to us, and encouraging us to use the gifts he has given us. Today, we, too, need to take time to listen, encourage, and help others.

Paul told the Jewish and Gentile believers in the church in Rome to accept one another and quit arguing. Today, we too must not tease or taunt others or look down on our brothers and sisters in Christ, even if they have different opinions or backgrounds than we do. Instead, we should grow in faith and in love for God and for each other.

> **Edification**
> The act of being uplifted or
> encouraged in one's faith

Topic 1—God's Righteousness and Our Response

Introduction: You already learned that Paul laid out the essential Christian doctrines related to salvation. Because the Romans understood slavery, Paul used the analogy of being a slave—either to sin or to Christ—to help them understand their need for salvation. Although Paul described the Law as "good," he also reminded the believers that no one can obey the Law perfectly in order to have right standing with God. Justification before God is only possible through faith. Paul further addressed the Jewish misunderstanding of righteousness in Romans 10:1–4:

¹ Dear brothers and sisters, the longing of my heart and my prayer to God is for the people of Israel to be saved. ² I know what enthusiasm they have for God, but it is misdirected zeal. ³ For they don't understand God's way of making people right with himself. Refusing to accept God's way, they cling to their own way of getting right with God by trying to keep the law. ⁴ For Christ has already accomplished the purpose for which the law was given. As a result, all who believe in him are made right with God.

Romans 10:1–4

Paul continued:

¹² Jew and Gentile are the same in this respect. They have the same Lord, who gives generously to all who call on him. ¹³ For "Everyone who calls on the name of the Lᴏʀᴅ will be saved."

Romans 10:12–13

Later he praised God with the following doxology (a brief praise to God):

³³ Oh, how great are God's riches and wisdom and knowledge! How impossible it is for us to understand his decisions and his ways!

³⁴ For who can know the Lᴏʀᴅ's thoughts?
   Who knows enough to give him advice?
³⁵ And who has given him so much
   that he needs to pay it back?

³⁶ For everything comes from him and exists by his power and is intended for his glory. All glory to him forever! Amen.

Romans 11:33–36

Part 1—Living Sacrifices

Paul continued his letter by pointing out practical applications of our right standing before God. Paul wrote that the Holy Spirit is in our hearts to help us glorify God. Paul taught that even our ordinary, everyday lives should be lived out as an offering to God.

By calling believers to live as holy sacrifices, Paul made another analogy. Under the Old Testament sacrificial system, there were five types of sacrifices, or offerings, commanded by God: burnt offerings, grain offerings, peace offerings, sin offerings, and guilt offerings (Leviticus 1–7). Each sacrifice had a purpose and specific requirements for the priests to follow, yet each one had to be repeated every time someone broke the Law. But Jesus laid down his life as the ultimate sacrifice for all time, ending the need to sacrifice grain or animals to the Lord as payment for sin. We are now freed from the sacrificial system and life under the Law. Therefore, we are free to sacrifice ourselves—not literally dying, but giving up our selfish ambitions—in gratitude for what Christ did for us. We can live to worship and glorify God in all that we do.

¹ And so, dear brothers and sisters, I plead with you to give your bodies to God because of all he has done for you. Let them be a living and holy sacrifice—the kind he will find acceptable. This is truly the way to worship him.

Romans 12:1

Like an airplane on autopilot, we tend to return to the way we lived before coming to Christ. So, how do we hear what God wants us to do and quickly respond? The culture we live in, like that of the Romans, can easily pull us down. Television, popular music, and the internet can cause our thought-life to sink, so that it is not much different from that of non-Christians. But as we rely on God, he brings out the best in us and helps us develop spiritual maturity. We need each other to stay on the right track so we will not return to worldly patterns of belief and behavior.

² Don't copy the behavior and customs of this world, but let God transform you into a new person by changing the way you think. Then you will learn to know God's will for you, which is good and pleasing and perfect.

³ Because of the privilege and authority God has given me, I give each of you this warning: Don't think you are better than you really are. Be honest in your evaluation of yourselves, measuring yourselves by the faith God has given us. ⁴ Just as our bodies have many parts and each part has a special function, ⁵ so it is with Christ's body. We are many parts of one body, and we all belong to each other.

Romans 12:2–5

Part 2—Spiritual Gifts

We all belong to each other. To help us live to glorify God, the Holy Spirit has given us everything we need, including spiritual gifts, which are very special strengths and abilities. All believers have spiritual gifts, but not all have the same gifts. When we all use our spiritual gifts, the church is at its most effective. Some of these gifts are prophecy, teaching, encouragement, showing kindness, and leadership. What gifts has God given you?

⁶ In his grace, God has given us different gifts for doing certain things well. So if God has given you the ability to prophesy, speak out with as much faith as God has given you. ⁷ If your gift is serving others, serve them well. If you are a teacher, teach well. ⁸ If your gift is to encourage others, be encouraging. If it is giving, give generously. If God has given you leadership ability, take the responsibility seriously. And if you have a gift for showing kindness to others, do it gladly.

Romans 12:6–8

Introduction: Paul emphasized how the gospel transforms believers when he said: Let God transform you into a new person by changing the way you think (Romans 12:2). In discussing this radical change, Paul used the Greek word *metamorphoō*, from which we get the English word *metamorphosis*. It describes a complete transformation, as when a caterpillar changes into a butterfly. We are no longer the same as we were before we accepted Christ as our Savior.

Paul described how we should live as redeemed people of God. Christians are no longer slaves to sin; they are free to serve God. No longer do we follow the Law and obey God because we have to; now we obey him because we want to! We don't fear God's wrath; we experience his love. As we allow the Holy Spirit to renew our minds, we will know what God wants us to do.

Loving Others. Having a deep and genuine love for others is evidence of a transformed life.

9 Don't just pretend to love others. Really love them. Hate what is wrong. Hold tightly to what is good. 10 Love each other with genuine affection, and take delight in honoring each other. 11 Never be lazy, but work hard and serve the Lord enthusiastically. 12 Rejoice in our confident hope. Be patient in trouble, and keep on praying. 13 When God's people are in need, be ready to help them. Always be eager to practice hospitality.

Romans 12:9–13

Paul understood that it is easy to love others who are good and kind to us, but that is not always how others treat us. He advised the church in Rome to love those who were not very lovable.

14 Bless those who persecute you. Don't curse them; pray that God will bless them. 15 Be happy with those who are happy, and weep with those who weep. 16 Live in harmony with each other. Don't be too proud to enjoy the company of ordinary people. And don't think you know it all!

17 Never pay back evil with more evil. Do things in such a way that everyone can see you are honorable. 18 Do all that you can to live in peace with everyone.

19 Dear friends, never take revenge. Leave that to the righteous anger of God. For the Scriptures say,

"I will take revenge;
  I will pay them back,"
  says the LORD.

20 Instead,

"If your enemies are hungry, feed them.
  If they are thirsty, give them something to drink.
In doing this, you will heap
  burning coals of shame on their heads."

21 Don't let evil conquer you, but conquer evil by doing good.

Romans 12:14–21

This passage of Scripture says not to curse others and never to take revenge. Such prohibitions do not mean that there is nothing we can do when someone is hurting us or seeking to harm us. Paul wrote that we should bless and pray for those who persecute us, seek peace, and conquer evil by doing good. Seeking peace means we can ask for help from others who can intervene. It also means we can try to avoid or escape from those

who are hurting us. One reason the early church spread out so quickly is that believers left situations where they were in danger. The Scripture tells us to feed our enemies if they are hungry, but this does not mean we can only do things our persecutors will like. Conquering evil by doing good might mean reporting a student who is threatening or bullying others so that he or she can be disciplined. This may not be easy, but obeying God is not always easy.

Recall that in his Sermon on the Mount, Jesus commanded us to love our enemies and pray for them. This is what Jesus said:

[43] "You have heard the law that says, 'Love your neighbor' and hate your enemy. [44] But I say, love your enemies! Pray for those who persecute you! [45] In that way, you will be acting as true children of your Father in heaven. For he gives his sunlight to both the evil and the good, and he sends rain on the just and the unjust alike. [46] If you love only those who love you, what reward is there for that? Even corrupt tax collectors do that much. [47] If you are kind only to your friends, how are you different from anyone else? Even pagans do that. [48] But you are to be perfect, even as your Father in heaven is perfect." Matthew 5:43–48

To be perfect as our Father in heaven is perfect requires us to love perfectly. This includes loving people whom we don't want to love. We need to be different from people in the world around us.

Topic 3—Life in the World

Introduction: After Paul addressed behavior toward enemies and those who persecute and make life difficult for Christians, he turned his attention to how believers should respond to authority. In the ancient world, Christians lived under the Roman empire—a government backed by force, with many soldiers. In Judea, the Christians lived under Jewish authority, which was itself under Roman authority. Neither the ruling Roman government nor the Pharisees and Sadducees in Jerusalem were favorable to Christians. Recall that the Jewish high council stoned Stephen; later, they had Paul arrested. A Jewish ruler, Herod Antipas, put James to death by the sword. Roman authorities under Caesar Claudius expelled all the Jews from Rome, including Aquila and Priscilla, Paul's friends and fellow believers. Paul and Silas suffered imprisonment and physical beatings under local magistrates in Philippi.

Paul called for all Christians to love each other and to shine for Christ no matter where they live. By our demonstrating holy love, nonbelievers will come to know Christ through us. Jesus himself taught his disciples, "Your love for one another will prove to the world that you are my disciples" (John 14:35).

Part 1—Respecting Authority

Remember that the early church existed during a time of intense persecution for both Jewish and Gentile believers. The authority of Rome was absolute and often merciless. Yet Paul addressed the subject of governmental authorities from a godly point of view that is just as true for us today as it was for believers nearly 2,000 years ago. The believers in Rome needed to treat authorities with respect, and so do we.

[1] Everyone must submit to governing authorities. For all authority comes from God, and those in positions of authority have been placed there by God. [2] So anyone who rebels against authority is rebelling against what God has instituted, and they will be punished. [3] For the authorities do not strike fear in people who are doing right, but in those who are doing wrong. Would you like to live without fear of the authorities? Do what is right, and they will honor you. [4] The authorities are God's servants, sent for your good. But if you are doing wrong, of course you should be afraid, for they have the power to punish you. They are God's servants, sent for the very purpose of punishing those who do what is wrong. [5] So you must submit to them, not only to avoid punishment, but also to keep a clear conscience.

[6] Pay your taxes, too, for these same reasons. For government workers need to be paid. They are serving God in what they do. [7] Give to everyone what you owe them: Pay your taxes and government fees to those who collect them, and give respect and honor to those who are in authority.   Romans 13:1–7

It is important to respect and obey civil authorities. However, if what an authority demands of us is contrary to God's Word, we must adhere to what God says. Paul knew that Peter and the other apostles had told the high council in Jerusalem, "We must obey God rather than any human authority" (Acts 5:29).

In writing to the Romans, Paul taught believers to submit to the government. But through his own life, Paul also taught that you can use the law to seek fair treatment (Acts 16:35–40, 22:25). We can work to change unjust laws (Esther 8:5–6) and help those who are hurt by such laws (Proverbs 24:11). In the United States and in many other countries around the world, Christians have the privilege of voting for legislators who we hope will enact fair and just laws. Many good laws we have today, such as requiring children to be educated or prohibiting child labor, are due in part to the work of believers. The legal systems of countries in Europe and in America were largely based on ancient Roman and Germanic laws as well as on Christian religion and ethics.

Part 2—Loving One Another

"Wake up!" Paul commanded. Why? Because we are closer to the return of Christ today than ever before in history. We need to shine for him in the dark culture in which we live. Nonbelievers do watch us. When we act, speak, and live just as they do, they don't see any reason to follow Christ. They may even call us hypocrites because we say we're different, but we act just the same as everyone else. However, when we follow Christ's command to love our neighbors as we love ourselves, we will win others to Christ.

8 Owe nothing to anyone—except for your obligation to love one another. If you love your neighbor, you will fulfill the requirements of God's law. 9 For the commandments say, "You must not commit adultery. You must not murder. You must not steal. You must not covet." These—and other such commandments—are summed up in this one commandment: "Love your neighbor as yourself." 10 Love does no wrong to others, so love fulfills the requirements of God's law.

11 This is all the more urgent, for you know how late it is; time is running out. Wake up, for our salvation is nearer now than when we first believed. 12 The night is almost gone; the day of salvation will soon be here. So remove your dark deeds like dirty clothes, and put on the shining armor of right living. 13 Because we belong to the day, we must live decent lives for all to see. Don't participate in the darkness of wild parties and drunkenness, or in sexual promiscuity and immoral living, or in quarreling and jealousy. 14 Instead, clothe yourself with the presence of the Lord Jesus Christ. And don't let yourself think about ways to indulge your evil desires.

Romans 13:8–14

Part 3—Comparing Views on Authority

The biblical Christian worldview holds that governing authorities are placed in their positions by God and we are to respect and obey our leaders. We must respect everyone, because every person bears God's image. The apostle Peter put it this way: "You are free, yet you are God's slaves, so don't use your freedom as an excuse to do evil. Respect everyone, and love the family of believers. Fear God, and respect the king" (1 Peter 2:16–17). Government officials, police officers, firefighters, school officials, and all others who have authority over us should be respected. We should honor them as God's servants (Romans 13:4), regardless of our opinion of their worthiness to hold office. We should pray for our leaders (1 Timothy 2:2), and at the same time seek justice and help the oppressed (Isaiah 1:17).

Muslims also respect authority. They, too, obey the laws of the land unless those laws contradict the Quran or the Hadith. "It is obligatory for one to listen to and obey (the ruler's orders) unless these orders involve one disobedience (to Allah); but if an act of disobedience (to Allah) is imposed, he should not listen to or obey it." (Sahih al-Bukhari 2955). In the centuries after Islam began, Muslims developed a system of laws called *shariah*

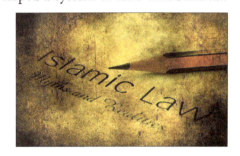

law, based on the teachings of the Quran and on the Hadith. But in the 19th century, when European powers gained influence in the Middle East and Africa, the legal systems in some countries were replaced with systems more like those in Europe. Today, where the laws of the land are not based on shariah law, Muslims may seek to make shariah the law of the land, or to arrange for Muslim populations to be allowed to have their own courts and judicial systems based on shariah law.

Naturalists also believe in obeying the law. Some seek to change laws that they see as unfairly favoring religious groups. American Atheists "support evidenced-based [sic] public policy that uses science, reason, and . . . shared humanity as its guiding principles rather than religious dogma."[1] Similarly, "humanists believe in a secular legal system, where the law applies equality to all people, regardless of religion or belief, and laws are made on the basis of reason, empathy, and evidence, and not upon religious or doctrinal considerations."[2]

People who believe in new spirituality tend not to focus on legal systems; instead, they emphasize personal transformation. They argue that if society understood that everyone is part of the divine all, laws would not be necessary. New spirituality author Neale David Walsh wants "to change the world's mind about God," because "our entire legal system is based [on] our Cultural Story of a God . . . who has His ideas of Right and Wrong, and punishes us for ignoring them."[3] Instead of being concerned about right, wrong, sin, rules, laws, crime, punishment, justice, government, or authority, new spiritualists say you should realize you are god and do whatever seems good to you. Author Shakti Gawain put it this way: "If you promise to feel or behave by a certain set of rules, eventually you are going to have to choose between being true to yourself and being true to those rules."[4] Because you are god, according to new spirituality, you are above any rules, authorities, or laws.

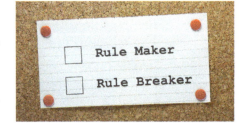

☐ Rule Maker

☐ Rule Breaker

Topic 4—Building Each Other Up

Introduction: Paul previously stressed the importance of loving others. Then he shifted the focus to how we should treat other believers. He made it clear that arguing with other believers over matters such as which day to worship, or which foods to avoid, can destroy harmony within the church. We need not condemn each other. Instead, we should be mindful of our own actions so that we do not cause other Christians to fall or doubt their faith.

Part 1—Causing Others to Stumble

In the ancient Roman world, religion was practiced to gain the blessing of the gods and thereby gain prosperity for oneself, one's family, and one's community. Each god or goddess had his or her own statue, image, or temple where sacrifices were offered. After offering a sacrifice to a god (burning a small portion of meat) and giving some meat to the priests, worshippers could sell the leftover meat at the local marketplace. Meat that was sold after first being offered to a god could be bought and served at any family meal. The practice of buying meat that had previously been dedicated to an idol caused a controversy in the Roman church.

DIANA, ROMAN GODDESS OF THE HUNT

[1] Accept other believers who are weak in faith, and don't argue with them about what they think is right or wrong. [2] For instance, one person believes it's all right to eat anything. But another believer with a sensitive conscience will eat only vegetables. [3] Those who feel free to eat anything must not look down on those who don't. And those who don't eat certain foods must not condemn those who do, for God has accepted them. [4] Who are you to condemn someone else's servants? Their own master will judge whether they stand or fall. And with the Lord's help, they will stand and receive his approval.

Romans 14:1–4

Paul addressed traditional days to fast in order to honor God. He was not advising the congregation to stop worshipping on the Sabbath, but he was addressing the Jewish custom of fasting on certain days of the week, a practice that would have seemed strange to Gentile believers.

[5] In the same way, some think one day is more holy than another day, while others think every day is alike. You should each be fully convinced that whichever day you choose is acceptable. [6] Those who worship the Lord on a special day do it to honor him. Those who eat any kind of food do so to honor the Lord, since they give thanks to God before eating. And those who refuse to eat certain foods also want to please the Lord and

give thanks to God. ⁷ For we don't live for ourselves or die for ourselves. ⁸ If we live, it's to honor the Lord. And if we die, it's to honor the Lord. So whether we live or die, we belong to the Lord. ⁹ Christ died and rose again for this very purpose—to be Lord both of the living and of the dead.

¹⁰ So why do you condemn another believer? Why do you look down on another believer? Remember, we will all stand before the judgment seat of God. ¹¹ For the Scriptures say,

"'As surely as I live,' says the LORD,
'every knee will bend to me,
    and every tongue will declare allegiance to God.'"

Romans 14:5–11

Paul reminded believers that each person will have to give a personal account to God for his or her actions, including how they treat others. Therefore, they should avoid controversial practices, like eating certain foods in front of people who abstain from such foods. God will also judge whether we encourage others in their faith. You remember that giving encouragement or building each other up in the faith is known as *edification*, and it is important for all Christians to do. Think about how other people have encouraged your faith.

¹² Yes, each of us will give a personal account to God. ¹³ So let's stop condemning each other. Decide instead to live in such a way that you will not cause another believer to stumble and fall.

¹⁴ I know and am convinced on the authority of the Lord Jesus that no food, in and of itself, is wrong to eat. But if someone believes it is wrong, then for that person it is wrong. ¹⁵ And if another believer is distressed by what you eat, you are not acting in love if you eat it. Don't let your eating ruin someone for whom Christ died. ¹⁶ Then you will not be criticized for doing something you believe is good. ¹⁷ For the Kingdom of God is not a matter of what we eat or drink, but of living a life of goodness and peace and joy in the Holy Spirit. ¹⁸ If you serve Christ with this attitude, you will please God, and others will approve of you, too. ¹⁹ So then, let us aim for harmony in the church and try to build each other up.

²⁰ Don't tear apart the work of God over what you eat. Remember, all foods are acceptable, but it is wrong to eat something if it makes another person stumble. ²¹ It is better not to eat meat or drink wine or do anything else if it might cause another believer to stumble. ²² You may believe there's nothing wrong with what you are doing, but keep it between yourself and God. Blessed are those who don't feel guilty for doing something they have decided is right.

²³ But if you have doubts about whether or not you should eat something, you are sinning if you go ahead and do it. For you are not following your convictions. If you do anything you believe is not right, you are sinning.

Romans 14:12–23

Part 2—Comparing Views on Diets

The biblical Christian worldview allows Christians to eat anything they wish as long as it does not violate one's conscience. Paul made this clear by saying "no food, in and of itself, is wrong to eat. But if someone believes it is wrong, then for that person it is wrong" (Romans 14:23). Believers with a Jewish background may want to keep on observing dietary restrictions such as those on shellfish or pork to honor God's past commands and relationship with Israel. Others may follow the advice of the apostles in Jerusalem and avoid eating foods like blood sausage (Acts 21:25). With compassion for those who struggle with alcoholism, some believers choose not to drink alcohol. Out of concern for animals, some Christians avoid eating meat. In other countries or cultures, believers may choose not to eat or drink certain things because they do not want to offend those around them. But for Christians, salvation is by faith and not dependent on what we eat or drink. Jesus "declared that every kind of food is acceptable in God's eyes" (Mark 7:19).

Muslims have dietary restrictions similar to what the Jews had in the Torah. They are forbidden to eat "carrion, blood, pig's meat, and animals over which any name other than God's has been invoked" (Quran 2:173). They also do not believe it is right to drink alcohol or other intoxicating substances. Recall, also, that one of the five pillars of Islam is *sawm*, or fasting. Muslims fast during the month of Ramadan. From sunrise to sunset, Muslims abstain from food and drink. During the fast, Muslims are to pray to Allah more often, asking for forgiveness of sins and trying not to commit new sins.

The naturalistic worldview does not prohibit or advocate specific foods or drinks. Naturalists who fast or restrict their diets usually do so for their health (to lose weight, to follow their doctors' orders, or because of allergies or sensitivity to specific foods). Naturalists may also fast for political reasons, as a form of protest. Naturalists' emphasis on science might mean they have an interest in genetically modified foods, organic foods, how much people spend to raise and preserve food, and whether the planet's resources can be used more effectively.

People who believe in the new spirituality worldview want to achieve enlightenment. To do so, they pursue all kinds of practices they believe will be helpful in their spiritual journey. Some new spiritualists use foods or other substances to bring about altered states of consciousness. Others try to follow a vegetarian or vegan diet.

The Vedas, religious scriptures in Hinduism, teach *ahimsa*, or nonviolence, which implies respect for all living things and avoidance of harm toward others. New spiritualists may avoid meat if they believe in reincarnation. Osho, an Indian guru who led the Rajneesh movement, said "You have lived for millennia in many forms. And if you remember that once you were a fish, it will become difficult for you to eat fish. Vegetarianism leads you into remembering your past lives. And . . . seeing that all are brothers and sisters . . . you cannot kill animals."[5]

Topic 5—Harmony with Others

Introduction: Paul closed his letter with several encouraging remarks. First, he reminded the Roman believers to look to the Scriptures for instruction in godliness and for hope. Paul insisted that the believers live like Christians, trusting God, giving him glory, and maintaining harmony with one another.

[1] We who are strong must be considerate of those who are sensitive about things like this [food sacrificed to idols]. We must not just please ourselves. [2] We should help others do what is right and build them up in the Lord. [3] For even Christ didn't live to please himself. As the Scriptures say, "The insults of those who insult you, O God, have fallen on me." [4] Such things were written in the Scriptures long ago to teach us. And the Scriptures give us hope and encouragement as we wait patiently for God's promises to be fulfilled.

Romans 15:1–4

Closing remarks: Notice that Paul called for the Roman believers to trust God for patience and encouragement in order to live in complete harmony with one another. As Christians, we accept one another. This does not mean that we tolerate sin, but it does mean that we treat others as we would like to be treated because we all bear God's image. This message was critical for the Jewish Christians to hear because they felt themselves to be superior to the Gentile believers. Paul called for all believers, both Jewish and Gentile, to praise God and live in peace, joy, and confident hope through the power of the Holy Spirit.

[5] May God, who gives this patience and encouragement, help you live in complete harmony with each other, as is fitting for followers of Christ Jesus. [6] Then all of you can join together with one voice, giving praise and glory to God, the Father of our Lord Jesus Christ.

[7] Therefore, accept each other just as Christ has accepted you so that God will be given glory. [8] Remember that Christ came as a servant to the Jews to show that God is true to the promises he made to their ancestors. [9] He also came so that the Gentiles might give glory to God for his mercies to them. That is what the psalmist meant when he wrote:

"For this, I will praise you among the Gentiles;
   I will sing praises to your name."

[10] And in another place it is written,

"Rejoice with his people,
   you Gentiles."

[11] And yet again,

"Praise the LORD, all you Gentiles.
   Praise him, all you people of the earth."

[12] And in another place Isaiah said,

"The heir to David's throne will come,
   and he will rule over the Gentiles.
They will place their hope on him."

[13] I pray that God, the source of hope, will fill you completely with joy and peace because you trust in him. Then you will overflow with confident hope through the power of the Holy Spirit.   Romans 15:6–13

ENDNOTES

1 "Issues," American Atheists, accessed May 7, 2019, https://www.atheists.org/issues/.

2 "Religious Courts," Humanists U.K., accessed May 8, 2019. https://humanism.org.uk/campaigns/human-rights-and-equality/religious-courts/.

3 Neale Donald Walsh, "What is My Purpose?", The CWG Foundation, September 26, 2014, http://cwg.org/index.php?b=612.

4 Shakti Gawain, with Laurel King, *Living in the Light: Following Your Inner Guidance to Create a New Life and a New World*, 25th ed., (Novato, CA: New World Library, 2011), 132.

5 Osho, *Philosophia Perennis, Series 2*, Osho Online Library, accessed May 9, 2019. https://www.osho.com/osho-online-library/osho-talks/alexander-the-great-pythagoras-self-remembrance-23d96bfe-24f?p=c78c55b6c0ebd9ab79c03e27daf3356e.

Getting Started—The Main Ideas

The books of 1 Corinthians and 2 Corinthians follow Paul's letter to the Romans in the New Testament. These books are letters that Paul wrote to the church in Corinth. Together, they contain 29 chapters, which is equal to about one-fourth of the total number of chapters in all of the letters in the New Testament.

Corinth was a center of commerce in the ancient world. It attracted wealthy visitors and poor people who were hoping to make their fortune there. The city was a religious center with many temples to Greek gods, including Aphrodite, the goddess of love and fertility. Corinth was well-known as a place of opportunity— and also immorality, great differences between social classes, and exorbitant, sinful behavior.

The Holy Spirit was fully aware that new believers in such a place would need extra help to grow and mature in Christ, so he inspired Paul to respond to the struggles the church faced. Paul wrote about the divisions the Corinthian believers experienced in boasting about who had more spiritual wisdom. He pointed out that their quarrels showed how immature they were. He warned the believers about judging others, especially leaders, and gave them advice on how to handle people who claimed to be believers but kept living in sin.

Topic 1—Introduction to Corinthians

Introduction: Corinth was a flourishing city in ancient Greece. Paul lived there for a year and a half, preaching the gospel to both Jews and Gentiles. After he left to plant more churches in other cities, the believers in Corinth wrote to him with many questions. Paul not only answered them in his letters but challenged the believers to stop quarreling and be united in Christ.

Part 1—Corinth

The city of Corinth was situated on a plateau at the base of an outcropping of rock almost 2,000 feet high. The top of the rock, known as *the Acrocorinth*, served as a fortress, with incredible views of the surrounding territory. Corinth was in the middle of an isthmus, a narrow strip of land with sea on either side. To the east, it had two harbors able to receive ships from Asia. To the west, its harbor could receive ships from Italy and the rest of Europe. To help ships avoid treacherous waters while navigating around Greece, the people of Corinth had an ingenious system that allowed ships, or their cargo, to be towed over land.

Because of its strategic location, Corinth was a wealthy city with visitors from many different lands. It was a trade center, known for its brass industry and for its unique style of pottery.

A century after the Romans conquered and destroyed Corinth in 146 BC, the Roman emperor Julius Caesar ordered that the city be rebuilt. Corinth gained fame for its architecture and the ornate columns of its temples. The most important temple was the one built to honor the goddess Aphrodite. Because of the rituals associated with worship at this temple, Corinth was associated with sexual immorality.

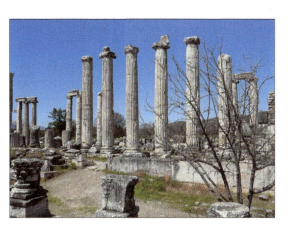

RUINS OF THE TEMPLE
OF APHRODITE

Paul knew about the city's reputation because he had lived there. God had spoken to Paul in a vision, telling him to preach boldly (Acts 18:10). Jews and Greeks there both came to know the Lord because of Paul's obedience to the Lord's calling.

What do you think would be helpful advice to new Christians living in a city known for its self-sufficiency, riches, and sin? Well, Paul, guided by the Holy Spirit, first affirmed that the Corinthian believers were called by God to be his own holy people (1 Corinthians 1:2). Later, he wrote to remind them to stand firm for Christ (2 Corinthians 1:21). In both of his letters, Paul responded to specific questions the church had about how to live a life that would please God.

Part 2—Greetings from Paul

Once the church was established in Corinth, Paul traveled to other cities to preach the gospel. He went to Jerusalem, back to Antioch in Syria, and many other places. Eventually he went to Ephesus, where he stayed for three years. While he was there, around AD 55, he and fellow believer Sosthenes (who may have been the same person mentioned in the book of Acts as the chief ruler of the Corinthian synagogue) wrote to the Corinthians. Paul began the letter by emphasizing that God calls every person to be holy.

[1] This letter is from Paul, chosen by the will of God to be an apostle of Christ Jesus, and from our brother Sosthenes. [2] I am writing to God's church in Corinth, to you who have been called by God to be his own holy people. He made you holy by means of Christ Jesus, just as he did for all people everywhere who call on the name of our Lord Jesus Christ, their Lord and ours.

[3] May God our Father and the Lord Jesus Christ give you grace and peace.

[4] I always thank my God for you and for the gracious gifts he has given you, now that you belong to Christ Jesus. [5] Through him, God has enriched your church in every way—with all of your eloquent words and all of your knowledge. [6] This confirms that what I told you about Christ is true. [7] Now you have every spiritual gift you need as you eagerly wait for the return of our Lord Jesus Christ. [8] He will keep you strong to the end so that you will be free from all blame on the day when our Lord Jesus Christ returns. [9] God will do this, for he is faithful to do what he says, and he has invited you into partnership with his Son, Jesus Christ our Lord.

1 Corinthians 1:1–9

Notice that Paul reminded the believers that they have two different types of gifts—natural gifts of eloquent words and knowledge and spiritual gifts, supernatural gifts from the Holy Spirit. Paul urged the believers to use both types of gifts as they partnered with Christ and looked forward to his return.

Part 3—Struggles in the Church

After Paul encouraged the Corinthians, he expressed his concern about the church there. Paul wanted the believers in Corinth to get along with each other and to be united. He reminded them that Christ died for every one of them. They were baptized in Jesus' name, not in Paul's (or anyone else's) name. Quarreling among themselves about which leader to follow did not help anyone! Paul wanted the believers to remember that what mattered most was sharing the good news—that through Christ's death on the cross, everyone could be reconciled to God.

[10] I appeal to you, dear brothers and sisters, by the authority of our Lord Jesus Christ, to live in harmony with each other. Let there be no divisions in the church. Rather, be of one mind, united in thought and purpose. [11] For some members of Chloe's household have told me about your quarrels, my dear brothers and sisters. [12] Some of you are saying, "I am a follower of Paul." Others are saying, "I follow Apollos," or "I follow Peter," or "I follow only Christ."

[13] Has Christ been divided into factions? Was I, Paul, crucified for you? Were any of you baptized in the name of Paul? Of course not! [14] I thank God that I did not baptize any of you except Crispus and Gaius, [15] for now no one can say they were baptized in my name. [16] (Oh yes, I also baptized the household of Stephanas, but I don't remember baptizing anyone else.) [17] For Christ didn't send me to baptize, but to preach the Good News—and not with clever speech, for fear that the cross of Christ would lose its power.   1 Corinthians 1:10–17

As the church grew and Gentile converts joined Jewish Christian believers, they began meeting in individual homes. Chloe (whose household was mentioned in 1 Corinthians 1:11) probably hosted one of the house churches in Corinth. Apollos was a Jewish Christian who went to Corinth to teach that Jesus was the Messiah. Peter was one of Jesus' 12 disciples and led the church in Jerusalem. Crispus, leader of the Jewish synagogue at Corinth, became a Christian and was baptized by Paul, who also baptized Gaius and Stephanas. Some years later, when Paul visited Corinth, he wrote to the Romans and mentioned that he stayed at Gaius' house. Stephanas and his household were the very first believers in Greece.

Topic 2—Spiritual Wisdom

Introduction: Corinth was a wealthy city with a lot of commerce and visitors from many parts of the world. Its population included rich and educated people, but also many more poor people and slaves. While the church in Corinth had people from all walks of life, most were ordinary people without much influence.

Paul wanted the believers to get along and work together. Instead of quarreling about the different leaders they followed, the Christians needed to focus on Christ. The story about Christ was new and strange in the ancient world. Who had ever heard of putting faith in someone who was killed on a cross? And who had ever heard of someone dying and then rising again? That was unusual!

But God's ways are not our ways (Isaiah 55:8–9), so Paul continued his letter to the Corinthians by comparing human thinking with God's wisdom. People—using merely human abilities—can be highly intelligent and able to speak eloquently about many different subjects. However, to be in a right relationship with a holy God, they have to trust in Jesus, who said, "I am the way, the truth, and the life. No one can come to the Father except through me" (John 14:6).

Wisdom is the ability to make decisions and do what is right for God, ourselves, others, and the earth. It is also the ability to use discernment and good judgment. Having faith in Jesus, of course, is the wisest decision that anyone can make. In the next part of 1 Corinthians, you will see how Paul distinguished between foolishness and wisdom.

> **Wisdom**
> The ability to make decisions and do what is right for God, ourselves, others, and the earth

Part 1—Foolishness and Wisdom

BUST OF EPICURUS,
A GREEK PHILOSOPHER

[18] The message of the cross is foolish to those who are headed for destruction! But we who are being saved know it is the very power of God. [19] As the Scriptures say,

"I will destroy the wisdom of the wise
and discard the intelligence of the intelligent."

[20] So where does this leave the philosophers, the scholars, and the world's brilliant debaters? God has made the wisdom of this world look foolish.

1 Corinthians 1:18–20

When Paul was in Athens, he preached in the synagogue, as usual, but he also debated the Epicurean and Stoic philosophers. Through his efforts, people came to Christ. Writing to the believers in Corinth, Paul emphasized that human judgment and intelligence are nothing compared with what God can do.

[21] Since God in his wisdom saw to it that the world would never know him through human wisdom, he has used our foolish preaching to save those who believe. [22] It is foolish to the Jews, who ask for signs from heaven. And it is foolish to the Greeks, who seek human wisdom. [23] So when we preach that Christ was crucified, the Jews are offended and the Gentiles say it's all nonsense.

[24] But to those called by God to salvation, both Jews and Gentiles, Christ is the power of God and the wisdom of God. [25] This foolish

plan of God is wiser than the wisest of human plans, and God's weakness is stronger than the greatest of human strength.

²⁶ Remember, dear brothers and sisters, that few of you were wise in the world's eyes or powerful or wealthy when God called you. ²⁷ Instead, God chose things the world considers foolish in order to shame those who think they are wise. And he chose things that are powerless to shame those who are powerful. ²⁸ God chose things despised by the world, things counted as nothing at all, and used them to bring to nothing what the world considers important. ²⁹ As a result, no one can ever boast in the presence of God.

³⁰ God has united you with Christ Jesus. For our benefit God made him to be wisdom itself. Christ made us right with God; he made us pure and holy, and he freed us from sin. ³¹ Therefore, as the Scriptures say, "If you want to boast, boast only about the LORD."

1 Corinthians 1:21–31

Part 2—God's Wisdom

Paul was a knowledgeable man, with a first-rate education in Jewish law (Acts 22:3). He was fluent in several languages, including Aramaic, Greek, and Hebrew. Besides this, he was well-traveled and had Roman citizenship. He could have boasted about his credentials, but he had just said that no one, not even he, could ever boast in God's presence. So instead of puffing himself up and arguing that he was a better teacher than the other teachers the Corinthian believers admired, Paul emphasized Jesus Christ and what God did through his Son.

¹ When I first came to you, dear brothers and sisters, I didn't use lofty words and impressive wisdom to tell you God's secret plan. ² For I decided that while I was with you I would forget everything except Jesus Christ, the one who was crucified. ³ I came to you in weakness—timid and trembling. ⁴ And my message and my preaching were very plain. Rather than using clever and persuasive speeches, I relied only on the power of the Holy Spirit. ⁵ I did this so you would trust not in human wisdom but in the power of God.

⁶ Yet when I am among mature believers, I do speak with words of wisdom, but not the kind of wisdom that belongs to this world or to the rulers of this world, who are soon forgotten. ⁷ No, the wisdom we speak of is the mystery of God—his plan that was previously hidden, even though he made it for our ultimate glory before the world began. ⁸ But the rulers of this world have not understood it; if they had, they would not have crucified our glorious Lord. ⁹ That is what the Scriptures mean when they say,

"No eye has seen, no ear has heard,
   and no mind has imagined
what God has prepared
   for those who love him."   1 Corinthians 2:1–9

Paul reminded the church that no one ever guessed God's plan to reconcile the whole world to himself through Jesus. But as believers, they now knew about this plan!

¹⁰ But it was to us that God revealed these things by his Spirit. For his Spirit searches out everything and shows us God's deep secrets. ¹¹ No one can know a person's thoughts except that person's own spirit, and no one can know God's thoughts except God's own Spirit. ¹² And we have received God's Spirit (not the world's spirit), so we can know the wonderful things God has freely given us.

¹³ When we tell you these things, we do not use words that come from human wisdom. Instead, we speak words given to us by the Spirit, using the Spirit's words to explain spiritual truths. . . . ¹⁶ But we understand these things, for we have the mind of Christ.   1 Corinthians 2:10–13, 16

Paul did not learn about God's plans on his own. The Holy Spirit worked in Paul and in the Corinthian believers and, as they trusted in Christ, the Spirit revealed his plan to them. Neither Paul nor any other Christian could boast, because understanding of spiritual truths comes from God alone. Therefore, the proper attitude for believers to have is not one of pride, but of humility. If we have the mind of Christ, then we should be imitators of his humble nature.

Topic 3—Jesus, the True Foundation

Introduction: The Corinthian believers had been quarreling among themselves, dividing into opposing groups. Instead of taking sides, Paul reminded the believers that God's wisdom is not like human wisdom and that God is the one who reveals spiritual things. Paul continued his letter by pointing out that the quarrels in the church showed the believers' immaturity.

¹ Dear brothers and sisters, when I was with you I couldn't talk to you as I would to spiritual people. I had to talk as though you belonged to this world or as though you were infants in Christ. ² I had to feed you with milk, not with solid food, because you weren't ready for anything stronger. And you still aren't ready, ³ for you are still controlled by your sinful nature. You are jealous of one another and quarrel with each other. Doesn't that prove you are controlled by your sinful nature? Aren't you living like people of the world? ⁴ When one of you says, "I am a follower of Paul," and another says, "I follow Apollos," aren't you acting just like people of the world?

⁵ After all, who is Apollos? Who is Paul? We are only God's servants through whom you believed the Good News. Each of us did the work the Lord gave us. ⁶ I planted the seed in your hearts, and Apollos watered it, but it was God who made it grow. ⁷ It's not important who does the planting, or who does the watering. What's important is that God makes the seed grow. ⁸ The one who plants and the one who waters work together with the same purpose. And both will be rewarded for their own hard work. ⁹ For we are both God's workers. And you are God's field. You are God's building.

¹⁰ Because of God's grace to me, I have laid the foundation like an expert builder. Now others are building on it. But whoever is building on this foundation must be very careful. ¹¹ For no one can lay any foundation other than the one we already have—Jesus Christ.

¹²Anyone who builds on that foundation may use a variety of materials—gold, silver, jewels, wood, hay, or straw. ¹³But on the judgment day, fire will reveal what kind of work each builder has done. The fire will show if a person's work has any value. ¹⁴If the work survives, that builder will receive a reward. ¹⁵But if the work is burned up, the builder will suffer great loss. The builder will be saved, but like someone barely escaping through a wall of flames.   1 Corinthians 3:1–15

Paul used word pictures to help the Corinthians understand his points. He first compared the believers to infants who need to be fed with milk, rather than with solid food. He continued by comparing the believers to a field where God's laborers work. And then he compared the believers to a building. This last word picture may have been especially meaningful to the Corinthians. Remember that much of their city had been destroyed and then rebuilt. They knew about architecture and construction.

The Corinthians also knew about temples. Their city had many of them! Besides the temple to Aphrodite, some of the other gods honored with temples included Apollo (the god of the sun), Asclepius (the god of healing), and Poseidon (the god of the sea).

The Jerusalem temple, however, was unlike Corinth's pagan shrines. God lived in the temple and showed his presence though a miraculous cloud of light. Christ, by his Spirit, lives in all believers (Colossians 3:11). The Hebrew temple was devoted to God and set apart by God for holy purposes. So, too, are all Christians set apart for service to God. Paul compared the Christians to the temple and warned them not to let their quarrels destroy it.

¹⁶Don't you realize that all of you together are the temple of God and that the Spirit of God lives in you? ¹⁷God will destroy anyone who destroys this temple. For God's temple is holy, and you are that temple.

¹⁸Stop deceiving yourselves. If you think you are wise by this world's standards, you need to become a fool to be truly wise. ¹⁹For the wisdom of this world is foolishness to God. As the Scriptures say,

SOSTHENES AND EARLY
CHURCH LEADERS

"He traps the wise
   in the snare of their own cleverness."

²⁰And again,

"The LORD knows the thoughts of the wise;
   he knows they are worthless."

²¹So don't boast about following a particular human leader. For everything belongs to you— ²²whether Paul or Apollos or Peter, or the world, or life and death, or the present and the future. Everything belongs to you, ²³and you belong to Christ, and Christ belongs to God.   1 Corinthians 3:16–23

Remember how Paul began this letter to the Corinthians? He said that God enriched the church in every way, graciously giving them all the spiritual gifts they needed. Paul once again emphasized the riches all believers have: everything belongs to them! So, the Corinthians didn't have to grasp for spiritual blessings or try to make themselves seem clever or quarrel and destroy each other. What they needed to do was to remember that God worked among them, that they belonged to Christ, and that they should behave in a way that would please him.

Topic 4—Attitude toward Leadership

Introduction: Have you ever heard of the term *praise sandwich*? It refers to a way to give people negative feedback so that they can receive and pay attention to what you have to say. This is done by first praising them, then stating what they need to change and why, and finally praising them again. The first three chapters of 1 Corinthians are a praise sandwich.

In the next chapter of 1 Corinthians, Paul returned to the topic of judging others. He told the Corinthian believers to remember that there was nothing they had that was not a gift from God. He reminded them not to boast. He compared their prideful attitudes with the attitudes of humble servants of Christ. Paul's approach was intended as a warning so that the believers in Corinth could have a clear conscience before the Lord.

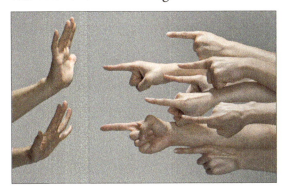

¹ So look at Apollos and me as mere servants of Christ who have been put in charge of explaining God's mysteries. ² Now, a person who is put in charge as a manager must be faithful. ³ As for me, it matters very little how I might be evaluated by you or by any human authority. I don't even trust my own judgment on this point. ⁴ My conscience is clear, but that doesn't prove I'm right. It is the Lord himself who will examine me and decide.

⁵ So don't make judgments about anyone ahead of time—before the Lord returns. For he will bring our darkest secrets to light and will reveal our private motives. Then God will give to each one whatever praise is due.

⁶ Dear brothers and sisters, I have used Apollos and myself to illustrate what I've been saying. If you pay attention to what I have quoted from the Scriptures, you won't be proud of one of your leaders at the expense of another. ⁷ For what gives you the right to make such a judgment? What do you have that God hasn't given you? And if everything you have is from God, why boast as though it were not a gift?

⁸ You think you already have everything you need. You think you are already rich. You have begun to reign in God's kingdom without us! I wish you really were reigning already, for then we would be reigning with you. ⁹ Instead, I sometimes think God has put us apostles on display, like prisoners of war at the end of a victor's parade, condemned to die. We have become a spectacle to the entire world—to people and angels alike.

¹⁰ Our dedication to Christ makes us look like fools, but you claim to be so wise in Christ! We are weak, but you are so powerful! You are honored, but we are ridiculed. ¹¹ Even now we go hungry and thirsty, and we don't have enough clothes to keep warm. We are often beaten and have no home. ¹² We work wearily with our own hands to earn our living. We bless those who curse us. We are patient with those who abuse us. ¹³ We appeal gently when evil things are said about us. Yet we are treated like the world's garbage, like everybody's trash—right up to the present moment.

1 Corinthians 4:1–13

How do you think the believers in Corinth felt when they read Paul's harsh words? Do you think they felt ashamed of the way they had been acting? Paul certainly thought they might feel that way. That is why he continued by reaffirming his love for them.

[14] I am not writing these things to shame you, but to warn you as my beloved children. [15] For even if you had ten thousand others to teach you about Christ, you have only one spiritual father. For I became your father in Christ Jesus when I preached the Good News to you. [16] So I urge you to imitate me.   1 Corinthians 4:14–16

Later in this same letter to the Corinthian church, Paul repeated this idea, saying, you should imitate me, just as I imitate Christ (1 Corinthians 11:1). And he sent the church a fellow brother to help.

That's why I have sent Timothy, my beloved and faithful child in the Lord. He will remind you of how I follow Christ Jesus, just as I teach in all the churches wherever I go.   1 Corinthians 4:17

A person who is a good leader doesn't just tell people what to do, but shows them how to do it and gives them extra help if they need it. The leader models the desired behavior so that others can copy it. Paul, a leader God chose to plant many new churches, modeled what he wanted believers to do. And because the Corinthians needed extra help, he sent them Timothy.

[18] Some of you have become arrogant, thinking I will not visit you again. [19] But I will come—and soon—if the Lord lets me, and then I'll find out whether these arrogant people just give pretentious speeches or whether they really have God's power. [20] For the Kingdom of God is not just a lot of talk; it is living by God's power. [21] Which do you choose? Should I come with a rod to punish you, or should I come with love and a gentle spirit?   1 Corinthians 4:18–21

Even though they had been led astray by sinful desires, Paul dearly loved the believers in Corinth. He showed his love by confronting them about their behavior, just as God shows his love for us when he disciplines us.

Topic 5—Sin in the Church

Introduction: Paul wrote 1 Corinthians in response to the news and questions he had received from the believers there. The church was not doing well. Besides quarreling about which leader to follow and having prideful attitudes, there were other problems, including sexual sin within the church.

You may remember that Corinth was famous not just for being a wealthy trade center between Asia and Europe, but also for its temples, especially the one to Aphrodite, the goddess of love, fertility, and the moon. Worship rituals often included inappropriate sexual activity. But the Corinthian Gentiles who trusted in Jesus had to learn how to worship in ways that were acceptable to a holy God. And it seems they had some trouble with this task. In fact, Paul said, "When I wrote to you before, I told you not to associate with people who indulge in sexual sin" (1 Corinthians 5:9), but they had not listened to him.

[1] I can hardly believe the report about the sexual immorality going on among you—something that even pagans don't do. I am told that a man in your church is living in sin with his stepmother. [2] You are so proud of yourselves, but you should be mourning in sorrow and shame. And you should remove this man from your fellowship.

© ⟋Ｓ Walking in Truth Grade 7

³ Even though I am not with you in person, I am with you in the Spirit. And as though I were there, I have already passed judgment on this man ⁴ in the name of the Lord Jesus. You must call a meeting of the church. I will be present with you in spirit, and so will the power of our Lord Jesus. ⁵ Then you must throw this man out and hand him over to Satan so that his sinful nature will be destroyed and he himself will be saved on the day the Lord returns.

1 Corinthians 5:1–5

Paul taught the Corinthian believers about all the things Jesus said and did. This may have included what Jesus taught about how to deal with a believer who sins and refuses to change. Jesus said:

¹⁵ "If another believer sins against you, go privately and point out the offense. If the other person listens and confesses it, you have won that person back. ¹⁶ But if you are unsuccessful, take one or two others with you and go back again, so that everything you say may be confirmed by two or three witnesses. ¹⁷ If the person still refuses to listen, take your case to the church. Then if he or she won't accept the church's decision, treat that person as a pagan or a corrupt tax collector."

Matthew 18:15–17

We do not know how many times faithful believers in the church in Corinth confronted this sinful man. But by the time Paul heard about the situation, it was a big problem.

⁶ Your boasting about this is terrible. Don't you realize that this sin is like a little yeast that spreads through the whole batch of dough? ⁷ Get rid of the old "yeast" by removing this wicked person from among you. Then you will be like a fresh batch of dough made without yeast, which is what you really are. Christ, our Passover Lamb, has been sacrificed for us. ⁸ So let us celebrate the festival, not with the old bread of wickedness and evil, but with the new bread of sincerity and truth.

⁹ When I wrote to you before, I told you not to associate with people who indulge in sexual sin. ¹⁰ But I wasn't talking about unbelievers who indulge in sexual sin, or are greedy, or cheat people, or worship idols. You would have to leave this world to avoid people like that.

¹¹ I meant that you are not to associate with anyone who claims to be a believer yet indulges in sexual sin, or is greedy, or worships idols, or is abusive, or is a drunkard, or cheats people. Don't even eat with such people.

¹² It isn't my responsibility to judge outsiders, but it certainly is your responsibility to judge those inside the church who are sinning. ¹³ God will judge those on the outside; but as the Scriptures say, "You must remove the evil person from among you."

1 Corinthians 5:6–13

Paul wanted the believers in Corinth to be holy. He wanted them to be able to reach the surrounding pagan culture with the good news of Jesus Christ and the power of the cross to make people right with God. But preaching this message would be very difficult if the Corinthians kept on quarreling and were allowed to keep indulging in sinful practices. So, Paul was direct and firm in addressing the problems the church faced. He didn't pretend the problems did not exist or did not matter. Instead, he lovingly told his readers what to do so that they could be free from all blame when Jesus returned.

Lesson 19 Stumbling Blocks

Getting Started—The Main Ideas

After planting the church in Corinth, Paul left to plant churches in other cities. But he still had friends in Corinth. Some of them came to see him when he was in Ephesus. Others wrote to him and asked him many questions, which he answered in 1 Corinthians.

Many of the questions had to do with food offered to idols. But all the Corinthians' questions showed the disunity and arguments in the congregation. Some of the believers had been Jews before they trusted in Christ, and others had been Gentiles. Some of the issues the congregation faced were due to its members' different cultural and religious backgrounds.

The believers wanted Paul to tell them who had the right views about these issues. Every group was looking for Paul's support for their opinions, which was the wrong thing to do. Paul told them that what they most needed to be concerned about was loving one another. This matched what Jesus told his followers when he said, "Your love for one another will prove to the world that you are my disciples" (John 13:35). Paul was concerned that the believers in Corinth would not grow strong and not be able to reach others if they kept fighting among themselves. He compared the fighting to placing stumbling blocks in front of others.

To help the church in Corinth see how serious a problem their disharmony was, Paul compared them to the people of Israel. He reminded them that God had judged Israel and could judge them too. He commanded them to not be concerned for their own sake, but to put others first. And he encouraged them to live for God's glory and to trust in him to help them resolve their problems and escape temptation.

Topic 1—Food Offered to Idols

Introduction: Recall that after Paul left Corinth to proclaim the gospel in Cenchrea and other places, he stayed in touch with the believers in the Corinthian church. He wrote to them and received a response from Chloe's household when he was in Ephesus. In Chapter 8 of 1 Corinthians, Paul answered questions about food offered to idols, a topic he also addressed in his letter to the Romans.

[1] Now regarding your question about food that has been offered to idols. Yes, we know that "we all have knowledge" about this issue. But while knowledge makes us feel important, it is love that strengthens the church. [2] Anyone who claims to know all the answers doesn't really know very much. [3] But the person who loves God is the one whom God recognizes.

1 Corinthians 8:1–3

Why did Paul talk about knowledge in his response to the Corinthians? You might remember that while the believers in Corinth were quarreling about who was the most clever or eloquent teacher, what they needed to do was live in harmony. Paul reminded them that love is paramount in their relationships with one another and with God.

⁴ So, what about eating meat that has been offered to idols? Well, we all know that an idol is not really a god and that there is only one God. ⁵ There may be so-called gods both in heaven and on earth, and some people actually worship many gods and many lords. ⁶ But for us,

There is one God, the Father,
    by whom all things were created,
    and for whom we live.
And there is one Lord, Jesus Christ,
    through whom all things were created,
    and through whom we live.   1 Corinthians 8:4–6

RUINS OF APOLLO'S TEMPLE IN CORINTH

The Corinthians knew that some people worshipped many gods. In fact, the city of Corinth was well-known for its temples dedicated to idols! Though some members of the church in Corinth had been Jews, believing in only one God, most members came from a Gentile background. That meant they had been polytheists, worshipping the many different gods and goddesses of the Greek and Roman pantheons. But when the Jews and Gentiles in Corinth received the good news of the gospel and formed the church there, they had to learn and accept Christian teaching. Paul reminded the Corinthians of what they already knew about God and his Son. Then he wrote:

⁷ However, not all believers know this. Some are accustomed to thinking of idols as being real, so when they eat food that has been offered to idols, they think of it as the worship of real gods, and their weak consciences are violated. ⁸ It's true that we can't win God's approval by what we eat. We don't lose anything if we don't eat it, and we don't gain anything if we do.   1 Corinthians 8:7–8

Does this remind you of anything else in the Bible? The apostle Peter had a vision of all kinds of animals lying on a sheet. God invited Peter to eat all the kinds of animals on that sheet. God sent this vision three times so Peter would be ready to share the gospel with Gentiles who then believed his message and were saved (Acts 10:9–35).

From Peter's vision we know that the Gentiles' approval before God did not depend on what they ate, or did not eat, but on their faith in Jesus. And from your study of Romans, you learned that there is only one God, and he makes people right with himself only by faith, whether they are Jews or Gentiles (Romans 3:30).

19TH CENTURY ENGRAVING OF PETER'S VISION

In writing to the church at Corinth, Paul reminded the Gentile believers that there is only one God, and he reminded the Jewish believers that God's approval did not depend on what they ate. He addressed both groups of believers because he wanted them to be united in love so that the church would be strengthened.

Topic 2—Respecting Weaker Believers

Introduction: The advice that Paul gave to the believers in Corinth about food offered to idols was similar to what he wrote to the believers in Rome. Paul emphasized edification, stating that those who believe it is all right to eat meat offered to idols should be considerate of those who avoid it. He told the Corinthians that each person must follow his or her own conscience and that Christ died even for the believers who are "weak," sensitive, or vulnerable to returning to the old lifestyle they lived before coming to Christ. He warned the "strong" believers to watch out that their attitudes and behaviors did not harm their brothers and sisters in the faith. If unbelievers saw Christians eating such meat, they might assume that Christians worshipped both the gods and goddesses as well as Christ!

⁹ But you must be careful so that your freedom does not cause others with a weaker conscience to stumble. ¹⁰ For if others see you—with your "superior knowledge"—eating in the temple of an idol, won't they be encouraged to violate their conscience by eating food that has been offered to an idol? ¹¹ So because of your superior knowledge, a weak believer for whom Christ died will be destroyed. ¹² And when you sin against other believers by encouraging them to do something they believe is wrong, you are sinning against Christ. ¹³ So if what I eat causes another believer to sin, I will never eat meat again as long as I live—for I don't want to cause another believer to stumble.   1 Corinthians 8:9–13

The principle of being considerate to others is very important. In the next chapter of 1 Corinthians, Paul extended this principle not just to relationships among believers (for unity in the church) but also to relationships with people who do not know Jesus (for evangelism).

²² When I am with those who are weak, I share their weakness, for I want to bring the weak to Christ. Yes, I try to find common ground with everyone, doing everything I can to save some. ²³ I do everything to spread the Good News and share in its blessings.   1 Corinthians 9:22–23

Paul's example and instructions show us that love and respect are important to help weak believers grow in faith and to win others to Christ. If someone treats you with love and respect, you are more likely to listen to and learn from him or her. And if you do not show love and respect toward others, you place a stumbling block in their way. They don't even listen to your message because you've shown yourself to be unworthy of their respect or time.

> **Stumbling block**
> Any act or attitude of a believer that causes someone to sin or to doubt God or his Word

Topic 3—Lessons from Israel's Past

Introduction: After discussing how the Corinthian believers needed to act in ways that would encourage and build one another up in faith, even if they had different opinions about eating food offered to idols, Paul included examples from the Hebrew Scriptures to support his teaching.

¹ I don't want you to forget, dear brothers and sisters, about our ancestors in the wilderness long ago. All of them were guided by a cloud that moved ahead of them, and all of them walked through the sea on dry

ground. ² In the cloud and in the sea, all of them were baptized as followers of Moses. ³ All of them ate the same spiritual food, ⁴ and all of them drank the same spiritual water. For they drank from the spiritual rock that traveled with them, and that rock was Christ.　　　　　　　　　　　　　　　　　1 Corinthians 10:1–4

The believers in Corinth could identify with the Israelites Paul described. Some Corinthian believers were Jewish, so they were descendants of the Israelites. Together with the Greek believers, they sought God's guidance in their spiritual journey. Like the Israelites, the Corinthian believers were baptized. Instead of being baptized as followers of Moses, they were baptized as followers of Christ. Like the Israelites, they ate and drank together. The believers shared spiritual food and drink when they celebrated communion. Knowing they were united in these ways, they must have noticed when Paul suddenly changed from using the word *all* to the word *most*.

ISRAELITES GATHERING MANNA

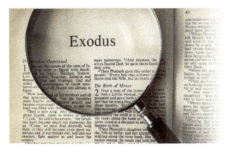

⁵ Yet God was not pleased with most of them, and their bodies were scattered in the wilderness.　　　　　　　　　　1 Corinthians 10:5

What brought this terrible consequence on the Israelites? Paul went on to give the Corinthians four different examples from the Old Testament. The first example comes from the book of Exodus.

⁶ These things happened as a warning to us, so that we would not crave evil things as they did, ⁷ or worship idols as some of them did. As the Scriptures say, "The people celebrated with feasting and drinking, and they indulged in pagan revelry."　　　　　　　　　　　　　　　　　1 Corinthians 10:6–7

The Scriptures Paul referred to in these verses came from Exodus 32:1–6. While Moses had been on Mount Sinai, talking to God and receiving the Ten Commandments, Moses' brother Aaron and the Jewish people had grown tired of waiting for Moses' return. So, Aaron made an idol shaped like a golden calf, and the people sacrificed food and drink to this idol and partied, feasting on the food and drink dedicated to the idol.

How do you think the Corinthian believers felt when they realized their behavior was like that of the Israelites? They had not made a golden calf, but they had been eating food sacrificed to idols and arguing about it!

ISRAELITES AND MOABITES OFFERING
SACRIFICES TO FALSE GODS

The next three examples of the Israelites' sin that Paul referred to came from the book of Numbers. Paul wrote:

And we must not engage in sexual immorality as some of them did, causing 23,000 of them to die in one day.

1 Corinthians 10:8

This verse referred to an event that happened many years before (Numbers 25:1–9). The women of Moab had invited Israelite men to attend sacrifices to their gods, involving feasts and sexual immorality. This resulted in a plague that killed many Jews.

The men and women in the church in Corinth faced a similar situation with their neighbors. Remember that the Corinthian believers lived in a city where worship of Aphrodite was highly encouraged. Such worship included inappropriate sexual activity. So, Paul's warnings to the church to avoid behaving like the Israelites made sense.

Paul gave the Corinthians two more examples, from the book of Numbers, of ways that the Israelites had sinned:

9 Nor should we put Christ to the test, as some of them did and then died from snakebites. 10 And don't grumble as some of them did, and then were destroyed by the angel of death.
1 Corinthians 10:9–10

Despite all God had done to provide for the Israelites in the wilderness on their way to the promised land, they complained. God sent a plague to punish them for their grumbling (Numbers 14:29). But they still didn't learn their lesson. They kept complaining, so on another occasion, God sent snakes to bite them (Numbers 21:4–6).

These things happened to them as examples for us. They were written down to warn us who live at the end of the age.
1 Corinthians 10:11

Paul's examples from Israel's history warned the church that inconsiderate and sinful behavior could result in terrible consequences. Imagine Paul as a construction worker carrying a big roll of yellow caution tape and wrapping it around all the places and behaviors where the Corinthians could stumble, fall, and hurt themselves. They crossed the tape at their own risk.

CAUTION   CAUTION   CAUTION

Topic 4—Warnings to God's People

Introduction: If you have ever been around a parent, or if you have ever had to take care of a child, you might have heard or said things like, "Don't put that in your mouth," "I said 'No'," "Don't bite," "Don't touch that," "Watch out," "Don't do that," and "Stop it." Parents and other adults do not say these kinds of things to children to be mean. They want to keep kids from doing things that could hurt them or those around them. Those who love their children care enough to discipline them (Proverbs 13:24). The number and types of warnings children receive from those around them as they get older changes, because the dangers in each stage of development also change.

Paul was the spiritual father of the Corinthian believers. Like any father, he warned and disciplined his children. He wanted the Corinthian church to grow and be strong until Jesus' return. He wanted the church to be holy. Paul continued his letter with more warnings and encouragement.

¹² If you think you are standing strong, be careful not to fall. ¹³ The temptations in your life are no different from what others experience. And God is faithful. He will not allow the temptation to be more than you can stand. When you are tempted, he will show you a way out so that you can endure.   1 Corinthians 10:12–13

Paul told the Corinthians not to make sinful choices. But Paul did not stop there. Like a good father who helps his children gain perspective when they think they are the only ones in the world facing a specific problem, Paul helped the believers understand that the temptations they experienced were normal. Paul also encouraged the Corinthians, reminding them of God's faithfulness and sharing two wonderful promises to help them stand strong. These are such precious truths that Christians often memorize 1 Corinthians 10:13. Paul continued his letter, writing:

So, my dear friends, flee from the worship of idols.   1 Corinthians 10:14

What temptations did the Corinthians face? In his letter to the church, Paul identified quite a few temptations, but he emphasized the worship of idols. You might think that this is a problem that only the Corinthians faced and that people today do not have this problem. But this is not so! Whenever people make something or someone else more important than God, they are worshipping an idol.

Paul continued his appeal by reminding the believers in Corinth that they are one body.

¹⁵ You are reasonable people. Decide for yourselves if what I am saying is true. ¹⁶ When we bless the cup at the Lord's Table, aren't we sharing in the blood of Christ? And when we break the bread, aren't we sharing in the body of Christ? ¹⁷ And though we are many, we all eat from one loaf of bread, showing that we are one body. ¹⁸ Think about the people of Israel. Weren't they united by eating the sacrifices at the altar?   1 Corinthians 10:15–18

Paul told the believers in Corinth that because they were one body, they should be united, like the people of Israel were when they worshipped the Lord. They should not grumble and complain against each other like the Israelites did when God judged them. They should not be arguing about the food offered to idols. Paul used even stronger language to rebuke the Corinthians:

¹⁹ What am I trying to say? Am I saying that food offered to idols has some significance, or that idols are real gods? ²⁰ No, not at all. I am saying that these sacrifices are offered to demons, not to God. And I don't want you to participate with demons. ²¹ You cannot drink from the cup of the Lord and from the cup of demons, too. You cannot eat at the Lord's Table and at the table of demons, too. ²² What? Do we dare to rouse the Lord's jealousy? Do you think we are stronger than he is?   1 Corinthians 10:19–22

Part 2—Glorifying God

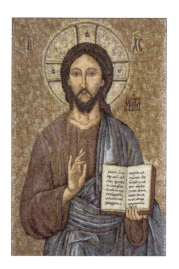

The first and most important commandment is ²⁹ The LORD our God is the one and only LORD ³⁰ And you must love the LORD your God with all your heart, all your soul, all your mind, and all your strength. (Mark 12:29–30). Paul showed how the Corinthians who were eating food offered to idols were violating that commandment. But he didn't stop there. Jesus said another commandment was just as important: Love your neighbor as yourself (Mark 12:31). So Paul showed that through arguing and disunity, the believers in Corinth were violating that commandment too.

²³ You say, "I am allowed to do anything"—but not everything is good for you. You say, "I am allowed to do anything"—but not everything is beneficial. ²⁴ Don't be concerned for your own good but for the good of others.

²⁵ So you may eat any meat that is sold in the marketplace without raising questions of conscience. ²⁶ For "the earth is the Lord's, and everything in it."

²⁷ If someone who isn't a believer asks you home for dinner, accept the invitation if you want to. Eat whatever is offered to you without raising questions of conscience. ²⁸ (But suppose someone tells you, "This meat was offered to an idol." Don't eat it, out of consideration for the conscience of the one who told you. ²⁹ It might not be a matter of conscience for you, but it is for the other person.) For why should my freedom be limited by what someone else thinks? ³⁰ If I can thank God for the food and enjoy it, why should I be condemned for eating it?

³¹ So whether you eat or drink, or whatever you do, do it all for the glory of God. ³² Don't give offense to Jews or Gentiles or the church of God.
1 Corinthians 10:23–32

The command to do "all" for God's glory is not limited to food or drink. It covers everything—anything that could offend people who do not know God, or offend brothers and sisters who do know him. We are free to eat, drink, dress, speak, or enjoy entertainment as we wish, but we must be also aware of how others are affected by our actions. Is what we do beneficial? Does it help or does it harm another's faith? If it harms others, it is a stumbling block.

Paul was not asking the Corinthians anything that he was not willing to do himself. He continued:

I, too, try to please everyone in everything I do. I don't just do what is best for me; I do what is best for others so that many may be saved.
1 Corinthians 10:33

And you should imitate me, just as I imitate Christ.
1 Corinthians 11:1

Paul was deliberate about his actions. He behaved a specific way because he wanted to accomplish a specific purpose. He was not perfect, but he did his best. And we can follow his example, as he followed Christ, loving others and seeking to glorify God.

Worship and Spiritual Gifts

Getting Started—The Main Ideas

The believers in the church in Corinth had many problems and many questions, so they wrote to Paul for help. When Paul was in Ephesus, Christians from Corinth came to visit him and tell him that the church was not doing very well. They said people were arguing and sinning. Paul wanted to help the church address these issues and wrote about how the believers should behave when they met together.

Paul began by focusing on the Lord's Supper, which is also called communion. When Christians take communion, they are commemorating Christ's death on the cross for our sins. This is done by eating bread and drinking wine or grape juice. This act is performed according to what Jesus taught his disciples during the Passover meal before his death. It is a sacrament, which is a religious ceremony considered to be very sacred. (Some Christians call the Lord's Supper *an ordinance* because it is required or ordered by Jesus.) The way that the Corinthians were behaving during the Lord's Supper was not respectful. It was completely unacceptable!

The Lord's Supper was also part of a communal meal, somewhat like a potluck in churches today. To show that they were better than others in the congregation, some of the Corinthian believers were disregarding others. Instead of waiting their turn and sharing with everyone, they took so much that there was nothing left for the poor. So, Paul reminded the Corinthians of what communion was all about. He told them that they needed to examine themselves and warned them that God would judge them if they continued in the same way.

The matter of showing off was not limited to communion, but also characterized the Corinthian believers' approach to spiritual gifts. They wanted to speak in unknown languages, or tongues, to interpret what was said, or to prophesy. Then everyone would know how important they were! In the temple of Apollo and the other temples that the city of Corinth was so famous for, the important people were the ones who gave the messages from the gods. So, the Corinthians wanted the spiritual gifts that would give them greater status. The believers did not understand that God wanted them to serve others. His gifts are intended to bless the church, not divide it.

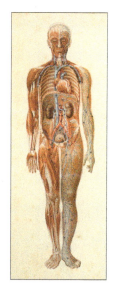

Paul explained that the church is like a body with many parts. Even though the parts are different, and some can be visible while others are not, every part is valuable. So, each person in the church, no matter what his or her gift or role might be, is valuable too. Paul wanted the believers to know that love is more important than spiritual gifts.

In English, the word *love* is used to describe a great many different feelings, from romantic love to the love someone might have for a parent, a friend, a pet, or even a possession or place. In contrast, the Greek language has many different words for love. The New Testament was written in Greek, and the Greek word that Paul used to describe love in 1 Corinthians 13 is *agape*. It refers to the kind of love that Jesus demonstrated when he died on the cross for our sake. Agape describes unconditional and unselfish love, a love that seeks the good of others.

After writing about love, Paul continued teaching the Corinthian believers about how they should handle spiritual gifts and corporate worship. He wanted the church to reflect God's own character, because God is not a God of disorder, but of peace (1 Corinthians 14:33). Having peaceful, orderly worship would also be a great testimony to the people of Corinth.

Communion
The act of commemorating Christ's death through a ritual using bread and wine

Sacrament
A religious ceremony that is considered very sacred

Agape
The Greek word for unconditional and unselfish love

Topic 1—The Lord's Supper

Introduction: Recall that Paul was writing to a church that was experiencing many problems. These included disunity, boasting, immaturity, idolatry, and sexual sin. In fact, the problems were so serious that some believers had taken each other to court (1 Corinthians 6:1–8). So, what did Paul say to these and other believers in the church in Corinth?

2 I am so glad that you always keep me in your thoughts, and that you are following the teachings I passed on to you. . . .
17 But in the following instructions, I cannot praise you. For it sounds as if more harm than good is done when you meet together. 18 First, I hear that there are divisions among you when you meet as a church, and to some extent I believe it. 19 But, of course, there must be divisions among you so that you who have God's approval will be recognized!
1 Corinthians 11:2, 17–19

Divisions were the result of the Corinthians' quarrels. These divisions did not win God's approval! What does God approve of? The Bible says the Lord approves of those who are good (Proverbs 12:2). It also says,

17 For the Kingdom of God is . . . a matter . . . of living a life of goodness and peace and joy in the Holy Spirit. 18 If you serve Christ with this attitude, you will please God, and others will approve of you, too.
Romans 14:17–18

Some believers behaved appropriately—according to what Jesus taught. God was pleased with them and other people approved of them. Other believers behaved inappropriately. Paul was concerned that the carelessness of those believers was harming the whole church in Corinth.

²⁰ When you meet together, you are not really interested in the Lord's Supper. ²¹ For some of you hurry to eat your own meal without sharing with others. As a result, some go hungry while others get drunk. ²² What? Don't you have your own homes for eating and drinking? Or do you really want to disgrace God's church and shame the poor? What am I supposed to say? Do you want me to praise you? Well, I certainly will not praise you for this!

1 Corinthians 11:20–22

Why was this kind of behavior wrong? Some believers were not waiting for everyone else. They did not share their food. They let others go hungry, humiliating those who were poor. Some even got drunk. Their behavior was a disgrace because it contradicted the whole purpose of meeting together, which was to remember Jesus and show that they were one body (1 Corinthians 10:16–17). No wonder Paul was appalled! So, he decided to remind the Corinthian believers what the Lord's Supper was all about. You have probably heard the following words recited in church:

²³ For I pass on to you what I received from the Lord himself. On the night when he was betrayed, the Lord Jesus took some bread ²⁴ and gave thanks to God for it. Then he broke it in pieces and said, "This is my body, which is given for you. Do this in remembrance of me." ²⁵ In the same way, he took the cup of wine after supper, saying, "This cup is the new covenant between God and his people—an agreement confirmed with my blood. Do this in remembrance of me as often as you drink it." ²⁶ For every time you eat this bread and drink this cup, you are announcing the Lord's death until he comes again.

1 Corinthians 11:23–26

What Jesus wanted his followers to announce, or proclaim, through communion was very different from what some of the Corinthians were proclaiming by their poor behavior. Therefore, Paul challenged each person to decide whether his or her actions would please the Lord or not.

²⁷ So anyone who eats this bread or drinks this cup of the Lord unworthily is guilty of sinning against the body and blood of the Lord. ²⁸ That is why you should examine yourself before eating the bread and drinking the cup. ²⁹ For if you eat the bread or drink the cup without honoring the body of Christ, you are eating and drinking God's judgment upon yourself. ³⁰ That is why many of you are weak and sick and some have even died.

1 Corinthians 11:27–30

Weakness, sickness, and death were serious consequences of the bad behavior that Paul described in the Corinthian church. Does this mean that God is like Zeus, the Greek god that many of the Corinthians believers had rejected, who was ready to hurl lightning bolts or other kinds of punishment at anyone who displeased him? No. God is merciful and compassionate, slow to get angry and filled with unfailing love . . . eager to relent and not punish (Joel 2:13).

Jesus taught that God judges his people for their own good. He said,

¹ "I am the true grapevine, and my Father is the gardener. ² He cuts off every branch of mine that doesn't produce fruit, and he prunes the branches that do bear fruit so they will produce even more."

John 15:1–2

God disciplines those he loves (Hebrews 12:5–13). So, Paul continued his warning to the Corinthians, explaining that God does not want to condemn us:

³¹ But if we would examine ourselves, we would not be judged by God in this way. ³² Yet when we are judged by the Lord, we are being disciplined so that we will not be condemned along with the world.

³³ So, my dear brothers and sisters, when you gather for the Lord's Supper, wait for each other. ³⁴ If you are really hungry, eat at home so you won't bring judgment upon yourselves when you meet together. I'll give you instructions about the other matters after I arrive.   1 Corinthians 11:31–34

Paul encouraged the believers in the Corinthian church to wait for one another when they gathered to celebrate the sacrament of the Lord's Supper. Paul also reminded them of his love for them and of his plan to visit them again.

Topic 2—Spiritual Gifts

Introduction: The next question that Paul answered in his letter had to do with spiritual gifts. Many of the believers in Corinth had been led astray and swept along in worshiping speechless idols (1 Corinthians 12:2), so they needed to know how spiritual gifts in Christian churches were different from what they had seen

in their previous worship of pagan deities. Such worship had included not only feasting, singing, and rituals, but also claims of miracles, exorcisms, and direct revelation from different gods. In fact, Greece was known in the ancient world for its oracles—the places and people through whom the deities supposedly spoke, either in tongues or with interpretation or prophecy. Therefore, Paul warned the new believers in Corinth that spiritual gifts in the church should come only from the Holy Spirit. Then he explained more about how spiritual gifts would function in their congregation.

THE ORACLE OF DELPHI IN GREECE

Part 1—One Giver

¹ Now, dear brothers and sisters, regarding your question about the special abilities the Spirit gives us. I don't want you to misunderstand this. ² You know that when you were still pagans, you were led astray and swept along in worshiping speechless idols. ³ So I want you to know that no one speaking by the Spirit of God will curse Jesus, and no one can say Jesus is Lord, except by the Holy Spirit.

⁴ There are different kinds of spiritual gifts, but the same Spirit is the source of them all. ⁵ There are different kinds of service, but we serve the same Lord. ⁶ God works in different ways, but it is the same God who does the work in all of us.   1 Corinthians 12:1–6

The polytheistic pagans in Corinth thought that each deity gave different gifts. In contrast, Paul emphasized that all spiritual gifts, service, and work are from the one true God. Christians worship one God in three Persons: the Father, the Son (the Lord Jesus Christ), and the Holy Spirit. The three Persons of the Trinity, who are one God, work together to equip believers so that they can help each other.

⁷A spiritual gift is given to each of us so we can help each other. ⁸To one person the Spirit gives the ability to give wise advice; to another the same Spirit gives a message of special knowledge. ⁹The same Spirit gives great faith to another, and to someone else the one Spirit gives the gift of healing. ¹⁰He gives one person the power to perform miracles, and another the ability to prophesy. He gives someone else the ability to discern whether a message is from the Spirit of God or from another spirit. Still another person is given the ability to speak in unknown languages, while another is given the ability to interpret what is being said. ¹¹It is the one and only Spirit who distributes all these gifts. He alone decides which gift each person should have.

1 Corinthians 12:7–11

Paul taught that even though there are many different kinds of gifts, they come from the one God, who gave them for believers to help each other. In another letter of the New Testament, the apostle Peter taught something very similar: God has given each of you a gift from his great variety of spiritual gifts. Use them well to serve one another (1 Peter 4:10).

Part 2—One Body

Recall that the Corinthian believers had been arguing about many things. They argued about their teachers. They argued about who had the right idea about what to eat or drink. They argued about how they could prove they were more spiritual than those around them. Paul explained to the Corinthians that the purpose of spiritual gifts was for Christians to help others. Then he continued his emphasis on unity with an analogy, or comparison.

¹²The human body has many parts, but the many parts make up one whole body. So it is with the body of Christ. ¹³Some of us are Jews, some are Gentiles, some are slaves, and some are free. But we have all been baptized into one body by one Spirit, and we all share the same Spirit.

¹⁴Yes, the body has many different parts, not just one part. ¹⁵If the foot says, "I am not a part of the body because I am not a hand," that does not make it any less a part of the body. ¹⁶And if the ear says, "I am not part of the body because I am not an eye," would that make it any less a part of the body? ¹⁷If the whole body were an eye, how would you hear? Or if your whole body were an ear, how would you smell anything?

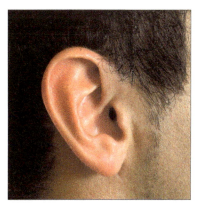

¹⁸But our bodies have many parts, and God has put each part just where he wants it. ¹⁹How strange a body would be if it had only one part! ²⁰Yes, there are many parts, but only one body. ²¹The eye can never say to the hand, "I don't need you." The head can't say to the feet, "I don't need you."

²²In fact, some parts of the body that seem weakest and least important are actually the most necessary. ²³And the parts we regard as less honorable are those we clothe with the greatest care. So we carefully protect those parts that should not be seen, ²⁴while the more honorable parts do not require this special care. So God has put the body together such that extra honor and care are given to those parts that have less dignity. ²⁵This makes for harmony among the members, so that all the members care for each other. ²⁶If one part suffers, all the parts suffer with it, and if one part is honored, all the parts are glad.

1 Corinthians 12:12–31

The church is like a body with many different parts. In the same way that the parts need each other for the whole body to function well, the church needs each of its members. Paul wanted all believers—Jews, Gentiles, slaves, free citizens, men, women, rich people, poor people, the old, and the young—to all support and encourage one another, regardless of their differences. He wanted them to help each other even if they each had different spiritual gifts.

²⁷ All of you together are Christ's body, and each of you is a part of it. ²⁸ Here are some of the parts God has appointed for the church:

first are apostles,
second are prophets,
third are teachers,
then those who do miracles,
those who have the gift of healing,
those who can help others,
those who have the gift of leadership,
those who speak in unknown languages.

²⁹ Are we all apostles? Are we all prophets? Are we all teachers? Do we all have the power to do miracles? ³⁰ Do we all have the gift of healing? Do we all have the ability to speak in unknown languages? Do we all have the ability to interpret unknown languages? Of course not! ³¹ So you should earnestly desire the most helpful gifts.

But now let me show you a way of life that is best of all.   1 Corinthians 12:27–31

Paul's list of parts included some, but not all, of the parts God appointed for the church. He did not include a complete list of every single gift that God gives to the church. But all the parts and gifts are given so that believers can honor God by seeking the best for each other.

Topic 3—Godly Love

Introduction: First Corinthians 13 is one of the most famous chapters of the Bible. Why? Because it explains the nature of God's love, or *agape*. It is often quoted in wedding ceremonies and referred to in sermons on Christian love.

Paul's discussion of love expands on what he previously said to the Corinthian believers. He had written that it is love that strengthens the church (1 Corinthians 8:1), commanding the Corinthians to be concerned . . . for the good of others (1 Corinthians 11:24), and adding that as members of one body, they should care for each other (1 Corinthians 12:25). Love would enable the believers to be united as they celebrated the Lord's Supper and took part in worship services. Paul explained love's importance in more detail.

¹ If I could speak all the languages of earth and of angels, but didn't love others, I would only be a noisy gong or a clanging cymbal. ² If I had the gift of prophecy, and if I understood all of God's secret plans and possessed all knowledge, and if I had such faith that I could move mountains, but didn't love others, I would be nothing. ³ If I gave everything I have to the poor and even sacrificed my body, I could boast about it; but if I didn't love others, I would have gained nothing.   1 Corinthians 13:1–3

Love is a common topic. There are poems and books devoted to the subject, songs about love on the radio, and movies and much more about it on the internet. But the messages that are broadcast about love often do not match what Paul wrote about love to the Corinthians. A song might tell about lustful love. A movie might portray a story about a jealous lover. These types of love are often selfish. Paul explained that agape love is not self-serving; it is the kind of love that considers what is best for others.

⁴ Love is patient and kind. Love is not jealous or boastful or proud ⁵ or rude. It does not demand its own way. It is not irritable, and it keeps no record of being wronged. ⁶ It does not rejoice about injustice but rejoices whenever the truth wins out. ⁷ Love never gives up, never loses faith, is always hopeful, and endures through every circumstance.   1 Corinthians 13:4–7

This kind of love is the kind of love that God has for us and that he wants us to show to one another. It is the kind of love that Paul wanted for the believers in Corinth. He wanted them to have this love even more than spiritual gifts. Even though such gifts as miracles, healing, and prophecies are desirable, love is more important.

⁸ Prophecy and speaking in unknown languages and special knowledge will become useless. But love will last forever! ⁹ Now our knowledge is partial and incomplete, and even the gift of prophecy reveals only part of the whole picture! ¹⁰ But when the time of perfection comes, these partial things will become useless.

¹¹ When I was a child, I spoke and thought and reasoned as a child. But when I grew up, I put away childish things. ¹² Now we see things imperfectly, like puzzling reflections in a mirror, but then we will see everything with perfect clarity. All that I know now is partial and incomplete, but then I will know everything completely, just as God now knows me completely.

¹³ Three things will last forever—faith, hope, and love—and the greatest of these is love.   1 Corinthians 13:8–13

Exhibiting agape love is a mark of Christian maturity. It is a fruit of the Holy Spirit. When you love unselfishly, this shows that the Holy Spirit is at work in you, transforming your character, so that you are becoming the person God wants you to be. Love is what Jesus considered was most important (Matthew 22:36–40). The more you love, the more this shows that you have the same priorities that Jesus had. This love was what Paul was trying to model for the believers in Corinth (1 Corinthians 11:1), and what he hoped they would have for one other.

Introduction: Paul wanted the believers in Corinth to be "united in thought and purpose" (1 Corinthians 1:10). But because the Corinthians had differences of opinion, Paul had to teach them again about how they should behave when they celebrated the Lord's Supper, and how they should think about the spiritual gifts that were present among them. He emphasized that love should guide the believers' actions and described what godly love is like. Then he returned to teaching about spiritual gifts.

[1] Let love be your highest goal! But you should also desire the special abilities the Spirit gives—especially the ability to prophesy. [2] For if you have the ability to speak in tongues, you will be talking only to God, since people won't be able to understand you. You will be speaking by the power of the Spirit, but it will all be mysterious. [3] But one who prophesies strengthens others, encourages them, and comforts them. [4] A person who speaks in tongues is strengthened personally, but one who speaks a word of prophecy strengthens the entire church.

[5] I wish you could all speak in tongues, but even more I wish you could all prophesy. For prophecy is greater than speaking in tongues, unless someone interprets what you are saying so that the whole church will be strengthened.

1 Corinthians 14:1–5

Paul's priority was for believers to behave in ways that strengthened, encouraged, and comforted others. Instead of arguing among themselves about whether it was greater to speak in tongues or to interpret or prophesy, Paul wanted the Corinthians to understand that in group settings, they should use their spiritual gifts to edify those around them.

Well, my brothers and sisters, let's summarize. When you meet together, one will sing, another will teach, another will tell some special revelation God has given, one will speak in tongues, and another will interpret what is said. But everything that is done must strengthen all of you.

1 Corinthians 14:26

Paul continued by giving the Corinthian believers specific instructions about how to maintain order in church as they exercised the spiritual gifts they received from the Spirit:

[27] No more than two or three should speak in tongues. They must speak one at a time, and someone must interpret what they say. [28] But if no one is present who can interpret, they must be silent in your church meeting and speak in tongues to God privately.

[29] Let two or three people prophesy, and let the others evaluate what is said. [30] But if someone is prophesying and another person receives a revelation from the Lord, the one who is speaking must stop. [31] In this way, all who prophesy will have a turn to speak, one after the other, so that everyone will learn and be encouraged. [32] Remember that people who prophesy are in control of their spirit and can take turns. [33] For God is not a God of disorder but of peace, as in all the meetings of God's holy people.

1 Corinthians 14:27–33

Peace, order, and holiness would certainly have made Christians' meetings in Corinth stand out from the worship practiced by the pagans around them. Recall that Corinth was a city full of temples to different idols, each requiring special homage. Rather than having Christians copy the temples and rituals of their past, Paul wanted believers to understand that, all together, they were "the temple of God" (1 Corinthians 3:16) and that their behavior as a group should reflect God's character. So he repeated himself:

[39] So, my dear brothers and sisters, be eager to prophesy, and don't forbid speaking in tongues. [40] But be sure that everything is done properly and in order.   1 Corinthians 14:39–40

Throughout history, Christians have agreed that several key elements are important in worship:

1. Praise, which is honoring or glorifying God through words, music, or artwork.
2. Confession, which involves admitting and repenting of our sins and accepting God's forgiveness.
3. Prayer and petitions, which include speaking directly to God about our needs and the needs of others.
4. Hearing God's Word through the reading of Scripture, the sermon, the words of the hymns or songs, and all aspects of the service.
5. Remembering Christ's sacrifice by taking communion. Many churches observe communion weekly, but others do so monthly or even less often.
6. Responding to God's love by honoring him with tithes and offerings. It also involves obeying and serving him throughout the week.

Topic 5—Comparing Views on Worship

Introduction: Do you remember the first time you ever went to church? If you grew up in a Christian home, you probably have many memories of worship. If you were invited to church when you were very young, you might have only a faint memory of what it was like. And because Christianity is the major religion in the United States, even people who are not Christians—because of what they have seen, read, or heard from the media or Christians around them—have some idea of what to expect if they visit a Christian church.

But imagine that you are inviting someone to church who has no background in what church is like. What would you tell that person? You might begin by explaining what is acceptable to wear to church. (Many Christian churches do not have a formal dress code, but they do encourage people to dress modestly.) You might describe what your friend should expect upon entering the church building. Will there be a greeter or an information desk? Where should your friend go? Do people wear name tags? Then you might want to explain what happens in church. Who speaks to the congregation? When

do people stand up, sit down, or kneel? How do you know which song to sing and what the tune is? What is communion? Can everyone eat the bread and drink the grape juice? How long are the worship services?

Remember that the Corinthians had questions about worship too. Much of what Paul addressed in 1 Corinthians answered questions the believers had about what they should do when they got together, including questions about what to wear, what to eat and how to eat it, whether to give an offering, and who should speak and how. And these are the same kinds of questions that you might have if a Muslim asks you to visit a mosque, a naturalist asks you to attend an atheist meeting, or a practitioner of new spirituality invites you to observe one of their rituals or ceremonies.

Part 1—Islam

When you studied *salat*, the second pillar of the Islamic faith, you learned that Muslims are expected to pray five times a day, preferably in a mosque. Because of this, mosques are open every day of the week. Many of them have places where Muslim believers can wash before they worship.

Muslims follow a dress code when they attend prayer or services at a mosque, and they encourage visitors to do the same. Traditionally, Muslim men avoid wearing silk or gold. Women are required to wear head coverings and to dress very modestly.

MAIN PRAYER HALL INSIDE THE
GRAND MOSQUE IN KUWAIT

Men and women worship in different sections of a mosque. Both must pray in the direction of Mecca (in Saudi Arabia). The salat prayers are recited in Arabic—led by the *imam*, who conducts the service—and the people respond. As men and women pray, they stand, bow, lie prostrate, or sit as instructed, so there are no pews and few or no chairs in the prayer space (these are for elderly or disabled people only). To maintain hygiene and be considerate of others, mosques do not allow people to wear shoes in the worship area; they have places for people to leave their shoes before entering.

While daily prayers last about 10 minutes, Muslims gather for a longer time during the noon prayers on Friday, considered the day of assembly (Quran 62:9). At that time, the imam preaches a sermon for the congregation. The sermon has two parts, allowing Muslims a few minutes for personal prayer as they reflect on the imam's words. In Islam, there are fewer opportunities for believers to participate than there are for Christians in their congregations. There are no elders or deacons or people using the gifts of the Holy Spirit to strengthen the whole church. There is no worship band or choir. Unlike Christians, Muslims generally do not sing or use musical instruments in their services. Worship in Islam is very different from what Paul described in 1 Corinthians.

Part 2—Naturalism

Most naturalists avoid religious gatherings. Journalist Tom Roston, an atheist, explains: "We're talking about a group of people who are primarily skeptics, fiercely individualistic, and mostly non-joiners—those who identify themselves by what they don't believe in. This is not a crowd that easily rallies around any person or precept."[1] Atheist, freethinker, and humanist meetings generally include announcements, a lecture or group discussion, and some refreshments. They do not include worship, prayer, music, communion, or other elements that we associate with church, or that Paul described as he wrote to the Corinthians.

Although people who hold naturalist beliefs do not tend to go to church, there are increasing numbers of naturalist organizations that offer community, singing, and discussion in a church-like format. One such example is the First Church of Atheism. It declares that "Nothing exists besides natural phenomena. Thought is merely a function of those natural phenomena. Death is complete, and irreversible. We have faith solely in humankind, nature, and the facts of science."[2]

Appreciation for humankind, nature, and science is good, but falls short of what Paul promised when he wrote to the Corinthians. Paul recognized that we human beings have limitations, so he wrote: All that I know now is partial and incomplete, but . . . God . . . knows me completely (1 Corinthians 13:12). And, no eye has seen, no ear has heard, and no mind has imagined what God has prepared for those who love him (1 Corinthians 2:6, 9). We have so much to look forward to with God!

Part 3—New Spirituality

What should you expect to see or experience if you go to a gathering with people who practice new spirituality? This is a very difficult question to answer due to the nature of this worldview because it is "an extremely large, loosely structured network of organizations . . . bound together by common values (based in mysticism and monism—the [belief] that "all is one") and a common vision (a coming "new age" of peace and mass enlightenment, the "Age of Aquarius").["]3 The network is quite diverse, so much so that it is impossible to describe what constitutes an average ritual or ceremony.

A lot of new spiritualist rituals are self-guided, done in solitude, and often in nature. They might involve using crystals, amulets, meditation, automatic writing, prayers to the universe, and many other items or actions. Other rituals or ceremonies involve only two people: the new spiritualist, and a teacher, guru, healer, or

TIBETAN SINGING BOWL

medium. A new spiritualist whose *reiki* healer is manipulating her spiritual energies through massage will describe this experience very differently from a new spiritualist who asks a counselor to help him access memories of a past life. There are, of course, events that bring new spiritualists together, such as a lecture where a medium claims to channel a spirit who speaks to those present or a retreat where a shaman and his followers use drugs and other means to induce altered states of consciousness. But there is no group gathering for new spiritualists that brings them all together in the same way that church unites Christians, because each gathering promotes different things.

In contrast, Christians are united in proclaiming that "Jesus is Lord" (1 Corinthians 12:3). When we celebrate communion, we proclaim a single message, as Paul taught the Corinthians: Every time you eat this bread and drink this cup, you are announcing the Lord's death until he comes again (1 Corinthians 11:26). And no one can lay any foundation other than the one we already have—Jesus Christ. (1 Corinthians 3:11).

ENDNOTES
1 Tom Roston, "Atheism has finally found its spiritual leader," *Quartz*, September 15, 2014. https://qz.com/265152/atheism-has-finally-found-its-spiritual-leader/.
2 FAQ, First Church of Atheism, accessed Friday, May 31, 2019, from https://firstchurchofatheism.com/faq/.
3 Elliot D. Miller, "The New Age Movement: What Is It?" *Christian Research Journal*, June 9, 2009, https://www.equip.org/article/the-new-age-movement-what-is-it/.

Getting Started—The Main Ideas

Believers in Corinth were in a unique situation. The city of Corinth was a political, commercial, cultural, and spiritual center. This meant that the church there had people with different levels of wealth, power, and education, as well as different religious traditions. Those differences led to disagreements and questions.

Paul wrote 1 Corinthians to help the church. He wrote about divisions and sin in the church. He answered questions about food offered to idols. He explained how the believers should celebrate the Lord's Supper, love one another, and use spiritual gifts for the benefit of the church. Because the Corinthian believers had disagreements about Jesus' resurrection and the resurrection of the dead, Paul wrote about these matters too.

Paul emphasized that he and other leaders who had taught in the church all proclaimed the same message: God's plan of salvation, accomplished when Jesus died for our sins, was buried, and rose again. Paul reminded the Corinthian believers of the many times that Jesus appeared to his disciples after his resurrection. He wanted the church to understand that Jesus' resurrection was essential to the faith. Because Jesus rose from the dead, those who put their faith in him have the hope of eternal life.

Paul explained that God will transform the bodies of all who are raised in Christ. God will change our bodies so that they are fit to live forever and inherit the kingdom of God. This will happen in an instant, fulfilling God's promise of victory over sin and death.

The believers in Corinth needed to understand the resurrection so that they could faithfully proclaim the gospel to those around them. People like the Sadducees, the Epicureans, and the Stoics did not believe that Jesus rose from the dead or that resurrection was even possible. Today, Muslims, naturalists, and new spiritualists have beliefs about Jesus' resurrection, and the resurrection of the dead, that are different from what Christians believe. Understanding what the Bible teaches about this topic is as important for us today as it was for the first-century Corinthian church.

Topic 1—Jesus' Resurrection

Introduction: Have you ever played the telephone game? This game is also known by other names, such as *broken telephone* or *pass the message*. If you have played the game, you know someone begins it by whispering a phrase to one person, who whispers it to the next, and so on. The more people there are to pass on the phrase, the more likely it is that someone will mishear it and change the wording. The changes can lead to hilarious results. That's the fun of the game!

Like the message in the telephone game, the good news of salvation in Jesus Christ spread from one person to another. It spread from Jerusalem all the way to Corinth and beyond! But unlike the message in the telephone game, the good news did not change along the way. Paul told the believers in Corinth that the good news he preached to them was the same message as he had received and the same that the other apostles preached.

THE GARDEN TOMB, WHERE MANY BELIEVE JESUS WAS BURIED

What was the message? It was that Christ died for our sins, was buried, and then rose from the dead. That message is still taught today in the Apostles' Creed. A creed is a statement that summarizes the core beliefs or principles guiding a group or an individual.

Jesus' resurrection was essential to the good news. Many people found it difficult to believe that it had happened because people who die usually stay dead. Why would Jesus be the exception? But Paul reminded the church in Corinth that even though Jesus had died and been buried, he was later seen alive on several occasions by many witnesses and in different locations.

¹ Let me now remind you, dear brothers and sisters, of the Good News I preached to you before. You welcomed it then, and you still stand firm in it. ² It is this Good News that saves you if you continue to believe the message I told you—unless, of course, you believed something that was never true in the first place.

³ I passed on to you what was most important and what had also been passed on to me. Christ died for our sins, just as the Scriptures said. ⁴ He was buried, and he was raised from the dead on the third day, just as the Scriptures said. ⁵ He was seen by Peter and then by the Twelve. ⁶ After that, he was seen by more than 500 of his followers at one time, most of whom are still alive, though some have died. ⁷ Then he was seen by James and later by all the apostles. ⁸ Last of all, as though I had been born at the wrong time, I also saw him. ⁹ For I am the least of all the apostles. In fact, I'm not even worthy to be called an apostle after the way I persecuted God's church.

¹⁰ But whatever I am now, it is all because God poured out his special favor on me—and not without results. For I have worked harder than any of the other apostles; yet it was not I but God who was working through me by his grace. ¹¹ So it makes no difference whether I preach or they preach, for we all preach the same message you have already believed.

1 Corinthians 15:1–11

Paul thought it was very important for the believers in Corinth to understand that Jesus really rose from the dead. He affirmed that he preached the same things the other apostles preached. Paul had not been with the disciples chosen by Jesus at the start of his ministry; God called Paul to be an apostle later, after Jesus had risen from the dead. The exciting story of Paul's conversion is found in Acts 9.

Paul gave a list of appearances of the resurrected Lord, but his list is not complete. The first people to see the resurrected Christ were Mary Magdalene; Mary, the mother of James, and possibly their friend Salome (Matthew 28:1–10, Mark 16:1–8). The risen Jesus also spent time speaking on the road to Emmaus with two men, one of whom was named *Cleopas* (Luke 24:13–34).

There were many witnesses to Jesus' resurrection. And many people could confirm that the believers in Corinth received the same message as those who followed Jesus in Jerusalem and in other cities in the ancient world. If today we, as Christians, agree in this core belief that Jesus rose from the dead, we affirm the same creed.

Creed
A summary of the core beliefs or principles guiding a group or an individual

Topic 2—The Coming Resurrection

Introduction: In the first verses of 1 Corinthians 15, Paul emphasized that he taught the same message as the other apostles: that Jesus Christ died, was buried, and then rose again. Many witnesses saw Jesus after he rose again. Paul wanted the believers in Corinth to understand that the resurrection was an essential part of the message about Jesus.

STATUE OF A STOIC PHILOSOPHER

Recall that the church in Corinth had people from both Jewish and Gentile backgrounds. Some of its Jewish members may have been influenced by the Sadducees—religious leaders who taught that there was no resurrection of the dead (Mark 12:18). Some of the Gentiles may have been influenced by Epicurean and Stoic philosophers (Acts 17:18). The Epicureans did not believe in life after death, and the Stoics did not believe in any sort of resurrection. And both Jews and Gentiles in the church in Corinth were probably influenced by Greek and Jewish teachers who thought that because human bodies were made of matter, they were therefore evil.

So, in trying to sort out their faith in Jesus with what they had previously learned, some believers in Corinth taught that there was no resurrection of the dead. They also taught that although Jesus died and was buried, he did not rise again in bodily form. Paul wrote to the church in Corinth to correct these erroneous teachings.

¹² But tell me this—since we preach that Christ rose from the dead, why are some of you saying there will be no resurrection of the dead? ¹³ For if there is no resurrection of the dead, then Christ has not been raised either. ¹⁴ And if Christ has not been raised, then all our preaching is useless, and your faith is useless. ¹⁵ And we apostles would all be lying about God—for we have said that God raised Christ from the grave. But that can't be true if there is no resurrection of the dead. ¹⁶ And if there is no resurrection of the dead, then Christ has not been raised. ¹⁷ And if Christ has not been raised, then your faith is useless and you are still guilty of your sins. ¹⁸ In that case, all who have died believing in Christ are lost! ¹⁹ And if our hope in Christ is only for this life, we are more to be pitied than anyone in the world.

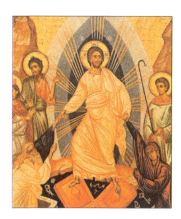

ICON OF JESUS HELPING
SAINTS RISE

[20] But in fact, Christ has been raised from the dead. He is the first of a great harvest of all who have died. *1 Corinthians 15:12–20*

Belief in Jesus' resurrection, and in the resurrection of the dead, is a key tenet of the Christian faith. When Paul wrote to the church in Rome, he said that believers *wait with eager hope for the day when God will give us our full rights as his adopted children, including the new bodies he has promised us. We were given this hope when we were saved. (Romans 8:23–24)*. Paul taught that believers *have been called to one glorious hope for the future (Ephesians 4:4)*. The resurrection is part of what Christians hope to receive because of their salvation, and Paul wrote to remind the believers in the Corinthian church about this. He further explained:

[21] So you see, just as death came into the world through a man, now the resurrection from the dead has begun through another man. [22] Just as everyone dies because we all belong to Adam, everyone who belongs to Christ will be given new life. [23] But there is an order to this resurrection: Christ was raised as the first of the harvest; then all who belong to Christ will be raised when he comes back.

FRESCO OF CHRIST AS
KING OF THE WORLD

[24] After that the end will come, when he will turn the Kingdom over to God the Father, having destroyed every ruler and authority and power. [25] For Christ must reign until he humbles all his enemies beneath his feet. [26] And the last enemy to be destroyed is death. [27] For the Scriptures say, "God has put all things under his authority." (Of course, when it says "all things are under his authority," that does not include God himself, who gave Christ his authority.) [28] Then, when all things are under his authority, the Son will put himself under God's authority, so that God, who gave his Son authority over all things, will be utterly supreme over everything everywhere. *1 Corinthians 15:21–28*

Paul believed that it was important for people to know that Jesus conquered death and that they could have new life in him. Because of this, he preached the message about Jesus' death and resurrection even at the risk of his own life.

[29] If the dead will not be raised, . . . [30] why should we . . . risk our lives hour by hour? [31] For I swear, dear brothers and sisters, that I face death daily. [32] . . . If there is no resurrection, "Let's feast and drink, for tomorrow we die!" [33] Don't be fooled by those who say such things, for "bad company corrupts good character." [34] Think carefully about what is right, and stop sinning. For to your shame I say that some of you don't know God at all. *1 Corinthians 15:29–34*

Topic 3—Raised to Life

Introduction: Paul said that Jesus rose from the dead, and that this was affirmed by the apostles and by the many witnesses who saw Jesus after his death. Then Paul explained that believers should also expect a physical resurrection. The Corinthian believers, therefore, had a lot of questions about what it would be like to rise from the dead and what their bodies would look like. It is a topic that has captured human imagination through the ages. People have pictured zombies, vampires, ghosts, mummies, and much more. But none of their speculations come close to the truth. Paul went on to explain more about the resurrection that is promised to those who believe in Jesus Christ as Lord.

35 But someone may ask, "How will the dead be raised? What kind of bodies will they have?" 36 What a foolish question! When you put a seed into the ground, it doesn't grow into a plant unless it dies first. 37 And what you put in the ground is not the plant that will grow, but only a bare seed of wheat or whatever you are planting. 38 Then God gives it the new body he wants it to have. A different plant grows from each kind of seed. 39 Similarly there are different kinds of flesh—one kind for humans, another for animals, another for birds, and another for fish.

40 There are also bodies in the heavens and bodies on the earth. The glory of the heavenly bodies is different from the glory of the earthly bodies. 41 The sun has one kind of glory, while the moon and stars each have another kind. And even the stars differ from each other in their glory.

42 It is the same way with the resurrection of the dead. Our earthly bodies are planted in the ground when we die, but they will be raised to live forever. 43 Our bodies are buried in brokenness, but they will be raised in glory. They are buried in weakness, but they will be raised in strength. 44 They are buried as natural human bodies, but they will be raised as spiritual bodies. For just as there are natural bodies, there are also spiritual bodies.

45 The Scriptures tell us, "The first man, Adam, became a living person." But the last Adam—that is, Christ—is a life-giving Spirit. 46 What comes first is the natural body, then the spiritual body comes later. 47 Adam, the first man, was made from the dust of the earth, while Christ, the second man, came from heaven. 48 Earthly people are like the earthly man, and heavenly people are like the heavenly man. 49 Just as we are now like the earthly man, we will someday be like the heavenly man.

50 What I am saying, dear brothers and sisters, is that our physical bodies cannot inherit the Kingdom of God. These dying bodies cannot inherit what will last forever.

1 Corinthians 15:35–50

What do we know about Jesus' body after he rose again, before he ascended into heaven? The Scriptures say he could appear in locked rooms (John 20:19, 20:26). He could also disappear at will (Luke 24:31). He looked like himself; those who had known him recognized him unless God kept them from doing so (Luke 24:16). Jesus explained that he was not a ghost and that he had a body (Luke 24:39). The disciples could see his wounds (John 20:20, 28). People could touch him (Matthew 28:9). He was able to eat (Luke 24:42–43).

We do not know the extent to which our resurrection bodies will be like Christ's, but we do know that our bodies will be raised to live forever . . . in glory . . . in strength . . . as spiritual bodies (1 Corinthians 15:42–44). This is a wonderful hope! But Paul had even more to say to the Corinthian believers, and to us:

⁵¹ But let me reveal to you a wonderful secret. We will not all die, but we will all be transformed! ⁵² It will happen in a moment, in the blink of an eye, when the last trumpet is blown. For when the trumpet sounds, those who have died will be raised to live forever. And we who are living will also be transformed. ⁵³ For our dying bodies must be transformed into bodies that will never die; our mortal bodies must be transformed into immortal bodies.

⁵⁴ Then, when our dying bodies have been transformed into bodies that will never die, this Scripture will be fulfilled:

"Death is swallowed up in victory.
⁵⁵ O death, where is your victory?
O death, where is your sting?"

⁵⁶ For sin is the sting that results in death, and the law gives sin its power. ⁵⁷ But thank God! He gives us victory over sin and death through our Lord Jesus Christ.

1 Corinthians 15:51–57

Because of Jesus' victory over death, death is never final for Christians. We have the promise that we will see believers again in a world where sin has no power and where there will be no more tears, pain, or sorrow. The wonder of this promise prompted Paul to thank God and to encourage the Corinthians to continue in their faith and in their service for Jesus.

So, my dear brothers and sisters, be strong and immovable. Always work enthusiastically for the Lord, for you know that nothing you do for the Lord is ever useless.   1 Corinthians 15:58

Topic 4—Comparing Views of the Resurrection

Introduction: The resurrection is central to the Christian faith. Without it, our faith is useless, our lives are all too brief, and everyone dies in the end. The resurrection shows God's power to save us from sin and to grant us eternal life. But people who are Muslims, naturalists, or new spiritualists do not believe what Christians believe.

Part 1—Did Jesus Rise from the Dead?

Muslims, naturalists, and new spiritualists all deny that Jesus physically rose from the dead, and they deny that Jesus' followers will be physically raised to life everlasting. They deny these truths in different ways, however.

1. The Islamic View: Islam teaches that Jesus did not rise from the dead. Recall that Muslims believe Allah has the authority and power to cancel some of his revelations and replace them with new ones. When Muhammad was in Mecca, he said that Jesus spoke about his birth, death, and resurrection (Quran 19:33), but this teaching was later nullified. In Medina, Allah revealed to Muhammad that Jesus never died on the cross. Someone who looked like him was crucified instead. Islam teaches that Allah took Jesus up into heaven and he will return to Earth before the day of Resurrection.

[157] [The People of the Book] said, 'We have killed the Messiah, Jesus, son of Mary, the Messenger of God.' (They did not kill him, nor did they crucify him, though it was made to appear like that to them; those that disagreed about him are full of doubt, with no knowledge to follow, only supposition: they certainly did not kill him- [158] God raised him up to Himself. God is almighty and wise. [159] There is not one of the People of the Book who will not believe in [Jesus] before his death, and on the Day of Resurrection he will be a witness against them.)   Quran 4:157–159

Instead of saving those who trust in him, the Quran teaches that Jesus will testify against them, saying that he never taught he should be worshipped as God (Quran 5:116).

2. The Naturalist View: Most naturalists believe that the Bible is unreliable, and that Jesus did not rise from the dead. Some even question that he ever existed at all. Regarding Jesus' resurrection, atheist author and physicist Lawrence M. Krauss once wrote:

> In the case of the claimed resurrection the scriptures were written decades after the claimed event, and the different accounts are not even consistent. Not only are there serious theologians who doubt the resurrection, there are historians who doubt the historical existence of Jesus himself.[1]

Other prominent atheists and organizations question the reliability of the gospels and the historicity of Jesus himself. Though "it is . . . possible to mount a serious, though not widely supported, historical case that Jesus never lived at all," says atheist author and biologist Richard Dawkins, "Jesus probably existed."[2]

3. New Spiritualist Views: Because new spirituality has a range of beliefs and practices, its practitioners answer the question of whether Jesus rose from the dead in different ways.

Some distinguish between the person of Jesus and the Christ force, or consciousness. For example, the Unity website teaches that "Christ, absolute Principle . . . is the true resurrecting power and life in each of us here and now. Jesus resurrected His body through the spiritual I AM dwelling in Him."[3]

Paramahansa Yogananda claimed that Jesus "was a realized yogi: one who knew and had mastered the spiritual science of life and death,"[4] so he rose again because yoga gave him the power to do so.

Others add that Jesus did not die on the cross but was buried alive, escaped, and continued his ministry in secret:

> When Jesus was crucified, he did not die. He entered the state of Nirvikalp Samadhi (the I-am-God state without bodily consciousness). On the third day, he again became conscious of his body, and he traveled secretly in disguise eastward (with some apostles) to India. This was called Jesus' resurrection. . . . When his work was finished on earth, he dropped his body and entered Nirvikalp Samadhi permanently.[5]

And still other new spiritualists teach that the facts of the resurrection do not matter, because "We have to transcend notions like birth, death, being, and non-being. Reality is free from all notions."[6]

Part 2—Is There Life after Death?

Christians rejoice in believing that Jesus conquered death and that through him, we also will live forever. But people with other worldviews do not see things the same way. Even though Muslims do believe in a physical resurrection to come, their expectations are somewhat different than ours. Naturalists have no hope for a resurrection and new spiritualists redefine what the resurrection is.

1. The Islamic View: Islam, like Christianity, teaches that there is a physical resurrection followed by judgment. The Quran teaches that time and history end with the Day of Resurrection, when all will be raised to life and face judgment. Muslims believe that everyone will be judged on their belief in Allah and Islam and on their deeds. If they have done enough good deeds and Allah is merciful, they will be saved and enter paradise; if they have not believed in Allah and Islam and if they have not done enough good deeds, they will not escape the fires of hell.

[101] On that Day when the Trumpet is blown. . . [102] those whose good deeds weigh heavy will be successful, [103] but those whose balance is light will have lost their souls for ever and will stay in Hell.   Quran 23:101–103

[9] God has promised forgiveness and a rich reward to those who have faith [in Allah and Islam] and do good works; [10] those who reject faith and deny Our [Allah's] revelations will inhabit the blazing Fire.   Quran 5:9–10

2. The Naturalist View: Recall that naturalists believe that there is no God, no such thing as life after death, and no souls. Therefore, naturalists do not believe that the dead will hear Jesus' voice and rise from their graves at the final judgment. Atheists do not believe that people can rise from the dead at all.

For naturalists (atheists), belief in a resurrection is simply belief in a lie or myth that people use to comfort themselves in the face of inevitable death. In his book *Billions & Billions: Thoughts on Life and Death at the Brink of the Millennium*, the late astronomer Carl Sagan wrote,

> I would love to believe that when I die I will live again, that some thinking, feeling, remembering part of me will continue. But as much as I want to believe that, and despite the ancient and worldwide cultural traditions that assert an afterlife, I know of nothing to suggest that [such a belief] is more than wishful thinking.[7]

More recently, in an interview, the late physicist Stephen Hawking stated, "I regard the brain as a computer which will stop working when its components fail. There is no heaven or afterlife for broken down computers; that is a fairy story for people afraid of the dark."[8]

3. New Spiritualist Views: People who are involved in new spirituality do not believe in the resurrection. Rather, they believe in reincarnation. Each reincarnation provides an opportunity for people to work out their karma, that is, for a soul to be enlightened by understanding its divinity and oneness with all things. For example, Eckhart Tolle, an influential new spiritualist, teaches that Jesus' resurrection means that "we are capable of freeing ourselves from the cross of pain and suffering." Tolle replaces the concept of resurrection with reincarnation, the belief that a human soul is reborn multiple times, teaching:

When the ego dies, your own true self, which has been dormant in slumber, will be resurrected. Not necessarily all at once with a big noble transformation, no. It will happen many times in small measures, again and again. Many resurrections. And they will lead, in time, to a real and grounded transformation of your consciousness, one that will never leave you.[9]

Another view is that resurrection is inevitable as a result of the new age that will be ushered in by technological advancement. Some believe the universe will reach a state of self-awareness, at which time it will be omnipresent, omniscient, and omnipotent, able to re-create every human consciousness that ever existed:

Physics will permit the resurrection to eternal life of everyone who has lived, is living, and will live. . . This power to resurrect which modern physics allows will actually exist in the far future. If any reader has lost a loved one or is afraid of death, modern physics says: 'Be comforted, you and they shall live again.'[10]

All of these teachings are very different from what we learn in the Bible:

[10] Christ lives within you, so even though your body will die because of sin, the Spirit gives you life because you have been made right with God. [11] The Spirit of God, who raised Jesus from the dead, lives in you. And just as God raised Christ Jesus from the dead, he will give life to your mortal bodies by this same Spirit living within you.

Romans 8:10–11

Therefore, we can exclaim, just as Paul did when he wrote to the believers in Corinth, Thank God! He gives us victory over sin and death through our Lord Jesus Christ (1 Corinthians 15:57).

ENDNOTES

1 Lawrence M. Krauss, "A Response and Perspective on Debate with Craig," Thursday, April 5, 2011, https://new.exchristian. net/2011/04/response-and-perspective-on-debate-with.html.

2 Richard Dawkins, *The God Delusion* (NY: Houghton Mifflin Harcourt, 2006), 122–123:

3 Charles Fillmore, *The Revealing Word: A Dictionary of Metaphysical Terms* (Asheville, North Carolina: Bibliotech Press, 2019), 146.

4 Paramahansa Yogananda, "The Hidden Truths in the Gospels," adapted from *The Second Coming of Christ: The Resurrection of the Christ Within You* (Self-Realization Fellowship, 2004), https://yogananda.org/the-hidden-truths-in-the-gospels.

5 Meher Baba, *The Gospel of Jesus Christ According to Meher Baba*, http://www.meherbabadnyana.net/life_eternal/Jesus_life. html.

6 Thich Nhat Hanh, *Living Buddha, Living Christ*, (New York: Riverhead Books, 1999), 135.

7 Carl Sagan, *Billions & Billions: Thoughts on Life and Death at the Brink of the Millennium* (New York: Random House, 1997), 258.

8 Ian Sample, "Stephen Hawking: 'There is no heaven; it's a fairy story'," *The Guardian*, Sunday, May 15, 2011.

9 Eckhart Tolle, "The Meaning of the Death on the Cross," http://tolleteachings.com/death-on-the-cross.html

10 Frank J. Tipler, *The Physics of Immortality: Modern Cosmology, God, and the Resurrection of the Dead* (New York: Anchor Books, 1995), 1.

The Nature of Ministry

Getting Started—The Main Ideas

The letter of 2 Corinthians was written in AD 55 or 56 to believers in the province of Achaia (in modern-day Greece) about how to live out the Christian life. Paul and his co-author, Timothy, told the believers in Corinth to comfort others, forgive others, be sincere in preaching the Word, have irreproachable conduct, give praise where it is due, and be generous.

In the early chapters of 2 Corinthians, Paul and Timothy explained that trials and hardships should help us to become more understanding of others and become a resource and a blessing to them. The church should provide loving words of comfort and encouragement to those in need. Paul and Timothy added that when a believer repents in heartfelt sorrow for his or her sin, we should be ready to forgive and restore him or her to fellowship once more.

In writing, Paul and Timothy explained that through their actions and relationships, the Corinthian believers were spreading the news about Jesus. This was wonderful but also a great responsibility. Paul also reflected on what it means to be a minister of the gospel. He wanted the believers in Corinth to understand how to know who was doing God's work and who was not.

Lesson 22 closes with the admonishment to believers to enjoy the freedom of the new covenant, or new agreement with God leading to lives of freedom. As we live in this freedom, we become more like Jesus.

Topic 1—God of All Comfort

Introduction: Paul began this letter to the Corinthians by saying that it was from him and Timothy. You may recall that Timothy was Paul's young apprentice. Timothy's mother was Jewish, but his father was Greek. He had been instructed in the Jewish faith by his mother and grandmother, so he knew both the Law and the prophets. Paul often referred to Timothy as his "son." Paul seldom ministered alone; partnership was vitally important to his ministry. Timothy knew the Corinthian congregation and had ministered there before.

¹ This letter is from Paul, chosen by the will of God to be an apostle of Christ Jesus, and from our brother Timothy. I am writing to God's church in Corinth and to all of his holy people throughout Greece. ² May God our Father and the Lord Jesus Christ give you grace and peace. 2 Corinthians 1:1–2

To appreciate Paul and Timothy's greeting and prayer, it is helpful to remember what Paul had faced. The book of Acts tells us that Paul spent a year in Corinth, trying to convince Jews and Gentiles alike that Jesus was the Messiah. Then Paul went to other cities to plant churches and spread the gospel there. He went through a lot to proclaim the good news that Jesus died and rose again and that everyone could have new life through faith in him.

VIEW OF ROAD AND RUINS OF CORINTH

Have you ever had a bad day or even a bad week? Perhaps you felt as if nothing was going right. Yet, your bad day was probably never as tough as Paul's! He went through some of the worst trials imaginable—beatings, shipwrecks, imprisonment, and rejection. Yet, he kept preaching the gospel. Why? Because God was there to comfort him even on his lowest days.

The book of Acts describes how Paul and his missions partner Silas sang hymns of praise to God, even after a severe beating and having their feet clamped into stocks (Acts 16:24–25). In Ephesus, some Jews stubbornly rejected Paul's message. Then Gentile dealers of silver images rioted, causing trouble for some Christians— Alexander, Gaius, and Aristarchus in particular (Acts 19:29, 33). And these were not the only troubles Paul and others faced when the church was just beginning. God's abiding presence comforted believers through many other trials. So, Paul told the Corinthian church that God's comfort was not only to uplift them but to help them to be able to comfort others.

³ All praise to God, the Father of our Lord Jesus Christ. God is our merciful Father and the source of all comfort. ⁴ He comforts us in all our troubles so that we can comfort others. When they are troubled, we will be able to give them the same comfort God has given us. ⁵ For the more we suffer for Christ, the more God will shower us with his comfort through Christ. ⁶ Even when we are weighed down with troubles, it is for your comfort and salvation! For when we ourselves are comforted, we will certainly comfort you. Then you can patiently endure the same things we suffer. ⁷ We are confident that as you share in our sufferings, you will also share in the comfort God gives us.

⁸ We think you ought to know, dear brothers and sisters, about the trouble we went through in the province of Asia. We were crushed and overwhelmed beyond our ability to endure, and we thought we would never live through it. ⁹ In fact, we expected to die. But as a result, we stopped relying on ourselves and learned to rely only on God, who raises the dead. ¹⁰ And he did rescue us from mortal danger, and he will rescue us again. We have placed our confidence in him, and he will continue to rescue us. ¹¹ And you are helping us by praying for us. Then many people will give thanks because God has graciously answered so many prayers for our safety.   2 Corinthians 1:3–11

Paul set a standard for us to imitate: if we are patient as we go through trials, we can console others who may be facing a similar situation. True consolation begins with empathy, the understanding of and sensitivity to the feelings and experiences of another person.

After speaking about the way God consoles us so that we can console others, Paul remarked that he and his coworkers—Timothy, Titus, and Silas—had been honest and straightforward with the people of Corinth. This message was especially important because false teachers were active in the early church. Paul described such liars as "wolves" (Acts 20:29).

Although Paul had planned to visit this congregation, he changed his plans to save the believers from stern words of discipline. Many of the Corinthians had slid back into their old way of life—influenced, no doubt, by the pagan culture in which they lived. Paul felt that sending a letter would be gentler than a direct confrontation.

¹² We can say with confidence and a clear conscience that we have lived with a God-given holiness and sincerity in all our dealings. We have depended on God's grace, not on our own human wisdom. That is how we have conducted ourselves before the world, and especially toward you. ¹³ Our letters have been straightforward, and there is nothing written between the lines and nothing you can't understand. I hope someday you will fully understand us, ¹⁴ even if you don't understand us now. Then on the day when the Lord Jesus returns, you will be proud of us in the same way we are proud of you . . . . ¹⁸ As surely as God is faithful, our word to you does not waver between "Yes" and "No." ¹⁹ For Jesus Christ, the Son of God, does not waver between "Yes" and "No." . . . He always does what he says. ²⁰ For all of God's promises have been fulfilled in Christ with a resounding "Yes!" And through Christ, our "Amen" (which means "Yes") ascends to God for his glory.

²¹ It is God who enables us, along with you, to stand firm for Christ. He has commissioned us, ²² and he has identified us as his own by placing the Holy Spirit in our hearts as the first installment that guarantees everything he has promised us.

²³ Now I call upon God as my witness that I am telling the truth. The reason I didn't return to Corinth was to spare you from a severe rebuke. ²⁴ But that does not mean we want to dominate you by telling you how to put your faith into practice. We want to work together with you so you will be full of joy, for it is by your own faith that you stand firm.

2 Corinthians 1:12–14, 18–24

Empathy
The understanding of and sensitivity to the feelings and experiences of another person

Topic 2—Called to Be Ministers

Introduction: Paul, Timothy, and other leaders worked hard to teach people what Jesus had taught and how to put it into practice. They wanted the believers to live holy lives and to share their joy with others. But sometimes, the believers made mistakes which created problems. When Paul wrote to the Corinthian church, he talked about the mistakes and problems. He did this because of the love he had for them (2 Corinthians 2:4).

Part 1—Comfort after Repentance

APHRODITE,
GODDESS OF LOVE

It is evident from Paul's words in chapter 2 that a member of the congregation had caused the Corinthian church a great deal of heartache. Paul did not tell us exactly what this person did to hurt the believers. He did not even reveal the man's name, although he could have been the person referred to in 1 Corinthians 5:1, which talks about sexual sin. You might recall that Corinth was a city known for its idolatry and sexually permissive behavior. One of the goddesses esteemed in Corinth was Aphrodite, the goddess of love and fertility.

What Paul told the believers in Corinth is that they needed to forgive those who repent of having sinned against them personally or against the church. Since the man had responded to correction and repented, it was time for love and healing. The Corinthians needed to reaffirm their love and acceptance of this believer.

⁵ I am not overstating it when I say that the man who caused all the trouble hurt all of you more than he hurt me. ⁶ Most of you opposed him, and that was punishment enough. ⁷ Now, however, it is time to forgive and comfort him. Otherwise he may be overcome by discouragement. ⁸ So I urge you now to reaffirm your love for him.   2 Corinthians 2:5–8

Satan has specific schemes or strategies that he uses against us to take advantage of our sinful nature. In Corinth, Satan's scheme may have been for the people to ignore the sin as if it didn't exist, to treat it as

if it did not matter much, or to be overly severe in punishing the sinner. But that is not what happened. The brothers and sisters in the church took the problem seriously, sent Titus to Paul with a report (2 Corinthians 2:13), and then did what Paul recommended. When a problem occurs in our churches today, it is best to confront the person who is sinning and urge him or her to repent. If he or she does so, then we must truly forgive him or her. This thwarts Satan's plans to cause bitterness, hard feelings, and divisions in the church.

⁹ I wrote to you as I did to test you and see if you would fully comply with my instructions. ¹⁰ When you forgive this man, I forgive him, too. And when I forgive whatever needs to be forgiven, I do so with Christ's authority for your benefit, ¹¹ so that Satan will not outsmart us. For we are familiar with his evil schemes.

2 Corinthians 2:9–11

Part 2—A Triumphal Procession

A TRIUMPHAL PROCESSION

To understand the next few verses Paul wrote, you'll need to think about a Roman victory parade. When the Romans conquered a new territory, they paraded the spoils of war—gold, weapons, silver, and jewelry—through the main streets. Trumpets sounded and sweet fragrances (probably incense) filled the air. The battle commanders and their officers rode on horseback for all to see. But for those captives taken in battle, this parade was one of total humiliation. They were going to their deaths. What was perceived as the smell of victory for some was the smell of death for others. So, when Paul spoke of a triumphal procession, he compared our victory in Christ to those who are perishing because of their unbelief.

© Walking in Truth Grade 7

¹⁴ But thank God! He has made us his captives and continues to lead us along in Christ's triumphal procession. Now he uses us to spread the knowledge of Christ everywhere, like a sweet perfume. ¹⁵ Our lives are a Christ-like fragrance rising up to God. But this fragrance is perceived differently by those who are being saved and by those who are perishing. ¹⁶ To those who are perishing, we are a dreadful smell of death and doom. But to those who are being saved, we are a life-giving perfume.   2 Corinthians 2:14–16

Part 3—Living Letters

Paul explained that the job of preaching life to those who are perishing is a serious one. He and his coworkers did not approach the task for personal profit, but out of a desire to see more people come to faith in Christ. The desired outcome of a missionary's efforts is to see people who live godly lives as if God's Word were written on their hearts.

¹⁷ You see, we are not like the many hucksters [frauds]who preach for personal profit. We preach the word of God with sincerity and with Christ's authority, knowing that God is watching us.

¹ Are we beginning to praise ourselves again? Are we like others, who need to bring you letters of recommendation, or who ask you to write such letters on their behalf? Surely not! ² The only letter of recommendation we need is you yourselves. Your lives are a letter written in our hearts; everyone can read it and recognize our good work among you. ³ Clearly, you are a letter from Christ showing the result of our ministry among you. This "letter" is written not with pen and ink, but with the Spirit of the living God. It is carved not on tablets of stone, but on human hearts.

⁴ We are confident of all this because of our great trust in God through Christ. ⁵ It is not that we think we are qualified to do anything on our own. Our qualification comes from God. ⁶ He has enabled us to be ministers of his new covenant. This is a covenant not of written laws, but of the Spirit. The old written covenant ends in death; but under the new covenant, the Spirit gives life.   2 Corinthians 2:17–3:6

Topic 3—A Glorious New Covenant

Introduction: The Old Testament included several covenants—contracts or agreements. There were two major types of covenants in the Hebrew Bible. One type was a covenant where both parties were required to do something, known as a *conditional* or *bilateral* covenant. In God's covenant with Moses, the people were required to obey God's Law. So, when Paul spoke about "the old way," or "the old covenant," he was talking about the obligation of Jewish people to obey the law of Moses in order to be made right with God. The second type of covenant was *unconditional* or *unilateral*, where one party decided to do something for the other party. God had announced a new covenant with the people of Israel that would replace the previous covenant they had not been able to keep. In his new covenant, God promised to forgive the people's wickedness and to write his laws on their hearts (Jeremiah 31:31–34).

⁷ The old way, with laws etched in stone, led to death, though it began with such glory that the people of Israel could not bear to look at Moses' face. For his face shone with the glory of God, even though the brightness was already fading away. ⁸ Shouldn't we expect far greater glory under the new way, now that the Holy Spirit is giving life? ⁹ If the old way, which brings condemnation, was glorious, how much more glorious is the new way, which

makes us right with God! ¹⁰ In fact, that first glory was not glorious at all compared with the overwhelming glory of the new way. ¹¹ So if the old way, which has been replaced, was glorious, how much more glorious is the new, which remains forever!

2 Corinthians 3:7–11

The new way, or new covenant, differs from the old covenant in several ways. First, the old covenant required obedience to the Law, but the new covenant is through faith in the atoning sacrifice of Christ on the cross. When Jesus taught his disciples, he said that the new covenant would be "between God and his people—an agreement confirmed with my blood, which is poured out as a sacrifice for you" (Luke 22:20). The old covenant was between God and the descendants of Abraham, but the new covenant is available to all people regardless of race, nationality, gender, or status in the culture. The old covenant was transitory, but the new covenant is permanent. The old covenant depends on human effort, but the new covenant depends on the Spirit.

Paul understood that it was difficult for Jews to give up their hold on the old covenant despite the promise of a new one. He reminded the believers that Moses had to wear a veil when he came down from Mount Sinai because the radiance of God's presence caused his face to glow brightly (Exodus 34:29–35). The veil kept the people from seeing the glory of God.

¹² Since this new way gives us such confidence, we can be very bold. ¹³ We are not like Moses, who put a veil over his face so the people of Israel would not see the glory, even though it was destined to fade away. ¹⁴ But the people's minds were hardened, and to this day whenever the old covenant is being read, the same veil covers their minds so they cannot understand the truth. And this veil can be removed only by believing in Christ. ¹⁵ Yes, even today when they read Moses' writings, their hearts are covered with that veil, and they do not understand. ¹⁶ But whenever someone turns to the Lord, the veil is taken away.

2 Corinthians 3:12–16

When the veil is lifted, we are free to live in fellowship with God. When Jesus spoke in the synagogue in his hometown of Nazareth, he declared that he came to set people free. He read the words of the prophet Isaiah:

"The Spirit of the Lord is upon me,
    for he has anointed me to bring Good News to the poor.
He has sent me to proclaim that captives will be released,
    that the blind will see,
that the oppressed will be set free, . . ."

Luke 4:18

Paul wanted the believers in Corinth to remember that Jesus brings freedom—freedom from slavery to sin, freedom from forced obedience to the Law, and freedom to know God personally. He continued:

¹⁷ For the Lord is the Spirit, and wherever the Spirit of the Lord is, there is freedom. ¹⁸ So all of us who have had that veil removed can see and reflect the glory of the Lord. And the Lord—who is the Spirit—makes us more and more like him as we are changed into his glorious image.

2 Corinthians 3:17–18

What does the glory of the Lord look like? Notice that we, as believers, are undergoing a process of change. We are being changed to become more and more like Christ. The glory that shines through us will never fade away, as Moses' did. In fact, Jesus promised that the righteous will shine like the sun in their Father's Kingdom (Matthew 13:43). How can we, as Christians, reflect God's glory to others today?

The Sacrifice of Ministry

Getting Started—The Main Ideas

The epistle of 2 Corinthians highlights the clash of competing worldviews present in the early church. Paul begins the letter by stating that he'd heard the people in Corinth were beginning to accept all sorts of ideas that were opposed to Christianity. The Corinthians, after having been led to Christ by Paul, had begun to doubt the apostle's authority and to accept concepts they'd learned from other teachers. Paul, called by God to be the apostle to the Gentiles, was uniquely qualified to teach God's Word to both Jews and Gentiles, having learned Hebrew Scriptures as a child and been trained by Gamaliel, a well-known Pharisee. After his conversion, Paul received the message of the gospel by direct revelation from Jesus himself (Galatians 1:11–12). As a Roman citizen from Tarsus, a Greco-Roman city, Paul was able to evangelize,

preach, and write using various analogies that the Roman citizens would have understood at the time. Yet, because God's Word is timeless, Paul's letter is just as relevant to us today as it was in the first century.

Paul urged the Corinthian church to follow his example as an ambassador for Christ. He wanted them to persevere in the truth that they had been taught from the beginning and not give in to competing false worldviews. By standing firm in their faith, believers would receive a crown of everlasting life.

> **Evangelize**
> To bring the message of salvation to those who do not know it in order to win converts

Topic 1—Treasures in Clay Jars

Introduction: In chapter 4 of 2 Corinthians, Paul explained the reasons for establishing the church in Corinth and the sacrifices he and other evangelists had made on behalf of the congregation. He noted that he was honest and sincere in preaching the truth of the gospel; he did not preach for personal gain, and he had endured many hardships for the sake of the gospel. Paul compared his life to a treasure in a jar of clay—fragile and poor physically, but filled with the joy of knowing Christ. He urged believers to persevere in their faith because earthly problems are temporary compared to eternal life.

Because false preachers (hucksters) had come to the church "selling" a different gospel, some believers were confused about the way to be saved. These false teachers were Jewish men who told the Corinthian congregation that salvation was only for Jews, so Gentiles first had to become Jews in order to be forgiven for their sins and receive God's gift of salvation. This wasn't

true, but the Corinthians didn't know who was teaching correct doctrine and who wasn't. Paul emphasized that we are saved only through faith in Jesus Christ, the Son of God.

Paul used his analogy of a veil from 2 Corinthians 3 again in chapter 4. Moses had worn a veil over his face because the people couldn't bear to look at the brilliance of God's glory. Paul used the word *veil* in chapter 4 to mean a poor understanding of the gospel. Most Jews did not understand the message of salvation through faith in Jesus alone.

Part 1—Light in the Darkness

[1] Therefore, since God in his mercy has given us this new way, we never give up. [2] We reject all shameful deeds and underhanded methods. We don't try to trick anyone or distort the word of God. We tell the truth before God, and all who are honest know this.

[3] If the Good News we preach is hidden behind a veil, it is hidden only from people who are perishing. [4] Satan, who is the god of this world, has blinded the minds of those who don't believe. They are unable to see the glorious light of the Good News. They don't understand this message about the glory of Christ, who is the exact likeness of God.

[5] You see, we don't go around preaching about ourselves. We preach that Jesus Christ is Lord, and we ourselves are your servants for Jesus' sake. [6] For God, who said, "Let there be light in the darkness," has made this light shine in our hearts so we could know the glory of God that is seen in the face of Jesus Christ.

2 Corinthians 4:1–6

If you've ever put coins into a ceramic piggy bank, you know about treasures in clay. During the first century AD (and even earlier), people would keep coins in clay jars to keep their money hidden from thieves. The more ordinary-looking the jar, the easier it was to hide money. A treasure jar might also be buried in the ground to keep it safe, or as an offering to a god.

Jesus told a parable about a man who found a buried treasure and sold all his possessions to buy a field (Matthew 13:44). In the parable, Jesus used the image of an earthly treasure to highlight the treasure we have in knowing God. The Greek word for treasure, *thesauros*, used by Matthew is the same Greek word that Paul used in 2 Corinthians 4:7. Both apostles used this word to remind us of the unsurpassed treasure we have in our salvation and harmony with God. Paul contrasted simple, fragile, ordinary clay jars (us) with amazing riches (Christ's love for us).

[7] We now have this light shining in our hearts, but we ourselves are like fragile clay jars containing this great treasure. This makes it clear that our great power is from God, not from ourselves.

2 Corinthians 4:7

Paul urged believers to persevere, despite persecution, because of the glory yet to come. He reminded them of the hardships he had faced in bringing the good news to them when he first came to Corinth and the hardships he had gone through in recent days. In Acts 23, Luke wrote about how Paul was hunted by a group of Jewish men in Jerusalem who had taken an oath not to eat or drink until they had killed Paul. He had been rejected by his own people, beaten, and imprisoned, yet he brought the gospel message to the Corinthians. Paul faced death to bring eternal life to all people. He fixed his eyes on eternity, not his present suffering.

Other writers echoed Paul's remarks about having faith in a future we cannot see. Hebrews 11:1 tells us that faith is the reality of things we hope for. We can't yet see what life will be like in heaven, but we believe it exists. In John 20:29, Jesus told Thomas, the disciple who doubted, that future believers would be blessed because they would believe without seeing the risen Christ. Peter wrote in his first epistle that believers who trust Jesus, even though they have never seen him physically, will rejoice with glorious and inexpressible joy (1 Peter 1:8).

[8] We are pressed on every side by troubles, but we are not crushed. We are perplexed, but not driven to despair. [9] We are hunted down, but never abandoned by God. We get knocked down, but we are not destroyed. [10] Through suffering, our bodies continue to share in the death of Jesus so that the life of Jesus may also be seen in our bodies.

[11] Yes, we live under constant danger of death because we serve Jesus, so that the life of Jesus will be evident in our dying bodies. [12] So we live in the face of death, but this has resulted in eternal life for you.

[13] But we continue to preach because we have the same kind of faith the psalmist had when he said, "I believed in God, so I spoke." [14] We know that God, who raised the Lord Jesus, will also raise us with Jesus and present us to himself together with you. [15] All of this is for your benefit. And as God's grace reaches more and more people, there will be great thanksgiving, and God will receive more and more glory.   2 Corinthians 4:8–15

Renewal of one's spirit was a concept that Jewish believers would have understood. King David prayed in Psalm 51 for God to "renew a loyal spirit within me." God renewed the spiritual life of Israel each year on the Day of Atonement, Yom Kippur. Paul reminded the believers that as our body grows older and weaker, the same is not true of our spirit. Our spirits are renewed daily by the indwelling of the Holy Spirit as we strive to imitate Jesus.

Topic 2—Heavenly Bodies

Introduction: After explaining how he and his fellow missionaries had been subject to painful abuse, and faced martyrdom, Paul turned his attention to life in heaven. He explained that he and the other apostles never gave up telling others about salvation because they fixed their gaze on their future life with the Lord rather than on temporary troubles.

Paul used an analogy—a tent—to describe our current bodies. You may remember that tentmaking was Paul's vocation, and he worked with Aquila and Priscilla, two other tentmakers, during his second missionary journey. Tents were valuable in the ancient world because they were portable and could be used for a variety of purposes, including cargo protection onboard ships, shade for the marketplace, and temporary lodging. So, when Paul used the word *tent* to describe our present, earthly bodies, the Corinthian believers might have imagined a tent being put up or taken down.

Paul compared the change from our present body to our heavenly body to changing into brand-new clothing. In the first-century world of Corinth, people would have understood Paul's analogy because funeral rites in ancient Greece included dressing the deceased person in his or her best clothing. If the deceased had earned a special honor during life, he or she would be buried with a crown—a wreath placed on the forehead. In Revelation 2:10, Jesus refers to a similar crown for all believers saying, "'But if you remain faithful even when facing death, I will give you the crown of life.'" Imagine never getting sick again! No pain, no suffering! What joy will be ours when we receive our new bodies at the resurrection of the dead!

1 For we know that when this earthly tent we live in is taken down (that is, when we die and leave this earthly body), we will have a house in heaven, an eternal body made for us by God himself and not by human hands. 2 We grow weary in our present bodies, and we long to put on our heavenly bodies like new clothing. 3 For we will put on heavenly bodies; we will not be spirits without bodies. 4 While we live in these earthly bodies, we groan and sigh, but it's not that we want to die and get rid of these bodies that clothe us. Rather, we want to put on our new bodies so that these dying bodies will be swallowed up by life. 5 God himself has prepared us for this, and as a guarantee he has given us his Holy Spirit.   2 Corinthians 5:1–5

Paul added the true goal of our human existence: glorifying God in all that we do. Then, when we stand before Christ on the day of judgment, we will receive a reward according to what we have done on Earth.

6 So we are always confident, even though we know that as long as we live in these bodies we are not at home with the Lord. 7 For we live by believing and not by seeing. 8 Yes, we are fully confident, and we would rather be away from these earthly bodies, for then we will be at home with the Lord. 9 So whether we are here in this body or away from this body, our goal is to please him. 10 For we must all stand before Christ to be judged. We will each receive whatever we deserve for the good or evil we have done in this earthly body.   2 Corinthians 5:6–10

© Walking in Truth Grade 7

Introduction: Some aspects of the culture of the Greco-Roman world were not all that different from our world today. Status in the first century AD depended on a person's ability to achieve the goals of the society, much like people today try to achieve the goals of fame, popularity, or wealth in our society. Skill, especially skill in public speaking, was a way to gain praise or honor in the Roman world. Paul, on the other hand, was criticized for his public speaking (2 Corinthians 10:10). This may be because Paul spoke in order to bring glory to God and didn't boast about himself. Rather, he spoke sincerely, always putting Jesus first.

[11] Because we understand our fearful responsibility to the Lord, we work hard to persuade others. God knows we are sincere, and I hope you know this, too. [12] Are we commending ourselves to you again? No, we are giving you a reason to be proud of us, so you can answer those who brag about having a spectacular ministry rather than having a sincere heart. [13] If it seems we are crazy, it is to bring glory to God. And if we are in our right minds, it is for your benefit. [14] Either way, Christ's love controls us. Since we believe that Christ died for all, we also believe that we have all died to our old life. [15] He died for everyone so that those who receive his new life will no longer live for themselves. Instead, they will live for Christ, who died and was raised for them.

2 Corinthians 5:11–15

When we come to faith in Christ, our worldview changes. Our ideas change, and we begin to evaluate people from God's point of view. Now we see people as image-bearers of God. Each person has worth and value to God as proven by Christ's willingness to die for them.

The false teachers in Corinth tried to change the Corinthians' worldview to a human point of view, teaching that salvation was not through God's grace but through submission to the Law. They tried to talk the believers into leaving their new lives of freedom.

[16] So we have stopped evaluating others from a human point of view. At one time we thought of Christ merely from a human point of view. How differently we know him now! [17] This means that anyone who belongs to Christ has become a new person. The old life is gone; a new life has begun!   2 Corinthians 5:16–17

An ambassador is a representative of his or her own government who has a temporary diplomatic assignment. For example, a president of our country may send a representative to live in the United Kingdom as an ambassador. Paul and his ministry partners' roles as ambassadors were very different from the jobs of other ambassadors in the first century. Usually lesser political powers, such as colonies, sent their ambassadors to the greater political powers in order to gain their favor. For instance, Roman emperors often received ambassadors from Corinth, Ephesus, and Philippi, which were smaller states or provinces. Yet in 2 Corinthians, we can see an amazing reversal. God, the far greater power than human beings, sends his ambassadors to preach the good news of reconciliation between God and his sinful image-bearers.

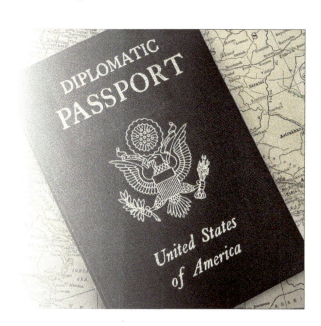

¹⁸ And all of this is a gift from God, who brought us back to himself through Christ. And God has given us this task of reconciling people to him. ¹⁹ For God was in Christ, reconciling the world to himself, no longer counting people's sins against them. And he gave us this wonderful message of reconciliation. ²⁰ So we are Christ's ambassadors; God is making his appeal through us. We speak for Christ when we plead, "Come back to God!" ²¹ For God made Christ, who never sinned, to be the offering for our sin, so that we could be made right with God through Christ.

2 Corinthians 5:18–21

Topic 4—Paul's Suffering

Introduction: Sadly, the Corinthians put Paul in an awkward position. Because of the many false teachers who had been allowed to persuade the people away from the truth, Paul had to reestablish his authority over them as an apostle. Paul decided to explain once again why he came to Corinth in the first place—to serve God.

Paul wasn't boasting when he shared his trials and troubles; he was merely stating the facts. He and his faithful companions in ministry suffered a great deal in order to bring salvation to the people of Corinth. Imagine how sad Paul must have felt to learn that some of the people were falling away from the truth!

Part 1—God's Partners

¹ As God's partners, we beg you not to accept this marvelous gift of God's kindness and then ignore it. ² For God says,

"At just the right time, I heard you.
  On the day of salvation, I helped you"

Indeed, the "right time" is now. Today is the day of salvation.

³ We live in such a way that no one will stumble because of us, and no one will find fault with our ministry. ⁴ In everything we do, we show that we are true ministers of God. We patiently endure troubles and hardships and calamities of every kind. ⁵ We have been beaten, been put in prison, faced angry mobs, worked to exhaustion, endured sleepless nights, and gone without food. ⁶ We prove ourselves by our purity, our understanding, our patience, our kindness, by the Holy Spirit within us, and by our sincere love. 2 Corinthians 6:1–6

Paul emphasized that he was able to endure trials because of God's power working through him. He described his mission as if it were a battle, and he was equipped with weapons of righteousness. Consider how a Roman soldier would have held his sword in this right hand (if righthanded) for offense and his shield in his left for defense. Then Paul used a series of contrasts beginning with serving God whether people honor them or despise them. See how many contrasting elements you can count in Paul's words.

[7] We faithfully preach the truth. God's power is working in us. We use the weapons of righteousness in the right hand for attack and the left hand for defense. [8] We serve God whether people honor us or despise us, whether they slander us or praise us. We are honest, but they call us impostors. [9] We are ignored, even though we are well known. We live close to death, but we are still alive. We have been beaten, but we have not been killed. [10] Our hearts ache, but we always have joy. We are poor, but we give spiritual riches to others. We own nothing, and yet we have everything.

2 Corinthians 6:7–10

Part 2—Missionaries Today

Missionaries today still face various hardships and dangers in order to take the gospel to the ends of the earth. Many missionaries must raise their own support, which generally requires writing letters, making phone calls, sending emails, and making personal appointments asking for donations. Often, they must rent or sell their homes before moving elsewhere.

Training is essential for long-term missionaries; they must learn the language and culture of the people they will be going to evangelize. They may need training in teaching the Bible to a different culture. Once they are in the country where they will minister, they will probably have to adjust to new foods, different clothing, a warmer or colder climate, inconveniences such as rough roads over long distances, and general changes in lifestyle. Missionary children must also adjust to change. They may be sent to boarding schools or need to take classes online.

Mike and Joanne Noel are American missionaries living in Tanzania, an African nation. There, Joanne helps the Tanzanian people learn good health habits to keep them from getting sick. Mike teaches spiritual leadership training classes. Both Mike and Joanne spread the good news to the people of Tanzania.

Topic 5—Comparing Views of Missions

Introduction: Muslims, naturalists, and new spirituality followers also practice evangelism. Each worldview seeks to influence others by sharing their philosophies in print, in the media, and in daily interactions.

The biblical Christian worldview sees evangelism and missionary efforts as obedience to Jesus' words in the Great Commission, "Therefore, go and make disciples of all the nations, baptizing them in the name of the Father and the Son and the Holy Spirit" (Matthew 28:19). Christians seek to reach everyone with the gospel—not just those who live in foreign countries but also those who live in our own land. All believers should be missionaries to those they meet.

Followers of Islam, naturalism, and new spirituality also practice evangelism in a variety of ways. According to former Muslim Ayman S. Ibrahim,

It [evangelism] is a duty in Islam, and is called da'wa. In Islamic dogma, da'wa means "to invite people to Islam." It is the act of making an appealing message, calling people to embrace the faith proclaimed by Muhammad, as described in the Quran (3:104; 3:110; 16:125; 41:33). The da'wa focuses on exclusive claims of Allah's strict monotheism and Muhammad's prophethood. Muslims are not shy about calling non-Muslims to Islam. Conversion to Islam is a goal. Just begin a religious conversation with a Muslim and, in a minute, you will be questioned about your faith and if you are open to receiving an open da'wa.[1]

The Black supremacist group Nation of Islam's efforts to recruit members provide an example of Islamic missionary activity in the United States. In the 1950s and 1960s, the Nation of Islam was the face of Islam in America. Malcolm X, Muhammad Ali, and Nation of Islam founder Elijah Muhammad's son, Warith Deen Mohammed, have been well-known leaders of the Nation of Islam movement. Sports celebrities have exerted a Muslim influence on our culture. Lew Alcindor Jr. was a college basketball player who converted to Islam, changing his name to Kareem Abdul-Jabbar. He had many successful seasons playing for the Los Angeles Lakers.[2]

Enes Kanter, who plays for the Portland Trail Blazers, fasts during Ramadan each year. Hakeem Olajuwon is one of the greatest centers to have ever played in the NBA and is also outspoken about his Muslim faith.[3]

Fencer Ibtihaj Muhammad wears her hijab while competing in fencing competitions. She made history at the 2016 Olympics as the first American to compete in a hijab and the first Muslim-American woman to win an Olympic medal. She is an outspoken advocate for her Muslim faith.[4]

Naturalists practice evangelism through their influence in the secular educational system as well in other areas of society. Naturalists publish books and magazines denouncing the practice of religion. They claim the ideas of creationism and intelligent design are untrue and should not be taught in public schools because they contradict true science. Dan Dana, a university professor and naturalist, claims that religion is illogical. He states that the world will be free of many of its problems when "secular education . . . and science education, in particular, is accessible worldwide. Not everyone must be a professional scientist, but everyone should have a science-based understanding of the natural world and its in habitants, and how to make reliable decisions based on critical evaluation of observational evidence."[5]

Followers of new spirituality believe that as the individual changes, the world around him or her will also change. They make the claim that as people "begin to feel the power of the universe" within their own bodies, other people will feel "a solid base of trust" and will "open up to more of their own power and truth." So for new spiritualists, the avenue for evangelizing the world is to change themselves which will, in some way, result in change in others. New spiritualists recognize the power of the universe at work and consider themselves channels through which the world's healing is being manifested.[6]

Not all new spiritualist groups evangelize on an individual basis. Scientology, a new spirituality cult, actively recruits members. Reading rooms and Scientology events appeal to people looking for a connection to each other and to the world.

ENDNOTES

1 Ayman S Ibrahim, "Proselytizing in Islam," accessed January 2, 2020 https://fullerstudio.fuller.edu/proselytizing-in-islam/.

2 "Missionary Work of Islam," Academic Room, accessed May 15, 2019, http://www.academicroom.com/topics/missionary-work-islam.

3 "Enes Kanter Ramadan: Fasting, Diet & Eating Schedule During Muslim Observance," Heavy.com Sports, accessed May 16, 2019, https://heavy.com/sports/2019/05/enes-kanter-ramadan-fasting-muslim-when-what-eat-drink/.

4 Sopan Deb, "Ibtihaj Muhammad: The Olympic Fencer Is Charting Her Own Path," *New York Times*, accessed January 2, 2020, https://www.nytimes.com/2018/07/24/books/ibtihaj-muhammad-fencing-hijab-olympics.html.

5 Dan Dana, *The Reason Revolution: Atheism, Secular Humanism, and the Collapse of Religion* (Dana, 2014) Kindle.

6 Shakti Gawain with Laurel King, *Living in the Light: Following Your Inner Guidance to Create a New Life and a New World* (Novato, CA: New World Library, 2011), 203, 207.

Giving and Exhortation

Getting Started—The Main Ideas

The subject of giving has always been a sensitive one for the church. Christians wonder how much to give, what to give, and when to give. Some even ask: Should we donate money? Volunteer our time? Give other possessions? How much should we save and how much should we give? These questions and others were also on the minds of believers in Corinth.

Recall what happened on the day of Pentecost, in Jerusalem, when the Holy Spirit came. On that day, as Luke wrote in the book of Acts, about 3,000 people came to faith in Jesus because of Peter's sermon. Later, the number swelled to over 5,000 people. Almost immediately, the new Christians began to share their possessions. Problems arose when the Greek-speaking widows were being neglected in the daily food distribution, so the disciples chose seven highly qualified men to make sure that all widows were treated fairly.

But 30 years later, when Paul wrote the book of 2 Corinthians, things weren't going so well in Jerusalem. Famine had hit Israel, and the believers badly needed food. Paul cared deeply for these poor people and called on the Gentile Christians to take up an offering for Israel. The Macedonian people, despite being poor themselves, had already contributed, and Paul called for the Corinthian church to be generous and add to the collection.

Islam, naturalism, and new spirituality followers donate to charity, but they do so for reasons other than those that motivate Christians. The biblical Christian worldview holds that giving is a natural response to what God has already given us.

After making his appeal for the Jerusalem church, Paul again urged the Corinthians to address the problems in their church before his next visit. He wanted to spend time with them in fellowship, not in discipline. Paul wanted to offer exhortation, or encouragement, to those who were weak or immature in their faith. Exhortation can also be an admonishment or gentle reprimand. Paul reasserted his apostolic authority with the statement that he would no longer go easy on those who continued to willfully sin.

> **Exhortation**
> An encouragement or
> admonishment

Topic 1—Giving

Introduction: All our physical and intellectual abilities are gifts from God, and we should use our God-given talents to glorify him. Generosity is one of the ways we can glorify God; God motivates us to give to others, especially those in need.

Giving generously does not depend on wealth. Jesus affirmed this when he pointed out a widow who only had two small coins left to live on but put them both in the temple offering box (Mark 12:42). Other worshippers put in much more money than the widow did, yet Jesus commended her generosity, declaring that she had given more than those who put in much larger amounts.

Part 1—Paul's Appeal for Generosity

Paul remarked that even the Macedonians, who could least afford it, gave generously. They trusted God to provide for their needs because they had first devoted their lives to Christ.

¹ Now I want you to know, dear brothers and sisters, what God in his kindness has done through the churches in Macedonia. ² They are being tested by many troubles, and they are very poor. But they are also filled with abundant joy, which has overflowed in rich generosity.

³ For I can testify that they gave not only what they could afford, but far more. And they did it of their own free will. ⁴ They begged us again and again for the privilege of sharing in the gift for the believers in Jerusalem. ⁵ They even did more than we had hoped, for their first action was to give themselves to the Lord and to us, just as God wanted them to do. 2 Corinthians 8:1–5

Titus, who was known to the Corinthian congregation, had been the first to ask the church for a gift to relieve the suffering of the Christians in Jerusalem. Notice how Paul made a well-worded appeal for funds by offering the people a chance to add another area of excellence to their reputation. Excellence in giving is just as important as excellence in showing compassion, using self-control, being loyal, or any other character trait.

⁶ So we have urged Titus, who encouraged your giving in the first place, to return to you and encourage you to finish this ministry of giving. ⁷ Since you excel in so many ways—in your faith, your gifted speakers, your knowledge, your enthusiasm, and your love from us—I want you to excel also in this gracious act of giving.

⁸ I am not commanding you to do this. But I am testing how genuine your love is by comparing it with the eagerness of the other churches. 2 Corinthians 8:6–8

Part 2—Sincere Giving

Jesus spoke about the difference between sincere giving motivated by love for others and giving in order to call attention to oneself. He said,

¹ "Watch out! Don't do your good deeds publicly, to be admired by others, for you will lose the reward from your Father in heaven. ² When you give to someone in need, don't do as the hypocrites do—blowing trumpets in the synagogues and streets to call attention to their acts of charity! I tell you the truth, they have received all the reward they will ever get. ³ But when you give to someone in need, don't let your left hand know what your right hand is doing. ⁴ Give your gifts in private, and your Father, who sees everything, will reward you"
Matthew 6:1–4

Paul reminded the believers that all the riches of heaven belonged to God's own Son, Jesus.

⁹ You know the generous grace of our Lord Jesus Christ. Though he was rich, yet for your sakes he became poor, so that by his poverty he could make you rich.

2 Corinthians 8:9

The Corinthian church had started a collection for the poor but had not yet sent it to Jerusalem. Paul advised the believers to finish the collection by giving in proportion to what they had. He emphasized that God expected them to follow through on their commitments. Many people in churches today practice proportional giving by sharing 10 percent of their income with others to honor God. Ten percent is called a tithe.

> **Tithe**
> Ten percent of one's income that
> is given to God

To drive home his point about giving wisely and unselfishly, Paul quoted a passage in Exodus where greedy people who gathered a lot of manna had none left over, but those who gathered proportionately to their needs had enough.

¹⁰ Here is my advice: It would be good for you to finish what you started a year ago. Last year you were the first who wanted to give, and you were the first to begin doing it. ¹¹ Now you should finish what you started. Let the eagerness you showed in the beginning be matched now by your giving. Give in proportion to what you have. ¹² Whatever you give is acceptable if you give it eagerly. And give according to what you have, not what you don't have. ¹³ Of course, I don't mean your giving should make life easy for others and hard for yourselves. I only mean that there should be some equality. ¹⁴ Right now you have plenty and can help those who are in need. Later, they will have plenty and can share with you when you need it. In this way, things will be equal. ¹⁵ As the Scriptures say,

"Those who gathered a lot had nothing left over,
  and those who gathered only a little had enough."

2 Corinthians 8:10–15

WOMAN GATHERING
MANNA

Topic 2—More on Giving

Introduction: Paul had encouraged the Corinthians to be as generous as the Macedonians. He encouraged the believers in Corinth to add excellence in giving to their virtues, and then he discussed giving in proportion to what they had. Next, Paul discussed how the offering would be handled, and he again encouraged the believers to be generous.

Part 1—Handling Money

Although Paul was planning to see the Corinthians, he did not want to arrive and find the believers unprepared for him. So, he sent a team in advance. They were supposed to see to it that the offering had been prepared. The team was made up of Titus and two other Christians. Paul made sure that the Corinthians knew that those brothers were elected by the Macedonian people, not chosen by Paul.

²³ If anyone asks about Titus, say that he is my partner who works with me to help you. And the brothers with him have been sent by the churches, and they bring honor to Christ. ²⁴ So show them your love, and prove to all the churches that our boasting about you is justified.   2 Corinthians 8:23–24

Multiple ministry partners were needed to handle the offering so that they could hold each other accountable. Leaders should be honorable, marked by integrity and a keen sense of duty to God. Security was also a concern when traveling in the first century, and the money or goods would have been safer with a larger group.

²⁰ We are traveling together to guard against any criticism for the way we are handling this generous gift. ²¹ We are careful to be honorable before the Lord, but we also want everyone else to see that we are honorable.
                                    2 Corinthians 8:20–21

Part 2—Sowing and Reaping

Paul continued, I thought I should send these brothers ahead of me to make sure the gift you promised is ready. But I want it to be a willing gift, not one given grudgingly (2 Corinthians 9:5).

In teaching about giving, Paul used the analogy of a farmer planting seeds and harvesting a crop. His point was that people who do not give much will not receive as many blessings as those who give generously: Remember this—a farmer who plants only a few seeds will get a small crop. But the one who plants generously will get a generous crop (2 Corinthians 9:6).

Jesus also encouraged his followers to give generously. He said, "Give, and you will receive. Your gift will return to you in full—pressed down, shaken together to make room for more, running over, and poured into your lap. The amount you give will determine the amount you get back" (Luke 6:38).

How much must you give to be considered generous? The believers in the church in Corinth had different opinions about this matter. Those who came from a Jewish background were used to the law of Moses, which prescribed tithes and offerings for different occasions. But the believers who were Gentiles did not have the custom of tithing. So Paul told the church:

⁷ You must each decide in your heart how much to give. And don't give reluctantly or in response to pressure. "For God loves a person who gives cheerfully." ⁸ And God will generously provide all you need. Then you will always have everything you need and plenty left over to share with others.   2 Corinthians 9:7–8

Topic 3—Comparing Views on Giving

Introduction: Christians, Muslims, naturalists, and new spiritualists all give to those in need, but they do not all share the same reasons for doing so. Christians base their charitable acts on Jesus' words, "Give to anyone who asks; and when things are taken away from you, don't try to get them back. Do to others as you would like them to do to you" (Luke 6:30–31). For Christians, giving is directly connected to the Golden Rule, to the love that we should have for our neighbors. Paul likewise encouraged believers to give as Jesus taught, saying, "Help those in need by working hard. You should remember the words of the Lord Jesus: 'It is more blessed to give than to receive'" (Acts 20:35). James taught that Christians give to minister to others. He said, "Pure and genuine religion in the sight of God the Father means caring for orphans and widows in their distress and refusing to let the world corrupt you" (James 1:27).

Christians give to people in need and to support the work of the church. Jesus and his disciples received support to preach the good news (Luke 8:1–3). Jesus taught that "those who work deserve their pay" (Luke 10:7). He also told his followers, "When you give to someone in need, don't let your left hand know what your right hand is doing. Give your gifts in private, and your Father, who sees everything, will reward you" (Matthew 6:3–4).

God wants us to give to others willingly and cheerfully, out of gratitude and love, not out of obligation or a desire to show off. And, according to the *Washington Times*, faith is a motivation for as much as 75% of all giving in the United States. While 62% of religious households donate to charity, only 46% of nonreligious households do.[1]

Giving is not an obligation for Christians, but it is a requirement for Muslims. The third pillar of Islam is to give alms to the poor; violating this requirement is considered a sin. Devout Muslims are expected to give a share of their income to charity annually. While Muslims make substantial donations, they give mainly to Muslim charities, such as Islamic Relief.

The Quran states:

Alms are meant only for the poor, the needy, those who administer them, those whose hearts need winning over, to free slaves and help those in debt, for God's cause, and for travellers in need. This is ordained by God; God is all knowing and wise.   Quran 9:60

The Quran also teaches:

If you give charity openly, it is good, but if you keep it secret and give to the needy in private, that is better for you, and it will atone for some of your bad deeds: God is well aware of all that you do.   Quran 2:271

While statistics show that atheists and agnostics tend to give less than religious households, naturalists do contribute money or volunteer time to aid organizations or other nonprofit agencies. According to one naturalist organization, the Kansas City Atheist Coalition, atheists are "committed to doing good purely for goodness' sake," and also "to show the larger community that atheists are moral without mythology [God or religion]."[2]

New spiritualists who follow a yogi consider giving a path to spiritual progress. However, giving may not be entirely beneficial if it makes the giver feel good. According to the Sri Aurobindo Society:

The urge to serve the poor and the under privileged [*sic*] and to give money for a higher cause . . . indicates moral awakening and when [service and giving] are pursued with a certain selflessness can lead to a rapid moral evolution of the individual . . . Spiritual progress comes from a progressive dissolution of the ego. But moral altruism, in most cases, does not dissolve the ego, but only shifts it to the moral plane. In altruism, serving others becomes a means for self-satisfaction of the moral ego.[3]

Other followers of new spirituality give because they see humanity as divine (god) and each individual as part of the whole. According to Humanity's Team, a new spirituality organization:

> When we see the Divine and Self in each other, we cannot help but nurture, love and support the other. When we embrace and embody our Oneness, we naturally care for the other person, place, or thing. The Divine and Self are in all of the other, so nothing is left out.[4]

Topic 4—A Genuine Faith

Introduction: Paul's first trip to Corinth, in about AD 50, was devoted to starting the church and staying with the believers for a fairly long period of time (Acts 18:1–11). The second trip, the "painful visit" mentioned in 2 Corinthians 2:1–2, was in the spring of AD 54. Paul told the believers that his third trip would have several purposes: to receive the collection for Jerusalem, to address charges that had been made against him, to confront those who were still living in sin, and to offer exhortation to the believers so that they could grow in faith.

Paul informed the believers that he wouldn't go easy on those who continued in sin; they'd better watch out! He wasn't timid about where his authority came from. Christ spoke through him and empowered him, so Paul had every right to reprove the church for not dealing correctly with ongoing sin.

1898 FRESCO OF THE APOSTLE PAUL, SACRED HEART CHURCH, BERLIN, GERMANY

[1] This is the third time I am coming to visit you (and as the Scriptures say, "The facts of every case must be established by the testimony of two or three witnesses"). [2] I have already warned those who had been sinning when I was there on my second visit. Now I again warn them and all others, just as I did before, that next time I will not spare them.   2 Corinthians 13:1–2

How do you think you might have felt if you were one of the members in the church in Corinth who had already been warned? Some sinners did not want to heed Paul's warnings. They questioned his authority. So Paul continued:

[3] I will give you all the proof you want that Christ speaks through me. Christ is not weak when he deals with you; he is powerful among you. [4] Although he was crucified in weakness, he now lives by the power of God. We, too, are weak, just as Christ was, but when we deal with you, we will be alive with him and will have God's power.

[5] Examine yourselves to see if your faith is genuine. Test yourselves. Surely you know that Jesus Christ is among you; if not, you have failed the test of genuine faith. [6] As you test yourselves, I hope you will recognize that we have not failed the test of apostolic authority.   2 Corinthians 13:3–6

Paul was not asking the Corinthian believers to do anything that he himself did not do. He examined his own heart for sin. In his previous letter, he had told the Corinthians,

24 Do you not know that in a race all the runners run, but only one receives the prize? So run that you may obtain it. 25 All athletes are disciplined in their training. They do it to win a prize that will fade away, but we do it for an eternal prize. 26 So I run with purpose in every step. I am not just shadowboxing. 27 I discipline my body and keep it under control, lest after preaching to others I myself should be disqualified.

1 Corinthians 9:24–27

Paul reminded the Corinthians that they needed to test their own faith and take responsibility for the way they lived as Jesus' disciples. He also reminded them that he cared about and prayed for them.

9 We pray that you will become mature. 10 I am writing this to you before I come, hoping that I won't need to deal severely with you when I do come. For I want to use the authority the Lord has given me to strengthen you, not to tear you down.

2 Corinthians 13:9–10

Paul did not want to waste a visit reprimanding the believers who hadn't changed their ways. He'd rather spend his time in teaching and edifying them. He exhorted them to grow, encourage each other, get along, and be at peace. Then, he prayed for God's blessing upon them.

11 Dear brothers and sisters, I close my letter with these last words: Be joyful. Grow to maturity. Encourage each other. Live in harmony and peace. Then the God of love and peace will be with you.

14 May the grace of the Lord Jesus Christ, the love of God, and the fellowship of the Holy Spirit be with you all.

2 Corinthians 13: 11, 14

ENDNOTES

1 Bradford Richardson, "Religious People More Likely to Give to Charity, Study Shows," modified October 30, 2017, https://www.washingtontimes.com/news/2017/oct/30/religious-people-more-likely-give-charity-study/.

2 "Positively Godless Philanthropy," accessed May 24, 2019, http://www.kcatheists.org/causes/philanthropy/.

3 M. S. Srinivasan "Social Service, Philanthropy, and Spirituality," accessed May 25, 2019, https://nextfuture.aurosociety.org/social-service-philanthropy-and-spirituality.

4 "A Civil Rights Movement for the Soul," accessed May 24, 2019, https://www.humanitysteam.org/objective.

Walking in Truth Grade 7 Student Textbook Index

Credits

Image: Christ the Redeemer (page 1)
Credit: KátiaLira
https://creativecommons.org/licenses/by-sa/3.0/deed.en

Image: Muslims entering the cave (page 42)
Credit: Seyfi Şeren
https://creativecommons.org/licenses/by/2.0/legalcode

Image: Men praying during Ramadan (page 100)
Credit: Vetman
https://creativecommons.org/licenses/by-sa/3.0/legalcode